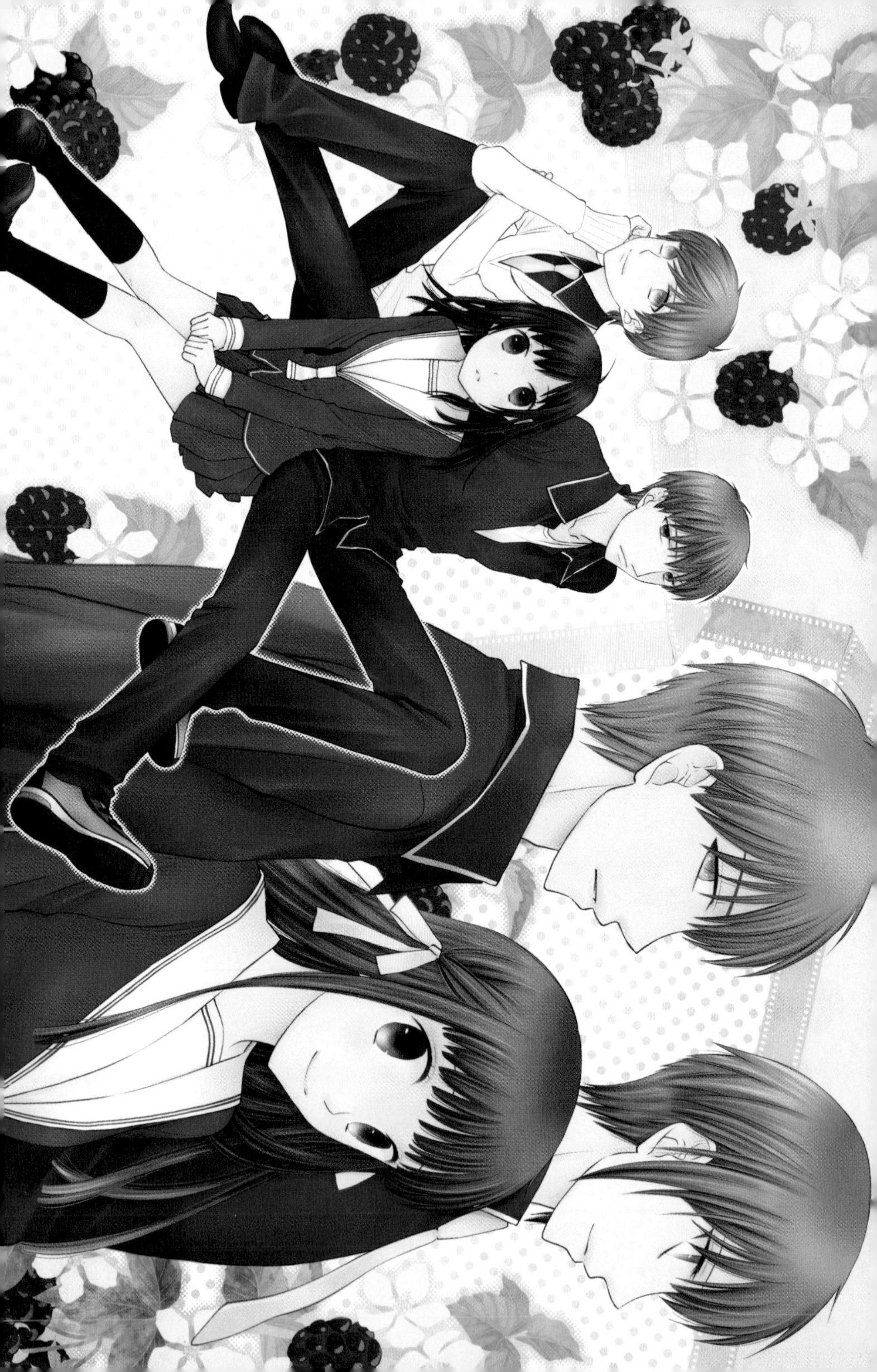

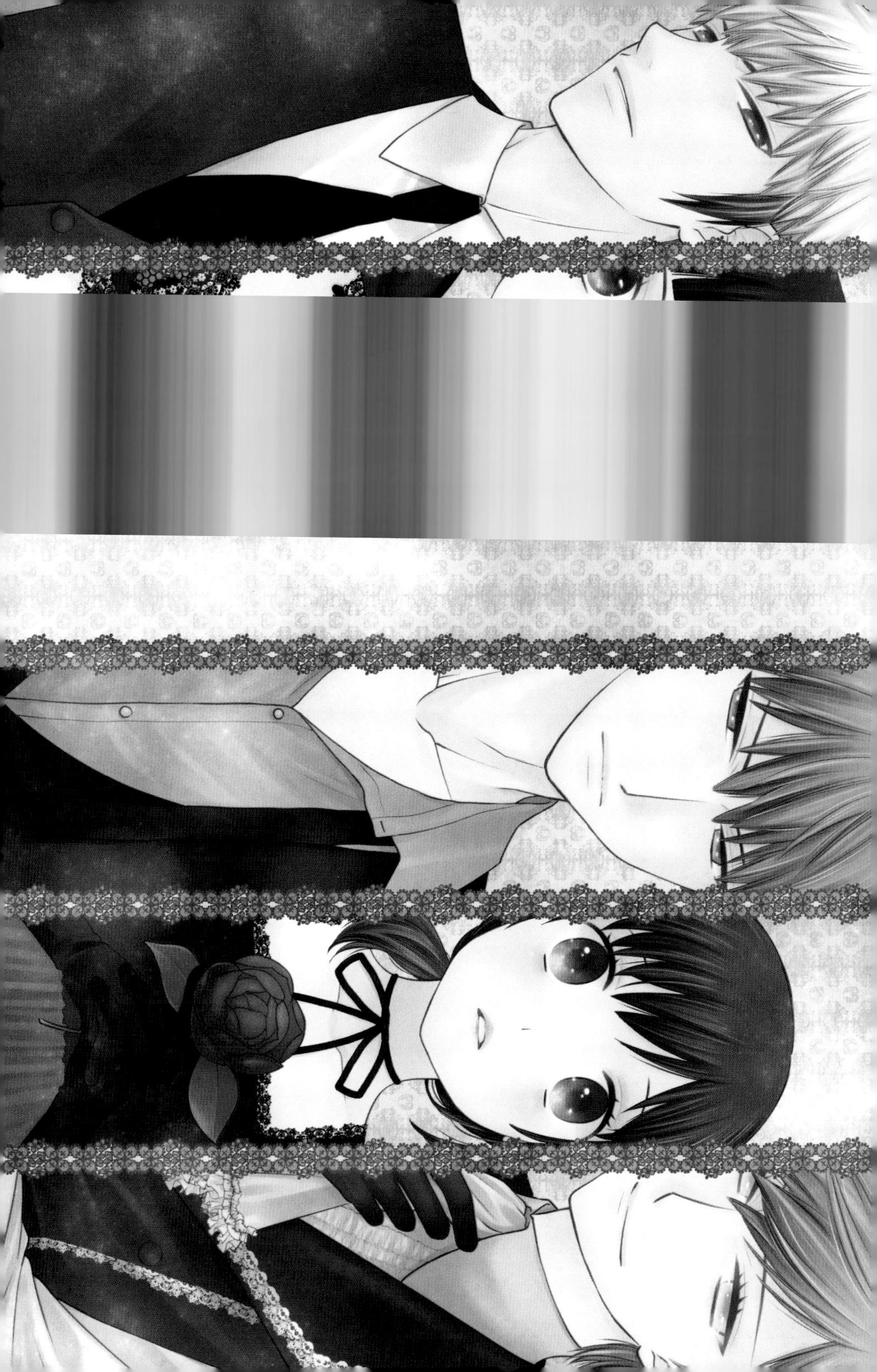

Fruits Basket another

NATSUKI TAKAYA

2

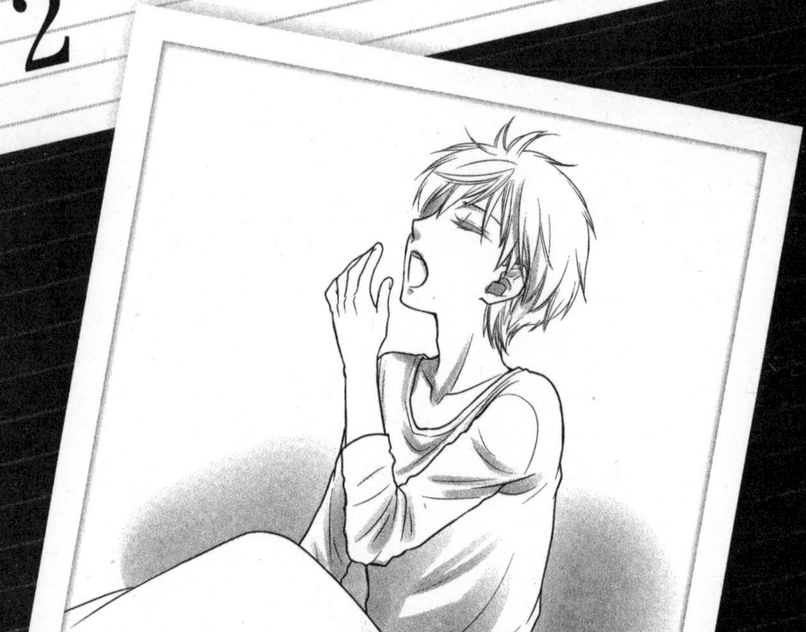

FRUITS BASKET another

Fruits Basket another

CONTENTS

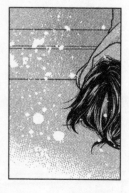

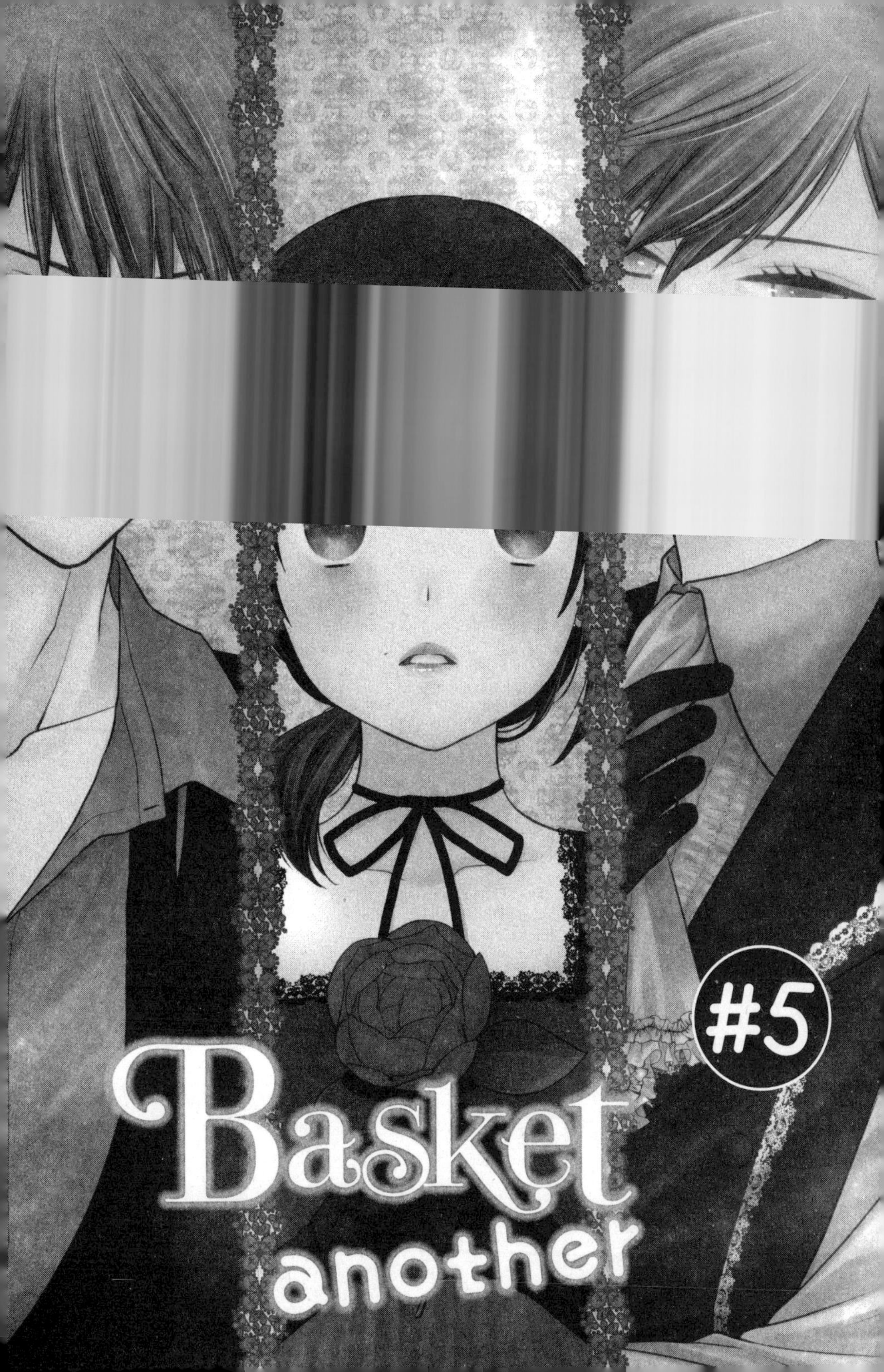
#5
Basket
another

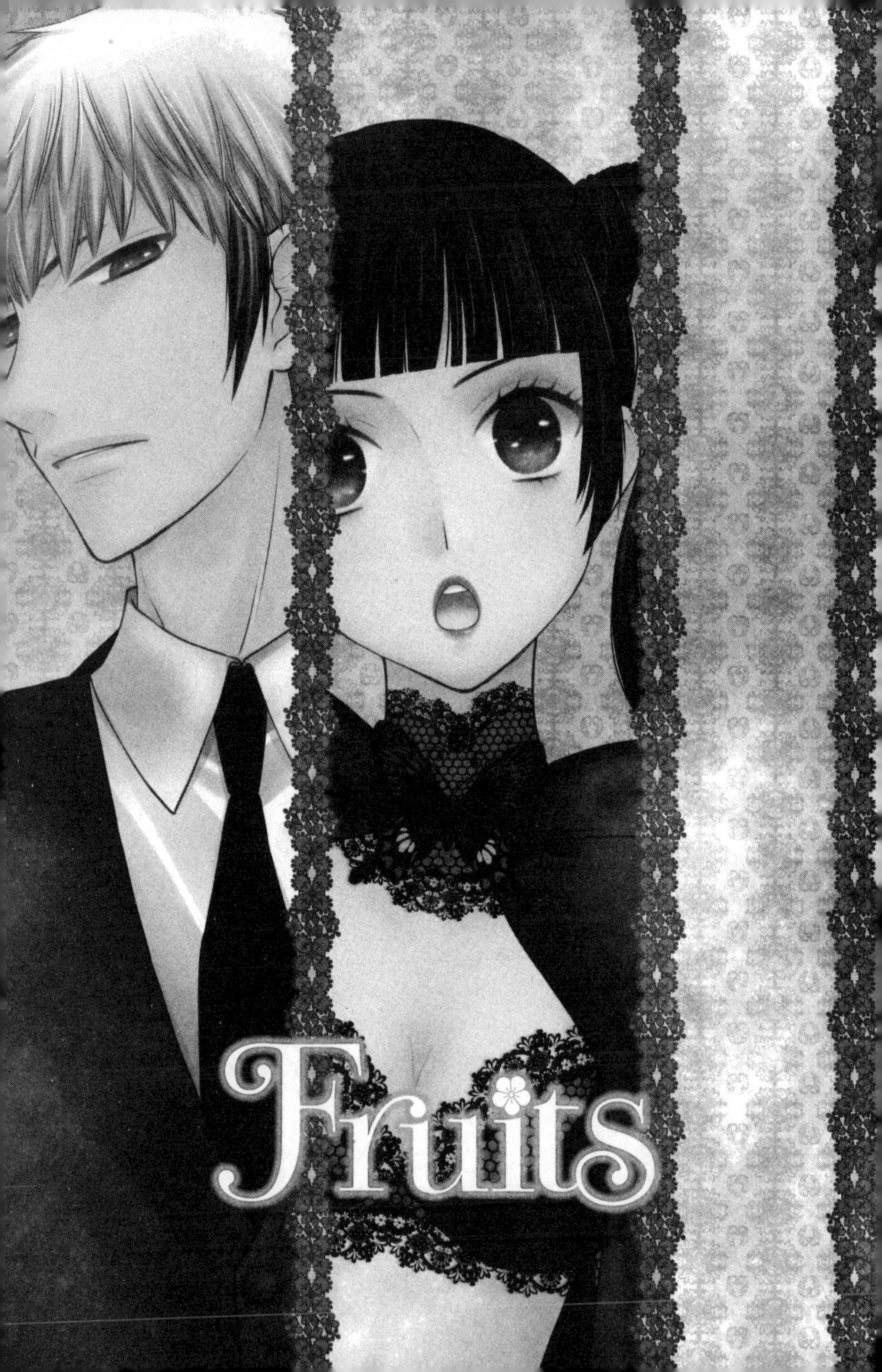
Fruits

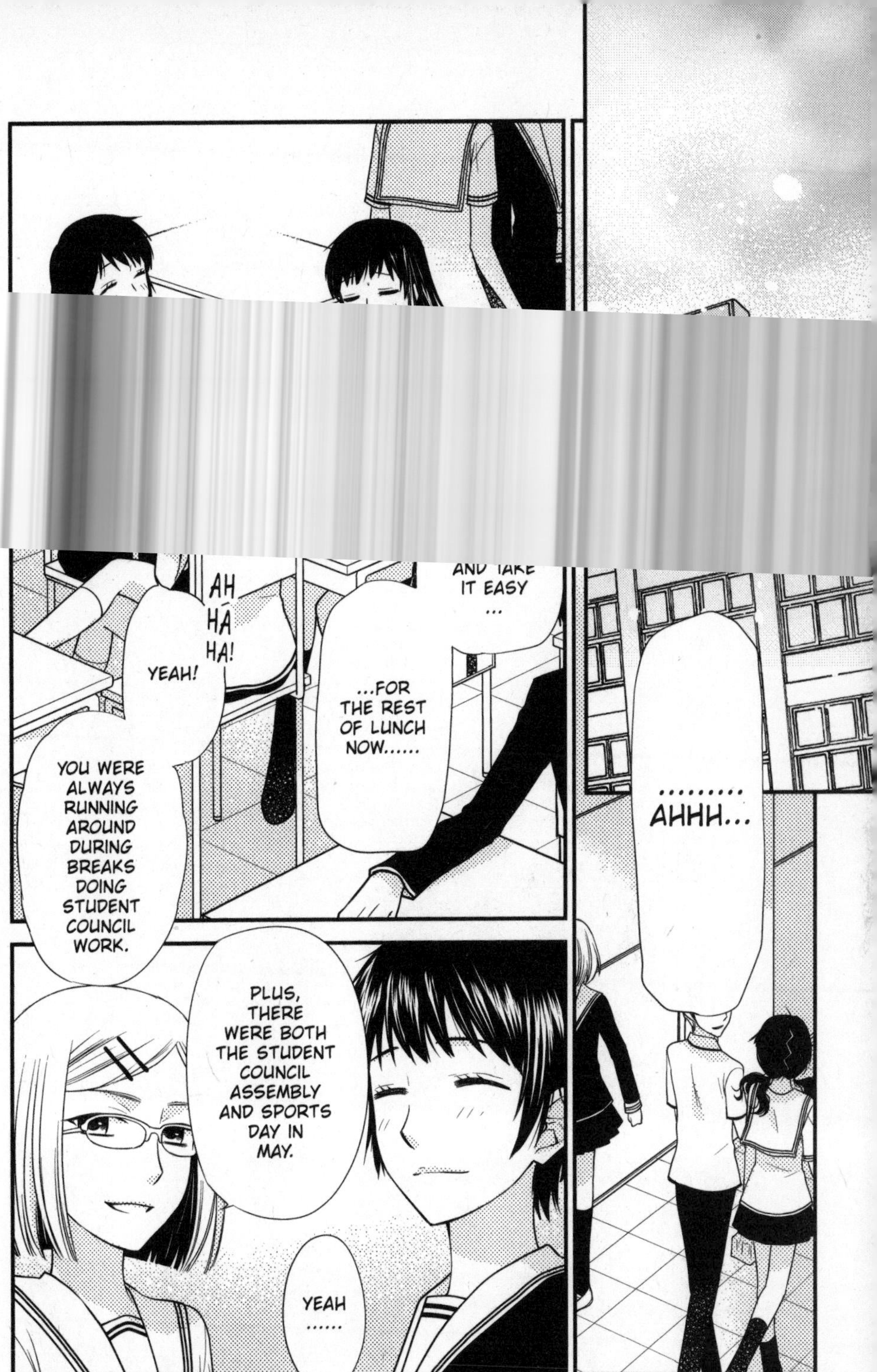

.... AHHH...
AND TAKE IT EASY ...
...FOR THE REST OF LUNCH NOW......
AH HA HA!
YEAH!
YOU WERE ALWAYS RUNNING AROUND DURING BREAKS DOING STUDENT COUNCIL WORK.
PLUS, THERE WERE BOTH THE STUDENT COUNCIL ASSEMBLY AND SPORTS DAY IN MAY.
YEAH ......

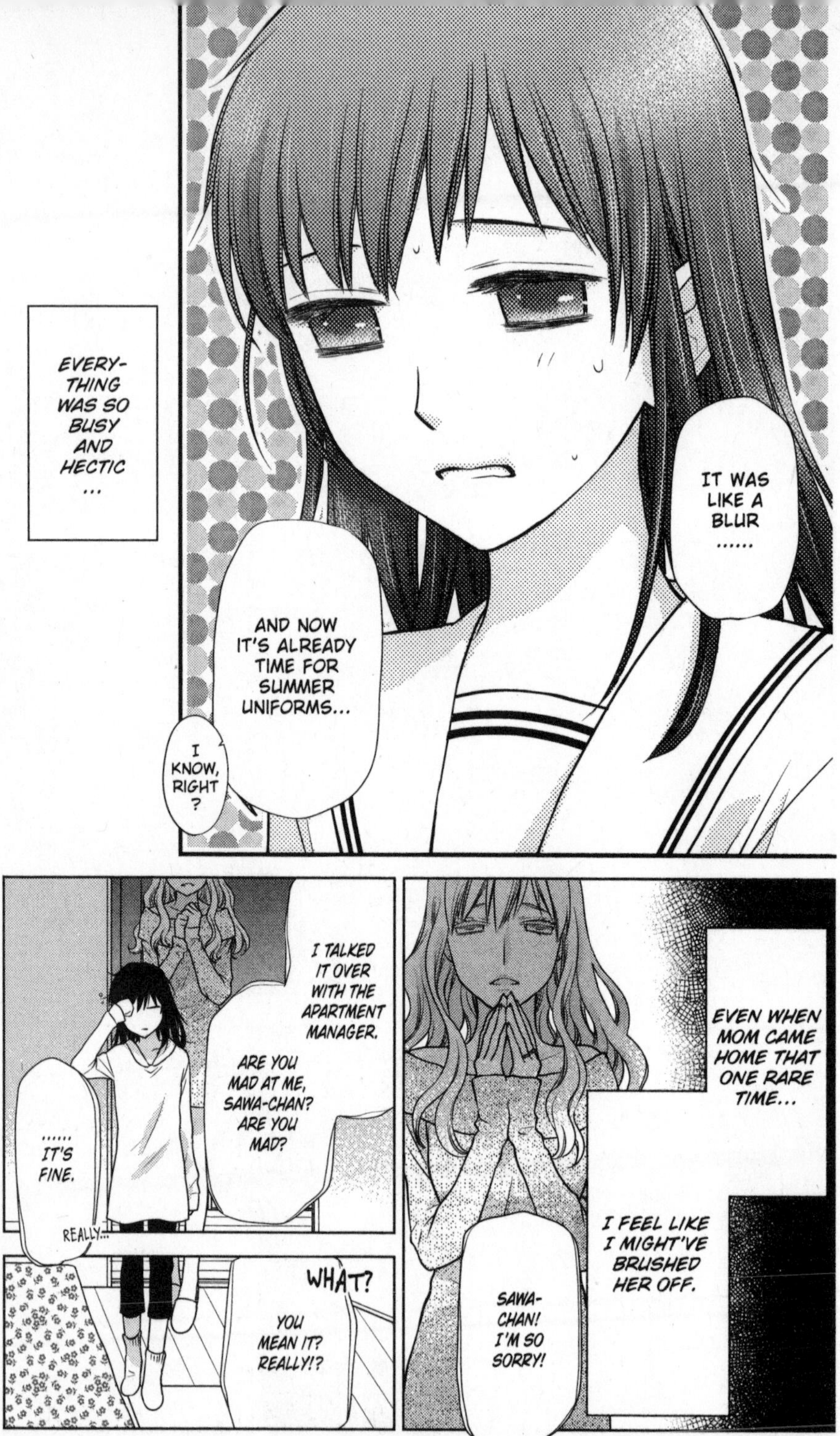
EVERY-THING WAS SO BUSY AND HECTIC...
IT WAS LIKE A BLUR......
AND NOW IT'S ALREADY TIME FOR SUMMER UNIFORMS...
I KNOW, RIGHT?
EVEN WHEN MOM CAME HOME THAT ONE RARE TIME...
I FEEL LIKE I MIGHT'VE BRUSHED HER OFF.
SAWA-CHAN! I'M SO SORRY!
I TALKED IT OVER WITH THE APARTMENT MANAGER.
ARE YOU MAD AT ME, SAWA-CHAN? ARE YOU MAD?
......IT'S FINE.
REALLY...
WHAT?
YOU MEAN IT? REALLY!?

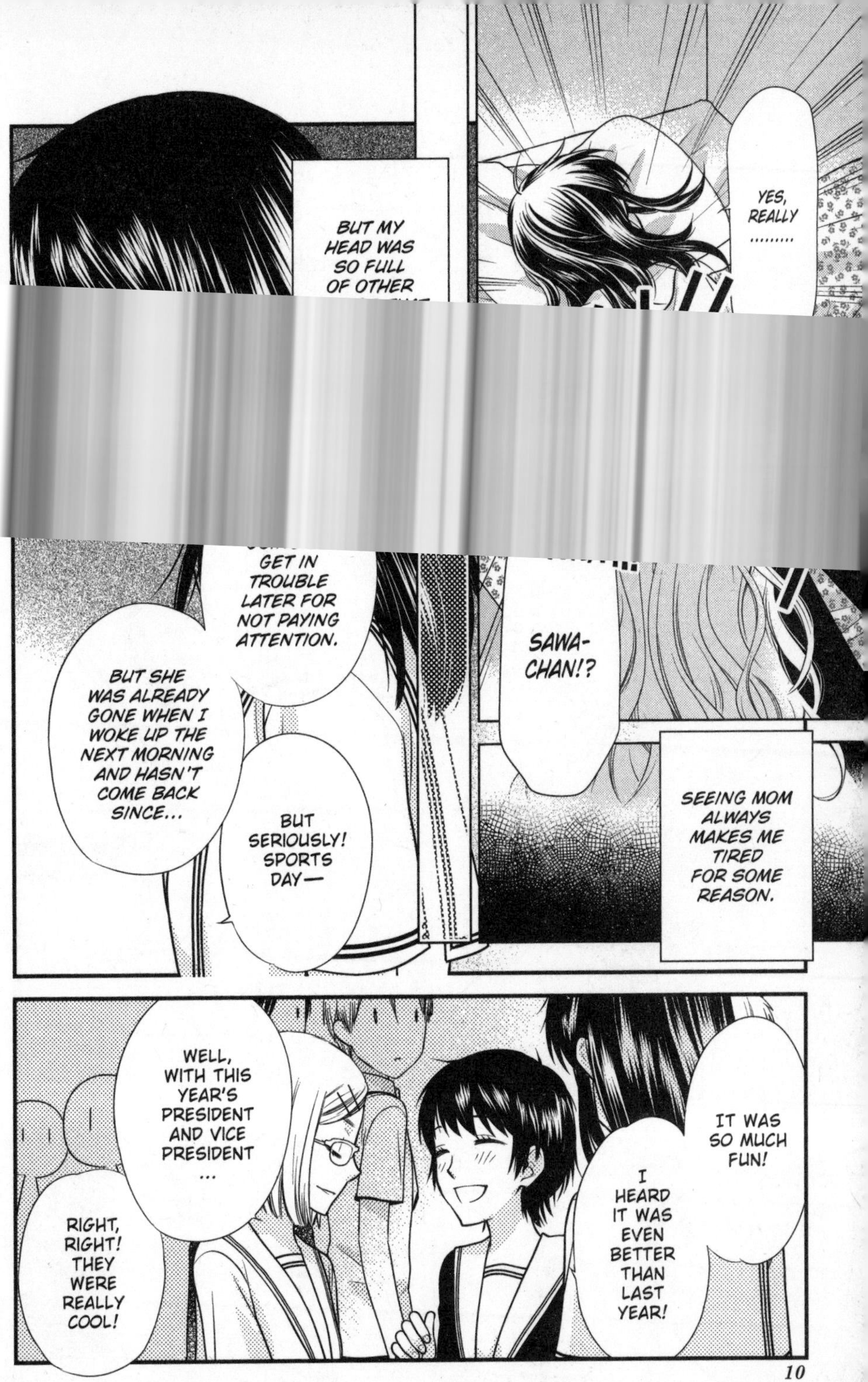
YES, REALLY ....
SAWA-CHAN!?
SEEING MOM ALWAYS MAKES ME TIRED FOR SOME REASON.
BUT MY HEAD WAS SO FULL OF OTHER
GET IN TROUBLE LATER FOR NOT PAYING ATTENTION.
BUT SHE WAS ALREADY GONE WHEN I WOKE UP THE NEXT MORNING AND HASN'T COME BACK SINCE...
BUT SERIOUSLY! SPORTS DAY—
IT WAS SO MUCH FUN!
I HEARD IT WAS EVEN BETTER THAN LAST YEAR!
WELL, WITH THIS YEAR'S PRESIDENT AND VICE PRESIDENT ...
RIGHT, RIGHT! THEY WERE REALLY COOL!

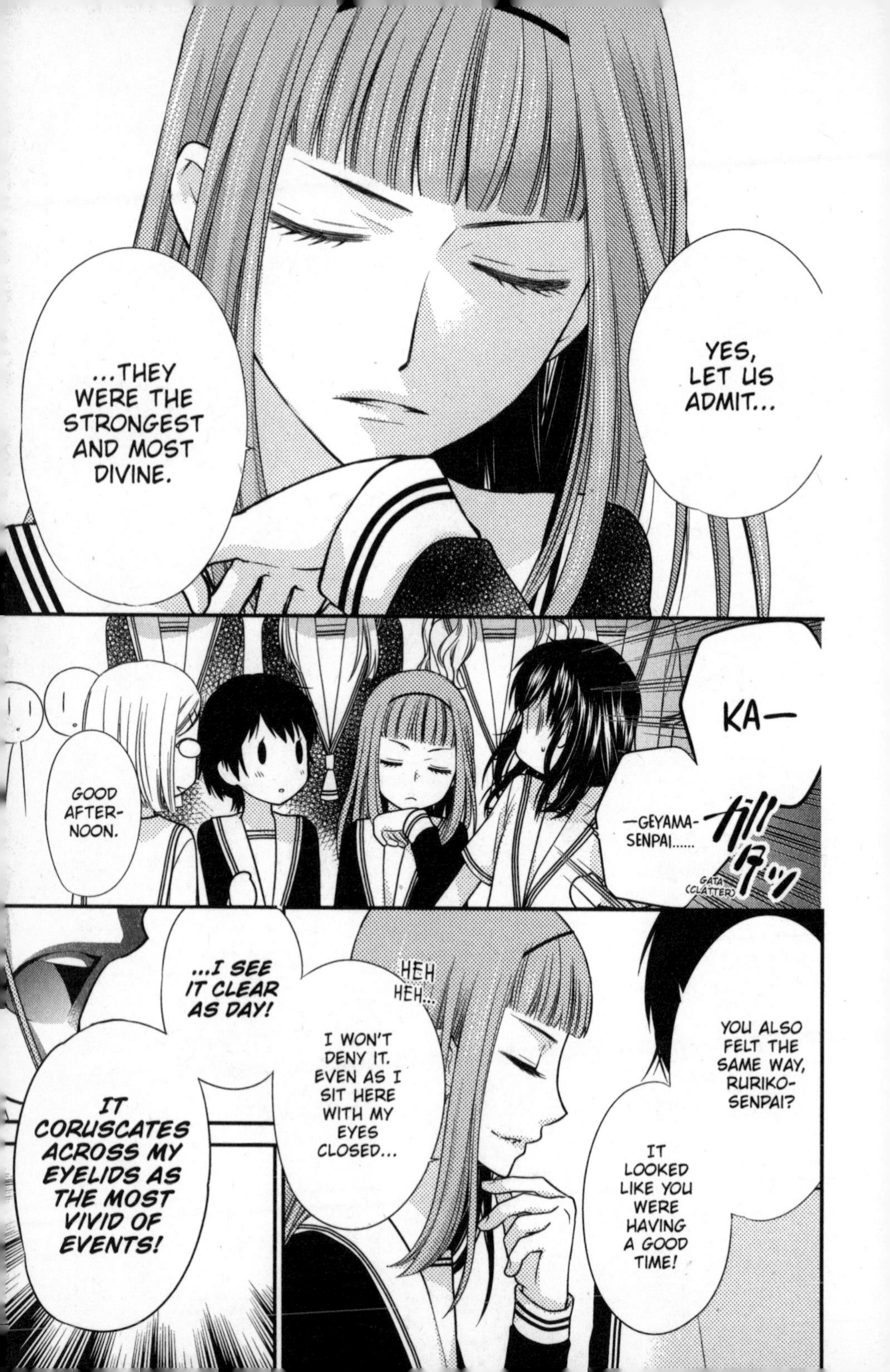
YES, LET US ADMIT...
...THEY WERE THE STRONGEST AND MOST DIVINE.
KA—
—GEYAMA-SENPAI......
GATA (CLATTER)
GOOD AFTERNOON.
YOU ALSO FELT THE SAME WAY, RURIKO-SENPAI?
IT LOOKED LIKE YOU WERE HAVING A GOOD TIME!
HEH HEH...
I WON'T DENY IT. EVEN AS I SIT HERE WITH MY EYES CLOSED...
...I SEE IT CLEAR AS DAY!
IT CORUSCATES ACROSS MY EYELIDS AS THE MOST VIVID OF EVENTS!

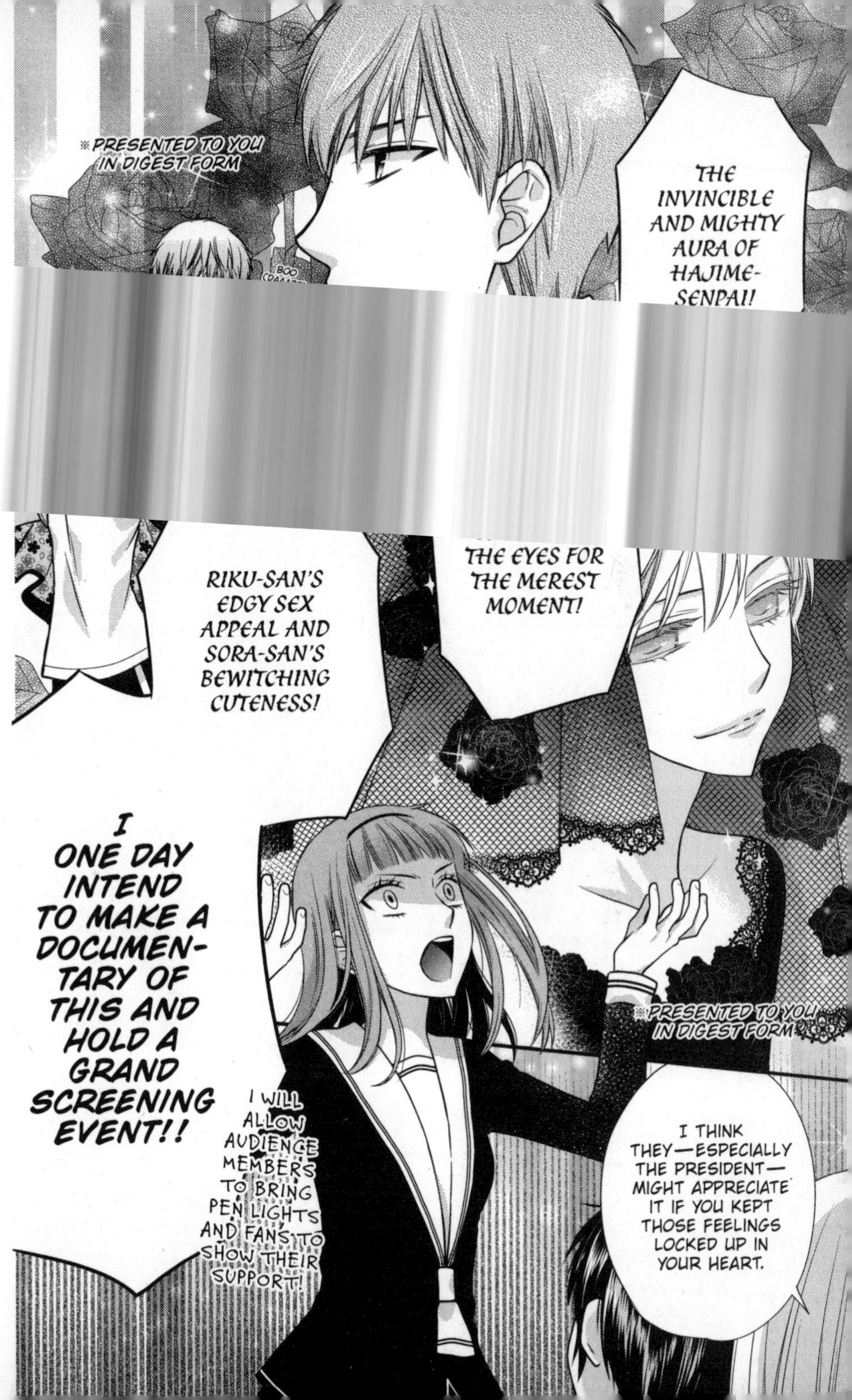
THE INVINCIBLE AND MIGHTY AURA OF HAJIME-SENPAI!
※PRESENTED TO YOU IN DIGEST FORM
THE EYES FOR THE MEREST MOMENT!
RIKU-SAN'S EDGY SEX APPEAL AND SORA-SAN'S BEWITCHING CUTENESS!
※PRESENTED TO YOU IN DIGEST FORM
I ONE DAY INTEND TO MAKE A DOCUMEN-TARY OF THIS AND HOLD A GRAND SCREENING EVENT!!
I WILL ALLOW AUDIENCE MEMBERS TO BRING PEN LIGHTS AND FANS TO SHOW THEIR SUPPORT!
I THINK THEY—ESPECIALLY THE PRESIDENT—MIGHT APPRECIATE IT IF YOU KEPT THOSE FEELINGS LOCKED UP IN YOUR HEART.

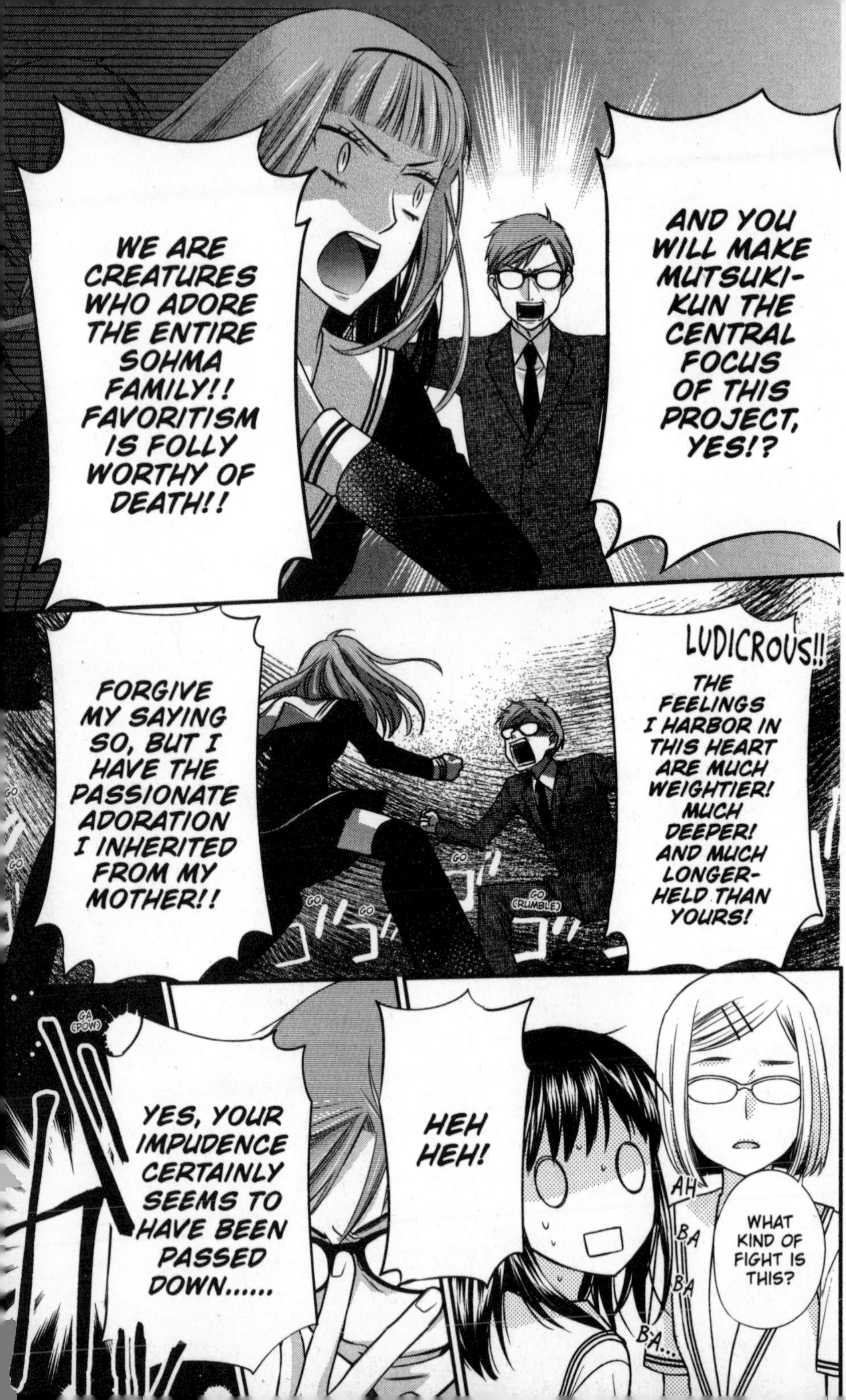
AND YOU WILL MAKE MUTSUKI-KUN THE CENTRAL FOCUS OF THIS PROJECT, YES!?
WE ARE CREATURES WHO ADORE THE ENTIRE SOHMA FAMILY!! FAVORITISM IS FOLLY WORTHY OF DEATH!!
LUDICROUS!!
THE FEELINGS I HARBOR IN THIS HEART ARE MUCH WEIGHTIER! MUCH DEEPER! AND MUCH LONGER-HELD THAN YOURS!
GO
GO (RUMBLE)
FORGIVE MY SAYING SO, BUT I HAVE THE PASSIONATE ADORATION I INHERITED FROM MY MOTHER!!
GO
GO
GO
GO
WHAT KIND OF FIGHT IS THIS?
AH
BA
BA
BA...
HEH HEH!
YES, YOUR IMPUDENCE CERTAINLY SEEMS TO HAVE BEEN PASSED DOWN......
GA (POW)

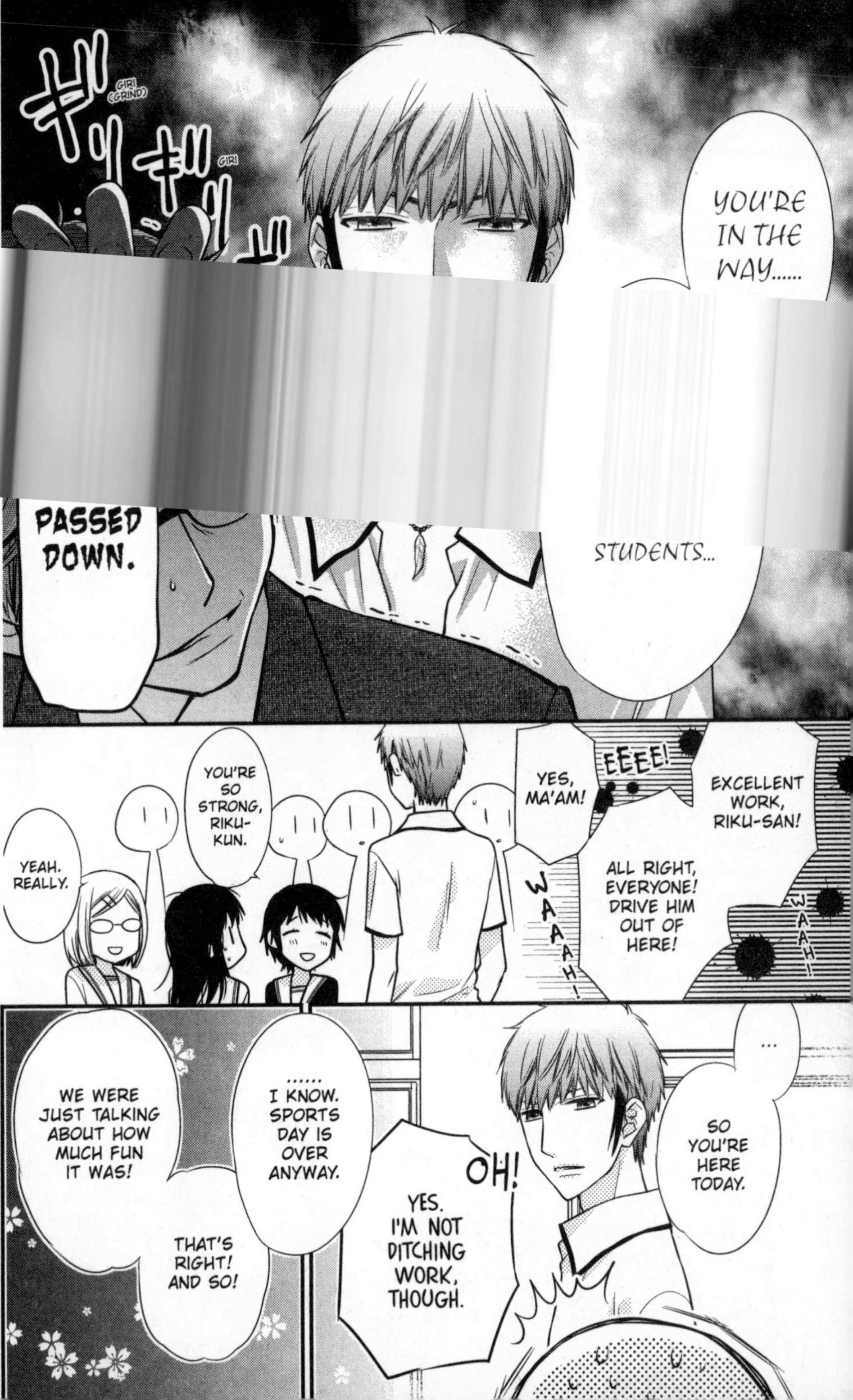
YOU'RE IN THE WAY......
GIRI (GRIND)
GIRI
STUDENTS...
PASSED DOWN.
EXCELLENT WORK, RIKU-SAN!
EEEE!
YES, MA'AM!
ALL RIGHT, EVERYONE! DRIVE HIM OUT OF HERE!
WAAH!
WAAAH!
YOU'RE SO STRONG, RIKU-KUN.
YEAH. REALLY.
...
SO YOU'RE HERE TODAY.
OH!
YES. I'M NOT DITCHING WORK, THOUGH.
...... I KNOW. SPORTS DAY IS OVER ANYWAY.
WE WERE JUST TALKING ABOUT HOW MUCH FUN IT WAS!
THAT'S RIGHT! AND SO!

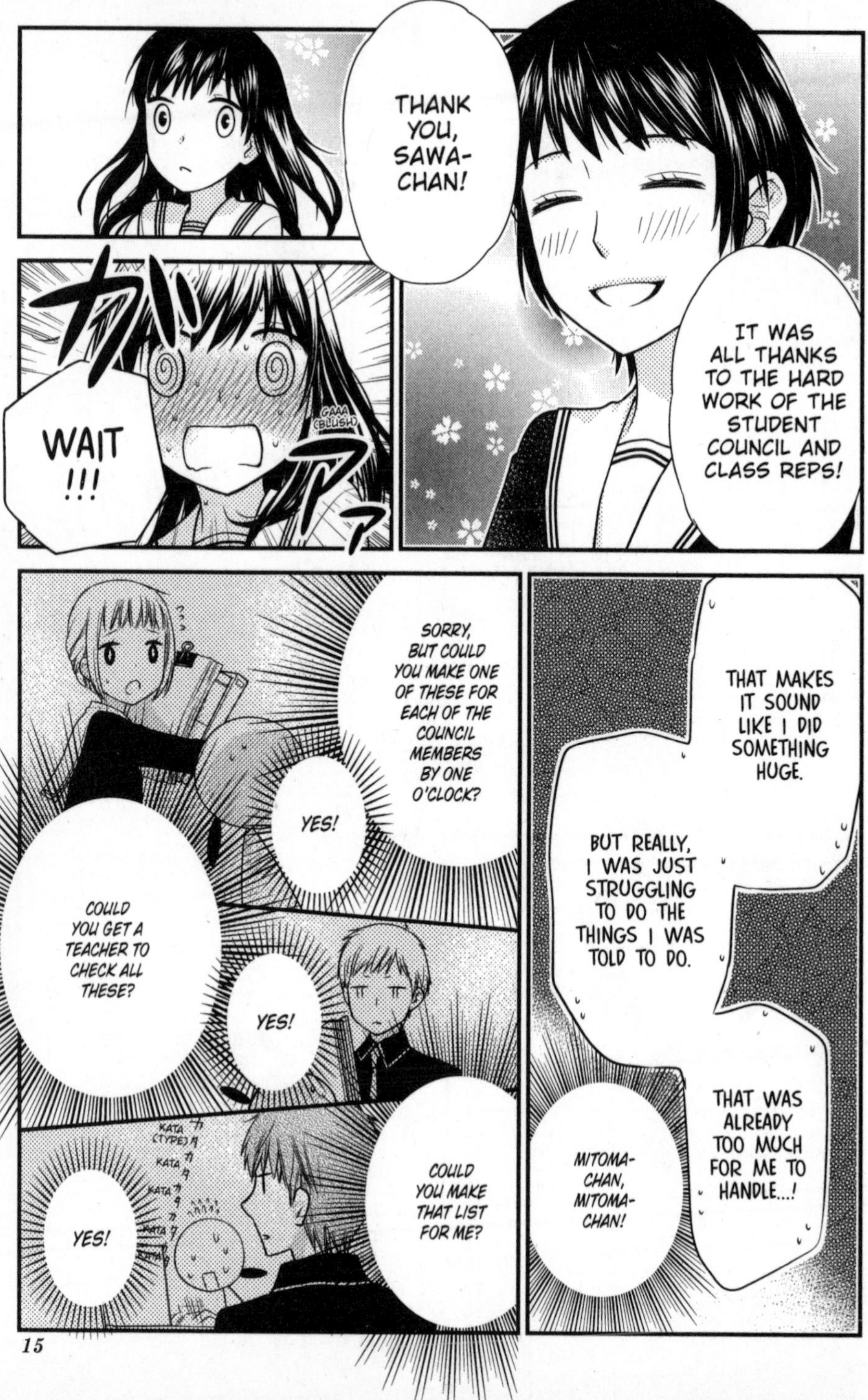
THANK YOU, SAWA-CHAN!
IT WAS ALL THANKS TO THE HARD WORK OF THE STUDENT COUNCIL AND CLASS REPS!
WAIT !!!
GAAA (BLUSH)
THAT MAKES IT SOUND LIKE I DID SOMETHING HUGE.
BUT REALLY, I WAS JUST STRUGGLING TO DO THE THINGS I WAS TOLD TO DO.
THAT WAS ALREADY TOO MUCH FOR ME TO HANDLE...!
MITOMA-CHAN, MITOMA-CHAN!
SORRY, BUT COULD YOU MAKE ONE OF THESE FOR EACH OF THE COUNCIL MEMBERS BY ONE O'CLOCK?
YES!
COULD YOU GET A TEACHER TO CHECK ALL THESE?
YES!
COULD YOU MAKE THAT LIST FOR ME?
YES!
KATA (TYPE)
KATA
KATA
KATA

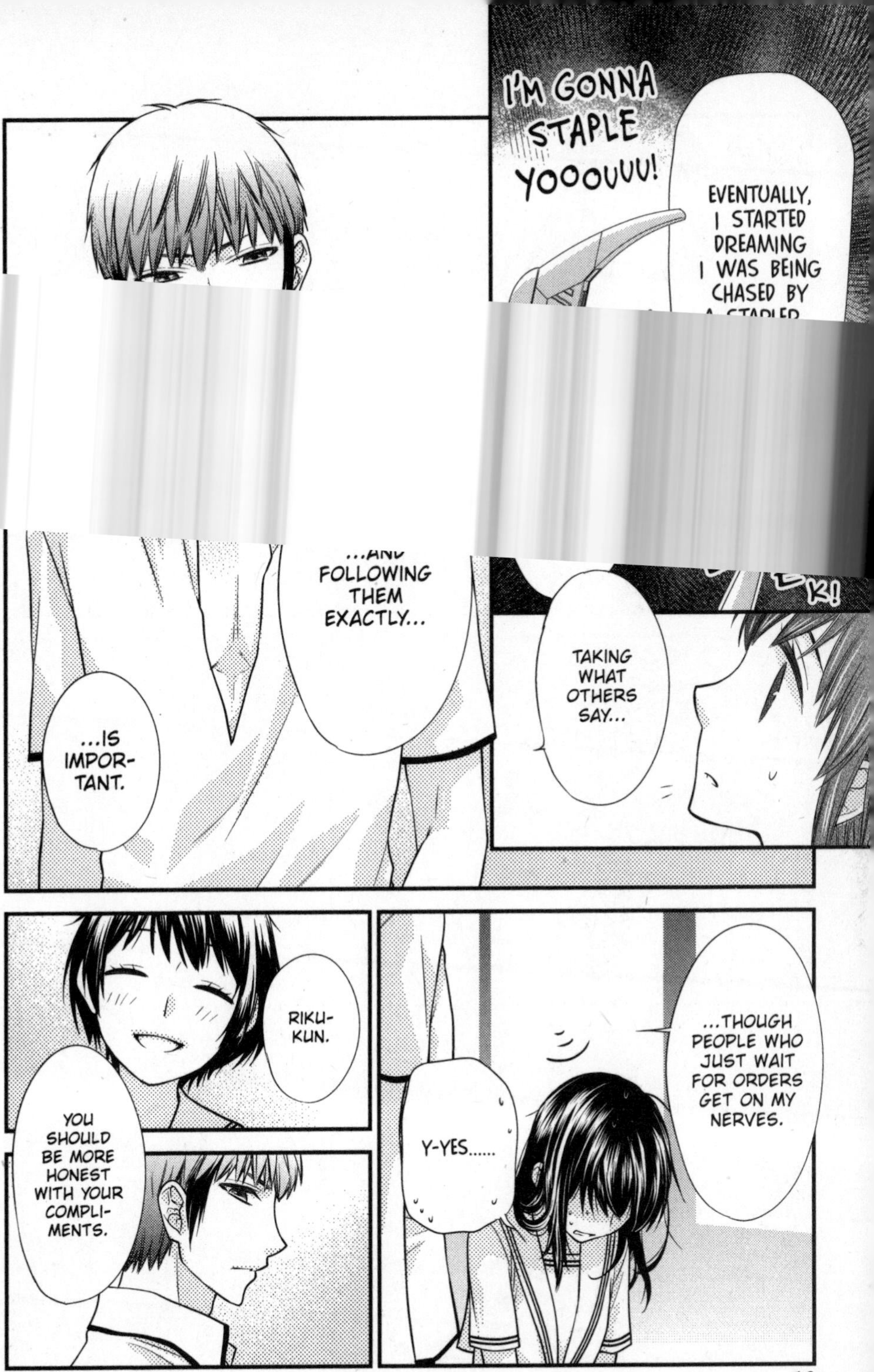
I'M GONNA STAPLE YOOOUUU!
EVENTUALLY, I STARTED DREAMING I WAS BEING CHASED BY
TAKING WHAT OTHERS SAY...
...AND FOLLOWING THEM EXACTLY...
...IS IMPORTANT.
...THOUGH PEOPLE WHO JUST WAIT FOR ORDERS GET ON MY NERVES.
Y-YES......
RIKU-KUN.
YOU SHOULD BE MORE HONEST WITH YOUR COMPLIMENTS.

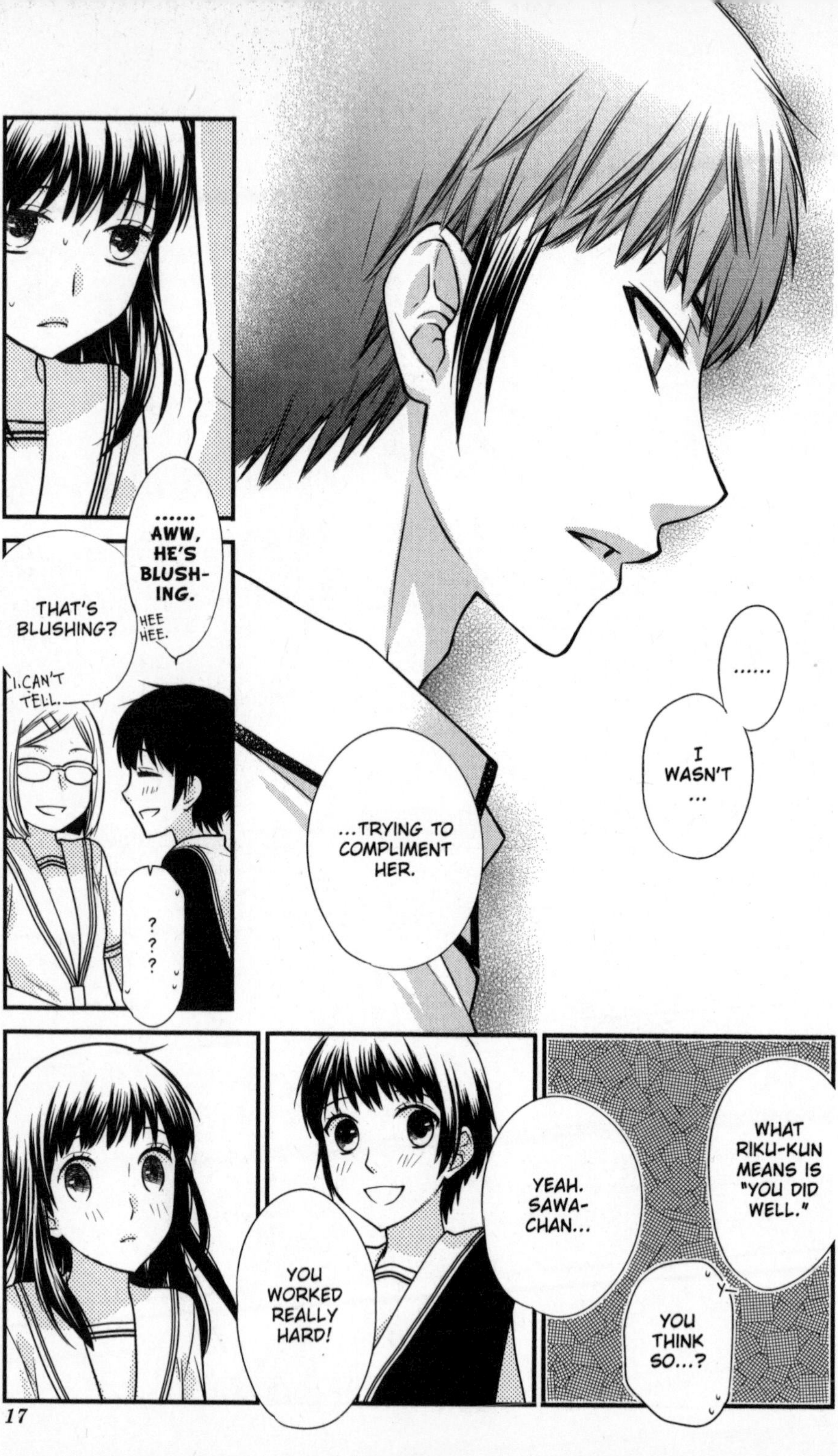

......
I WASN'T ...
...TRYING TO COMPLIMENT HER.
...... AWW, HE'S BLUSHING.
THAT'S BLUSHING?
HEE HEE.
I CAN'T TELL.
?.?.?
WHAT RIKU-KUN MEANS IS "YOU DID WELL."
Y-
YOU THINK SO...?
YEAH. SAWA-CHAN...
YOU WORKED REALLY HARD!

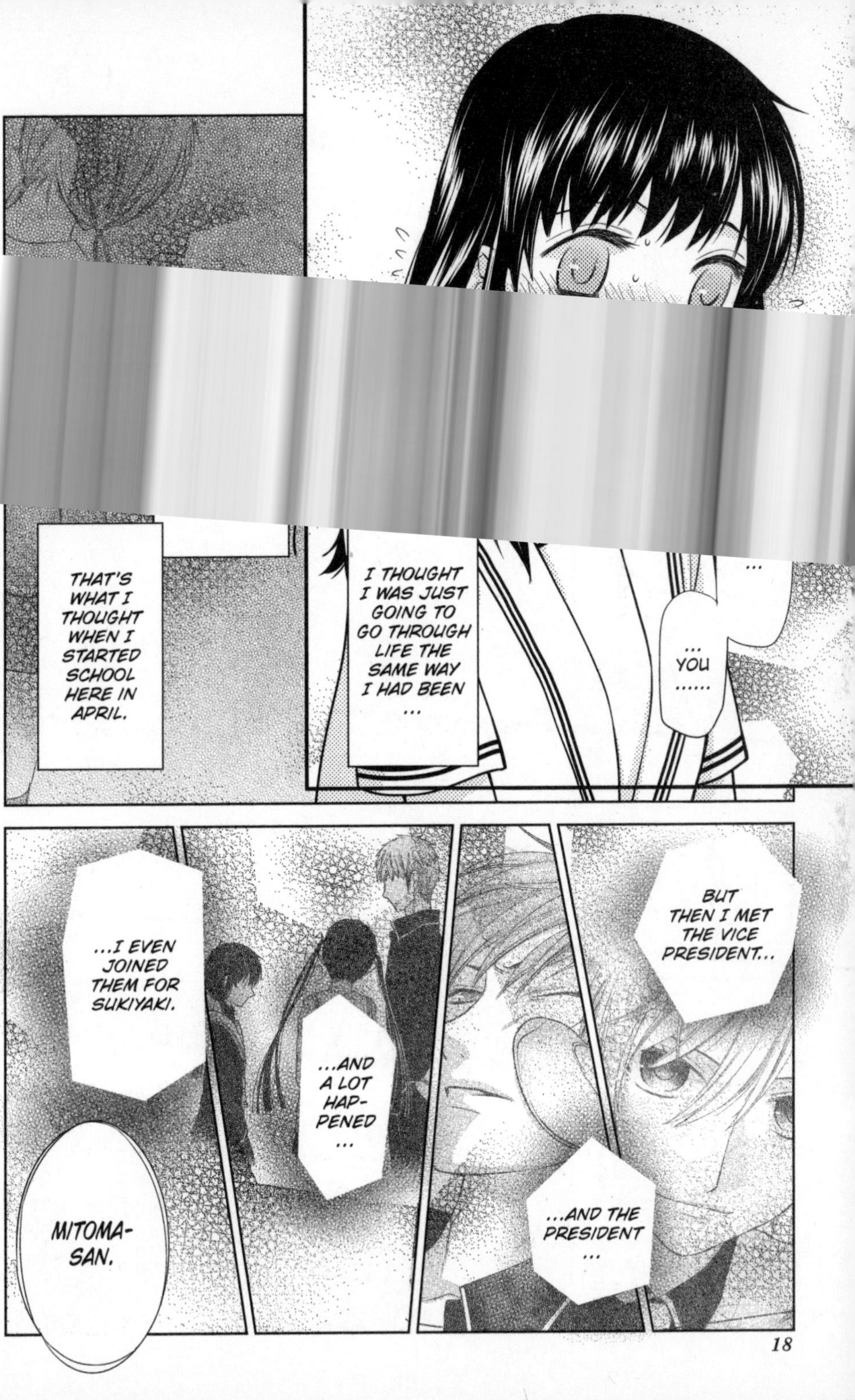
...
... YOU ......
I THOUGHT I WAS JUST GOING TO GO THROUGH LIFE THE SAME WAY I HAD BEEN ...
THAT'S WHAT I THOUGHT WHEN I STARTED SCHOOL HERE IN APRIL.
BUT THEN I MET THE VICE PRESIDENT...
...AND THE PRESIDENT ...
...AND A LOT HAP-PENED ...
...I EVEN JOINED THEM FOR SUKIYAKI.
MITOMA-SAN.

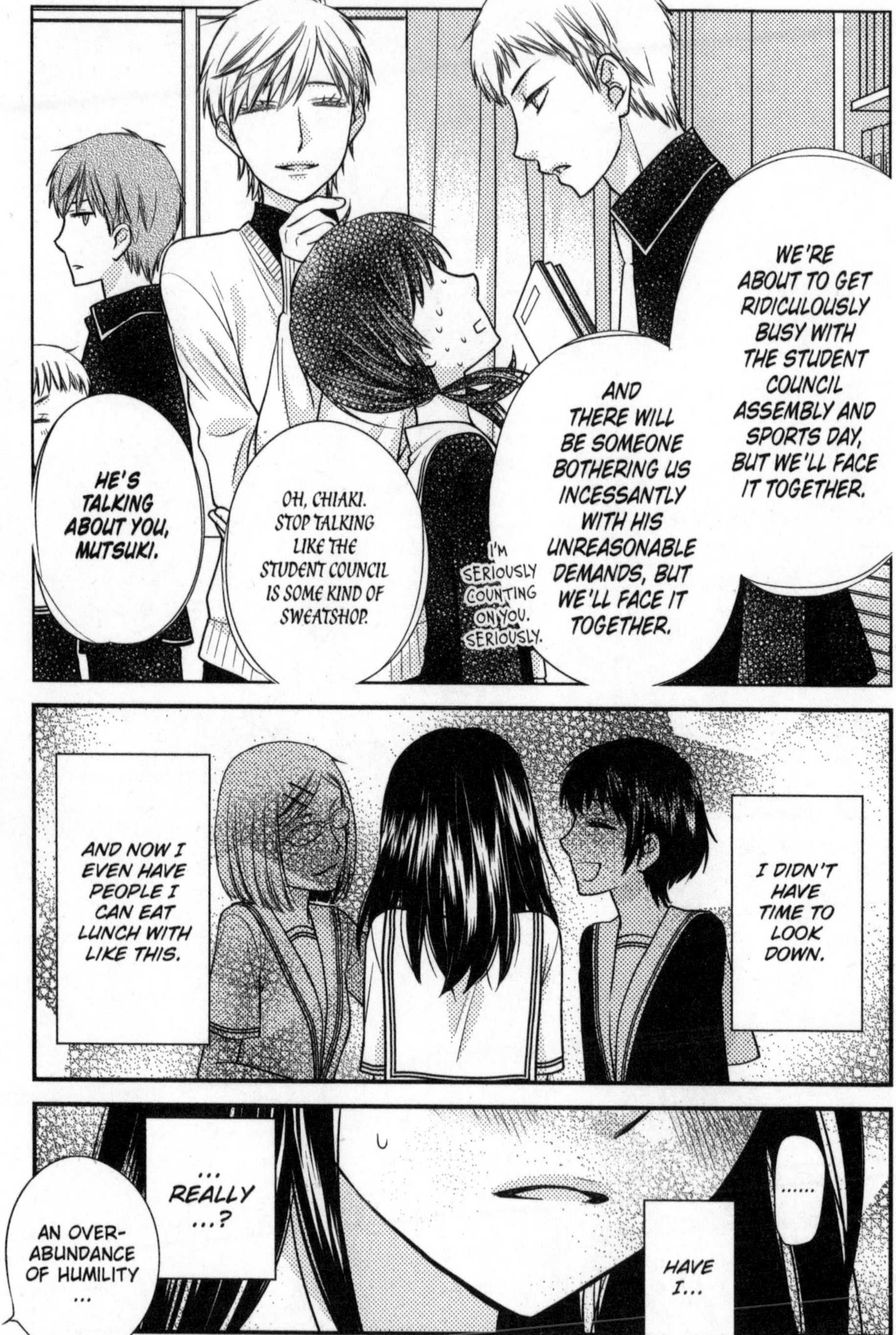

WE'RE ABOUT TO GET RIDICULOUSLY BUSY WITH THE STUDENT COUNCIL ASSEMBLY AND SPORTS DAY, BUT WE'LL FACE IT TOGETHER.
AND THERE WILL BE SOMEONE BOTHERING US INCESSANTLY WITH HIS UNREASONABLE DEMANDS, BUT WE'LL FACE IT TOGETHER.
I'M SERIOUSLY COUNTING ON YOU. SERIOUSLY.
OH, CHIAKI. STOP TALKING LIKE THE STUDENT COUNCIL IS SOME KIND OF SWEATSHOP.
HE'S TALKING ABOUT YOU, MUTSUKI.
I DIDN'T HAVE TIME TO LOOK DOWN.
AND NOW I EVEN HAVE PEOPLE I CAN EAT LUNCH WITH LIKE THIS.
......
HAVE I...
...REALLY...?
AN OVER-ABUNDANCE OF HUMILITY...

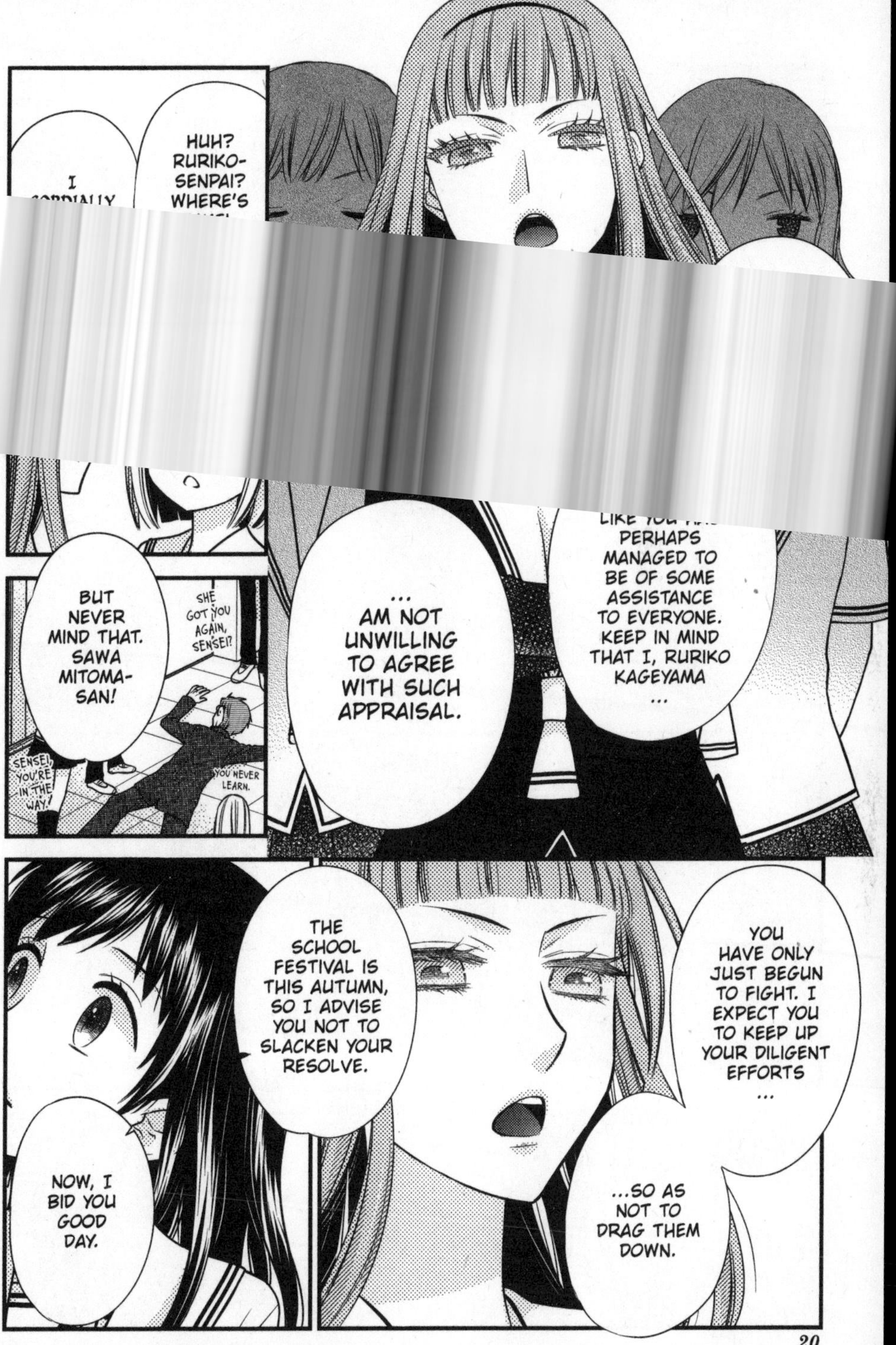
PERHAPS MANAGED TO BE OF SOME ASSISTANCE TO EVERYONE. KEEP IN MIND THAT I, RURIKO KAGEYAMA ...
... AM NOT UNWILLING TO AGREE WITH SUCH APPRAISAL.
HUH? RURIKO-SENPAI? WHERE'S
I
SHE GOT YOU AGAIN, SENSEI!?
BUT NEVER MIND THAT. SAWA MITOMA-SAN!
YOU NEVER LEARN.
SENSEI, YOU'RE IN THE WAY!
YOU HAVE ONLY JUST BEGUN TO FIGHT. I EXPECT YOU TO KEEP UP YOUR DILIGENT EFFORTS ...
...SO AS NOT TO DRAG THEM DOWN.
THE SCHOOL FESTIVAL IS THIS AUTUMN, SO I ADVISE YOU NOT TO SLACKEN YOUR RESOLVE.
NOW, I BID YOU GOOD DAY.

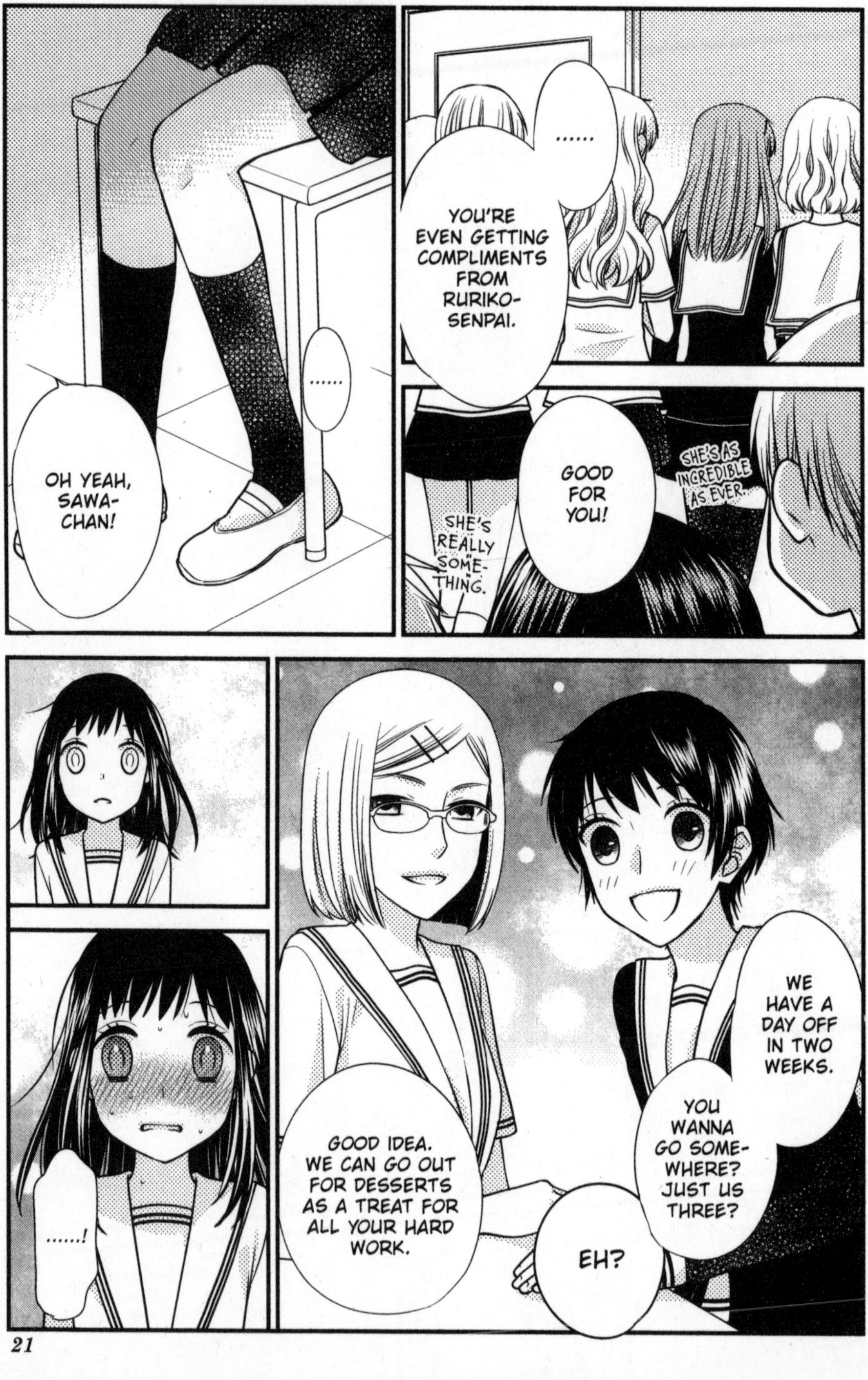
......
YOU'RE EVEN GETTING COMPLIMENTS FROM RURIKO-SENPAI.
SHE'S AS INCREDIBLE AS EVER.
GOOD FOR YOU!
SHE'S REALLY SOME-THING.
......
OH YEAH, SAWA-CHAN!
WE HAVE A DAY OFF IN TWO WEEKS.
YOU WANNA GO SOME-WHERE? JUST US THREE?
GOOD IDEA. WE CAN GO OUT FOR DESSERTS AS A TREAT FOR ALL YOUR HARD WORK.
EH?
......!

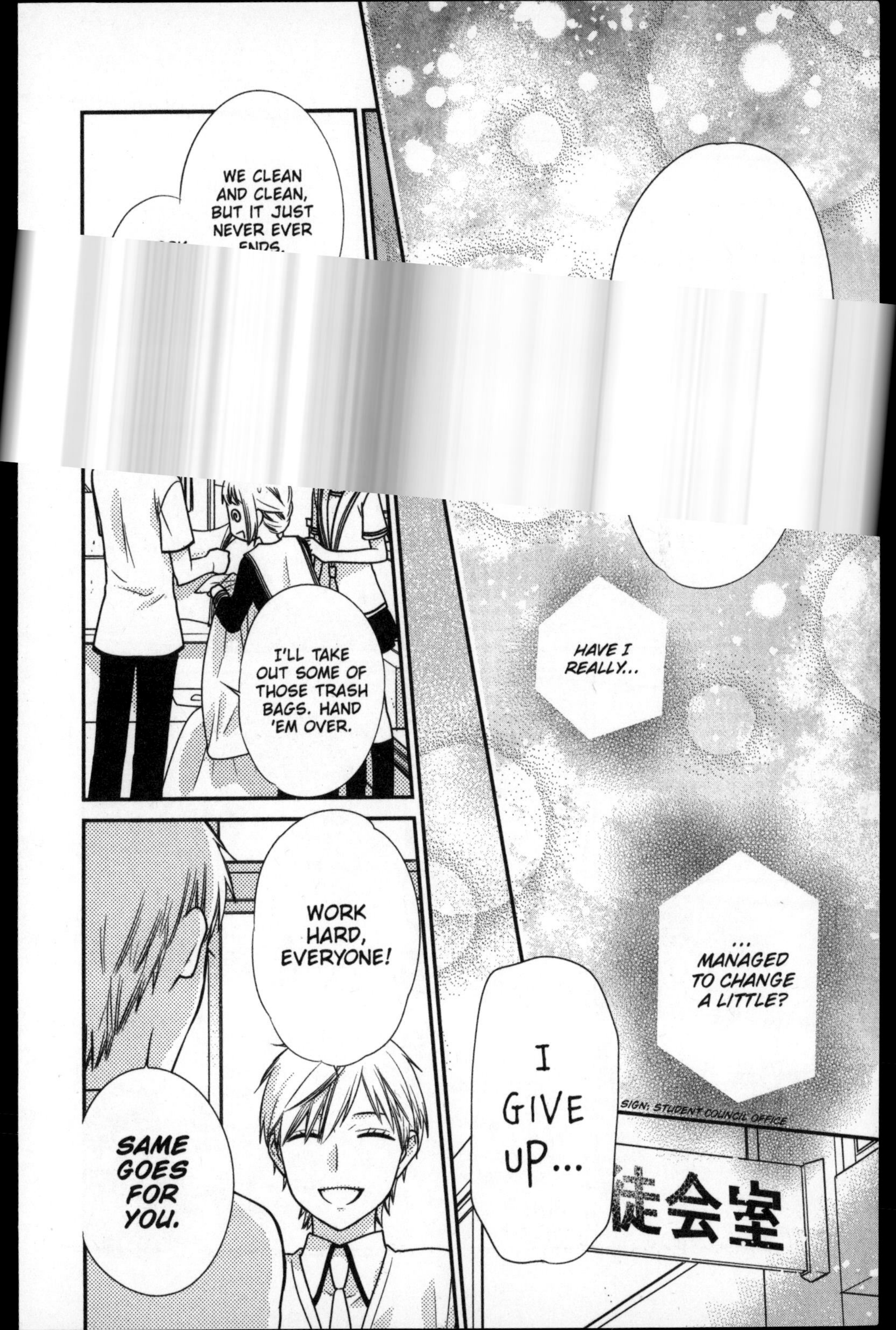
HAVE I REALLY...
... MANAGED TO CHANGE A LITTLE?
I GIVE UP...
SIGN: STUDENT COUNCIL OFFICE
徒会室
WE CLEAN AND CLEAN, BUT IT JUST NEVER EVER ENDS.
I'LL TAKE OUT SOME OF THOSE TRASH BAGS. HAND 'EM OVER.
WORK HARD, EVERYONE!
SAME GOES FOR YOU.

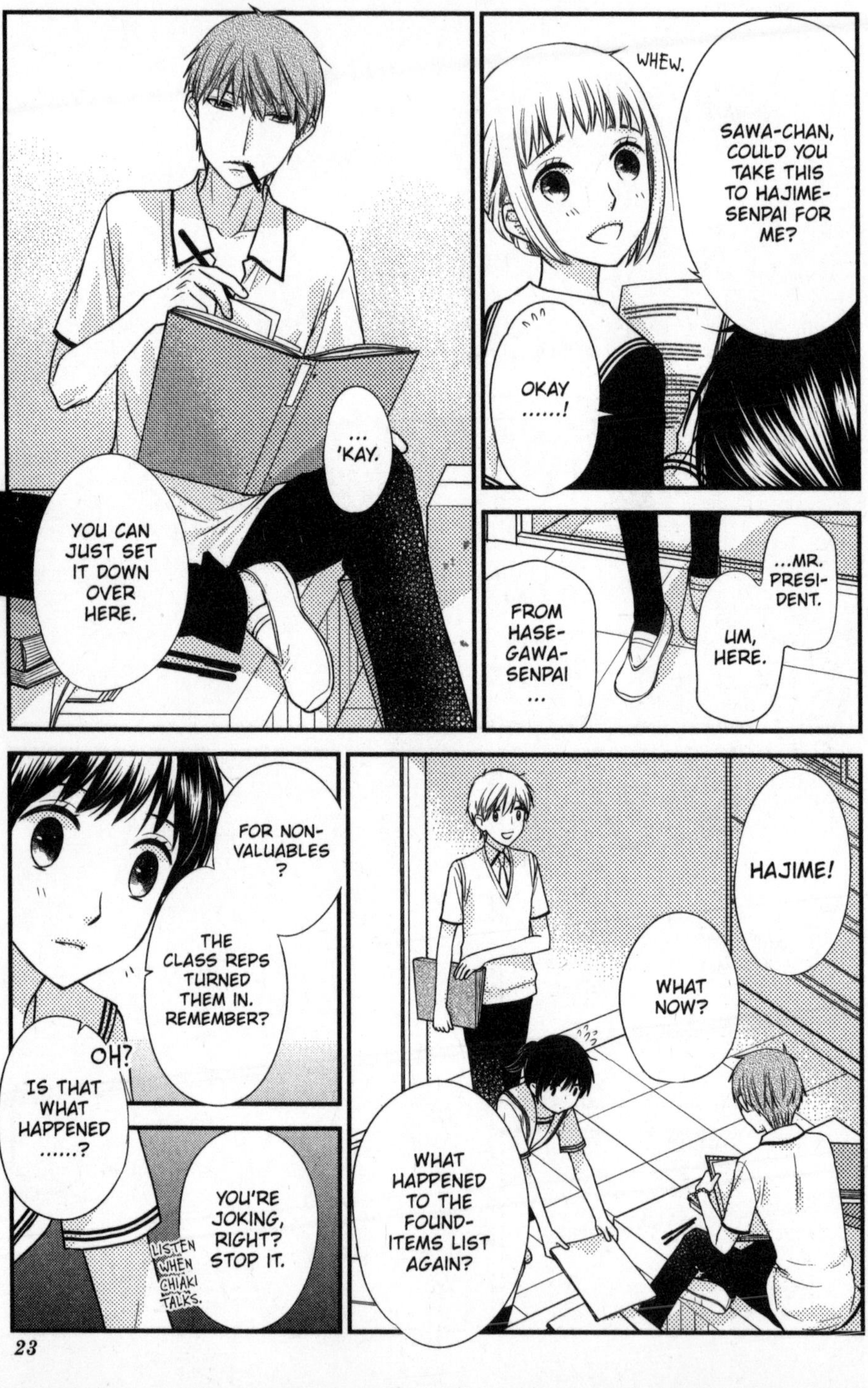
WHEW.
SAWA-CHAN, COULD YOU TAKE THIS TO HAJIME-SENPAI FOR ME?
OKAY ......!
...MR. PRESIDENT.
UM, HERE.
FROM HASEGAWA-SENPAI ...
... 'KAY.
YOU CAN JUST SET IT DOWN OVER HERE.
HAJIME!
WHAT NOW?
WHAT HAPPENED TO THE FOUND-ITEMS LIST AGAIN?
FOR NON-VALUABLES?
THE CLASS REPS TURNED THEM IN. REMEMBER?
OH? IS THAT WHAT HAPPENED ......?
YOU'RE JOKING, RIGHT? STOP IT.
LISTEN WHEN CHIAKI TALKS.

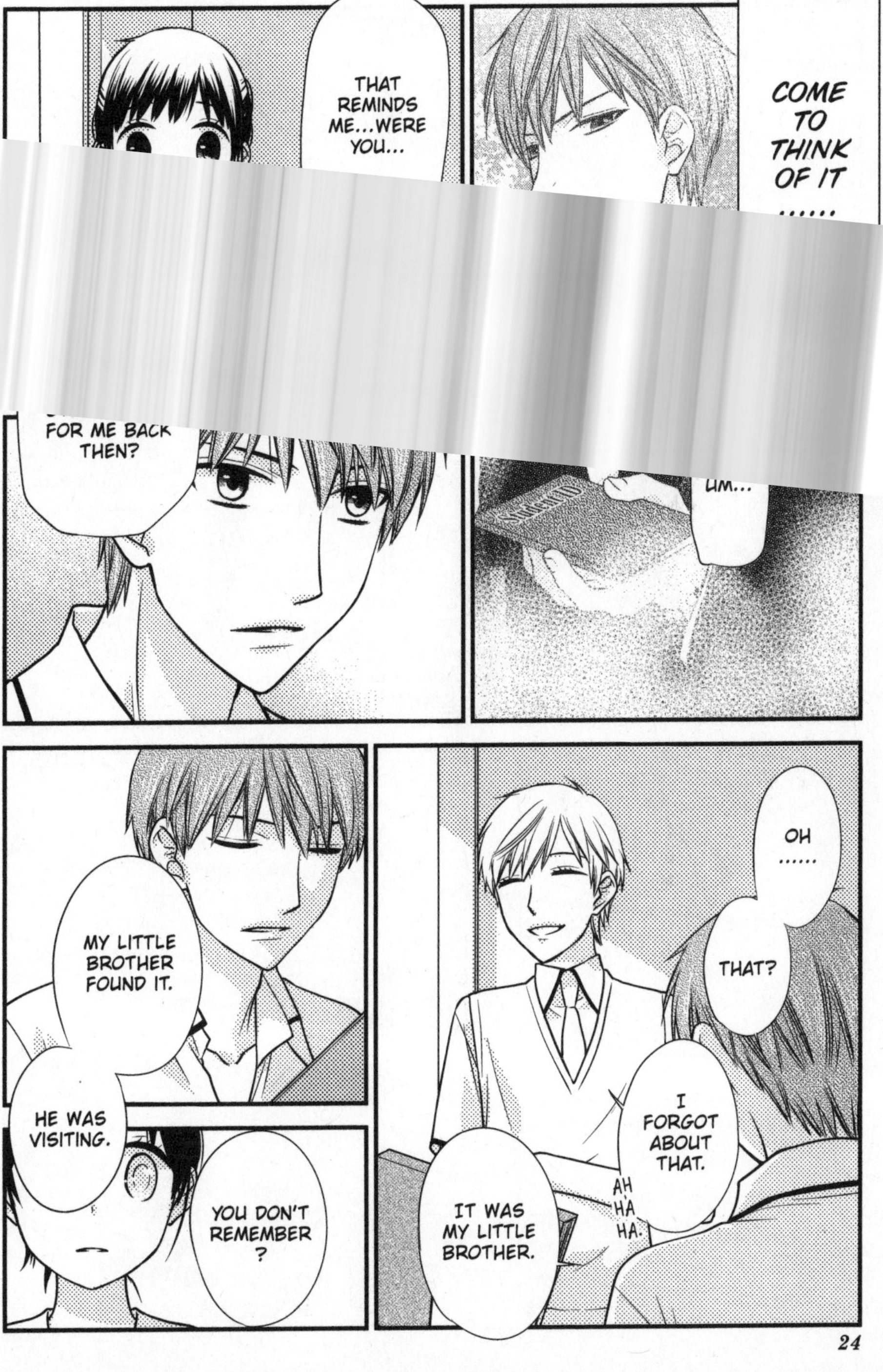
COME TO THINK OF IT......
THAT REMINDS ME...WERE YOU...
UM...
FOR ME BACK THEN?
OH......
THAT?
I FORGOT ABOUT THAT.
AH HA HA.
IT WAS MY LITTLE BROTHER.
MY LITTLE BROTHER FOUND IT.
HE WAS VISITING.
YOU DON'T REMEMBER?

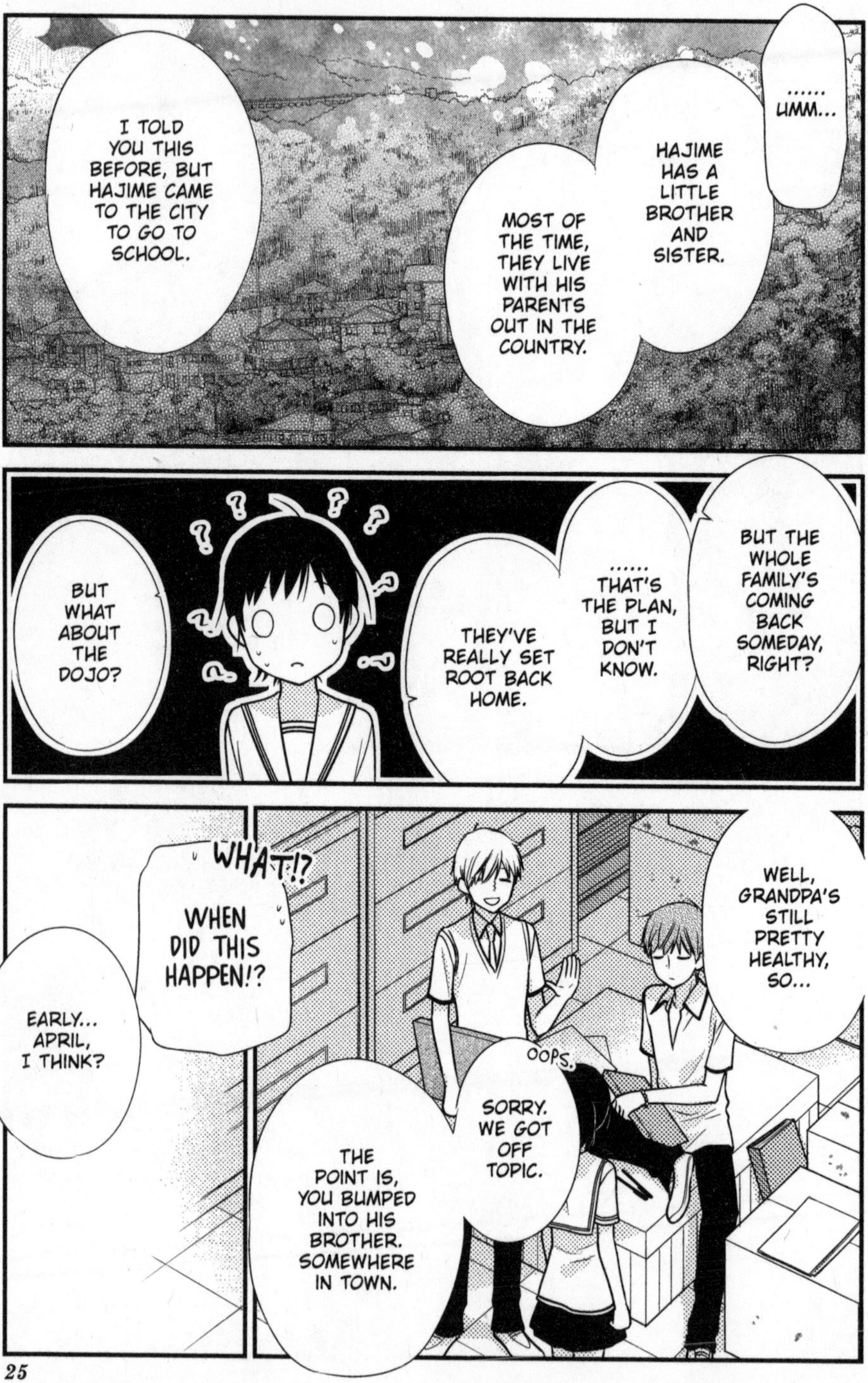
......UMM...
HAJIME HAS A LITTLE BROTHER AND SISTER.
MOST OF THE TIME, THEY LIVE WITH HIS PARENTS OUT IN THE COUNTRY.
I TOLD YOU THIS BEFORE, BUT HAJIME CAME TO THE CITY TO GO TO SCHOOL.
BUT THE WHOLE FAMILY'S COMING BACK SOMEDAY, RIGHT?
......THAT'S THE PLAN, BUT I DON'T KNOW.
THEY'VE REALLY SET ROOT BACK HOME.
BUT WHAT ABOUT THE DOJO?
WELL, GRANDPA'S STILL PRETTY HEALTHY, SO...
OOPS.
SORRY. WE GOT OFF TOPIC.
THE POINT IS, YOU BUMPED INTO HIS BROTHER. SOMEWHERE IN TOWN.
WHAT!?
WHEN DID THIS HAPPEN!?
EARLY... APRIL, I THINK?

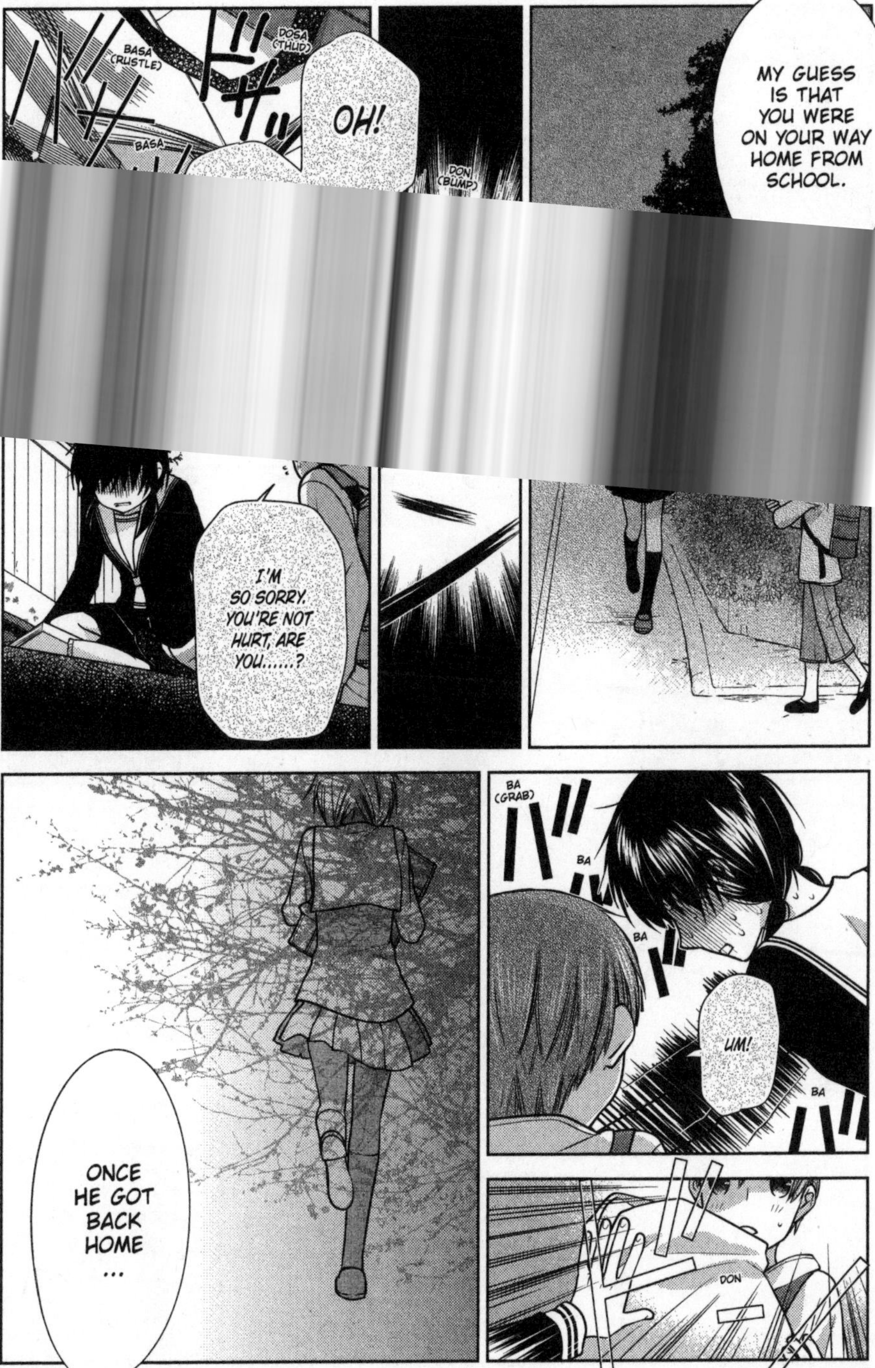
MY GUESS IS THAT YOU WERE ON YOUR WAY HOME FROM SCHOOL.
DON (BUMP)
DOSA (THUD)
OH!
BASA (RUSTLE)
BASA
I'M SO SORRY. YOU'RE NOT HURT, ARE YOU......?
BA (GRAB)
BA
BA
UM!
BA
DON
ONCE HE GOT BACK HOME ...

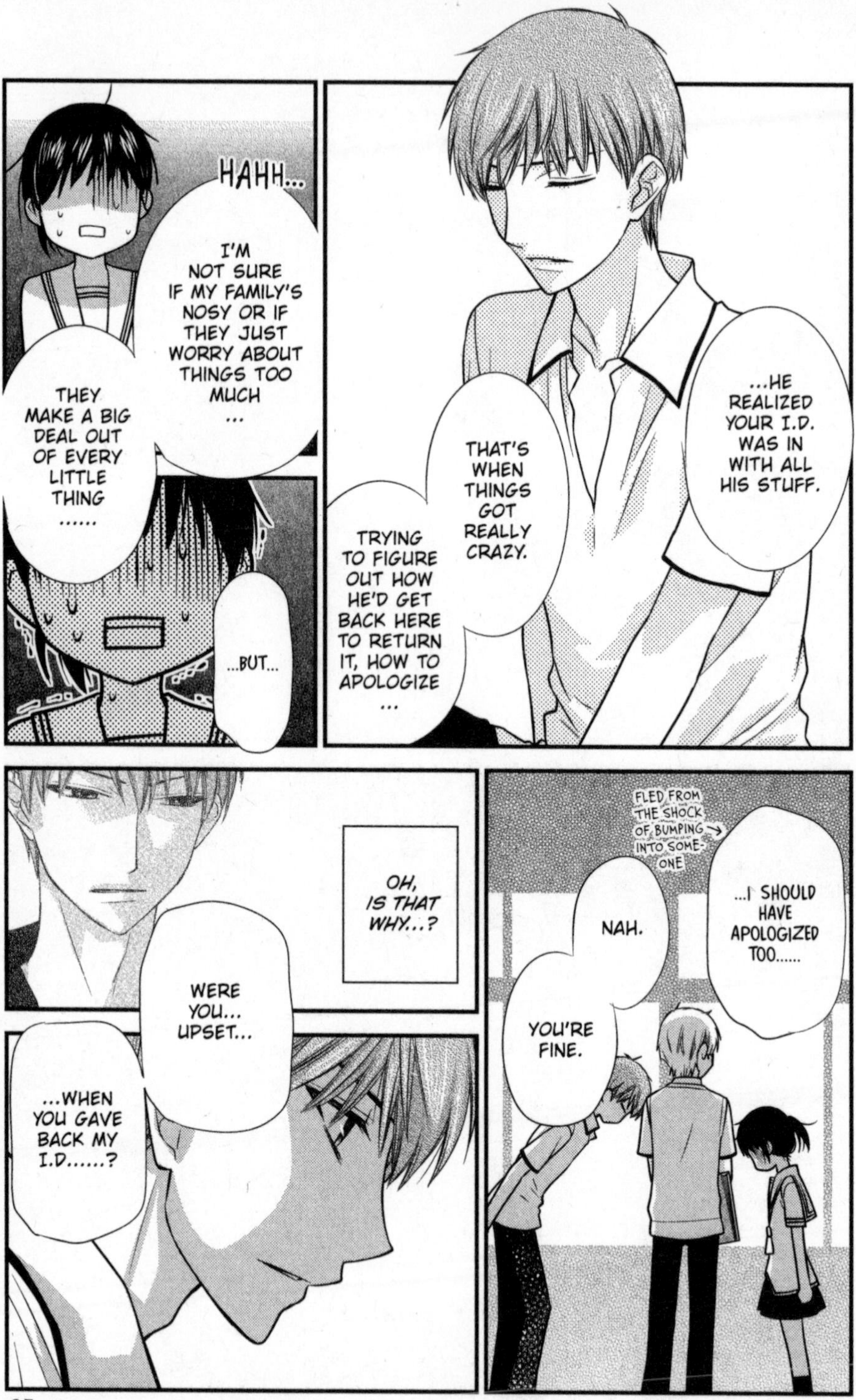
...HE REALIZED YOUR I.D. WAS IN WITH ALL HIS STUFF.
THAT'S WHEN THINGS GOT REALLY CRAZY.
TRYING TO FIGURE OUT HOW HE'D GET BACK HERE TO RETURN IT, HOW TO APOLOGIZE...
HAHH...
I'M NOT SURE IF MY FAMILY'S NOSY OR IF THEY JUST WORRY ABOUT THINGS TOO MUCH...
THEY MAKE A BIG DEAL OUT OF EVERY LITTLE THING......
...BUT...
FLED FROM THE SHOCK OF BUMPING INTO SOME-ONE
...I SHOULD HAVE APOLOGIZED TOO......
NAH.
YOU'RE FINE.
OH, IS THAT WHY...?
WERE YOU... UPSET...
...WHEN YOU GAVE BACK MY I.D......?

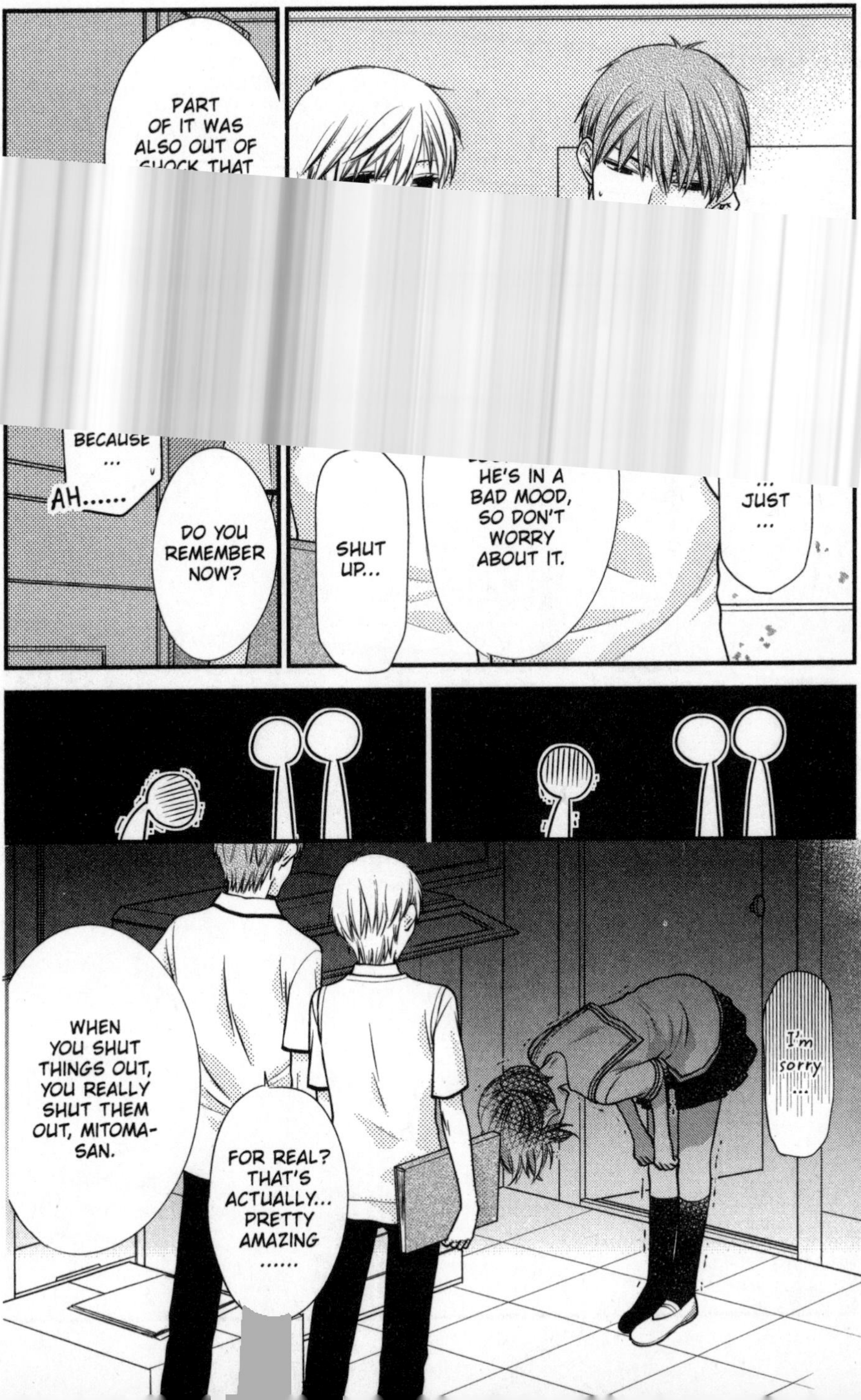
... JUST ...
HE'S IN A BAD MOOD, SO DON'T WORRY ABOUT IT.
SHUT UP...
PART OF IT WAS ALSO OUT OF
BECAUSE ...
AH......
DO YOU REMEMBER NOW?
I'm sorry ...
WHEN YOU SHUT THINGS OUT, YOU REALLY SHUT THEM OUT, MITOMA-SAN.
FOR REAL? THAT'S ACTUALLY... PRETTY AMAZING ......

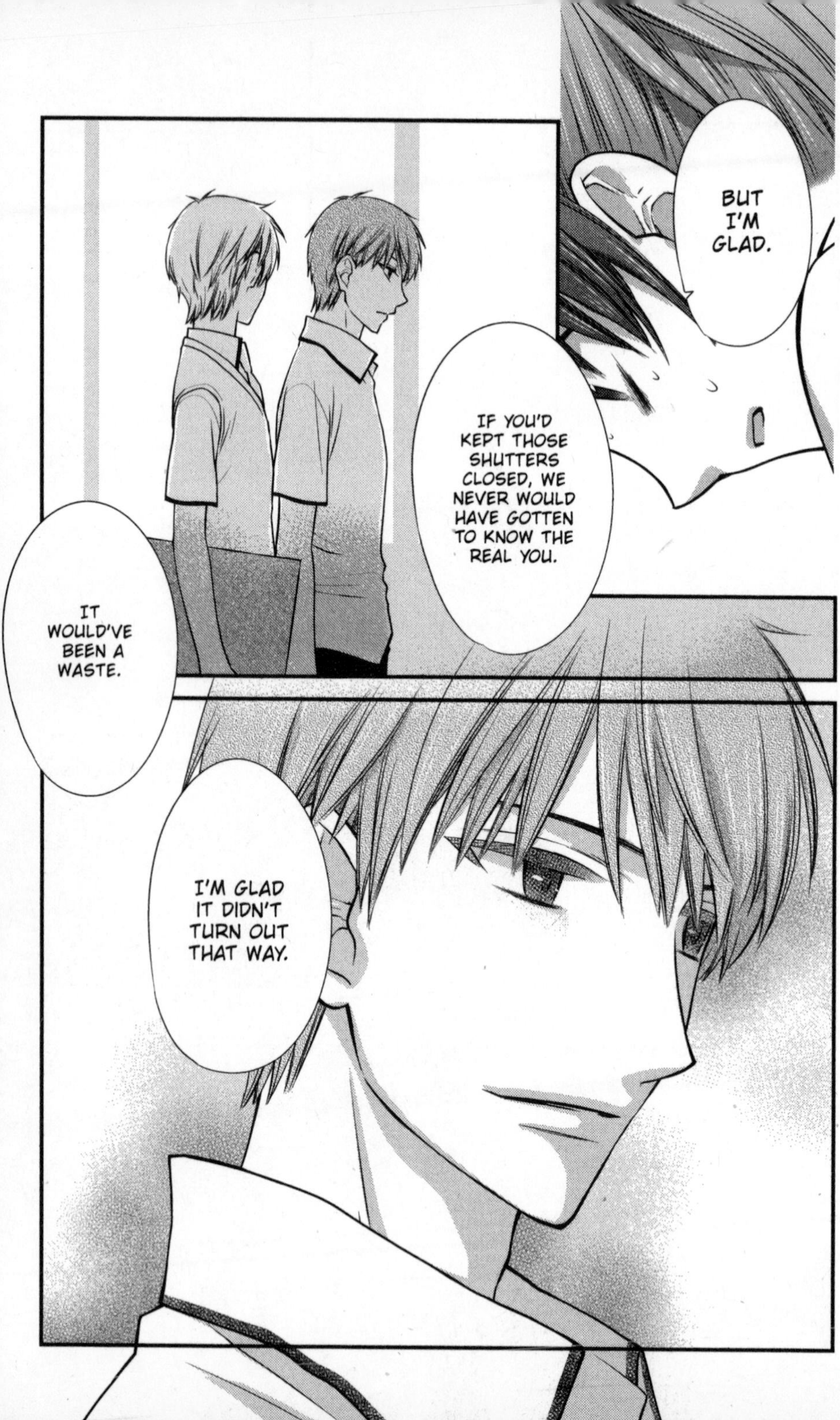
BUT I'M GLAD.
IF YOU'D KEPT THOSE SHUTTERS CLOSED, WE NEVER WOULD HAVE GOTTEN TO KNOW THE REAL YOU.
IT WOULD'VE BEEN A WASTE.
I'M GLAD IT DIDN'T TURN OUT THAT WAY.

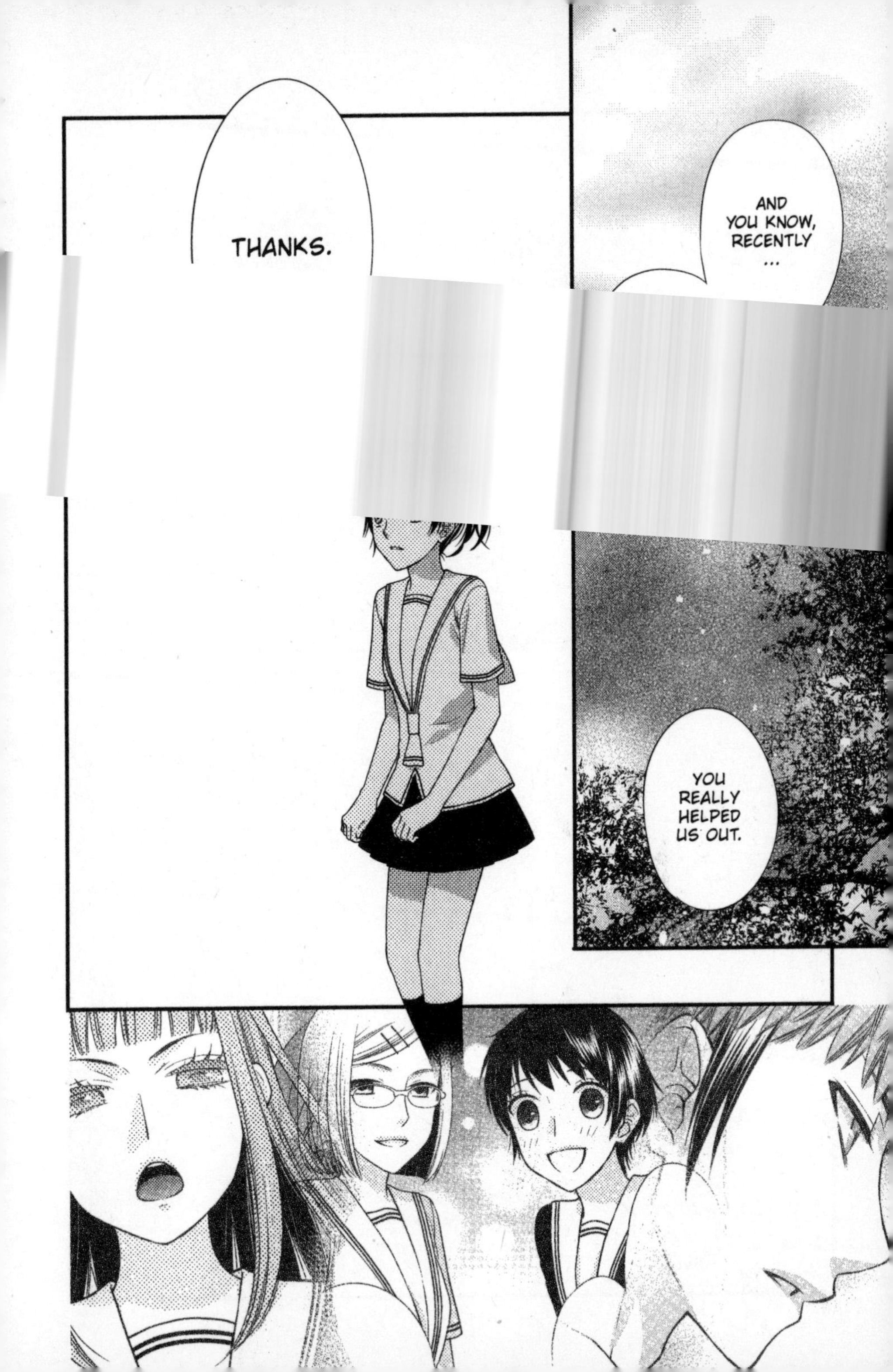
AND YOU KNOW, RECENTLY ...
YOU REALLY HELPED US OUT.
THANKS.

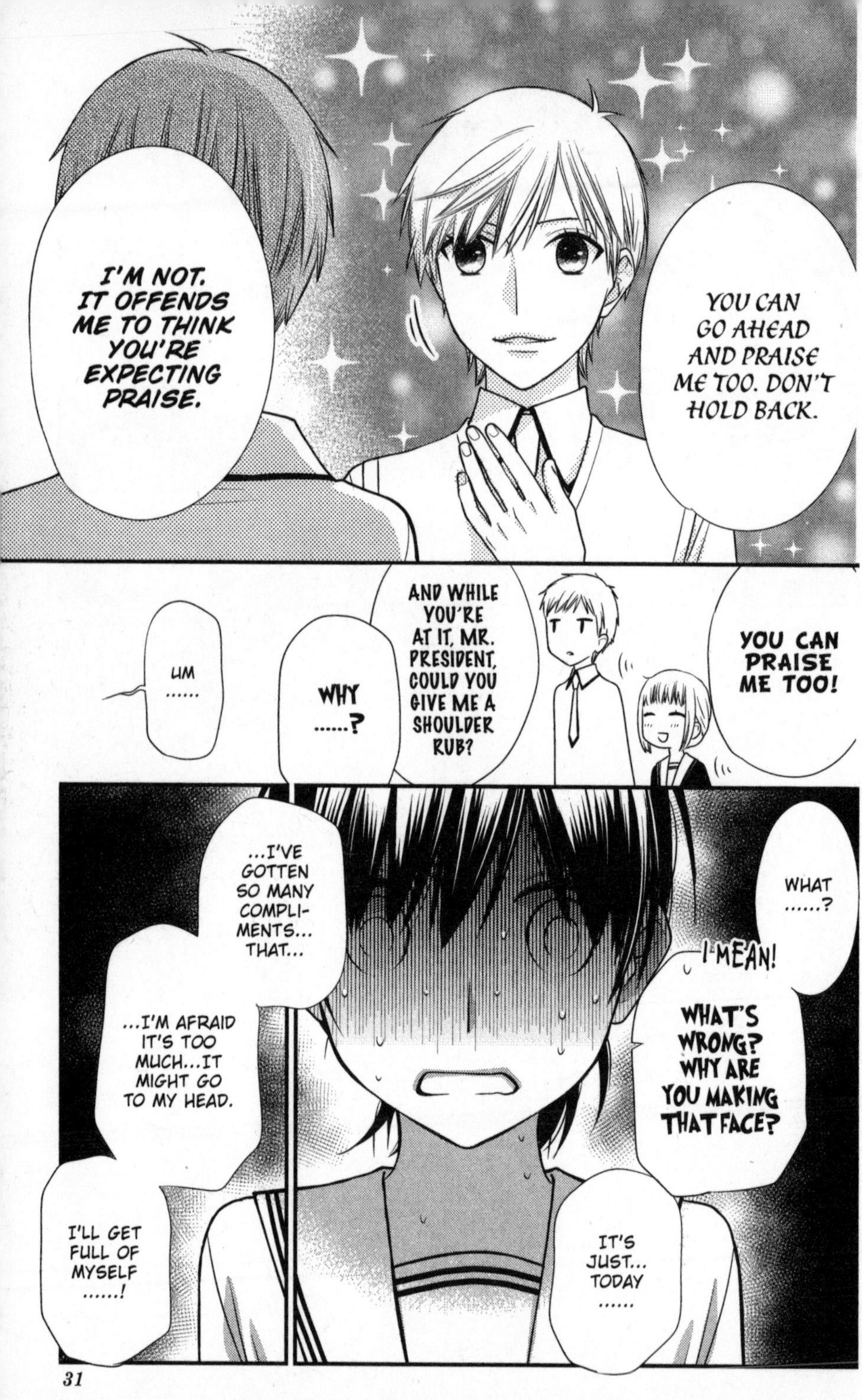
YOU CAN GO AHEAD AND PRAISE ME TOO. DON'T HOLD BACK.
I'M NOT. IT OFFENDS ME TO THINK YOU'RE EXPECTING PRAISE.
YOU CAN PRAISE ME TOO!
AND WHILE YOU'RE AT IT, MR. PRESIDENT, COULD YOU GIVE ME A SHOULDER RUB?
WHY......?
UM......
WHAT......?
I MEAN!
WHAT'S WRONG? WHY ARE YOU MAKING THAT FACE?
IT'S JUST... TODAY......
...I'VE GOTTEN SO MANY COMPLIMENTS... THAT...
...I'M AFRAID IT'S TOO MUCH...IT MIGHT GO TO MY HEAD.
I'LL GET FULL OF MYSELF......!

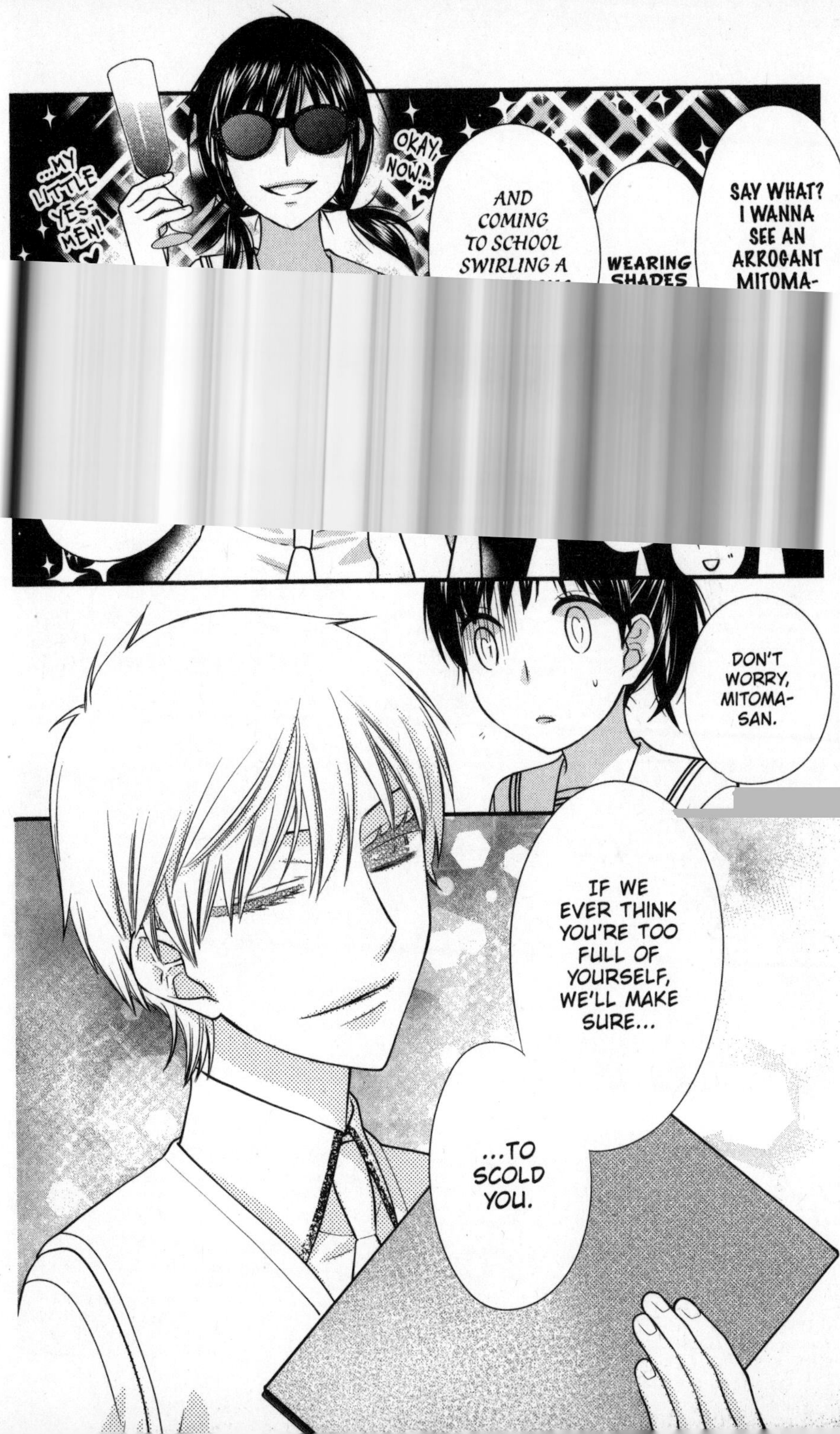
SAY WHAT? I WANNA SEE AN ARROGANT MITOMA-
WEARING
AND COMING TO SCHOOL SWIRLING A
OKAY, NOW...♥
...MY LITTLE YES-MEN! ♥
DON'T WORRY, MITOMA-SAN.
IF WE EVER THINK YOU'RE TOO FULL OF YOURSELF, WE'LL MAKE SURE...
...TO SCOLD YOU.

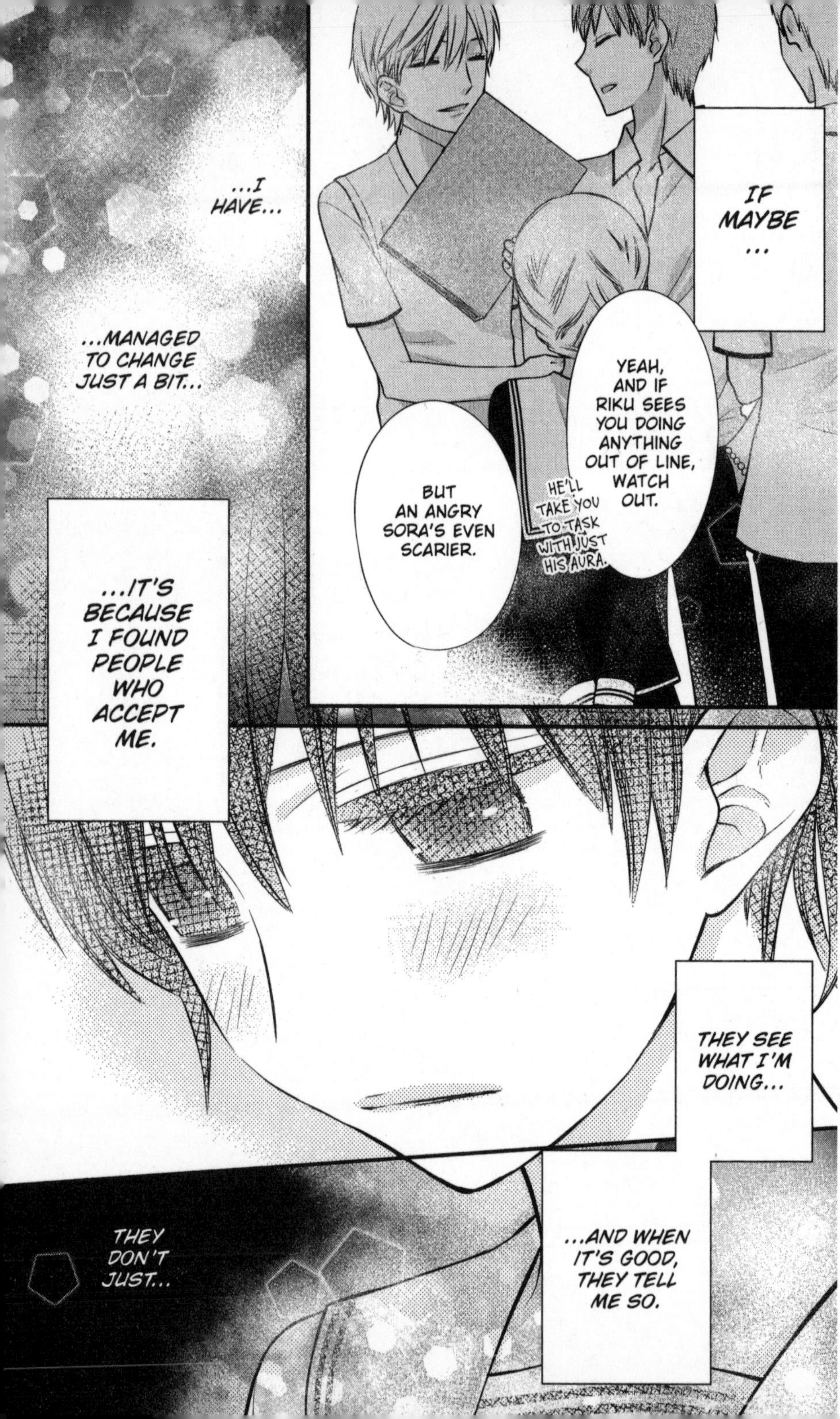
IF MAYBE...
YEAH, AND IF RIKU SEES YOU DOING ANYTHING OUT OF LINE, WATCH OUT.
HE'LL TAKE YOU TO TASK WITH JUST HIS AURA.
BUT AN ANGRY SORA'S EVEN SCARIER.
...I HAVE...
...MANAGED TO CHANGE JUST A BIT...
...IT'S BECAUSE I FOUND PEOPLE WHO ACCEPT ME.
THEY SEE WHAT I'M DOING...
THEY DON'T JUST...
...AND WHEN IT'S GOOD, THEY TELL ME SO.

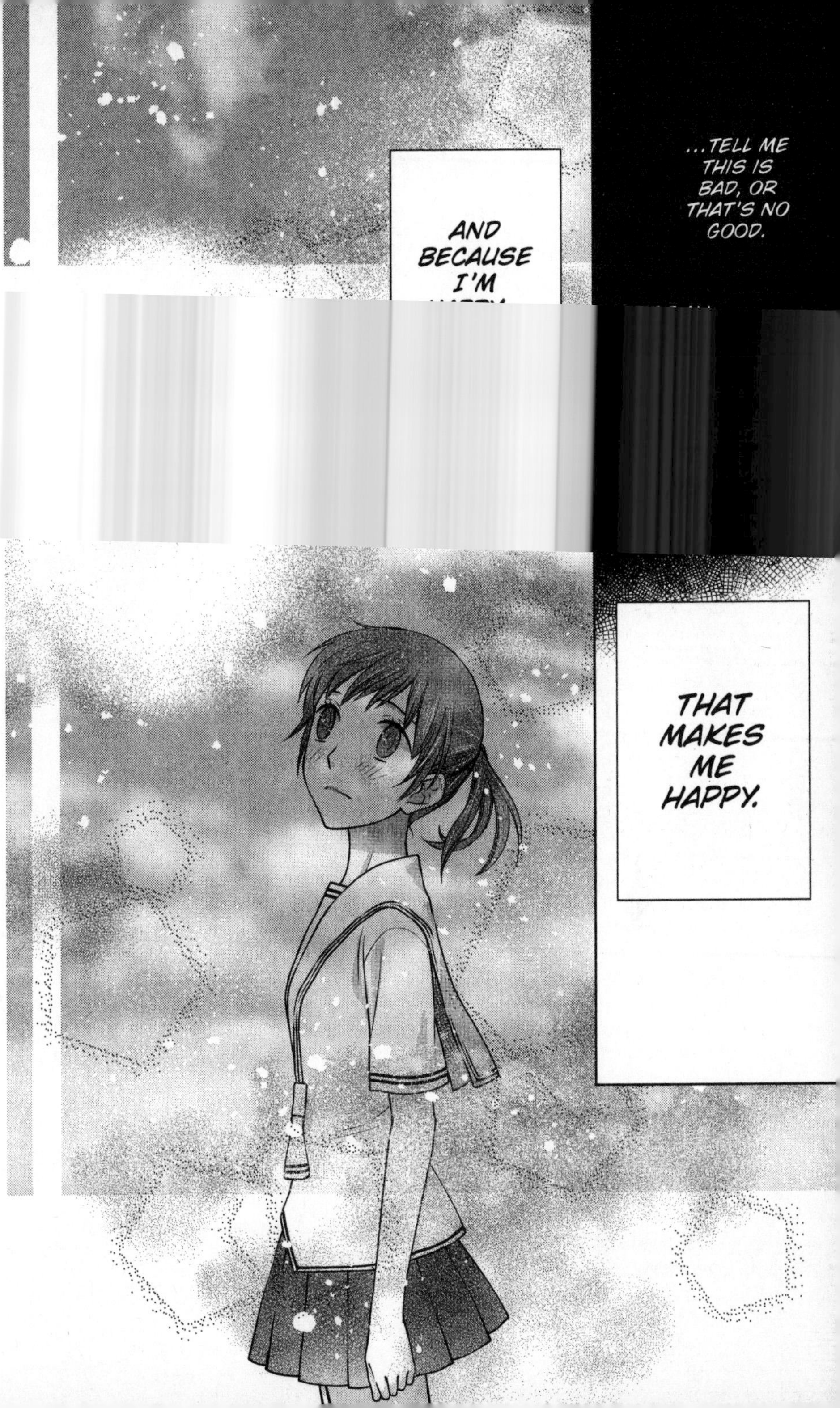
...TELL ME THIS IS BAD, OR THAT'S NO GOOD.
AND BECAUSE I'M
THAT MAKES ME HAPPY.

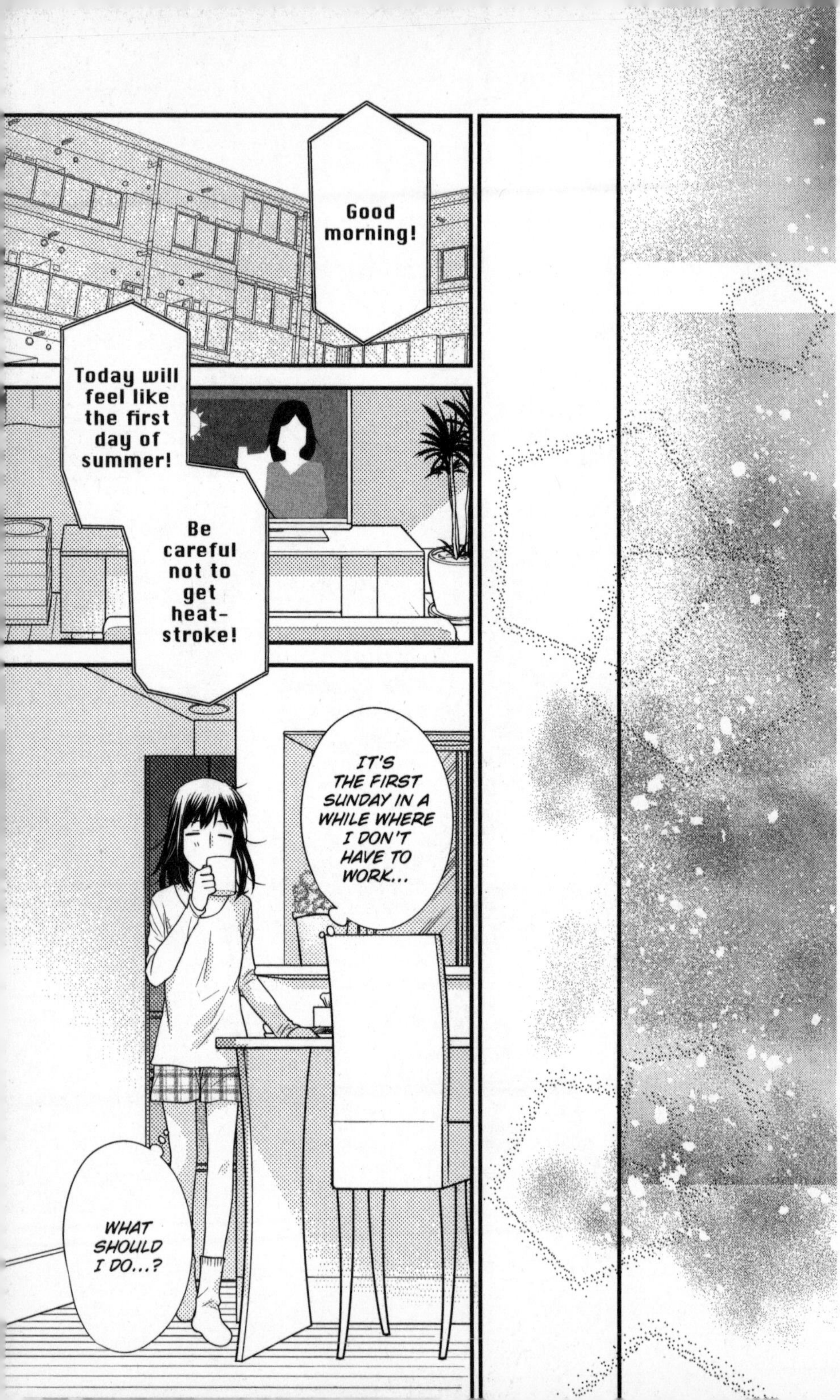
Good morning!
Today will feel like the first day of summer!
Be careful not to get heat-stroke!
IT'S THE FIRST SUNDAY IN A WHILE WHERE I DON'T HAVE TO WORK...
WHAT SHOULD I DO...?

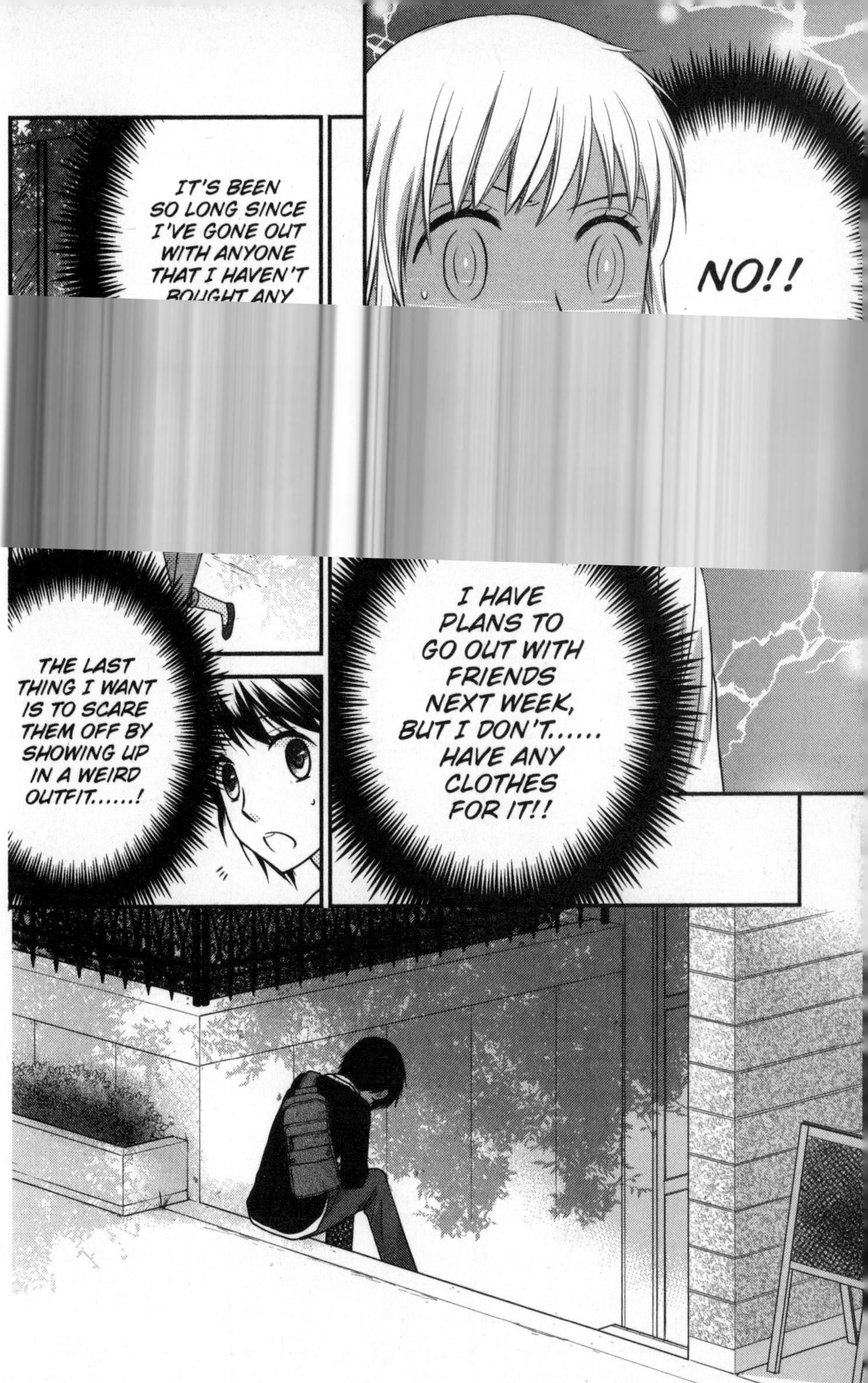
NO!!
IT'S BEEN SO LONG SINCE I'VE GONE OUT WITH ANYONE THAT I HAVEN'T BOUGHT ANY
I HAVE PLANS TO GO OUT WITH FRIENDS NEXT WEEK, BUT I DON'T...... HAVE ANY CLOTHES FOR IT!!
THE LAST THING I WANT IS TO SCARE THEM OFF BY SHOWING UP IN A WEIRD OUTFIT......!

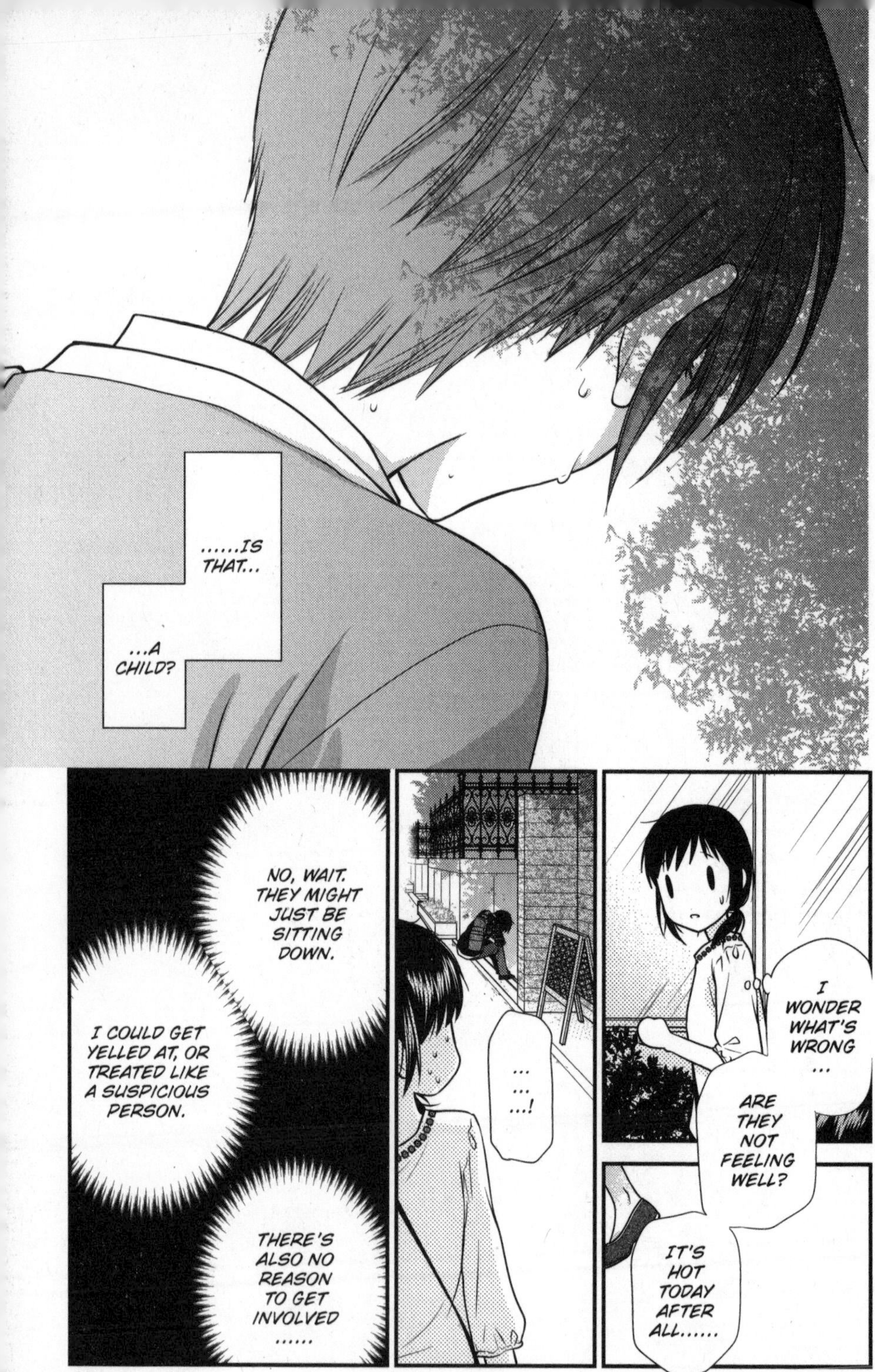
......IS THAT...
...A CHILD?
I WONDER WHAT'S WRONG...
ARE THEY NOT FEELING WELL?
IT'S HOT TODAY AFTER ALL......
... ...!
NO, WAIT. THEY MIGHT JUST BE SITTING DOWN.
I COULD GET YELLED AT, OR TREATED LIKE A SUSPICIOUS PERSON.
THERE'S ALSO NO REASON TO GET INVOLVED ......

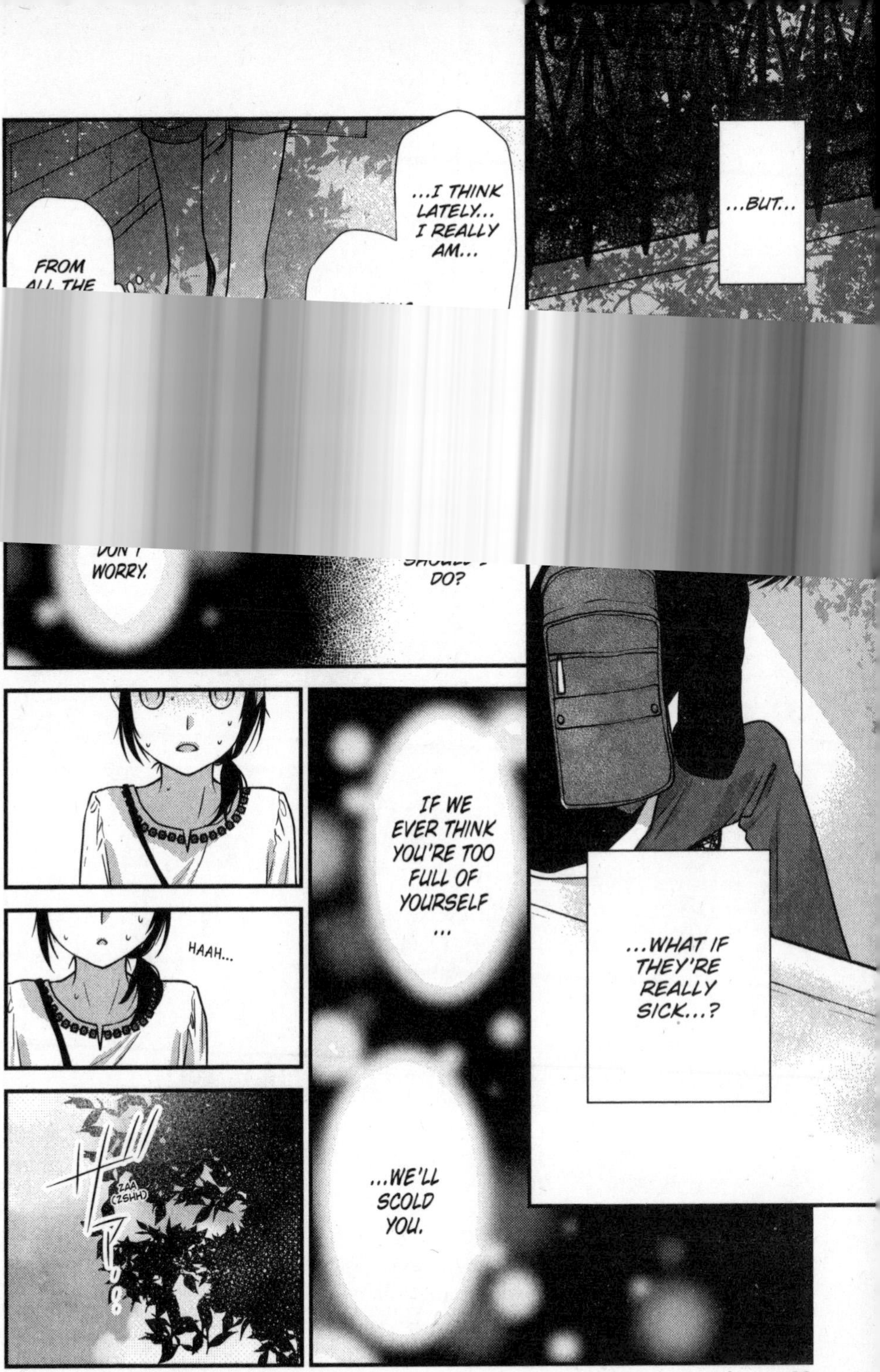
...BUT...
...WHAT IF THEY'RE REALLY SICK...?
...I THINK LATELY... I REALLY AM...
FROM ALL THE
DO?
WORRY.
IF WE EVER THINK YOU'RE TOO FULL OF YOURSELF ...
...WE'LL SCOLD YOU.
HAAH...
ZAA (ZSHH)

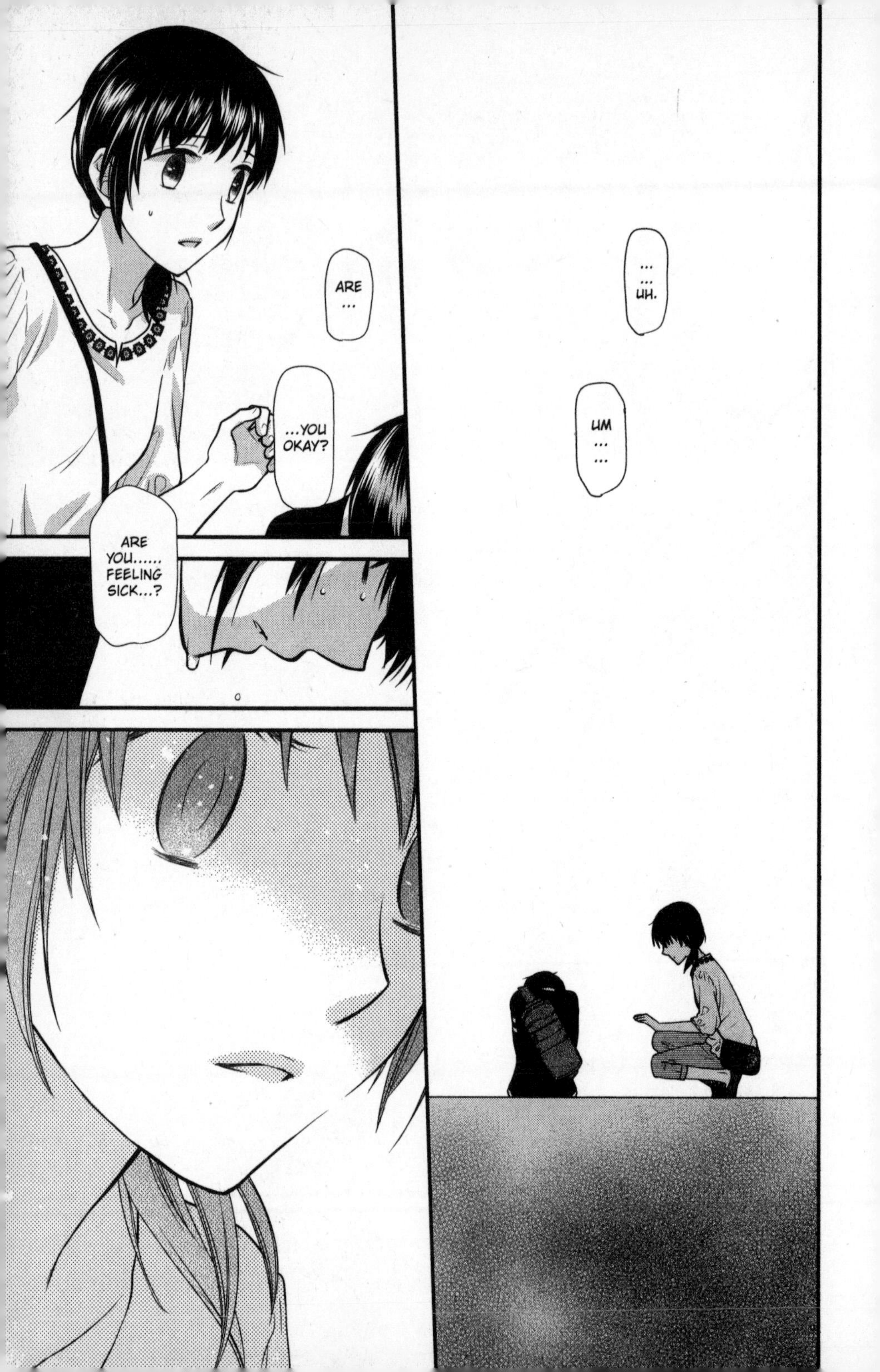
... ... UH.
UM ... ...
ARE ...
...YOU OKAY?
ARE YOU...... FEELING SICK...?

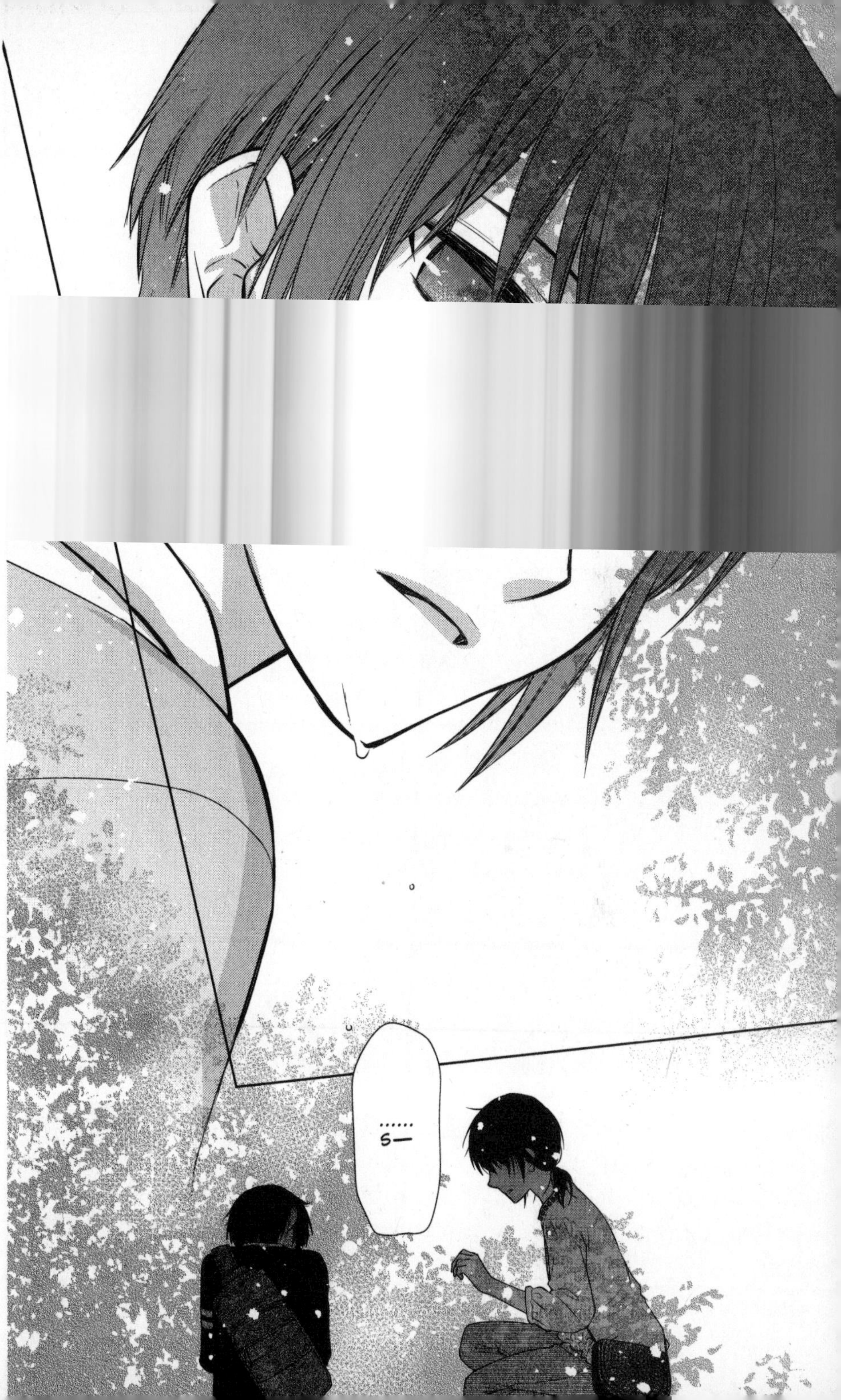
......S—

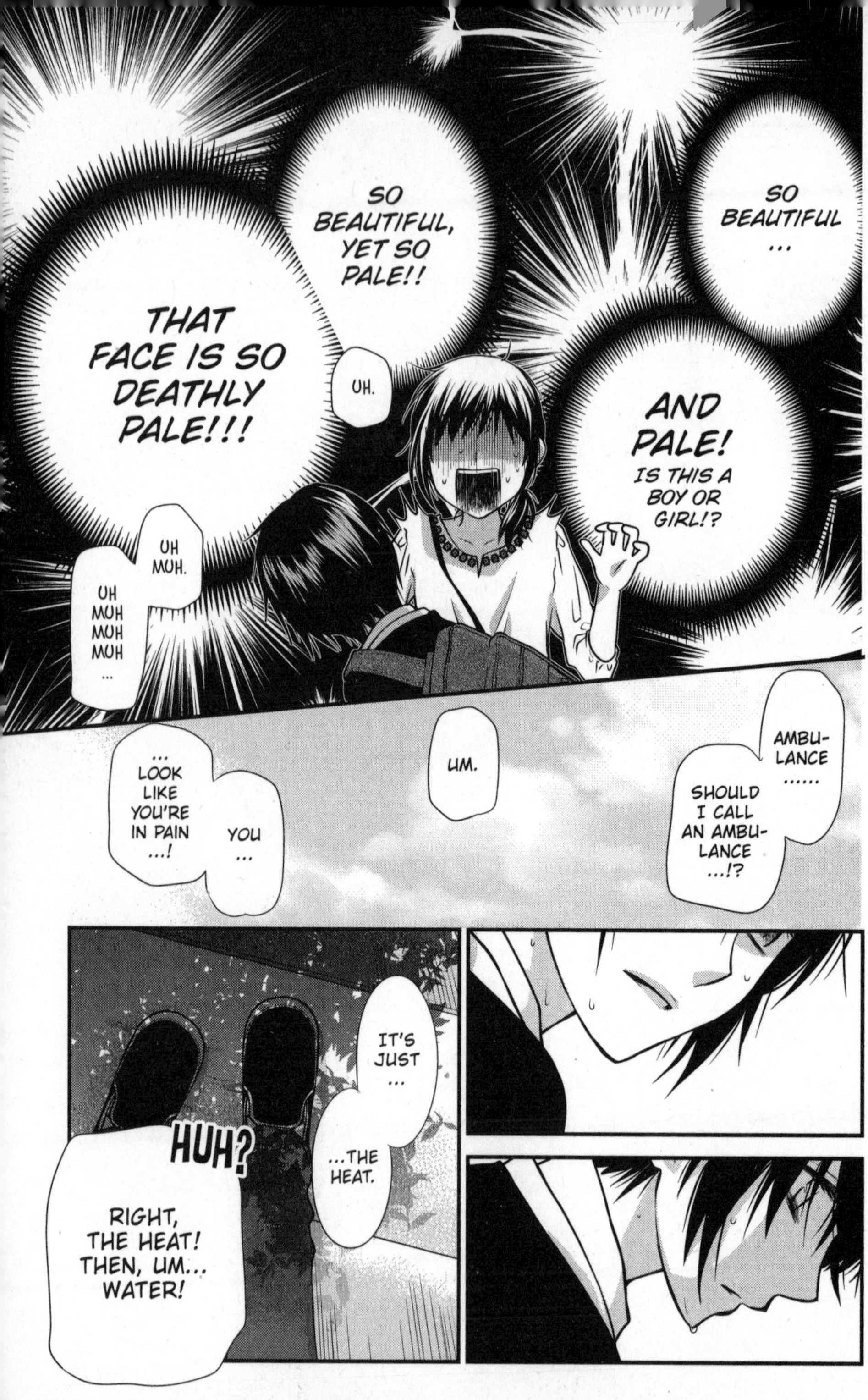
SO BEAUTIFUL ...
SO BEAUTIFUL, YET SO PALE!!
THAT FACE IS SO DEATHLY PALE!!!
AND PALE! IS THIS A BOY OR GIRL!?
UH.
UH MUH.
UH MUH MUH MUH ...
AMBULANCE ......
SHOULD I CALL AN AMBULANCE ...!?
UM.
YOU ...
... LOOK LIKE YOU'RE IN PAIN ...!
IT'S JUST ...
...THE HEAT.
HUH?
RIGHT, THE HEAT! THEN, UM... WATER!

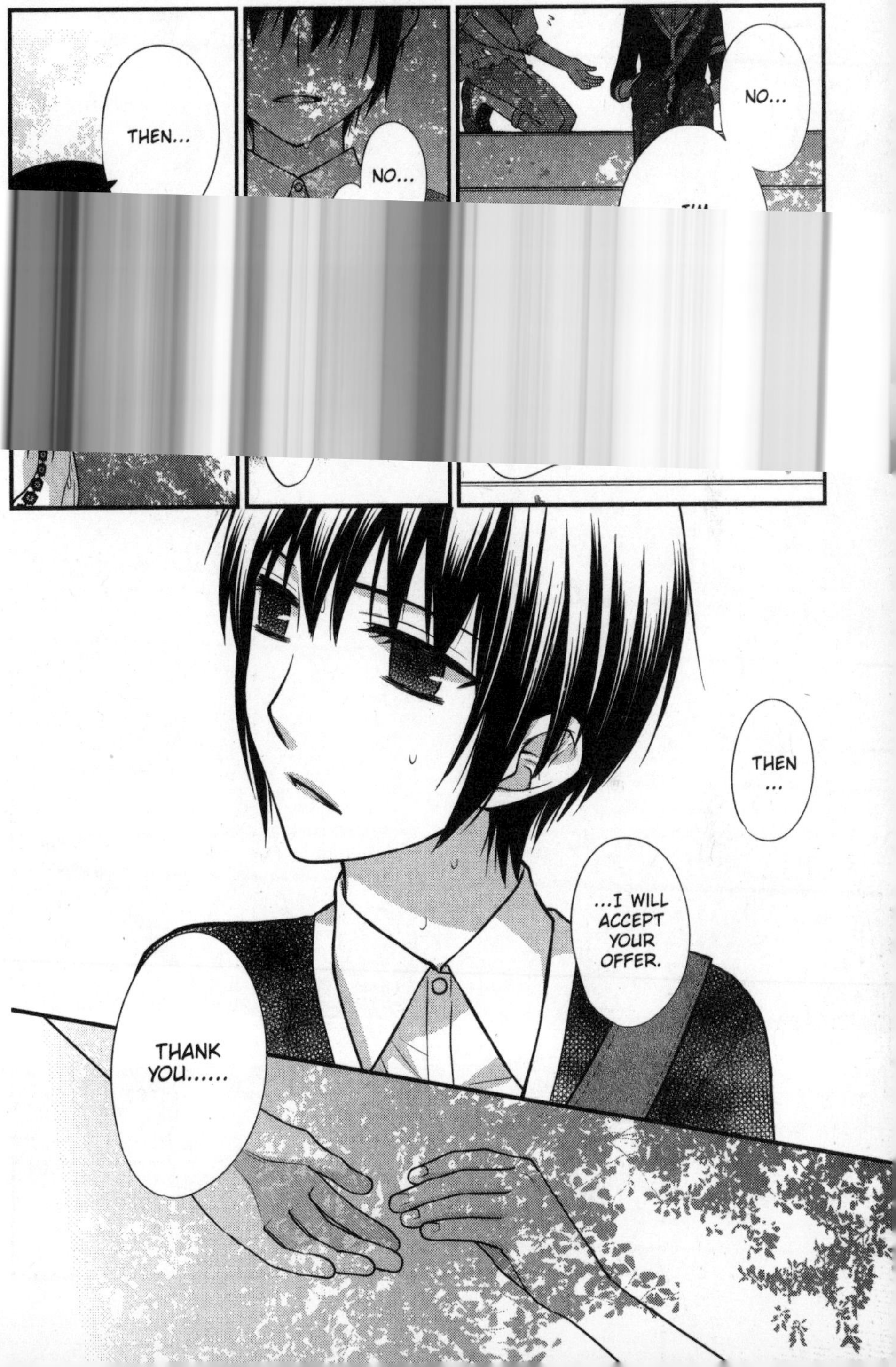
NO...
NO...
THEN...
THEN...
...I WILL ACCEPT YOUR OFFER.
THANK YOU......

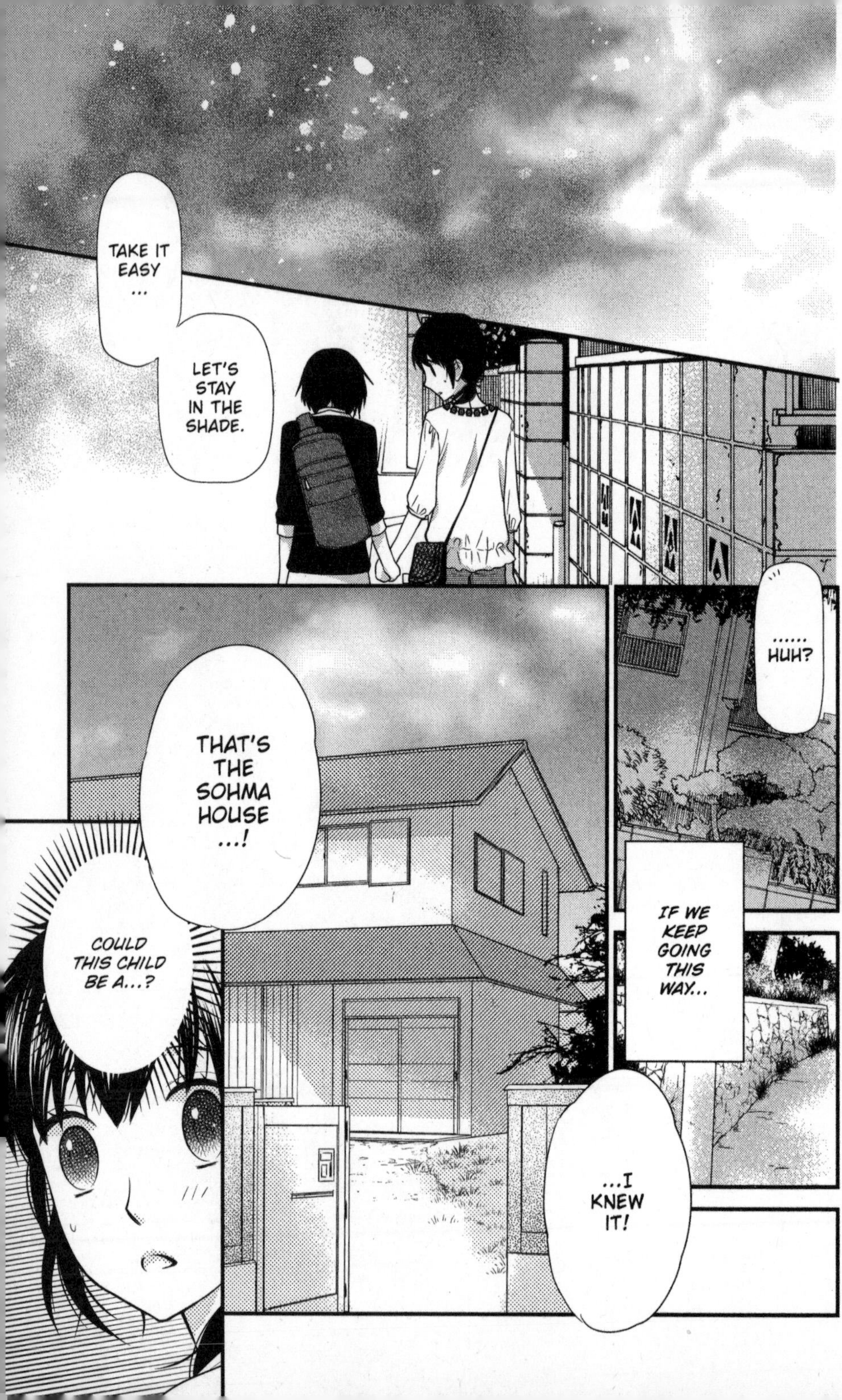
TAKE IT EASY...
LET'S STAY IN THE SHADE.
......HUH?
IF WE KEEP GOING THIS WAY...
...I KNEW IT!
THAT'S THE SOHMA HOUSE...!
COULD THIS CHILD BE A...?

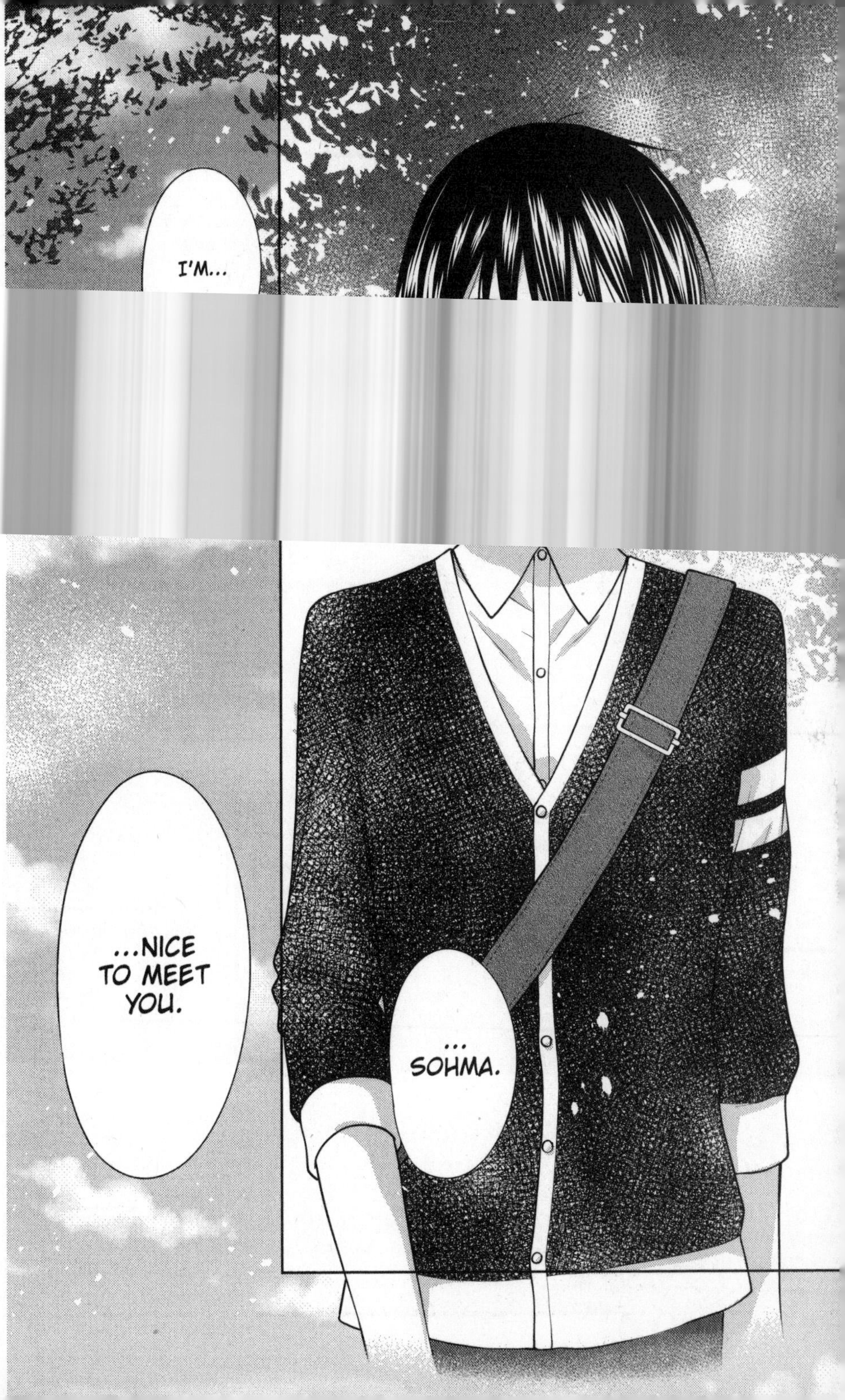
I'M...
...NICE TO MEET YOU.
... SOHMA.

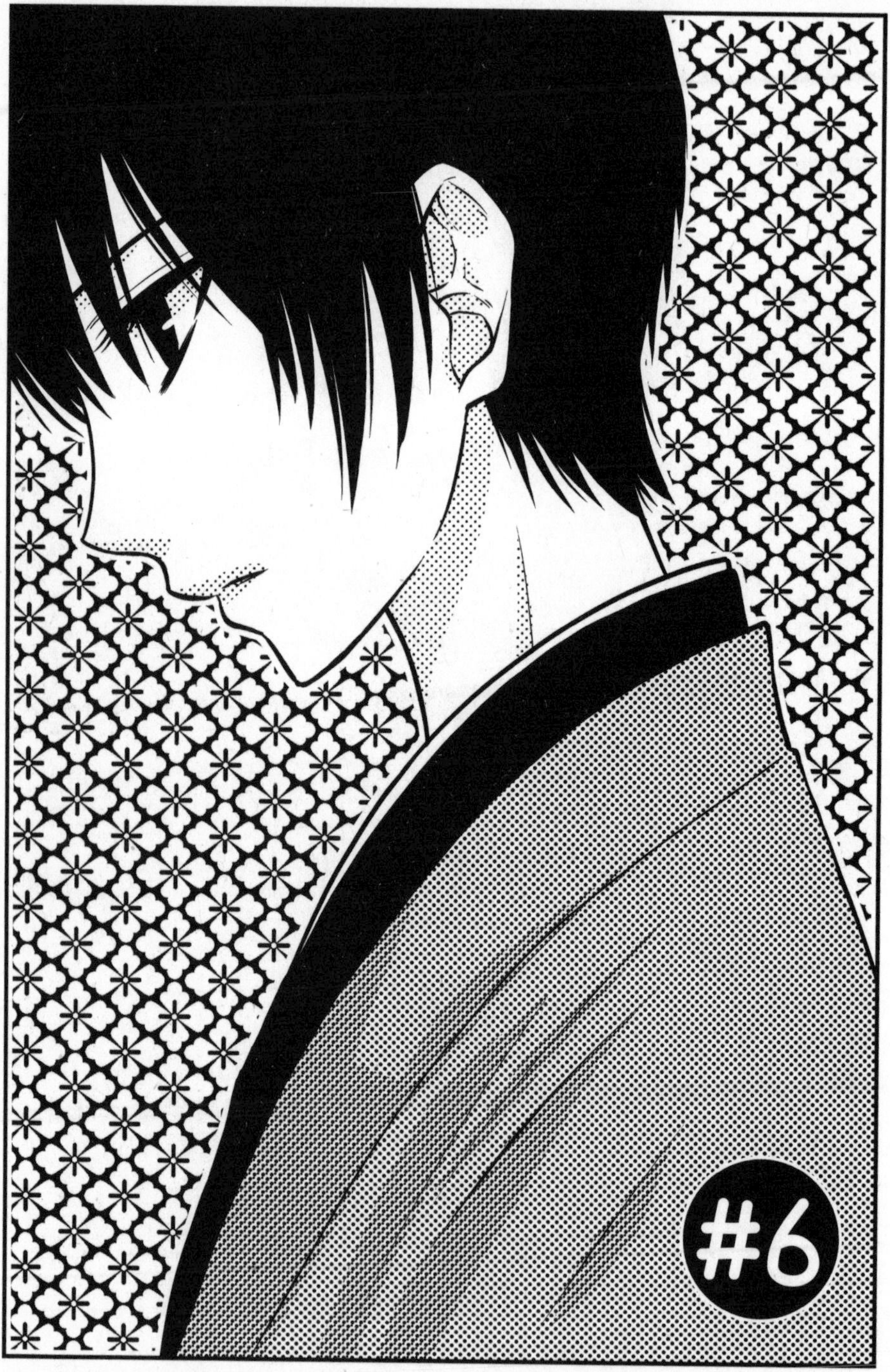
#6

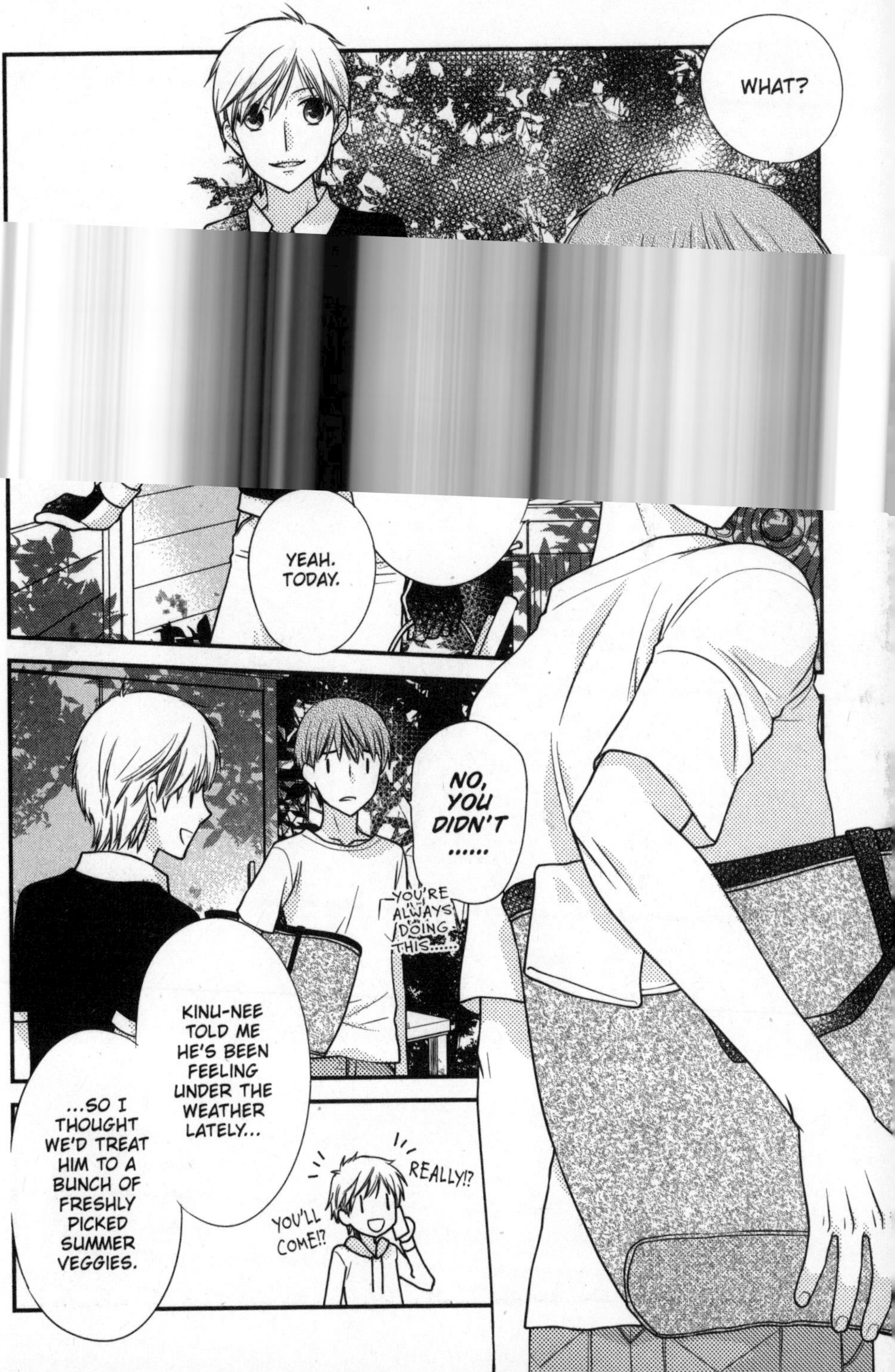
WHAT?
YEAH. TODAY.
NO, YOU DIDN'T ......
YOU'RE ALWAYS DOING THIS......
KINU-NEE TOLD ME HE'S BEEN FEELING UNDER THE WEATHER LATELY...
...SO I THOUGHT WE'D TREAT HIM TO A BUNCH OF FRESHLY PICKED SUMMER VEGGIES.
REALLY!?
YOU'LL COME!?

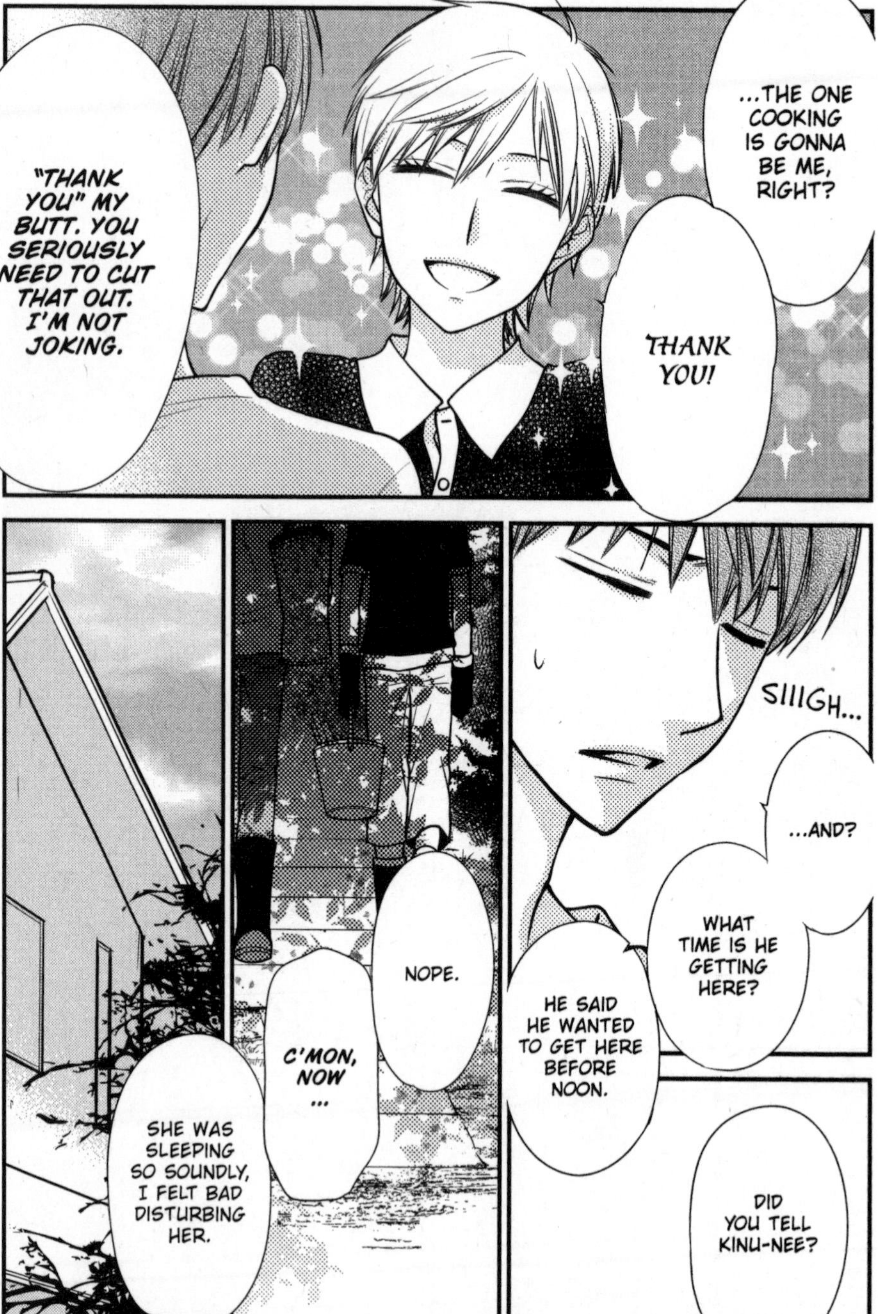
...THE ONE COOKING IS GONNA BE ME, RIGHT?
THANK YOU!
"THANK YOU" MY BUTT. YOU SERIOUSLY NEED TO CUT THAT OUT. I'M NOT JOKING.
SIIIGH...
...AND?
WHAT TIME IS HE GETTING HERE?
HE SAID HE WANTED TO GET HERE BEFORE NOON.
DID YOU TELL KINU-NEE?
NOPE.
C'MON, NOW...
SHE WAS SLEEPING SO SOUNDLY, I FELT BAD DISTURBING HER.

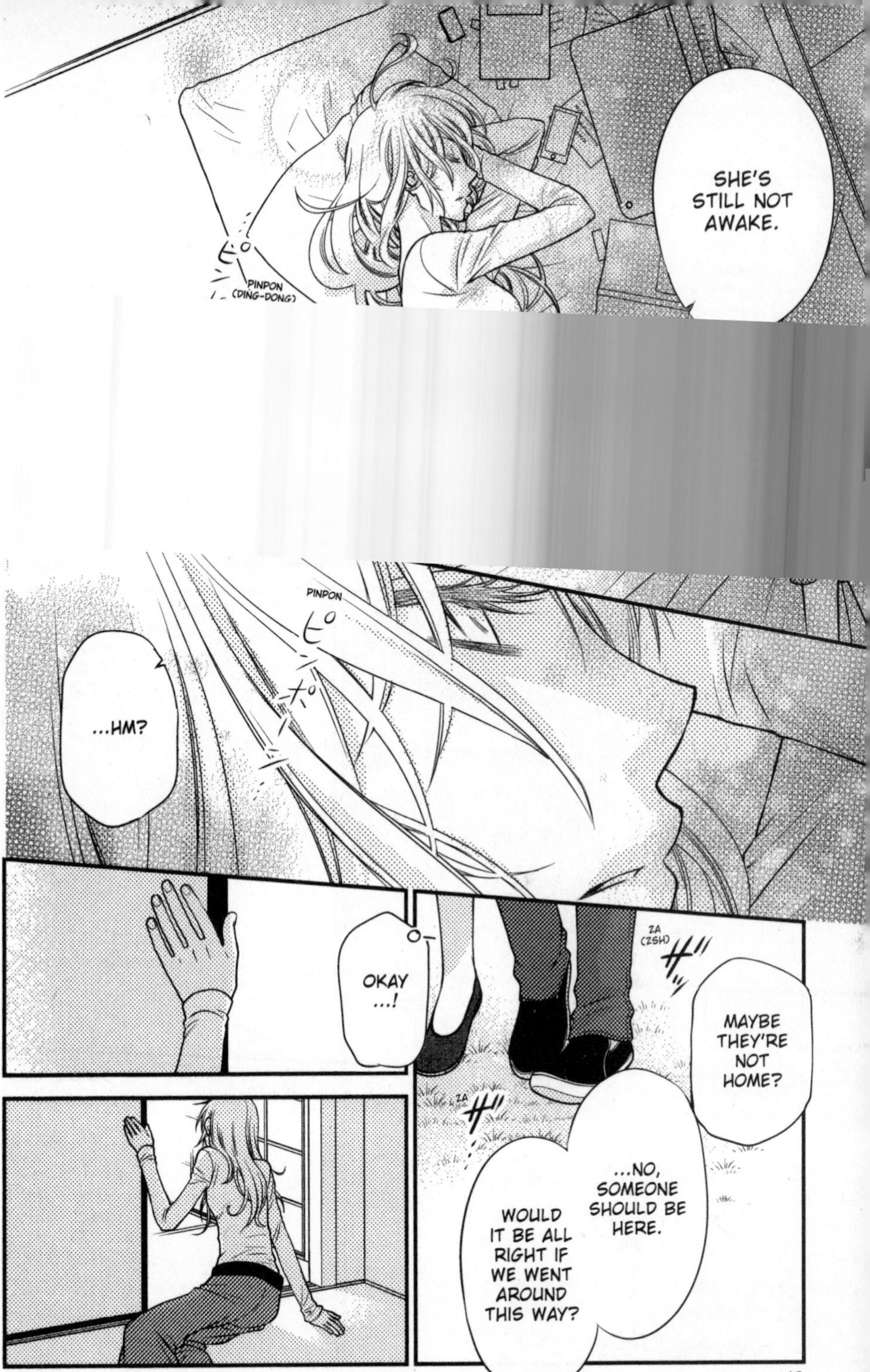
SHE'S STILL NOT AWAKE.
PINPON (DING-DONG)
PINPON
...HM?
ZA (ZSH)
MAYBE THEY'RE NOT HOME?
ZA
...NO, SOMEONE SHOULD BE HERE.
WOULD IT BE ALL RIGHT IF WE WENT AROUND THIS WAY?
OKAY ...!

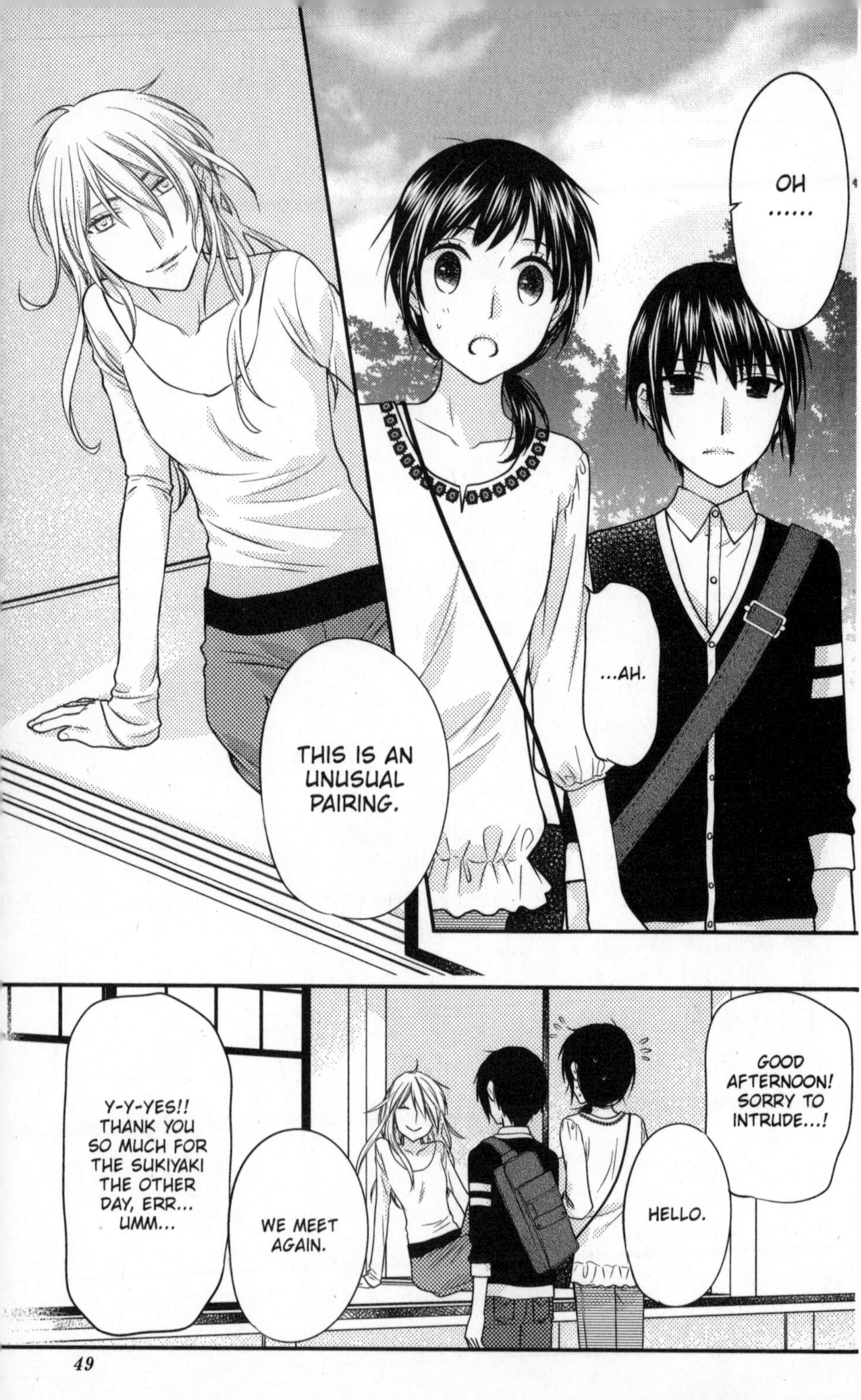
OH ......
...AH.
THIS IS AN UNUSUAL PAIRING.
GOOD AFTERNOON! SORRY TO INTRUDE...!
HELLO.
WE MEET AGAIN.
Y-Y-YES!! THANK YOU SO MUCH FOR THE SUKIYAKI THE OTHER DAY, ERR... UMM...

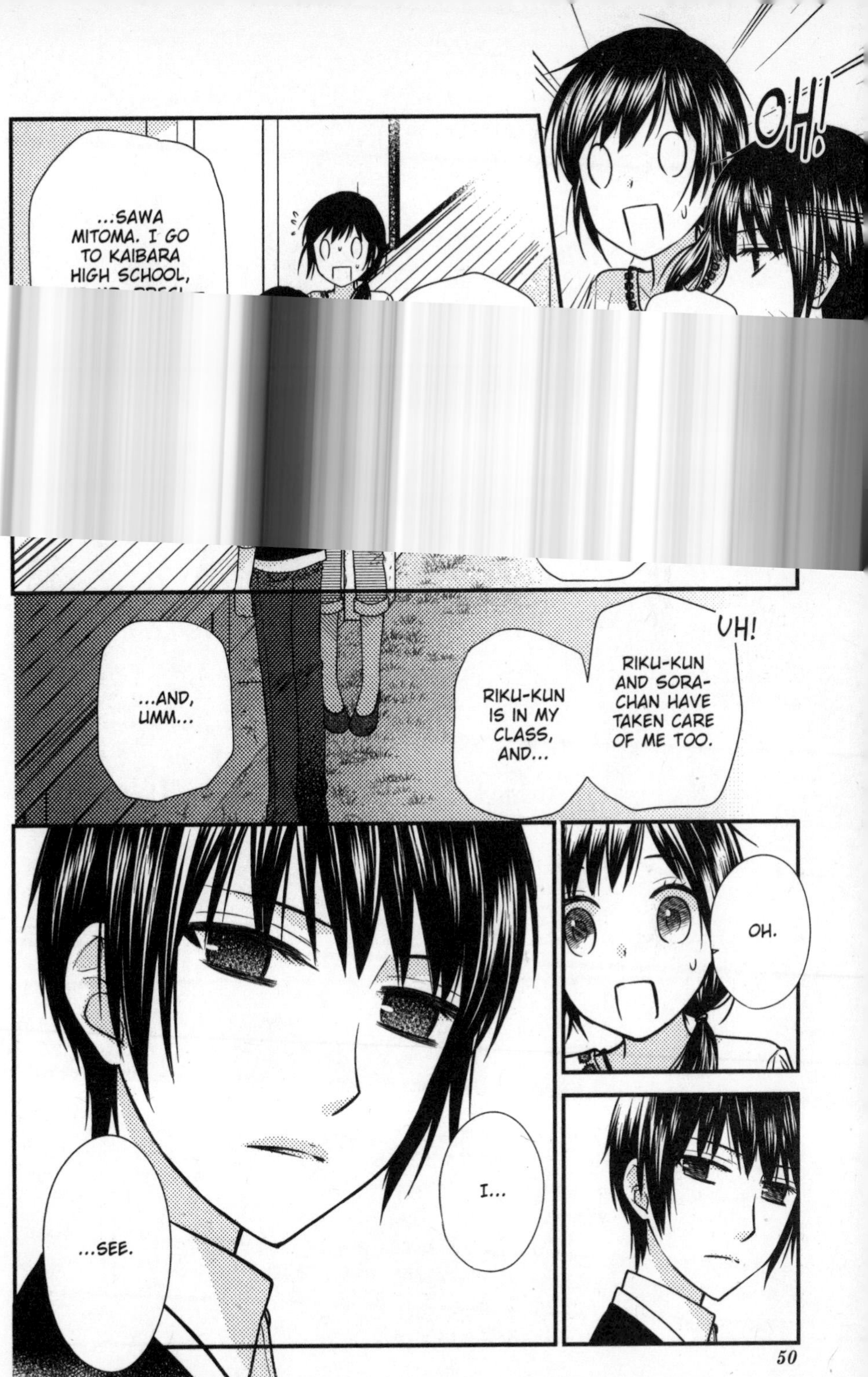
OH!
...SAWA MITOMA. I GO TO KAIBARA HIGH SCHOOL,
UH!
RIKU-KUN AND SORA-CHAN HAVE TAKEN CARE OF ME TOO.
RIKU-KUN IS IN MY CLASS, AND...
...AND, UMM...
OH.
I...
...SEE.

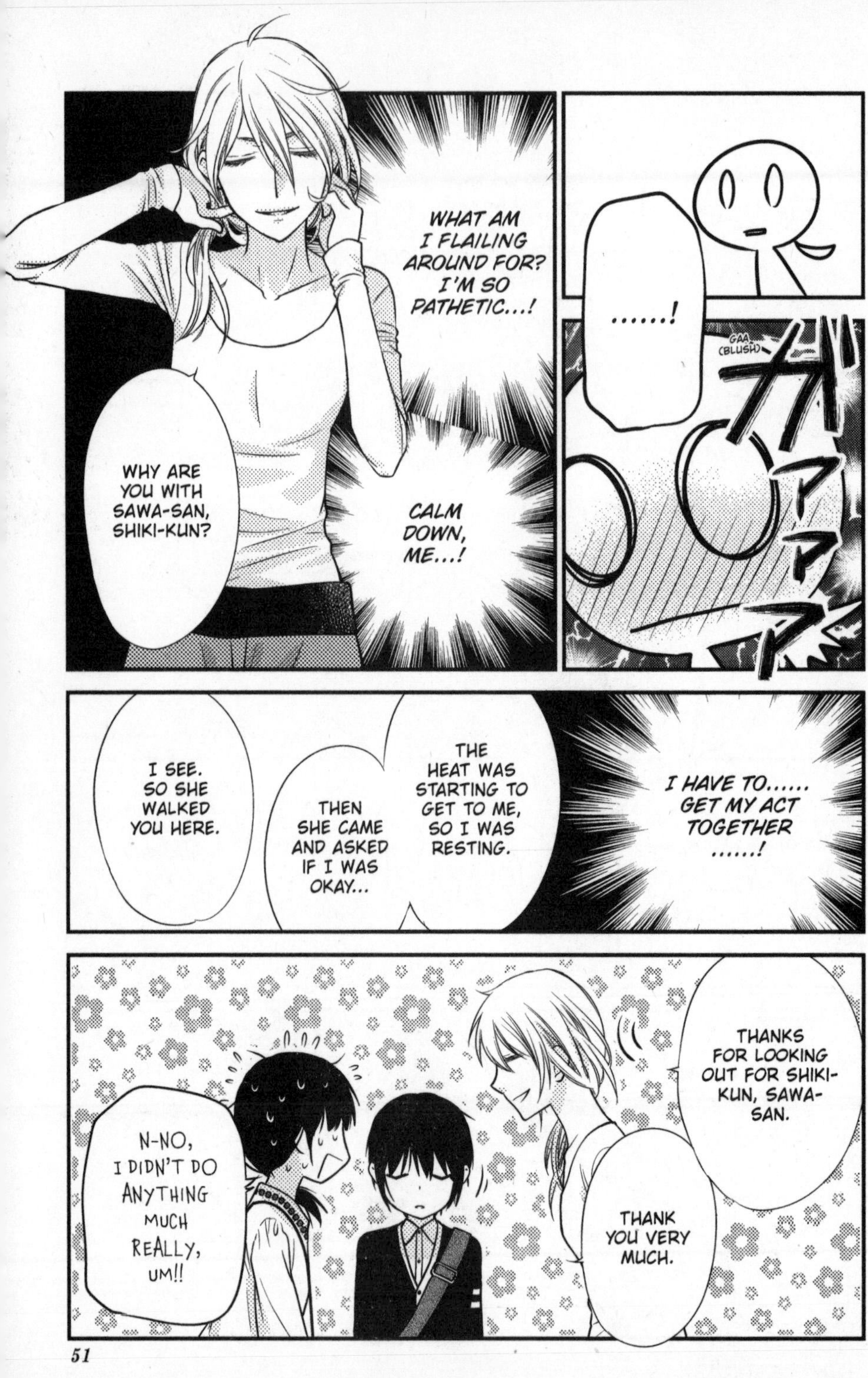
......!
GAA (BLUSH)
WHAT AM I FLAILING AROUND FOR? I'M SO PATHETIC...!
CALM DOWN, ME...!
WHY ARE YOU WITH SAWA-SAN, SHIKI-KUN?
I HAVE TO...... GET MY ACT TOGETHER ......!
THE HEAT WAS STARTING TO GET TO ME, SO I WAS RESTING.
THEN SHE CAME AND ASKED IF I WAS OKAY...
I SEE. SO SHE WALKED YOU HERE.
THANKS FOR LOOKING OUT FOR SHIKI-KUN, SAWA-SAN.
THANK YOU VERY MUCH.
N-NO, I DIDN'T DO ANYTHING MUCH REALLY, UM!!

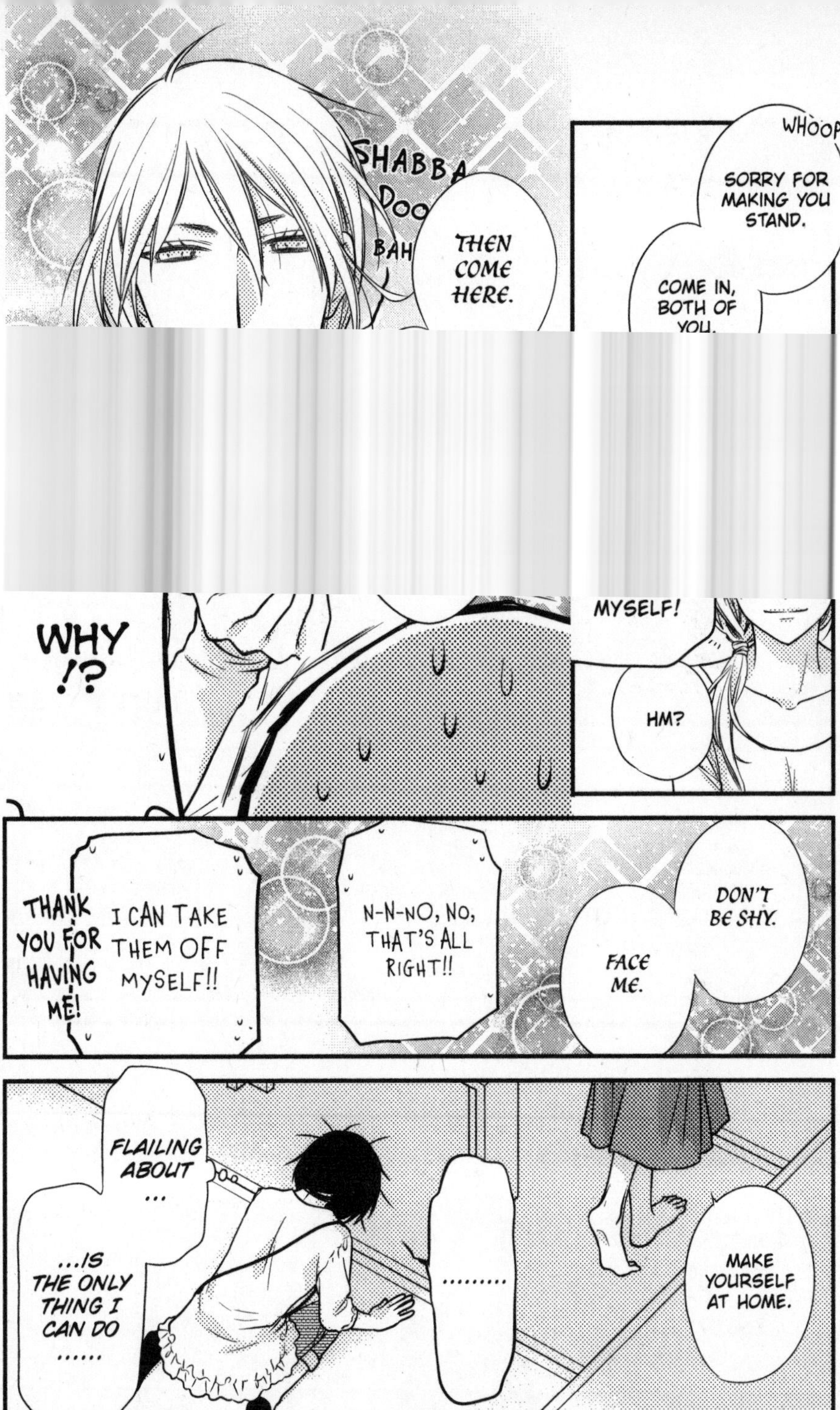
WHOOPS!
SORRY FOR MAKING YOU STAND.
COME IN, BOTH OF YOU.
MYSELF!
HM?
SHABBA DOO BAH
THEN COME HERE.
WHY !?
DON'T BE SHY.
FACE ME.
N-N-NO, NO, THAT'S ALL RIGHT!!
I CAN TAKE THEM OFF MYSELF!!
THANK YOU FOR HAVING ME!
MAKE YOURSELF AT HOME.
....
FLAILING ABOUT ...
...IS THE ONLY THING I CAN DO ......

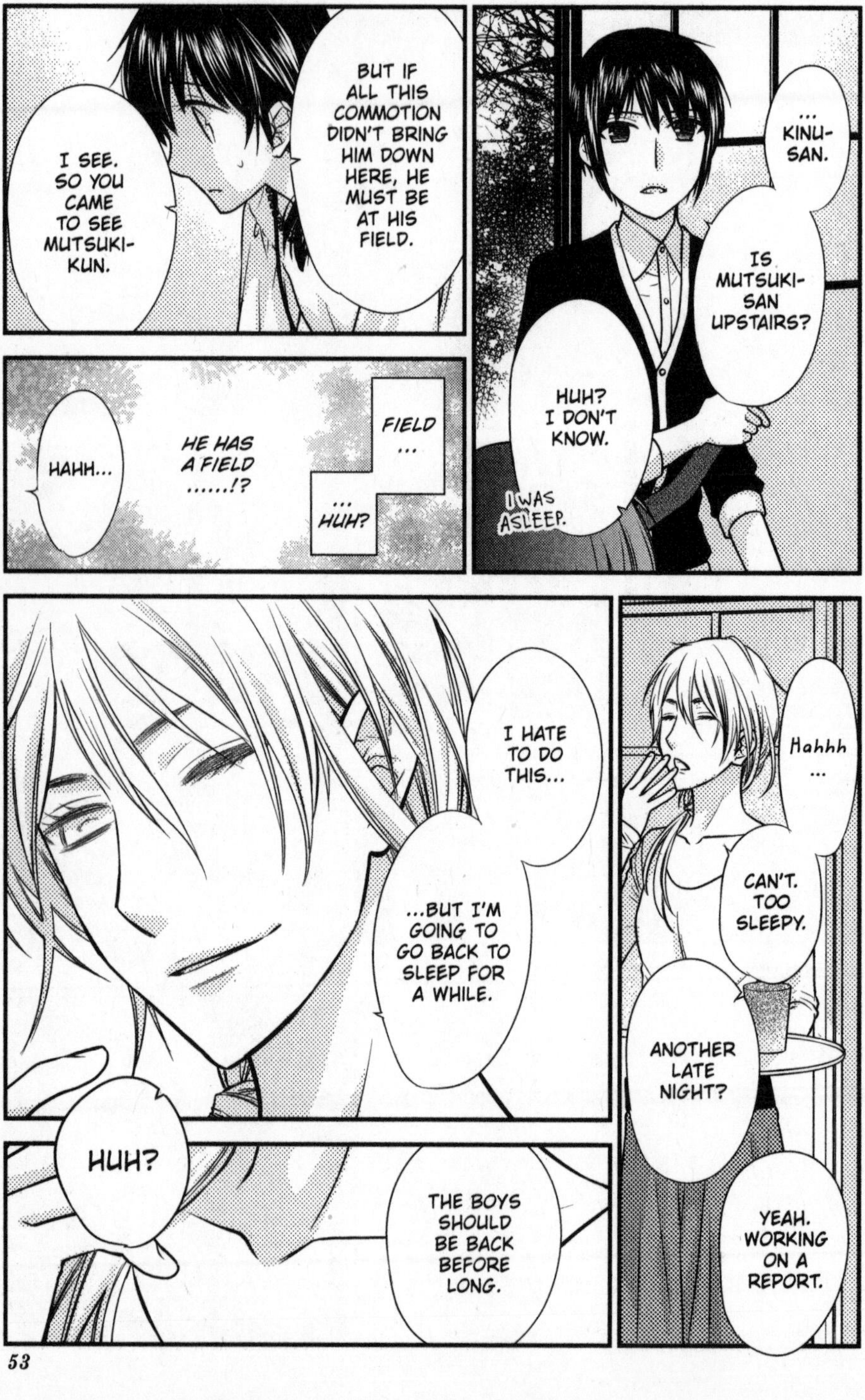
...KINU-SAN.
IS MUTSUKI-SAN UPSTAIRS?
HUH? I DON'T KNOW.
I WAS ASLEEP.
BUT IF ALL THIS COMMOTION DIDN'T BRING HIM DOWN HERE, HE MUST BE AT HIS FIELD.
I SEE. SO YOU CAME TO SEE MUTSUKI-KUN.
FIELD ...
... HUH?
HE HAS A FIELD ......!?
HAHH...
Hahhh ...
CAN'T. TOO SLEEPY.
ANOTHER LATE NIGHT?
YEAH. WORKING ON A REPORT.
I HATE TO DO THIS...
...BUT I'M GOING TO GO BACK TO SLEEP FOR A WHILE.
THE BOYS SHOULD BE BACK BEFORE LONG.
HUH?

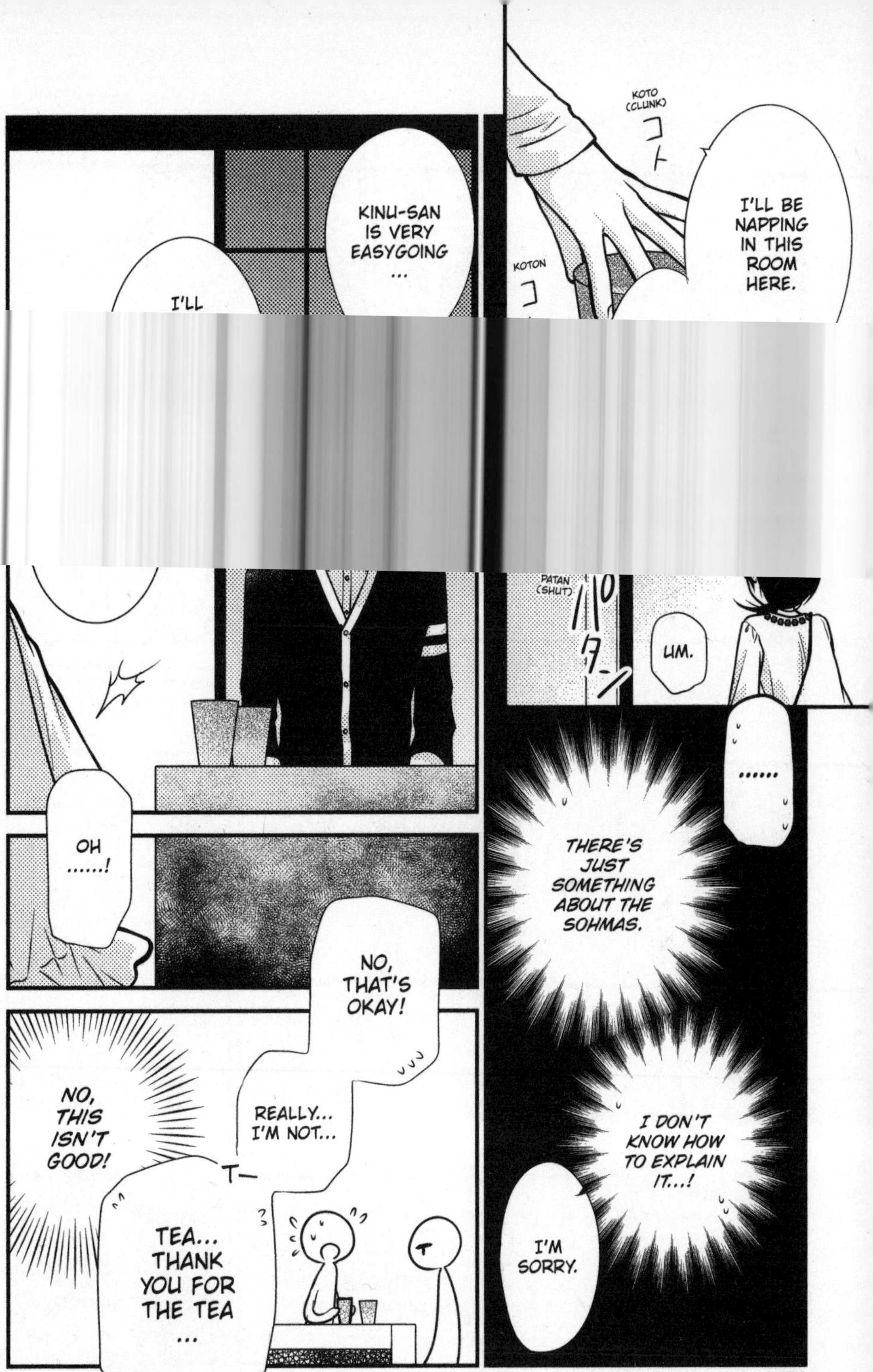
KOTO (CLUNK)
I'LL BE NAPPING IN THIS ROOM HERE.
KOTON
PATAN (SHUT)
UM.
......
THERE'S JUST SOMETHING ABOUT THE SOHMAS.
I DON'T KNOW HOW TO EXPLAIN IT...!
I'M SORRY.
KINU-SAN IS VERY EASYGOING ...
I'LL
OH ......!
NO, THAT'S OKAY!
REALLY... I'M NOT...
NO, THIS ISN'T GOOD!
T—
TEA... THANK YOU FOR THE TEA ...

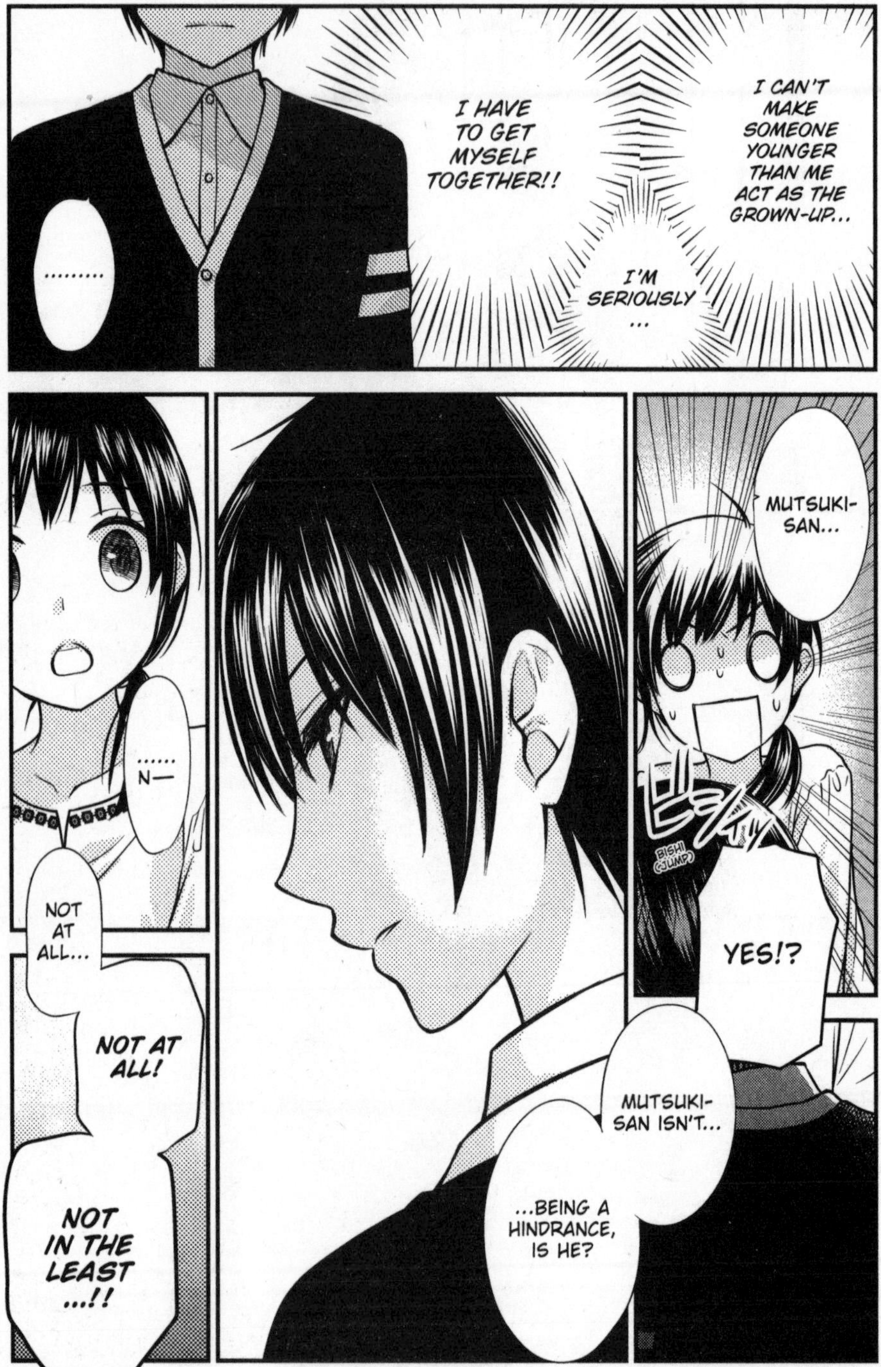
I CAN'T MAKE SOMEONE YOUNGER THAN ME ACT AS THE GROWN-UP...
I HAVE TO GET MYSELF TOGETHER!!
I'M SERIOUSLY ...
....
MUTSUKI-SAN...
BISHI (JUMP)
YES!?
MUTSUKI-SAN ISN'T...
...BEING A HINDRANCE, IS HE?
...... N—
NOT AT ALL...
NOT AT ALL!
NOT IN THE LEAST ...!!

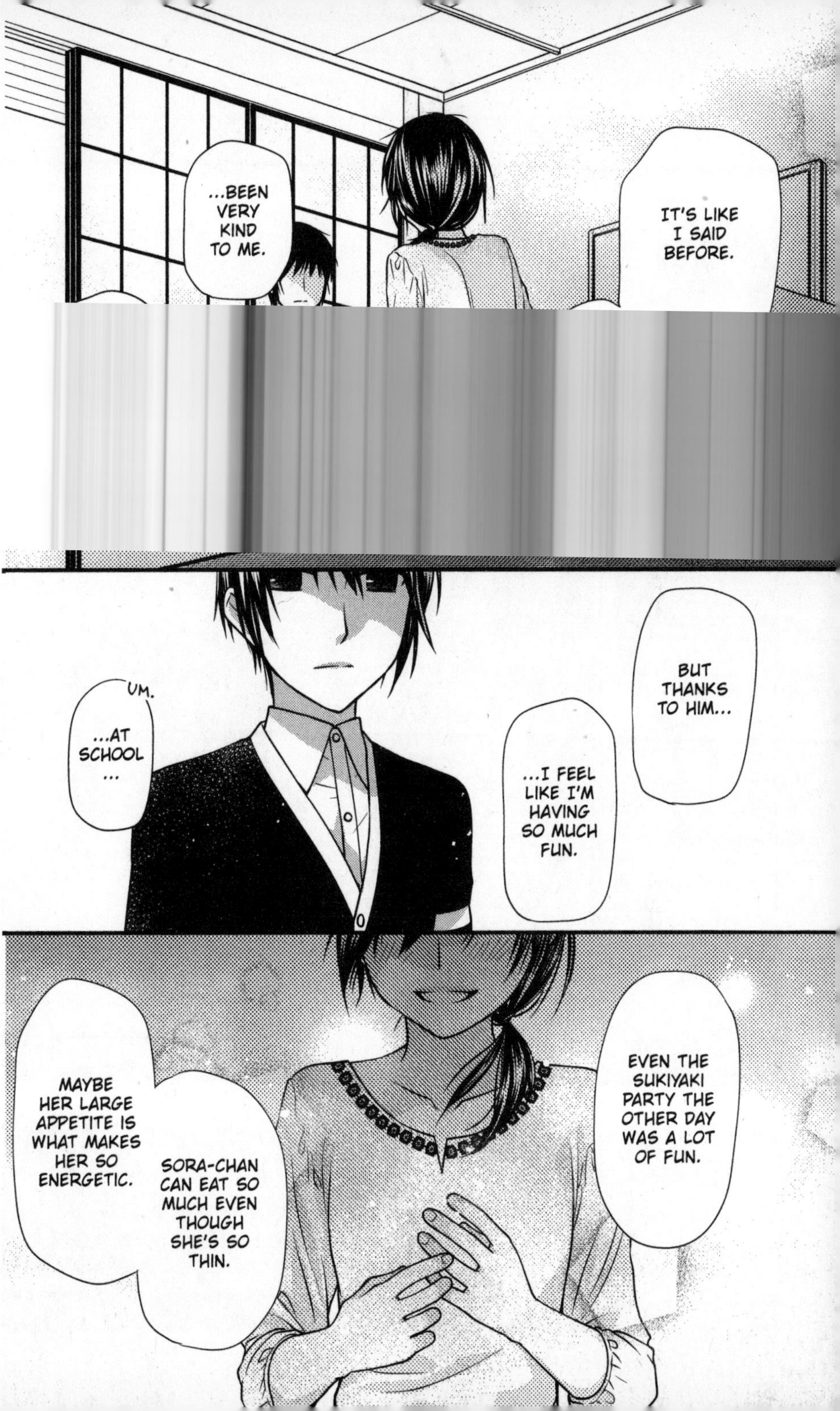
IT'S LIKE I SAID BEFORE.
...BEEN VERY KIND TO ME.
BUT THANKS TO HIM...
...I FEEL LIKE I'M HAVING SO MUCH FUN.
UM.
...AT SCHOOL ...
EVEN THE SUKIYAKI PARTY THE OTHER DAY WAS A LOT OF FUN.
SORA-CHAN CAN EAT SO MUCH EVEN THOUGH SHE'S SO THIN.
MAYBE HER LARGE APPETITE IS WHAT MAKES HER SO ENERGETIC.

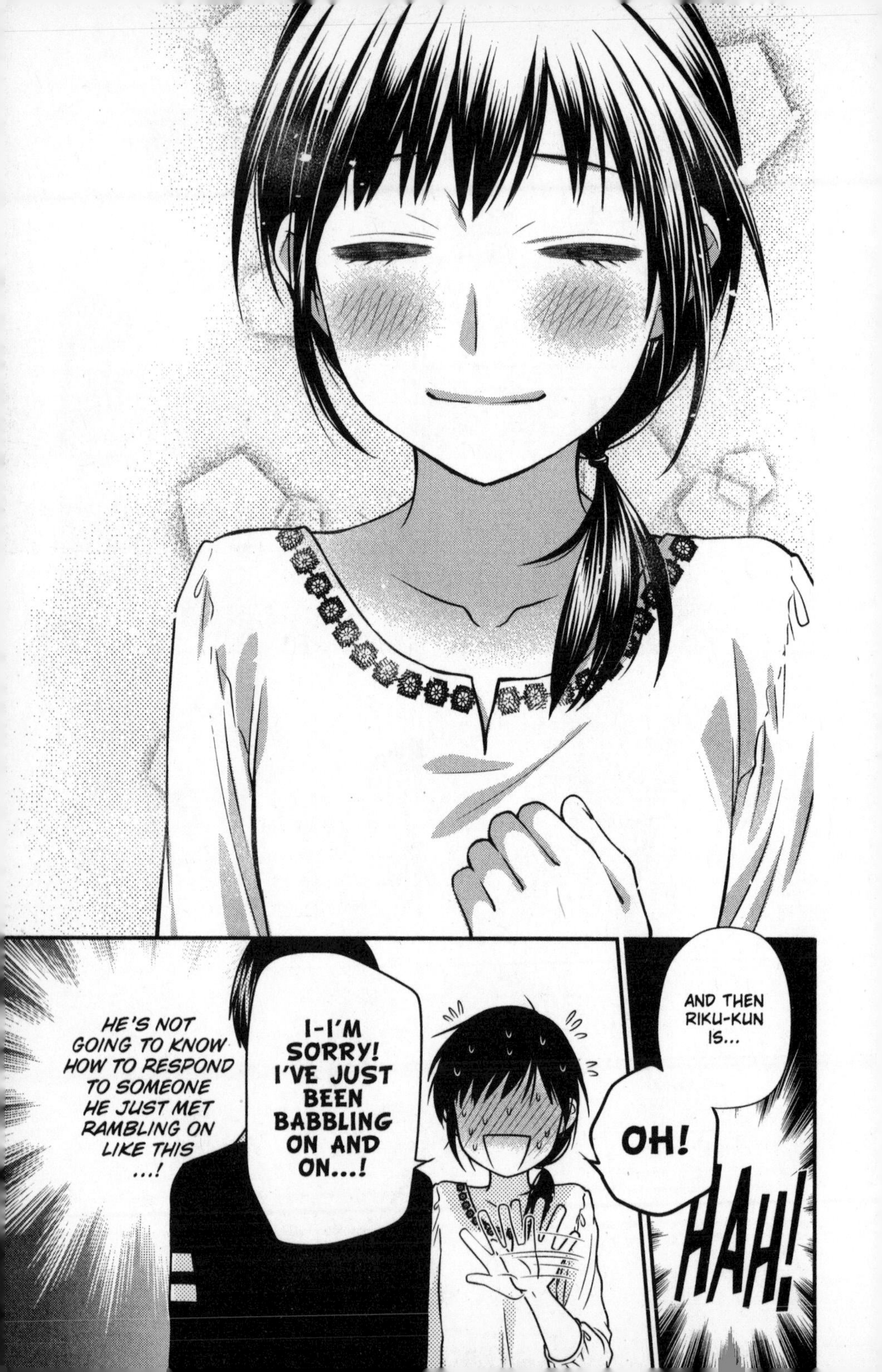
AND THEN RIKU-KUN IS...
OH!
HAH!
I-I'M SORRY! I'VE JUST BEEN BABBLING ON AND ON...!
HE'S NOT GOING TO KNOW HOW TO RESPOND TO SOMEONE HE JUST MET RAMBLING ON LIKE THIS ...!

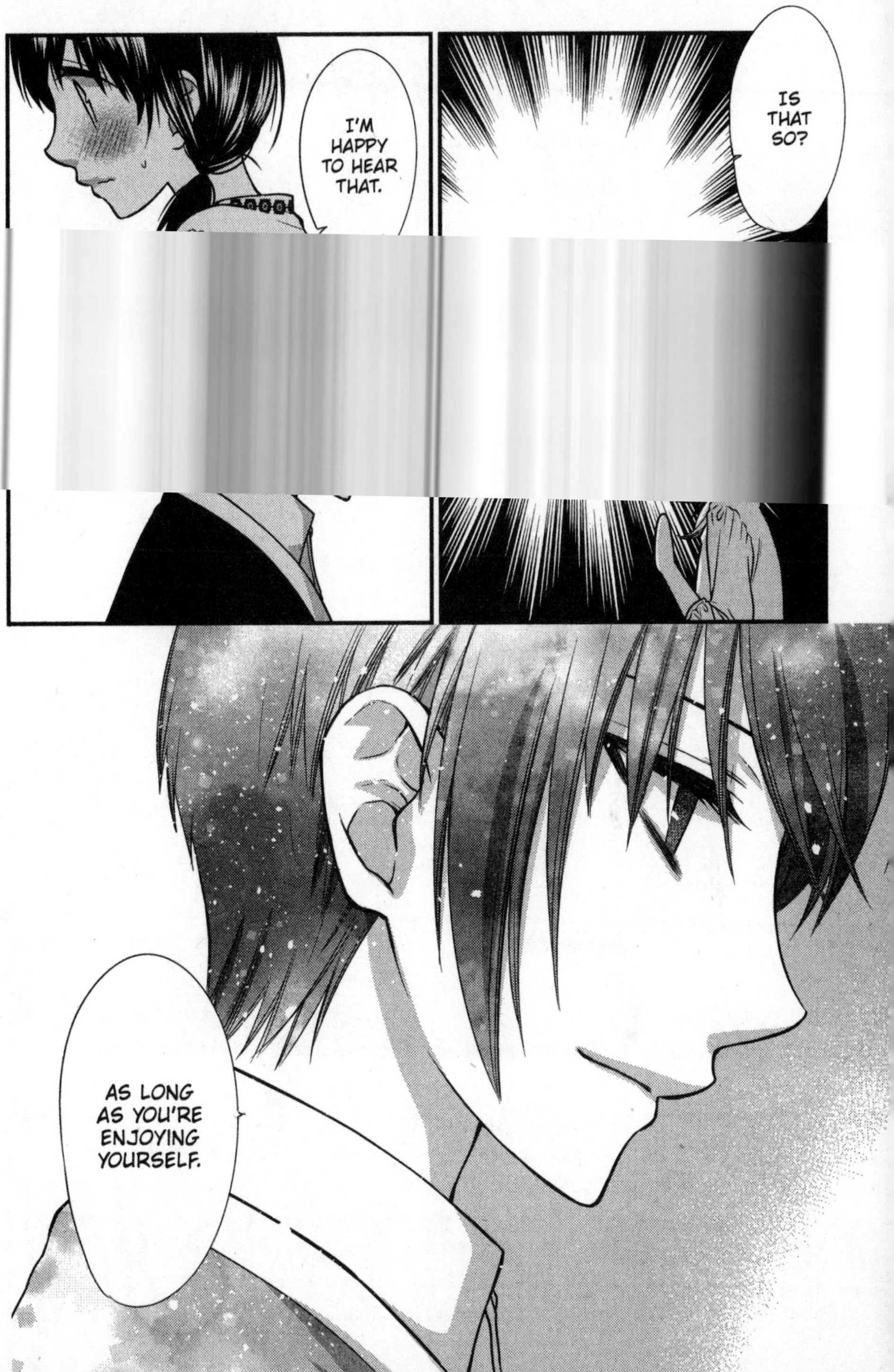
IS THAT SO?
I'M HAPPY TO HEAR THAT.
AS LONG AS YOU'RE ENJOYING YOURSELF.

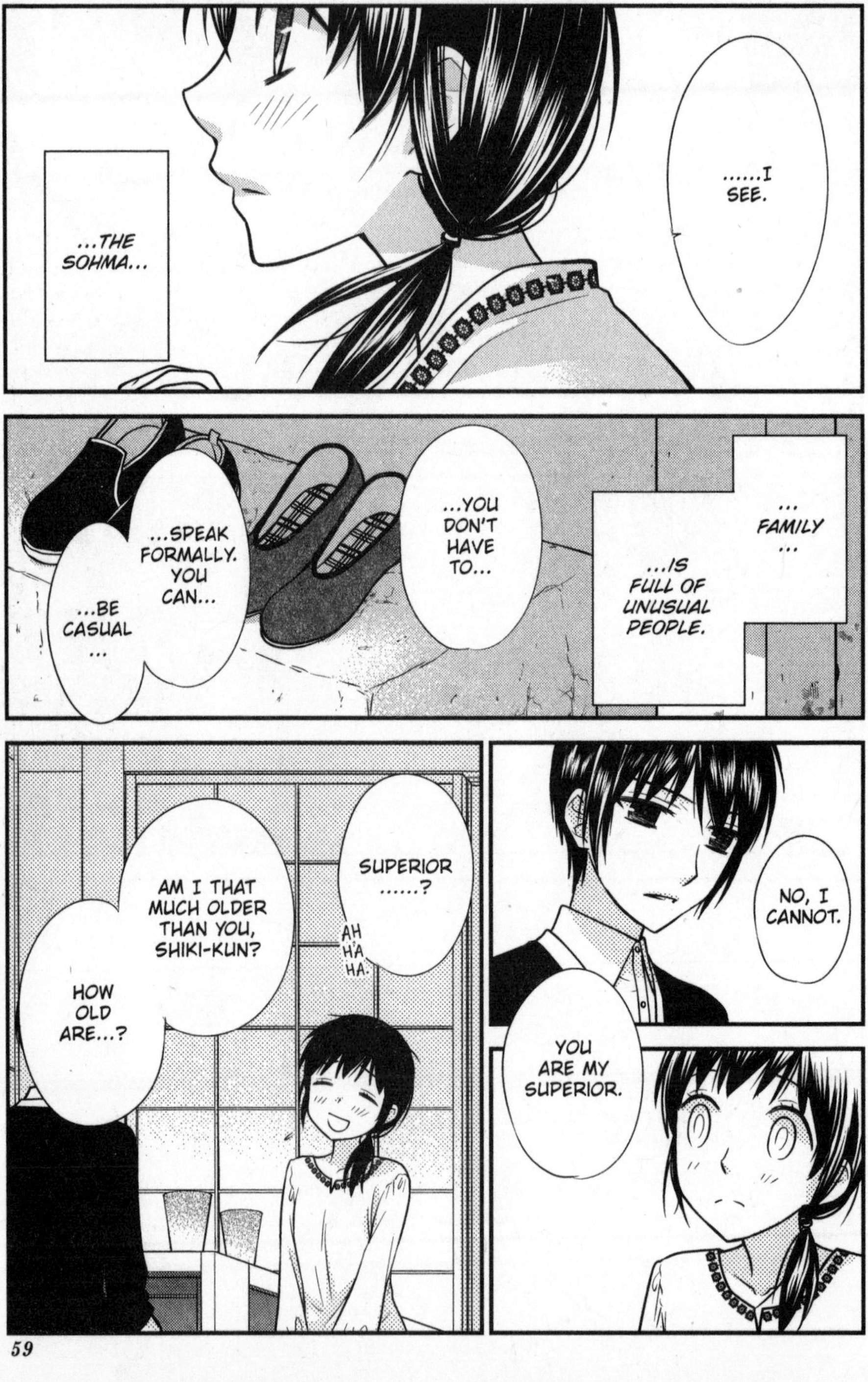
......I SEE.
...THE SOHMA...
... FAMILY ...
...IS FULL OF UNUSUAL PEOPLE.
...YOU DON'T HAVE TO...
...SPEAK FORMALLY. YOU CAN...
...BE CASUAL ...
NO, I CANNOT.
YOU ARE MY SUPERIOR.
SUPERIOR ......?
AH HA HA.
AM I THAT MUCH OLDER THAN YOU, SHIKI-KUN?
HOW OLD ARE...?

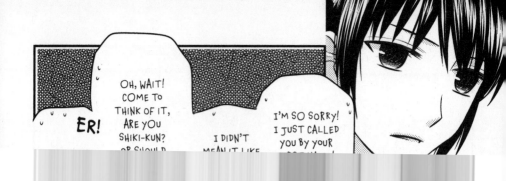

OH, WAIT! COME TO THINK OF IT, ARE YOU SHIKI-KUN? OR SHOULD

ER!

I DIDN'T MEAN IT LIKE

I'M SO SORRY! I JUST CALLED YOU BY YOUR

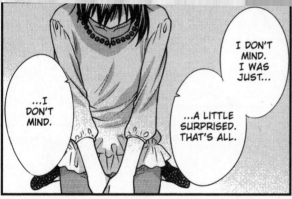

...I DON'T MIND.

I DON'T MIND. I WAS JUST...

...A LITTLE SURPRISED. THAT'S ALL.

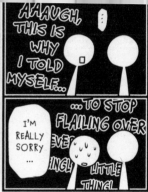

AAAUGH, THIS IS WHY I TOLD MYSELF...

...TO STOP FLAILING OVER EVERY LITTLE THING!

I'M REALLY SORRY...

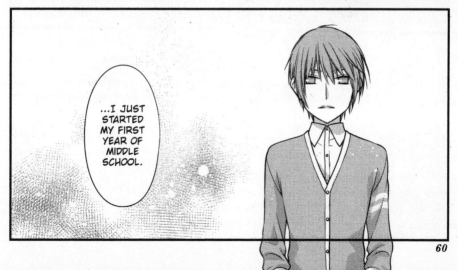

...I JUST STARTED MY FIRST YEAR OF MIDDLE SCHOOL.

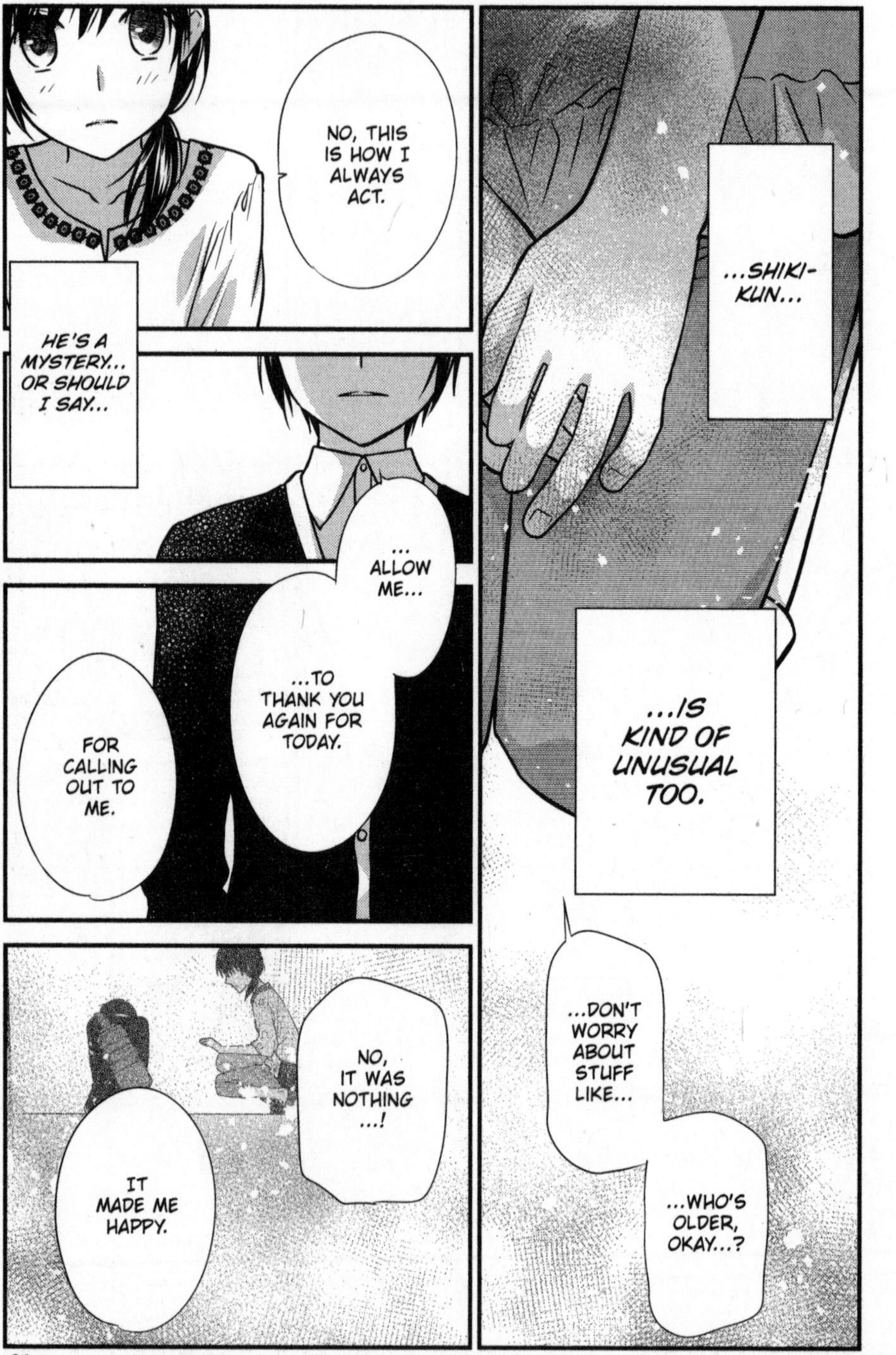
...SHIKI-KUN...
...IS KIND OF UNUSUAL TOO.
...DON'T WORRY ABOUT STUFF LIKE...
...WHO'S OLDER, OKAY...?
NO, THIS IS HOW I ALWAYS ACT.
HE'S A MYSTERY... OR SHOULD I SAY...
... ALLOW ME...
...TO THANK YOU AGAIN FOR TODAY.
FOR CALLING OUT TO ME.
NO, IT WAS NOTHING ...!
IT MADE ME HAPPY.

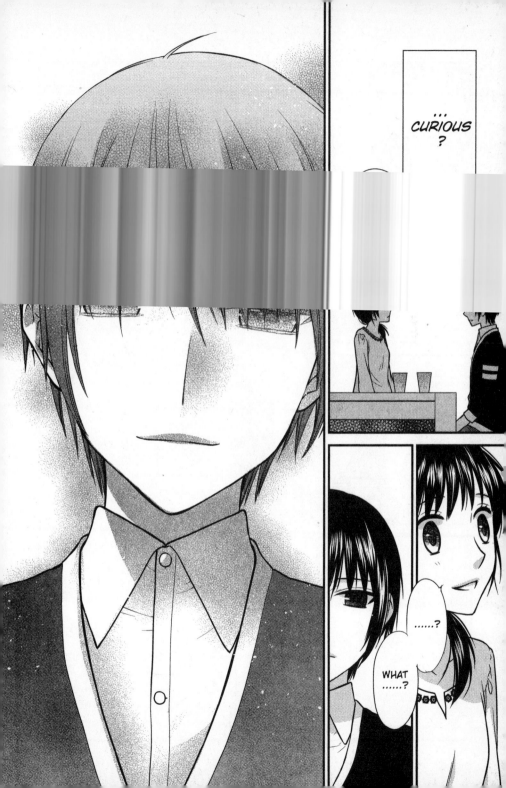

...CURIOUS?

.....?

WHAT
......?

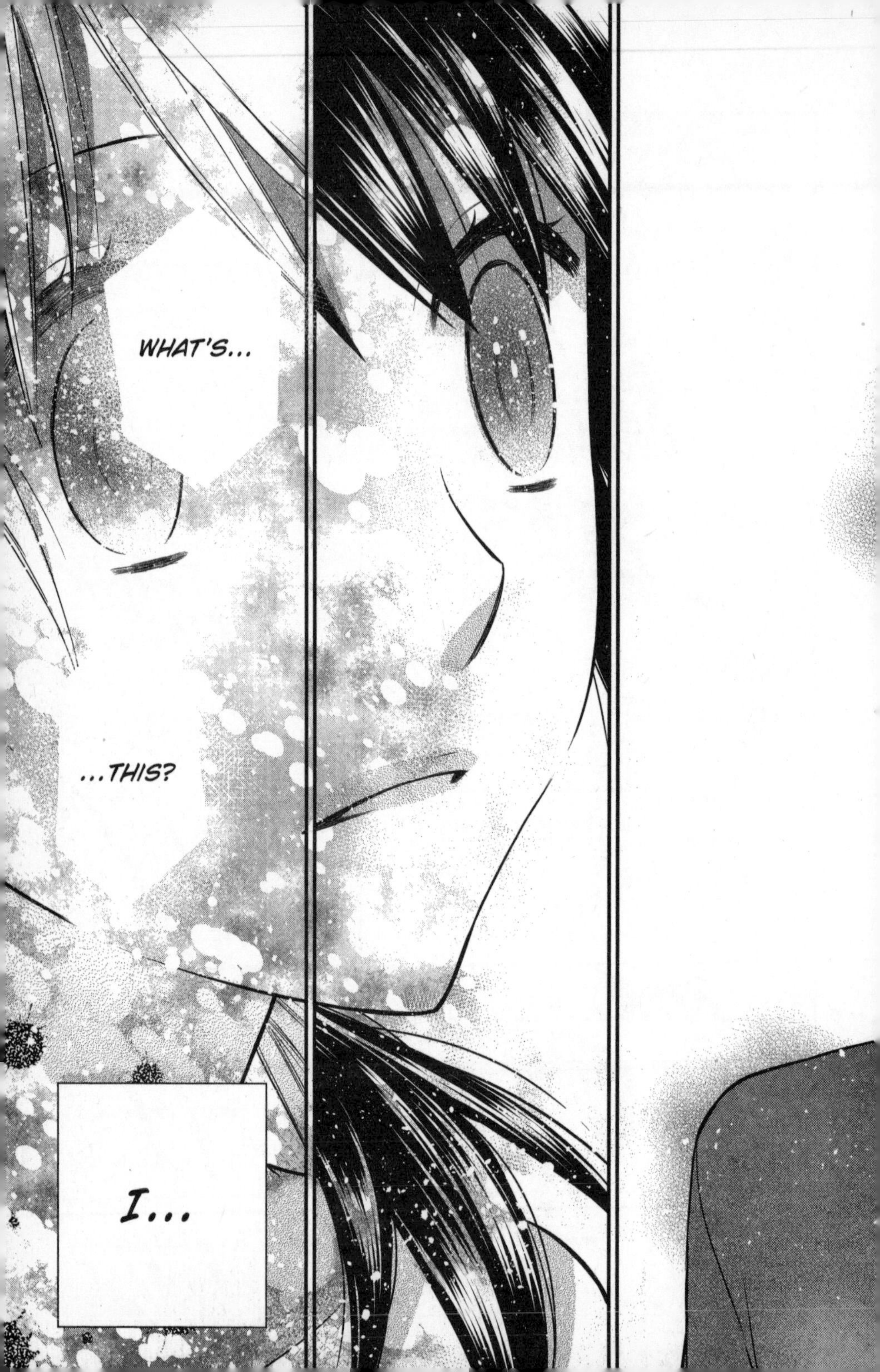
WHAT'S...
...THIS?
I...

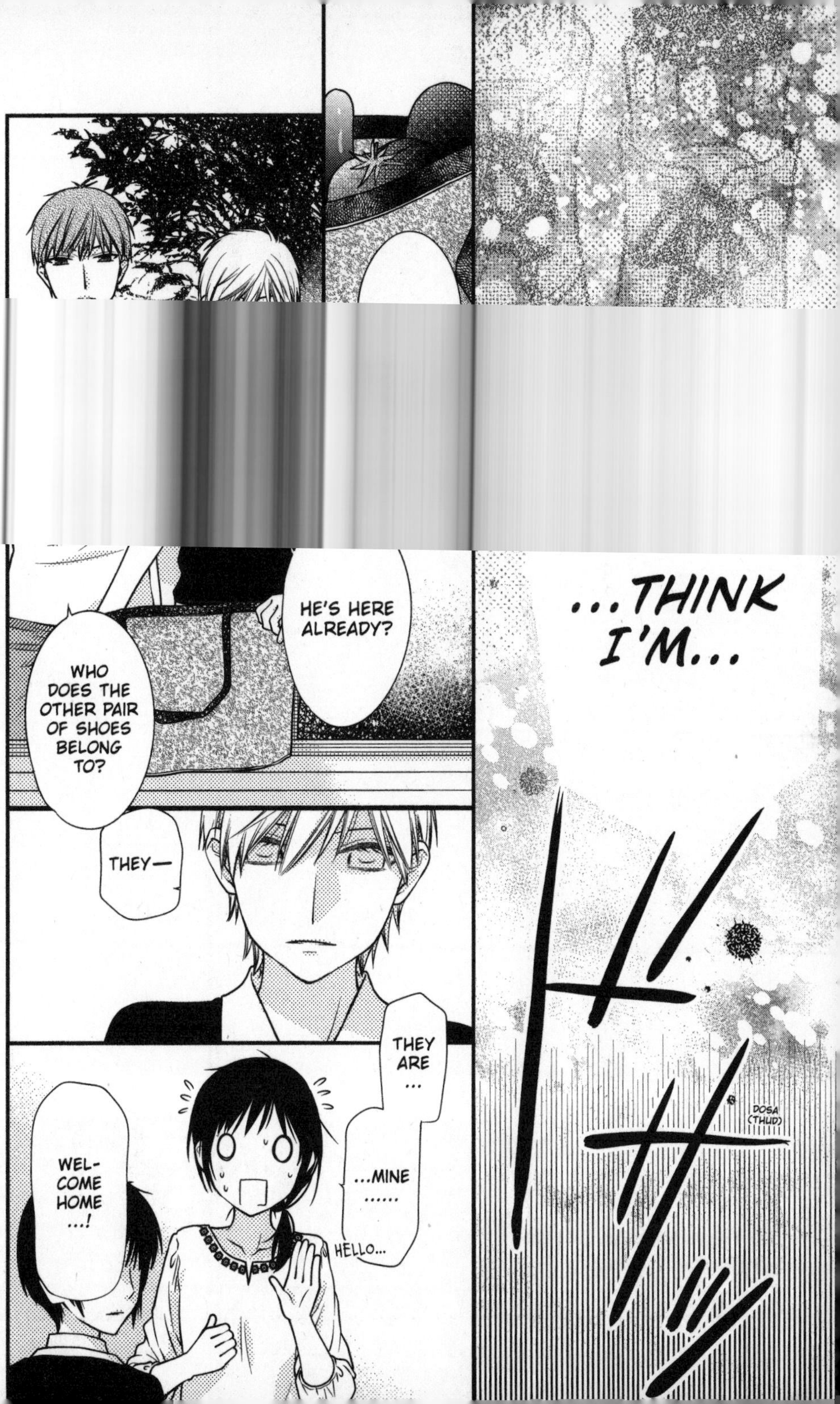
...THINK I'M...
DOSA (THUD)
HE'S HERE ALREADY?
WHO DOES THE OTHER PAIR OF SHOES BELONG TO?
THEY—
THEY ARE ...
...MINE ......
HELLO...
WEL-COME HOME ...!

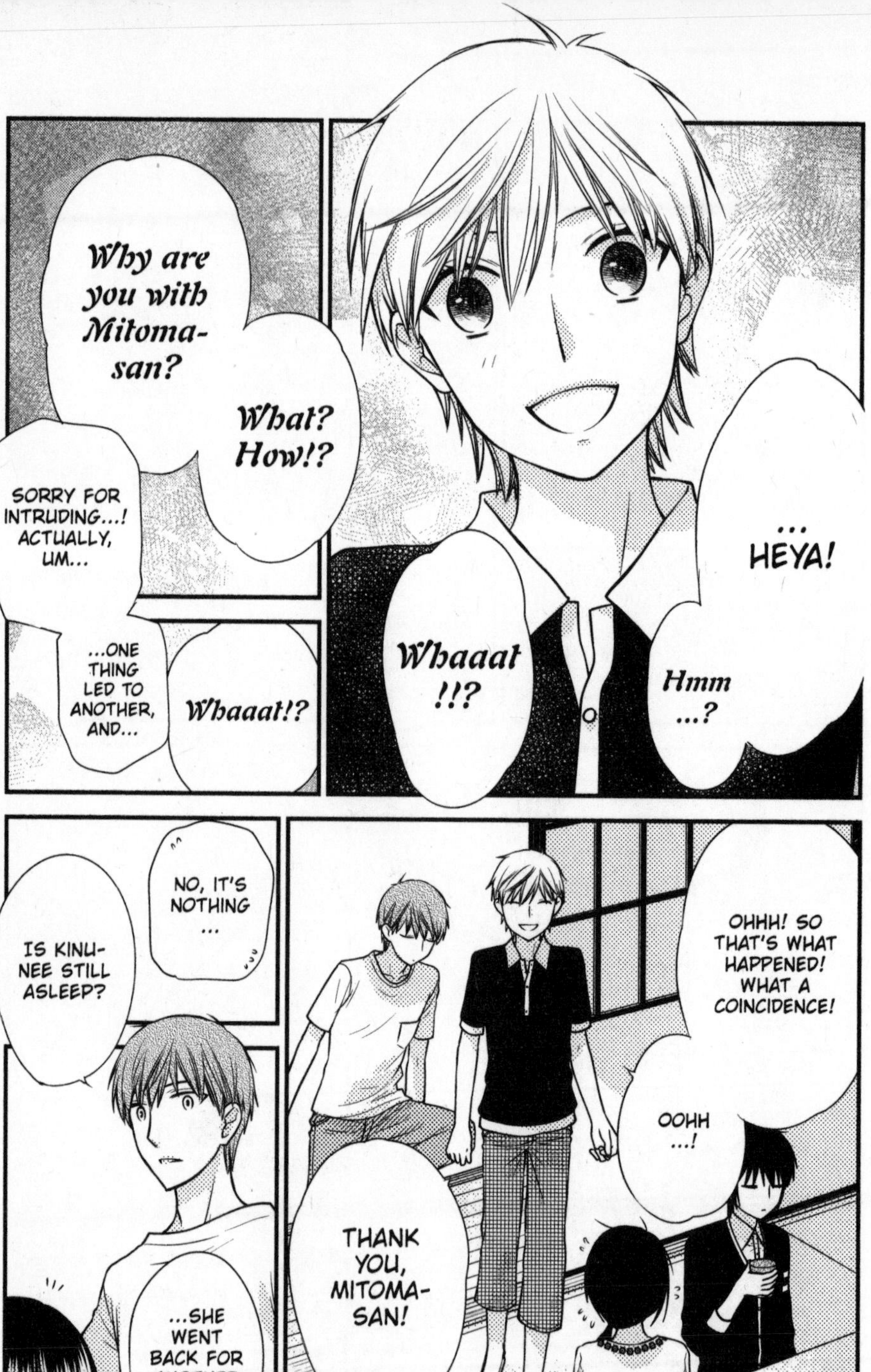
...HEYA!
Hmm...?
Whaaat!!?
Why are you with Mitoma-san?
What? How!?
SORRY FOR INTRUDING...! ACTUALLY, UM...
Whaaat!?
...ONE THING LED TO ANOTHER, AND...
OHHH! SO THAT'S WHAT HAPPENED! WHAT A COINCIDENCE!
OOHH...!
THANK YOU, MITOMA-SAN!
NO, IT'S NOTHING...
IS KINU-NEE STILL ASLEEP?
...SHE WENT BACK FOR ANOTHER NAP.

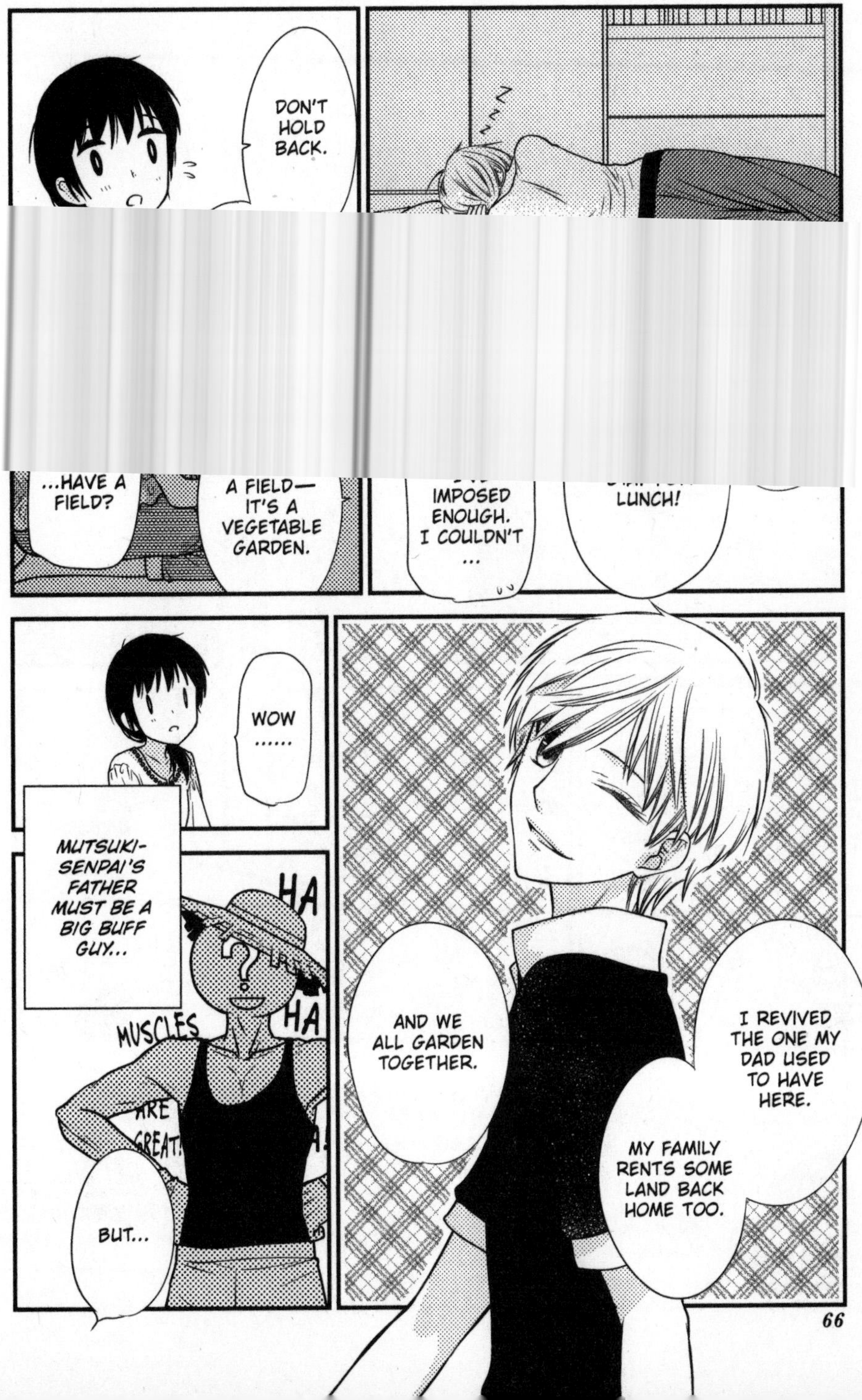

DON'T HOLD BACK.
LUNCH!
IMPOSED ENOUGH. I COULDN'T ...
A FIELD— IT'S A VEGETABLE GARDEN.
...HAVE A FIELD?
I REVIVED THE ONE MY DAD USED TO HAVE HERE.
MY FAMILY RENTS SOME LAND BACK HOME TOO.
AND WE ALL GARDEN TOGETHER.
WOW ......
MUTSUKI-SENPAI'S FATHER MUST BE A BIG BUFF GUY...
HA
HA
MUSCLES
ARE
GREAT!
BUT...

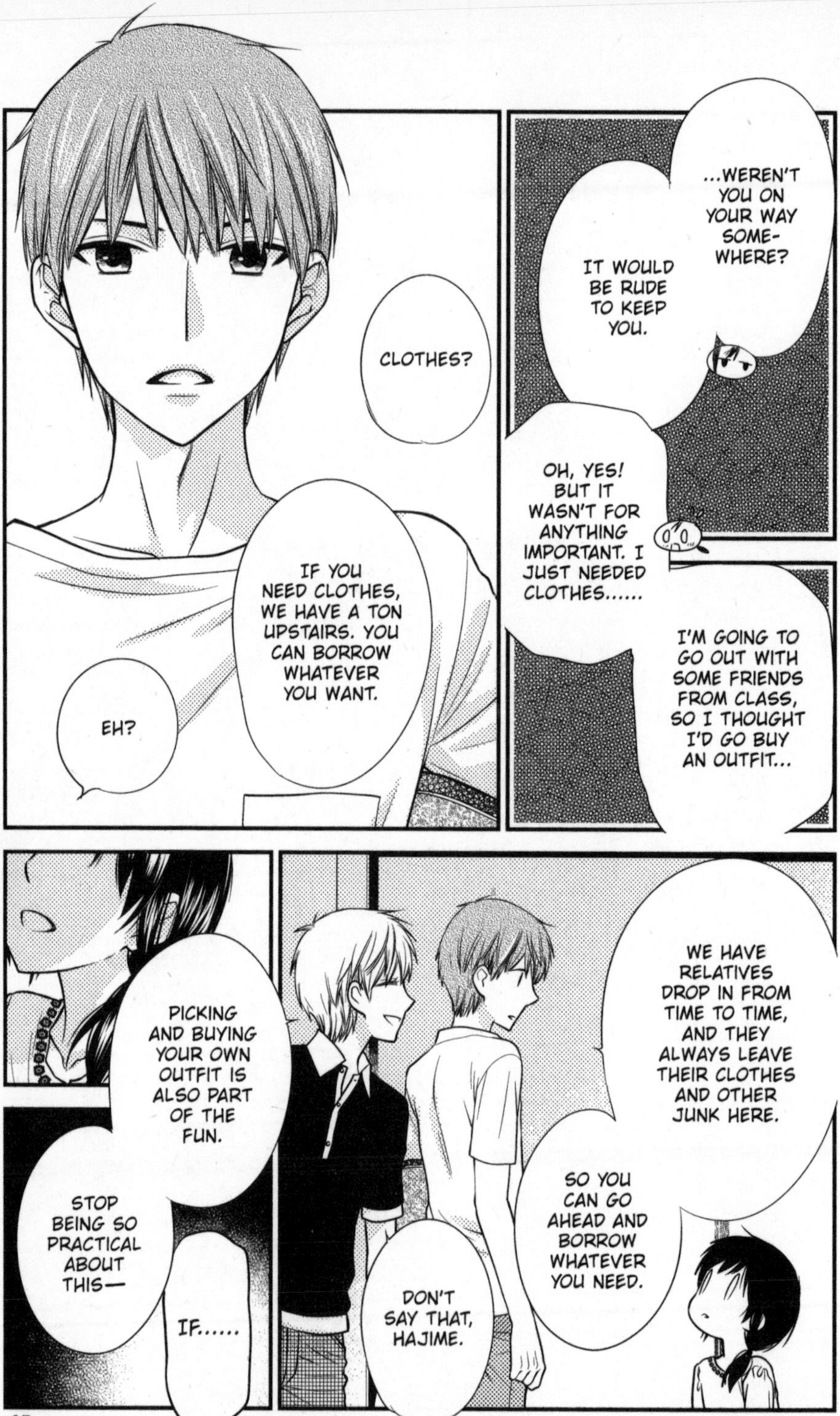
...WEREN'T YOU ON YOUR WAY SOME-WHERE?
IT WOULD BE RUDE TO KEEP YOU.
OH, YES! BUT IT WASN'T FOR ANYTHING IMPORTANT. I JUST NEEDED CLOTHES......
I'M GOING TO GO OUT WITH SOME FRIENDS FROM CLASS, SO I THOUGHT I'D GO BUY AN OUTFIT...
CLOTHES?
IF YOU NEED CLOTHES, WE HAVE A TON UPSTAIRS. YOU CAN BORROW WHATEVER YOU WANT.
EH?
WE HAVE RELATIVES DROP IN FROM TIME TO TIME, AND THEY ALWAYS LEAVE THEIR CLOTHES AND OTHER JUNK HERE.
SO YOU CAN GO AHEAD AND BORROW WHATEVER YOU NEED.
DON'T SAY THAT, HAJIME.
PICKING AND BUYING YOUR OWN OUTFIT IS ALSO PART OF THE FUN.
STOP BEING SO PRACTICAL ABOUT THIS—
IF......

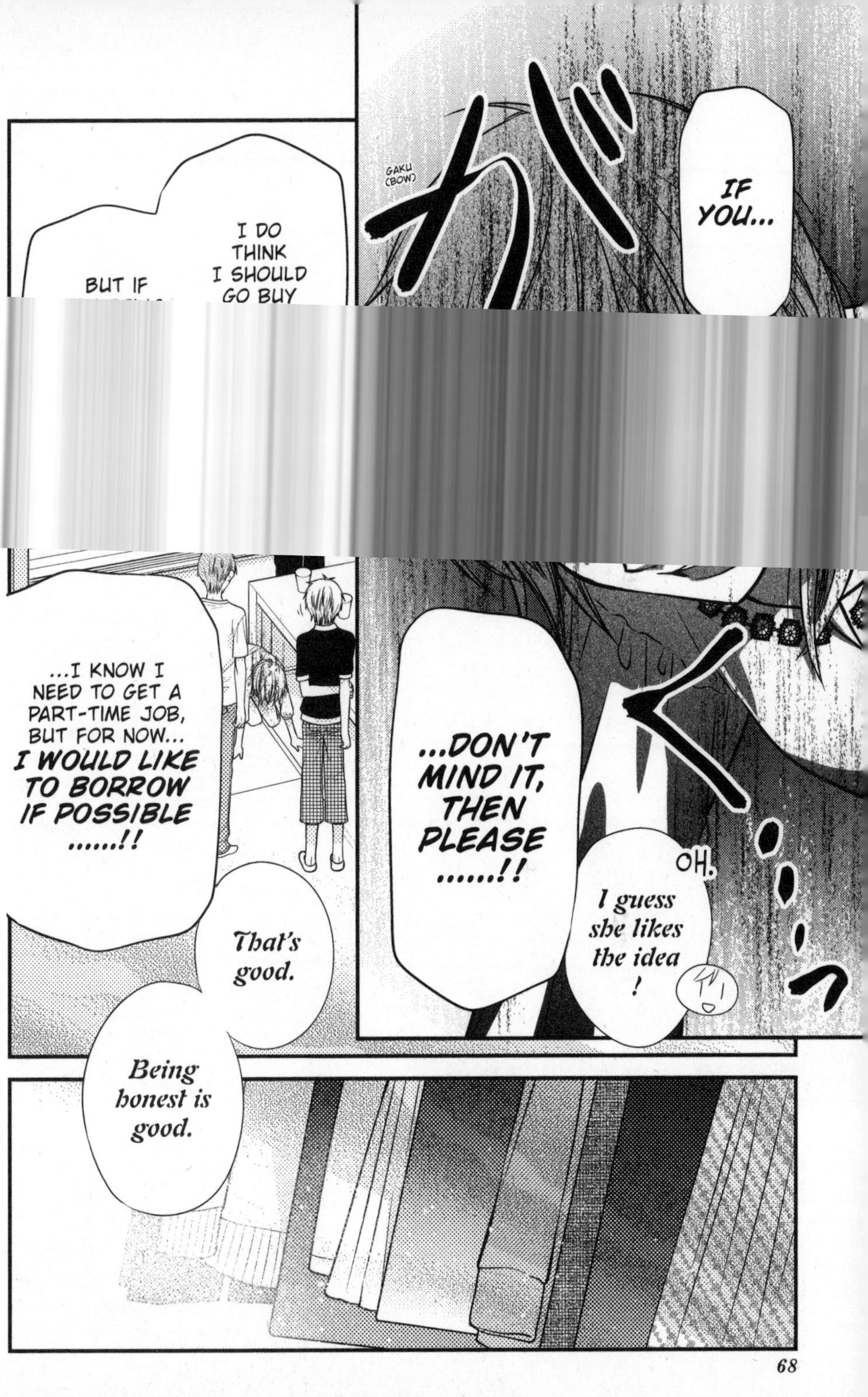
GAKU (BOW)
IF YOU...
...DON'T MIND IT, THEN PLEASE ......!!
OH.
I guess she likes the idea !
I DO THINK I SHOULD GO BUY
BUT IF
...I KNOW I NEED TO GET A PART-TIME JOB, BUT FOR NOW... I WOULD LIKE TO BORROW IF POSSIBLE ......!!
That's good.
Being honest is good.

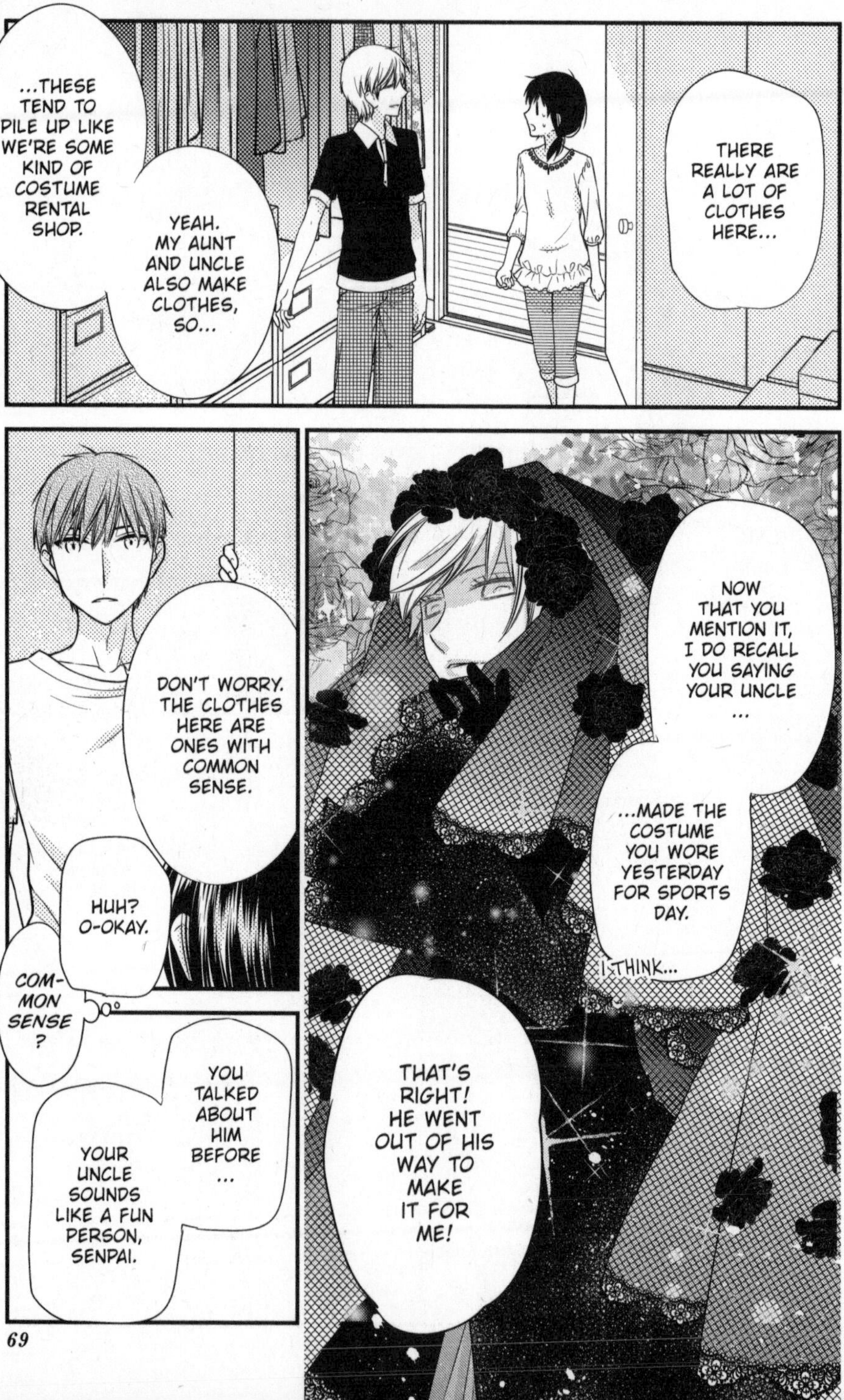
THERE REALLY ARE A LOT OF CLOTHES HERE...
YEAH. MY AUNT AND UNCLE ALSO MAKE CLOTHES, SO...
...THESE TEND TO PILE UP LIKE WE'RE SOME KIND OF COSTUME RENTAL SHOP.
NOW THAT YOU MENTION IT, I DO RECALL YOU SAYING YOUR UNCLE ...
...MADE THE COSTUME YOU WORE YESTERDAY FOR SPORTS DAY.
I THINK...
THAT'S RIGHT! HE WENT OUT OF HIS WAY TO MAKE IT FOR ME!
DON'T WORRY. THE CLOTHES HERE ARE ONES WITH COMMON SENSE.
HUH? O-OKAY.
COM-MON SENSE?
YOU TALKED ABOUT HIM BEFORE ...
YOUR UNCLE SOUNDS LIKE A FUN PERSON, SENPAI.

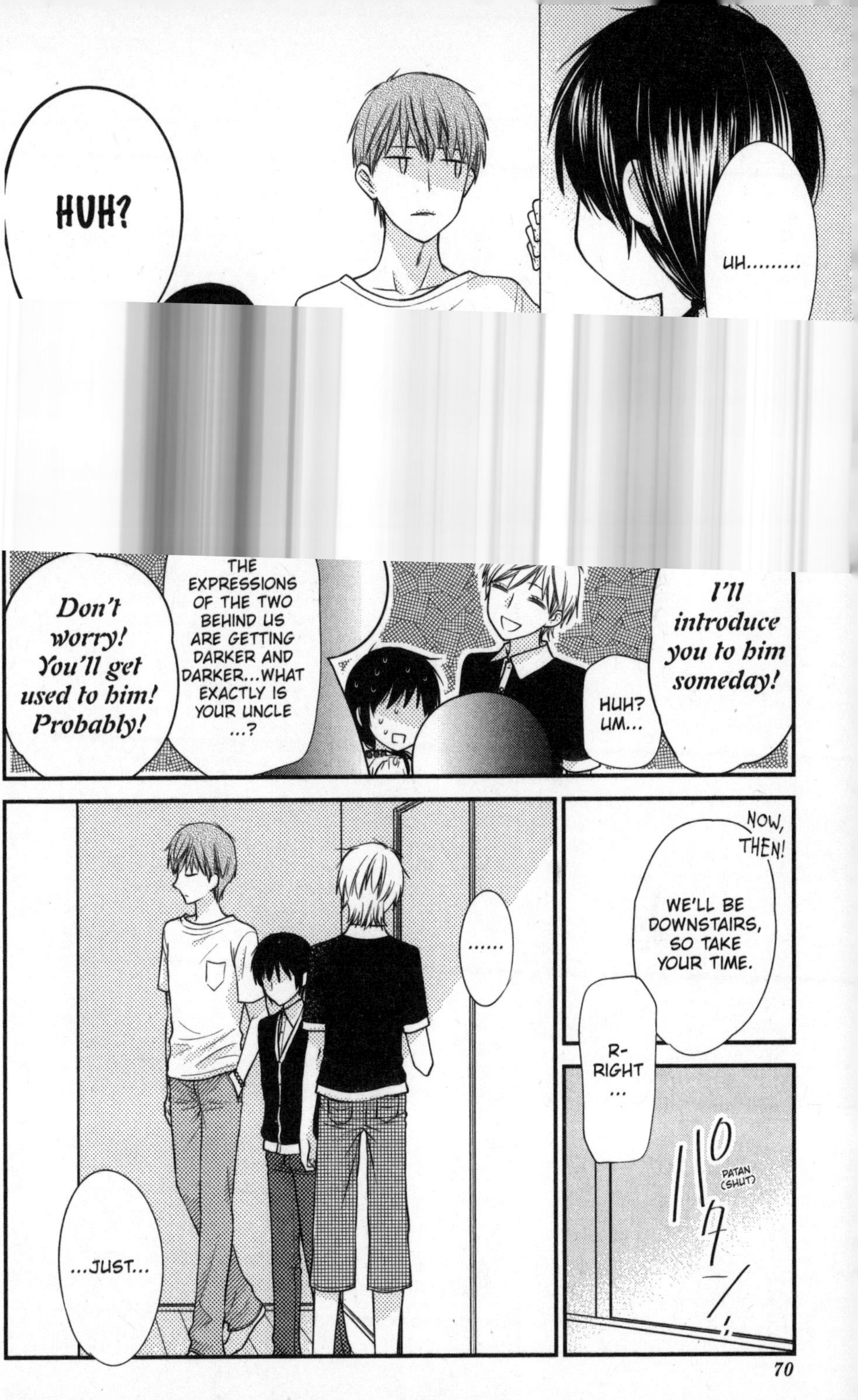
UH.........
HUH?
I'll introduce you to him someday!
HUH? UM...
THE EXPRESSIONS OF THE TWO BEHIND US ARE GETTING DARKER AND DARKER...WHAT EXACTLY IS YOUR UNCLE ...?
Don't worry! You'll get used to him! Probably!
NOW, THEN!
WE'LL BE DOWNSTAIRS, SO TAKE YOUR TIME.
R-RIGHT ...
PATAN (SHUT)
......
...JUST...

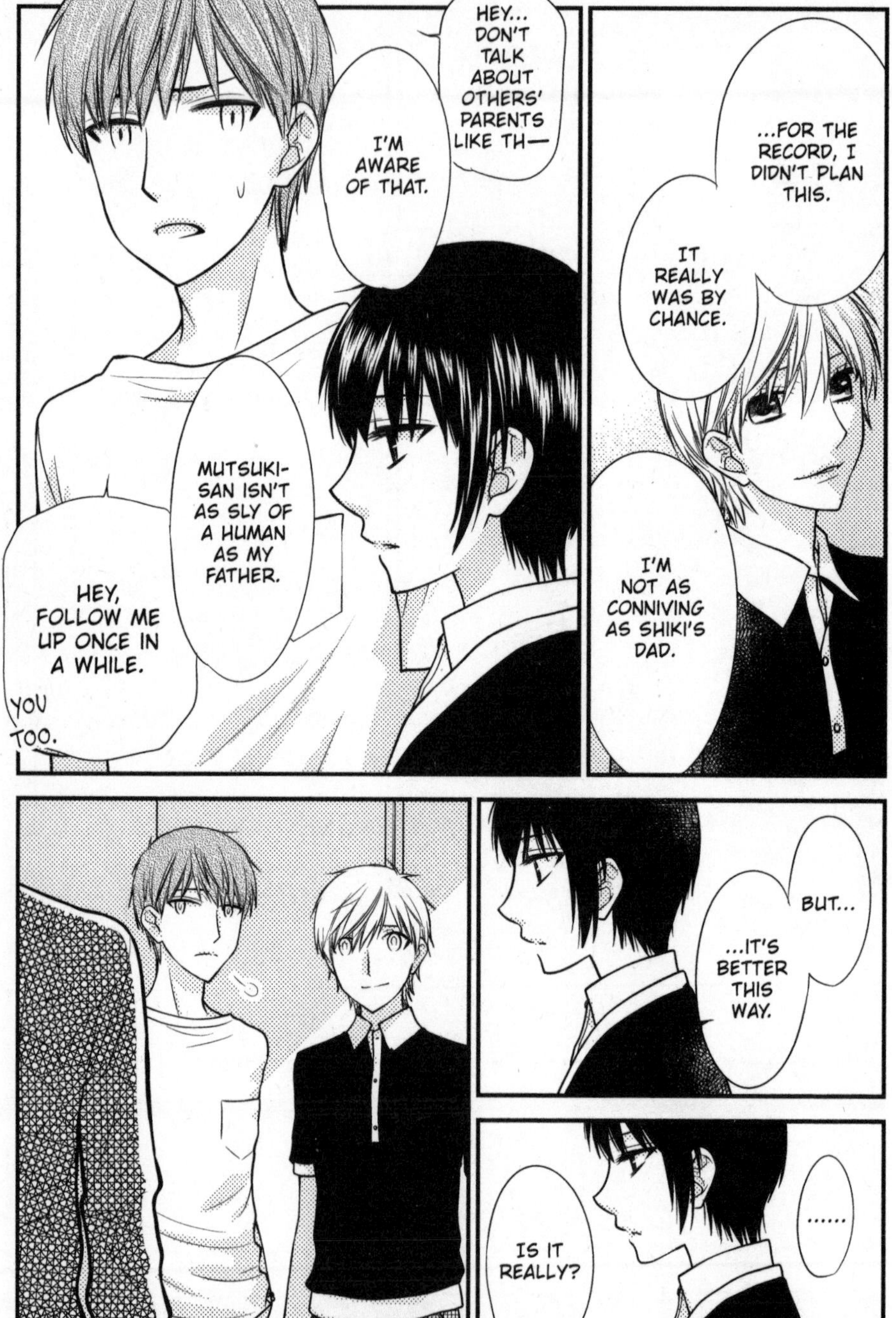
...FOR THE RECORD, I DIDN'T PLAN THIS.
IT REALLY WAS BY CHANCE.
I'M NOT AS CONNIVING AS SHIKI'S DAD.
HEY... DON'T TALK ABOUT OTHERS' PARENTS LIKE TH—
I'M AWARE OF THAT.
MUTSUKI-SAN ISN'T AS SLY OF A HUMAN AS MY FATHER.
HEY, FOLLOW ME UP ONCE IN A WHILE.
YOU TOO.
BUT...
...IT'S BETTER THIS WAY.
......
IS IT REALLY?

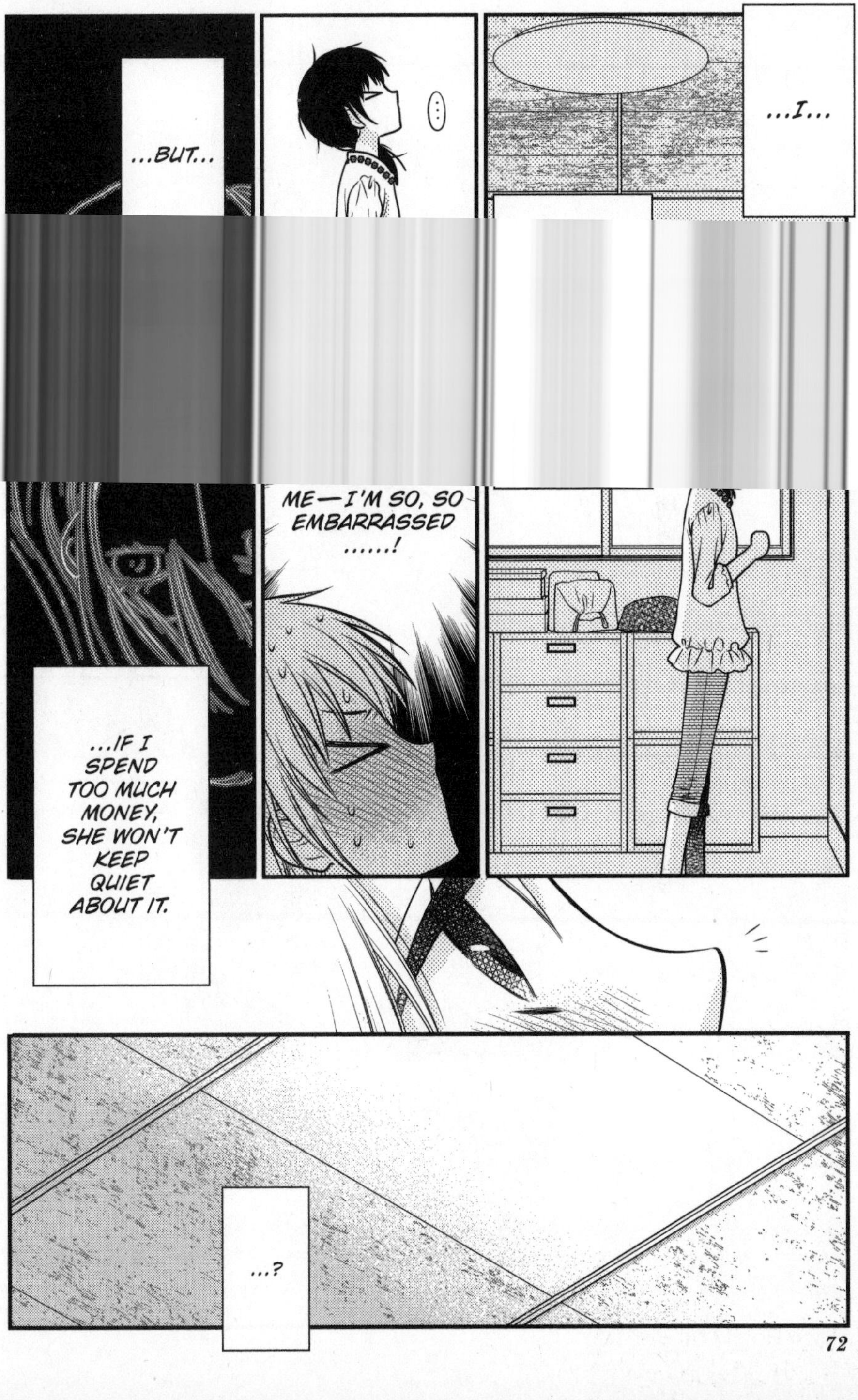
...I...
...
...BUT...
ME—I'M SO, SO EMBARRASSED ......!
...IF I SPEND TOO MUCH MONEY, SHE WON'T KEEP QUIET ABOUT IT.
...?

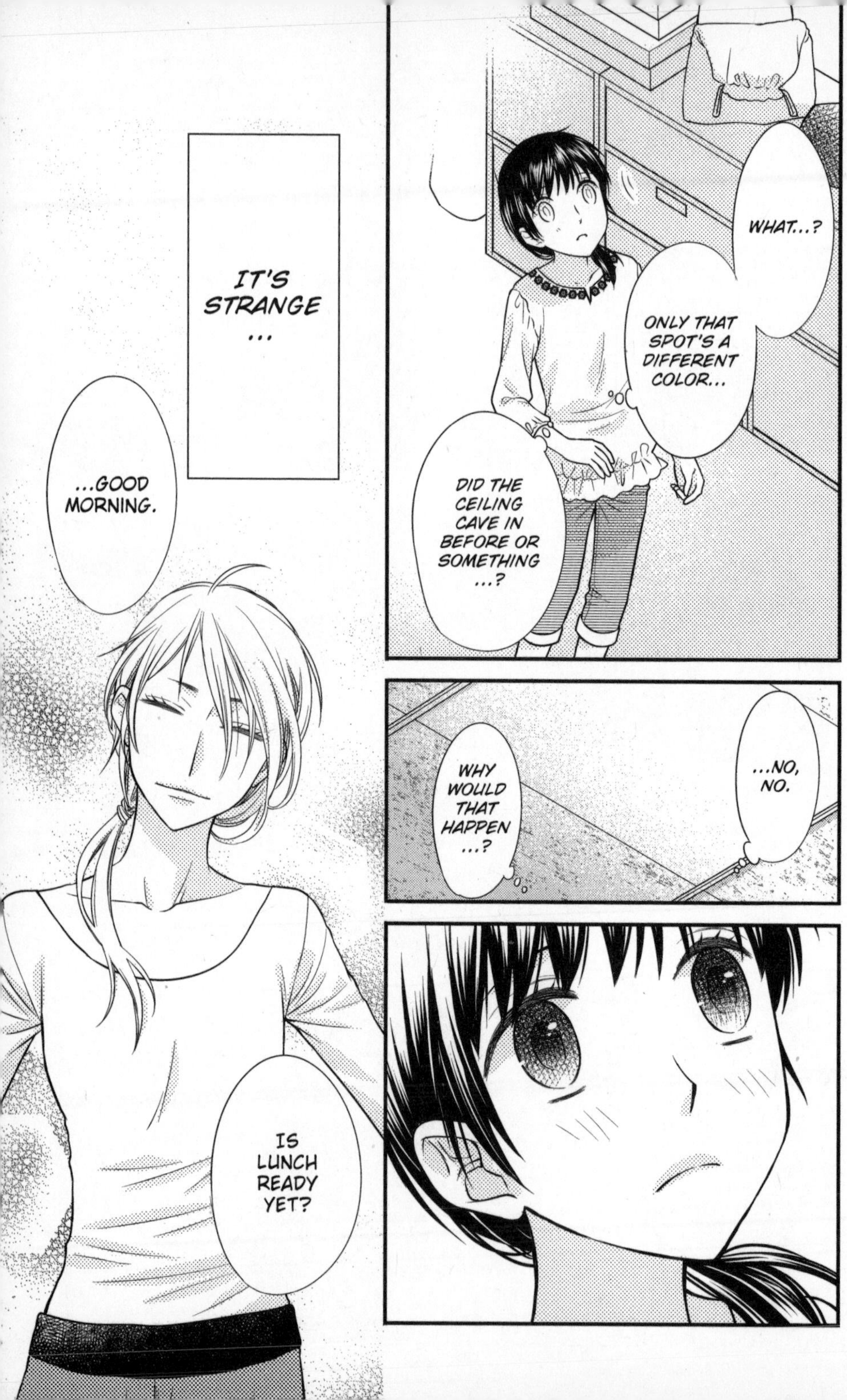
WHAT...?
ONLY THAT SPOT'S A DIFFERENT COLOR...
DID THE CEILING CAVE IN BEFORE OR SOMETHING...?
...NO, NO.
WHY WOULD THAT HAPPEN...?
IT'S STRANGE...
...GOOD MORNING.
IS LUNCH READY YET?

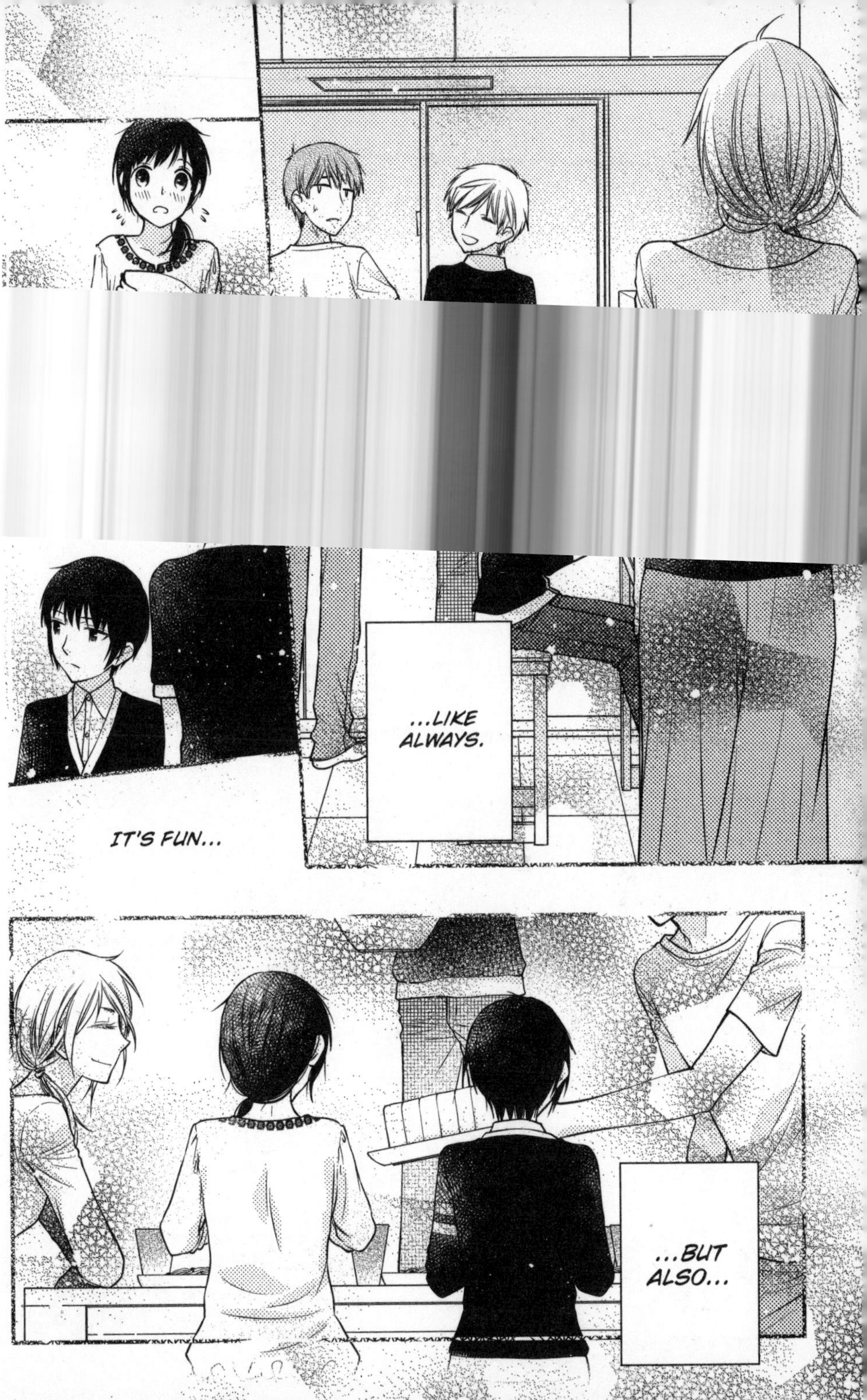
...LIKE ALWAYS.
IT'S FUN...
...BUT ALSO...

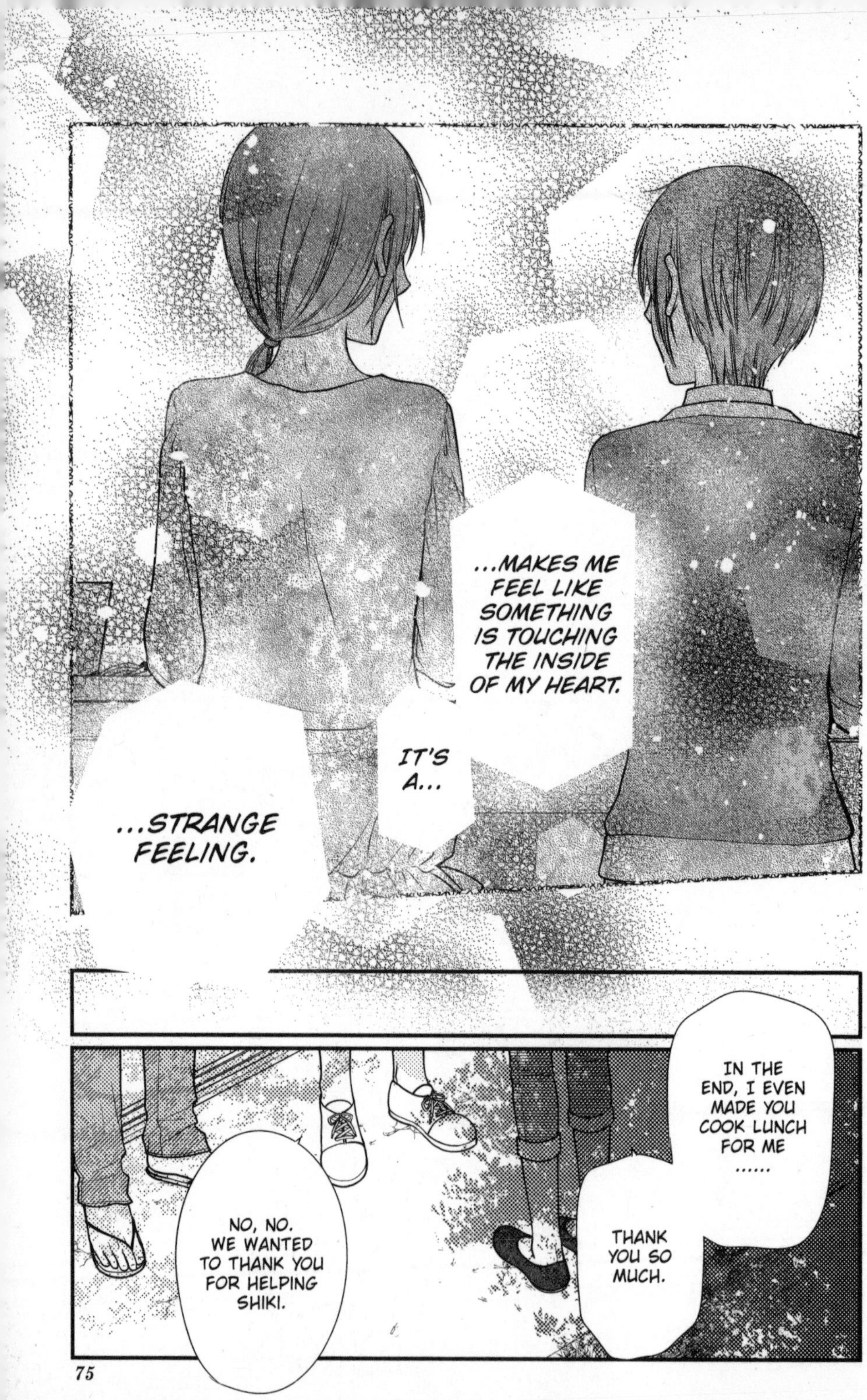
...MAKES ME FEEL LIKE SOMETHING IS TOUCHING THE INSIDE OF MY HEART.
IT'S A...
...STRANGE FEELING.
IN THE END, I EVEN MADE YOU COOK LUNCH FOR ME ......
THANK YOU SO MUCH.
NO, NO. WE WANTED TO THANK YOU FOR HELPING SHIKI.

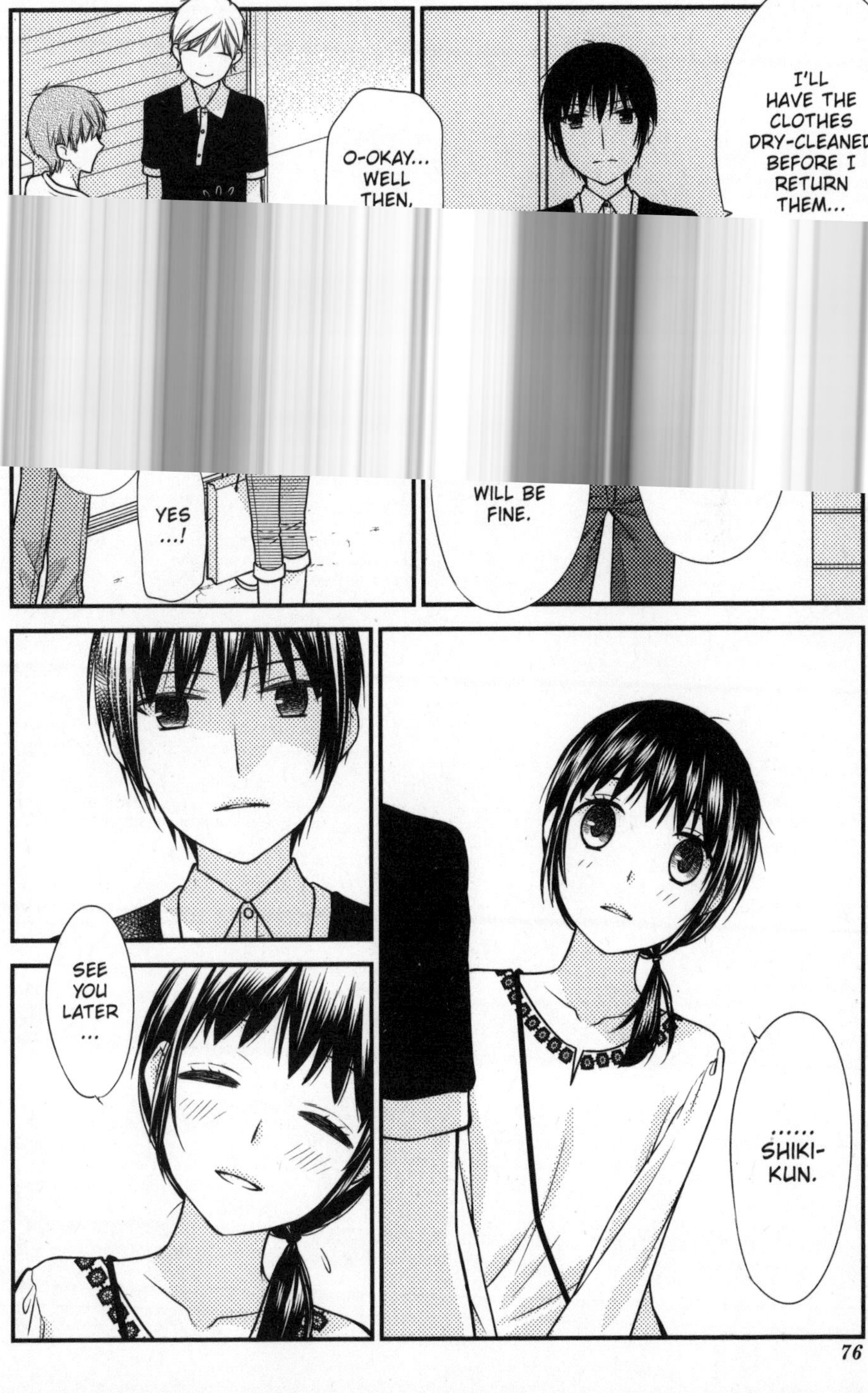
I'LL HAVE THE CLOTHES DRY-CLEANED BEFORE I RETURN THEM...
O-OKAY... WELL THEN,
WILL BE FINE.
YES ...!
...... SHIKI-KUN.
SEE YOU LATER ...

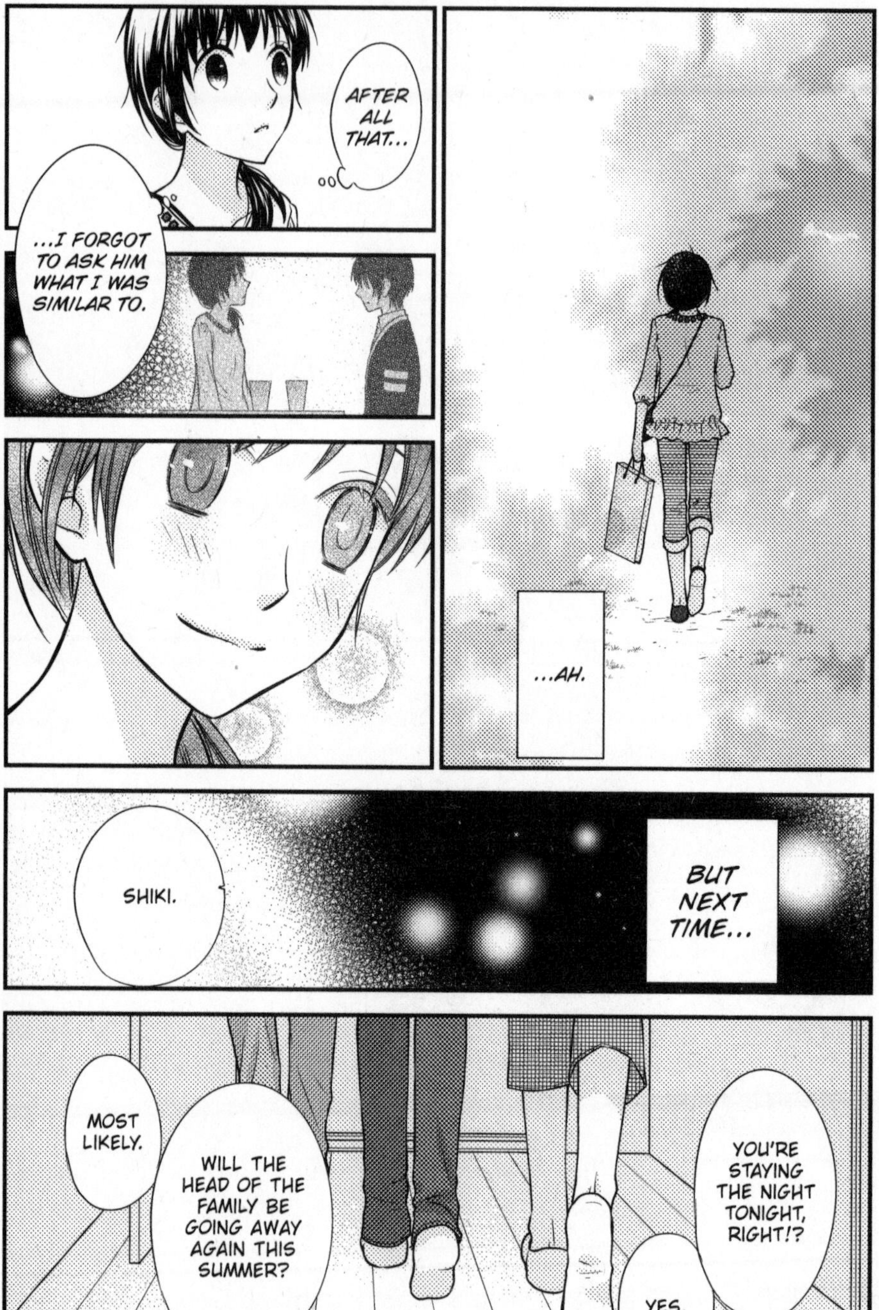
...AH.
AFTER ALL THAT...
...I FORGOT TO ASK HIM WHAT I WAS SIMILAR TO.
BUT NEXT TIME...
SHIKI.
YOU'RE STAYING THE NIGHT TONIGHT, RIGHT!?
YES.
WILL THE HEAD OF THE FAMILY BE GOING AWAY AGAIN THIS SUMMER?
MOST LIKELY.

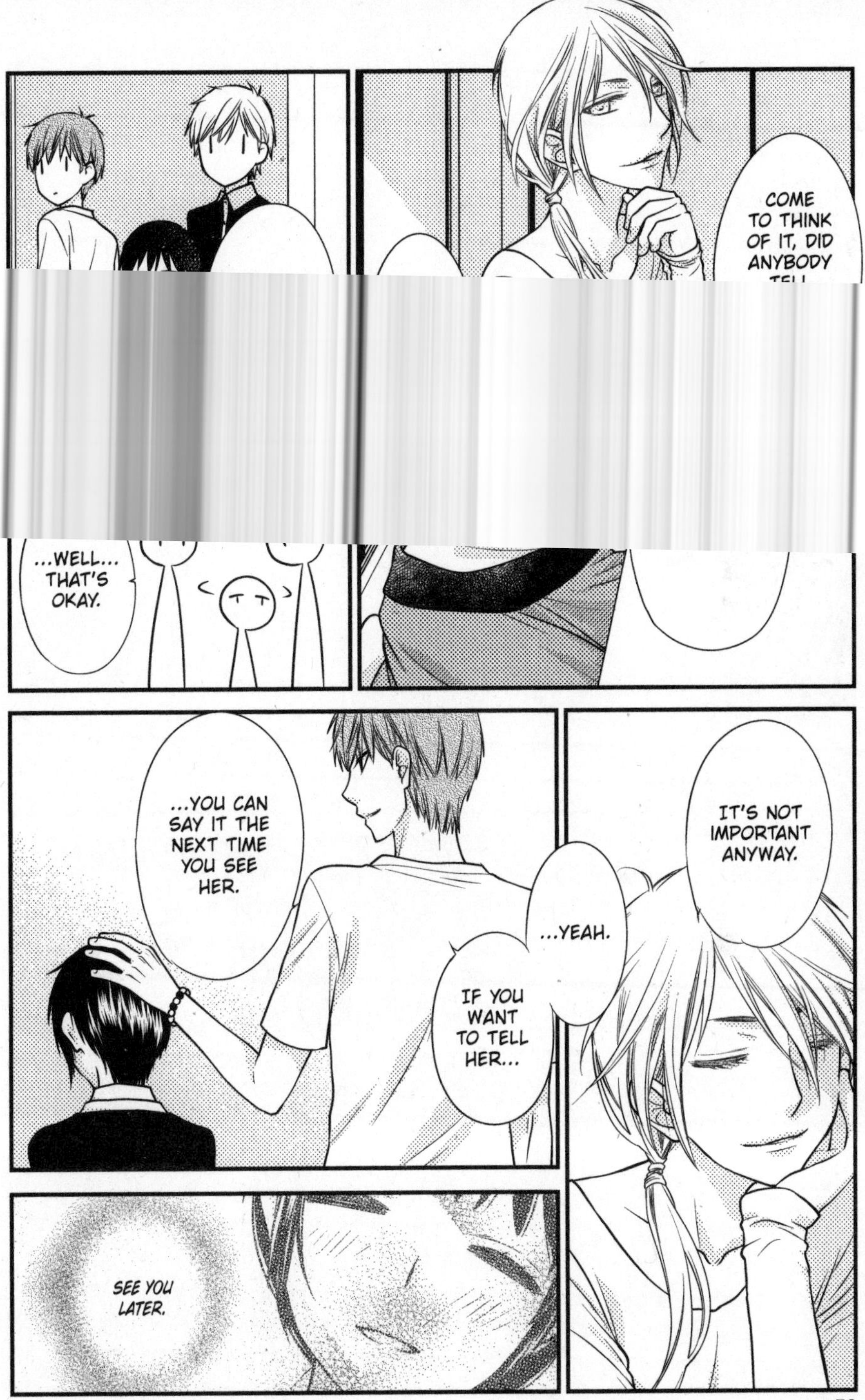
COME TO THINK OF IT, DID ANYBODY
...WELL... THAT'S OKAY.
IT'S NOT IMPORTANT ANYWAY.
...YEAH.
IF YOU WANT TO TELL HER...
...YOU CAN SAY IT THE NEXT TIME YOU SEE HER.
SEE YOU LATER.

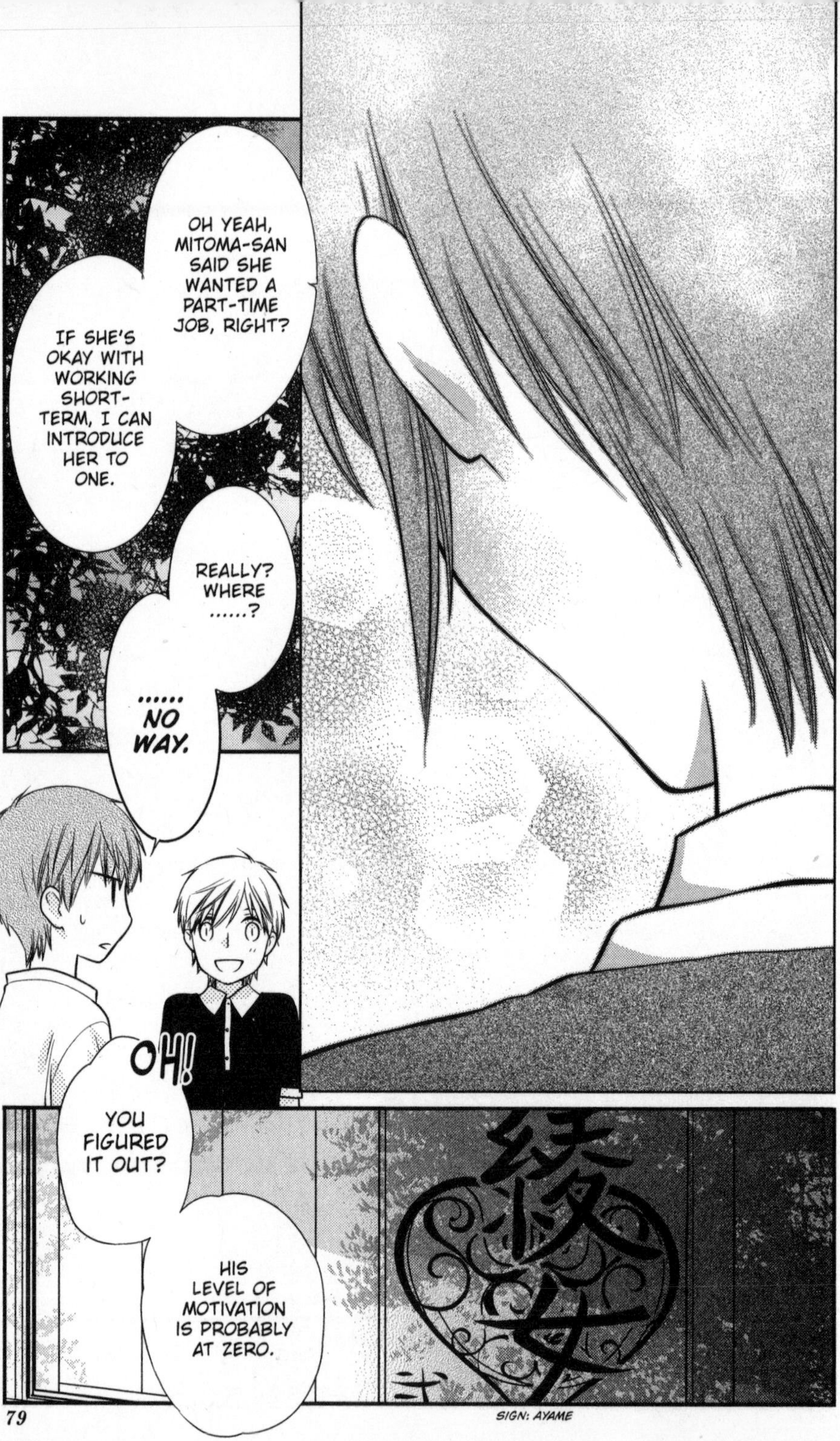
OH YEAH, MITOMA-SAN SAID SHE WANTED A PART-TIME JOB, RIGHT?
IF SHE'S OKAY WITH WORKING SHORT-TERM, I CAN INTRODUCE HER TO ONE.
REALLY? WHERE ......?
...... NO WAY.
OH!
YOU FIGURED IT OUT?
HIS LEVEL OF MOTIVATION IS PROBABLY AT ZERO.

SIGN: AYAME

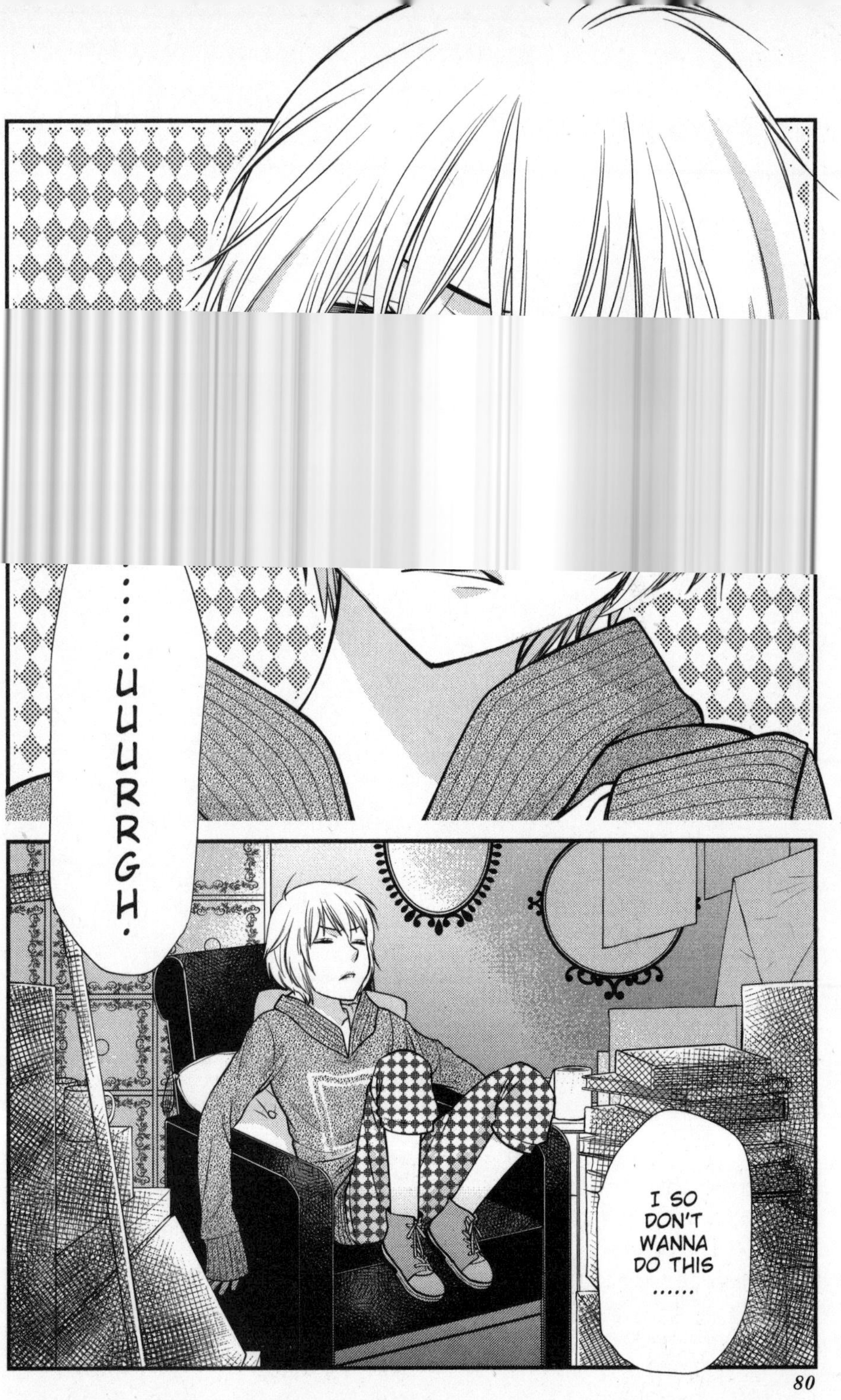
......UUURRGH.
I SO DON'T WANNA DO THIS ......

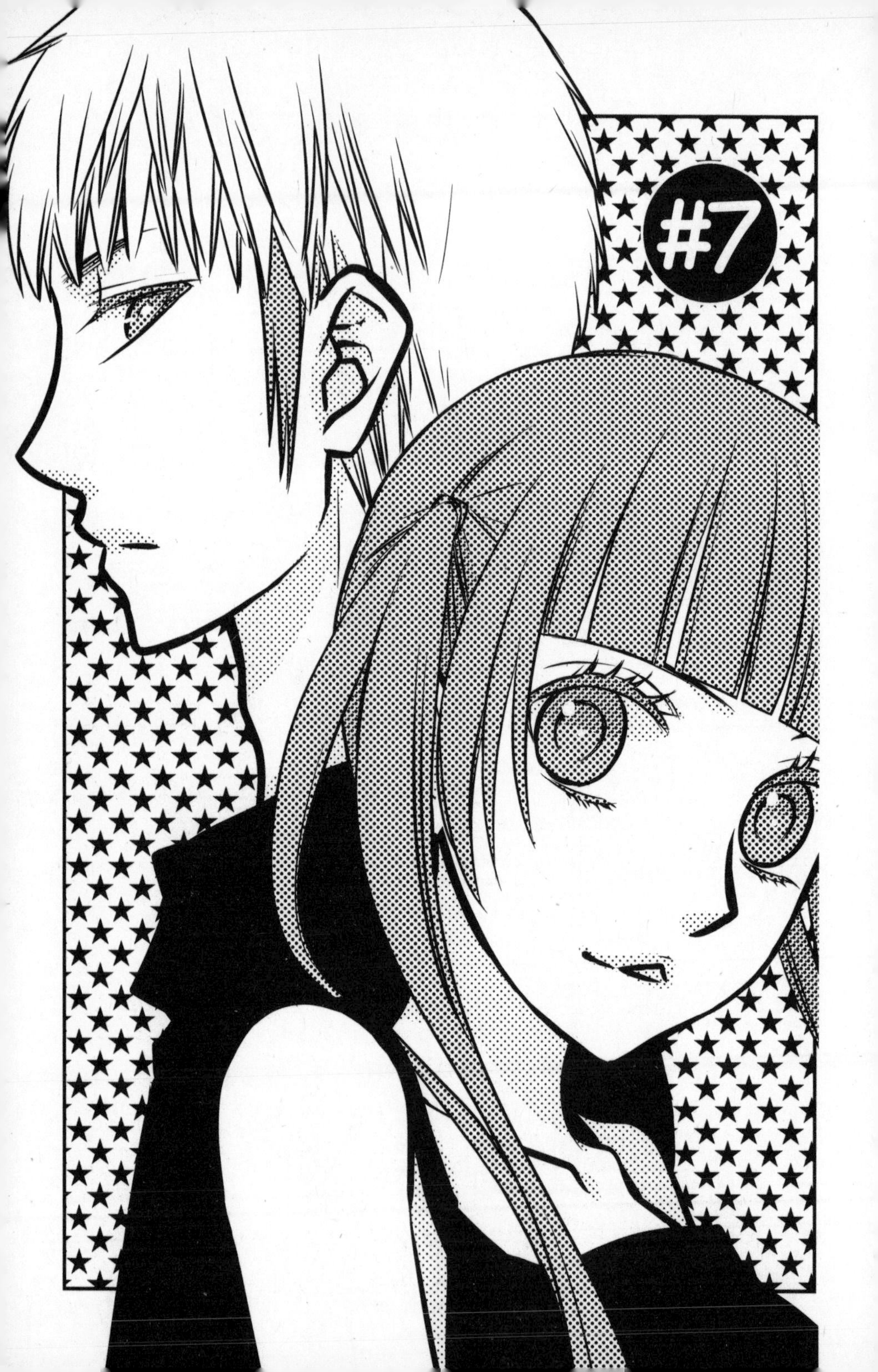
#7

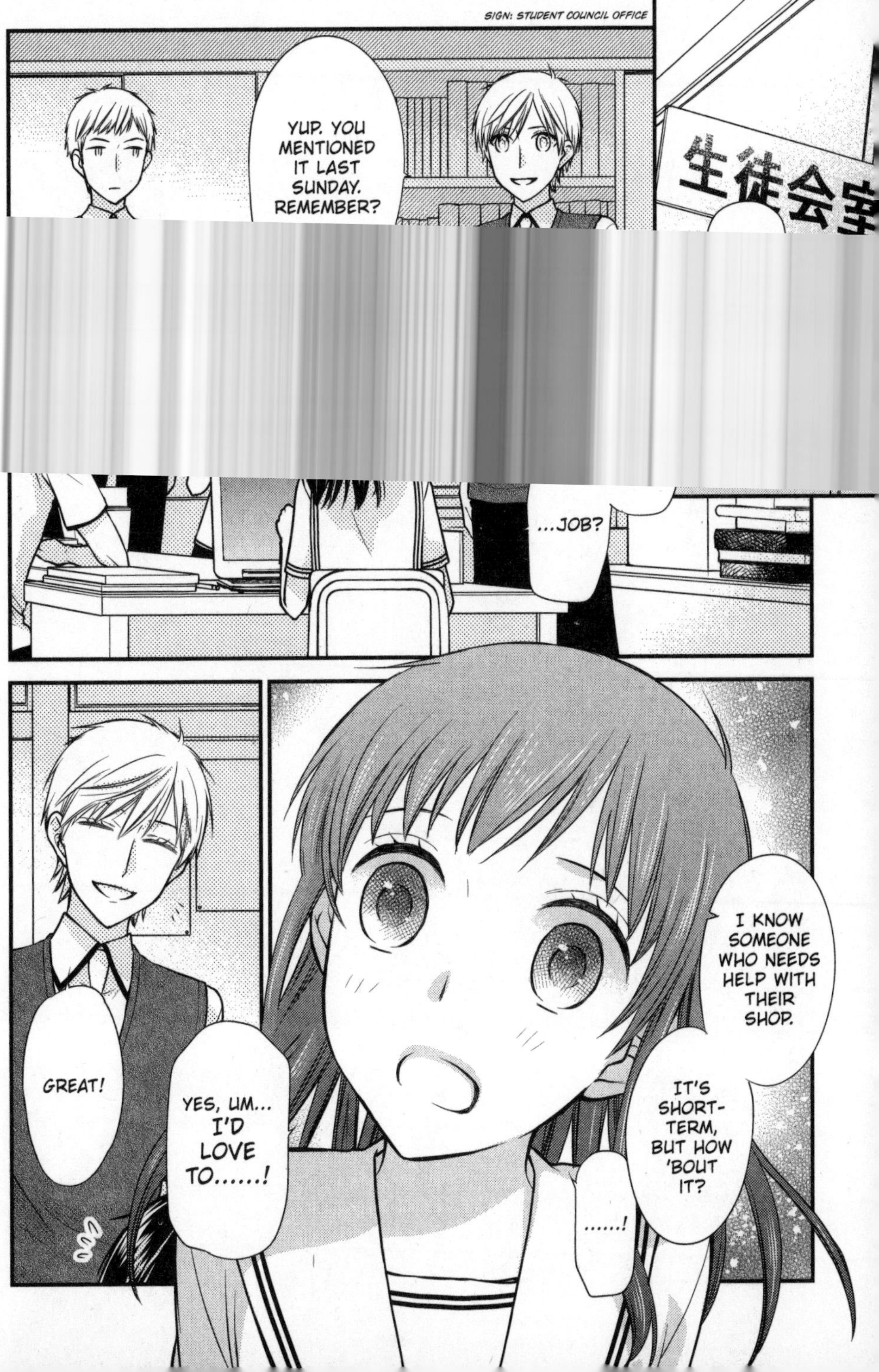
SIGN: STUDENT COUNCIL OFFICE
生徒会室
YUP. YOU MENTIONED IT LAST SUNDAY. REMEMBER?
...JOB?
I KNOW SOMEONE WHO NEEDS HELP WITH THEIR SHOP.
IT'S SHORT-TERM, BUT HOW 'BOUT IT?
......!
YES, UM... I'D LOVE TO......!
GREAT!

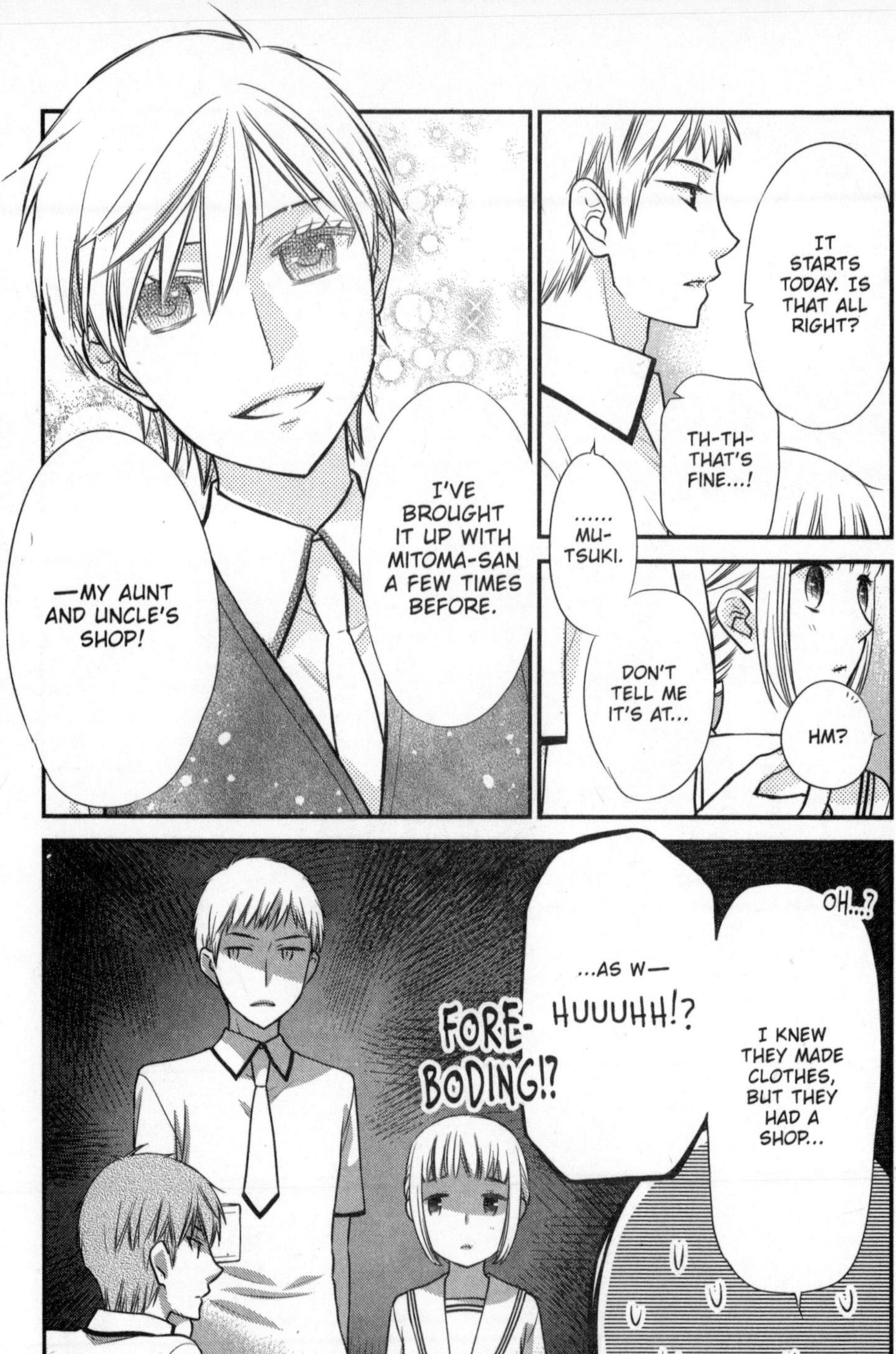

IT STARTS TODAY. IS THAT ALL RIGHT?
TH-TH-THAT'S FINE...!
...... MU-TSUKI.
HM?
DON'T TELL ME IT'S AT...
I'VE BROUGHT IT UP WITH MITOMA-SAN A FEW TIMES BEFORE.
—MY AUNT AND UNCLE'S SHOP!
OH...?
I KNEW THEY MADE CLOTHES, BUT THEY HAD A SHOP...
...AS W—
HUUUHH!?
FORE-BODING!?

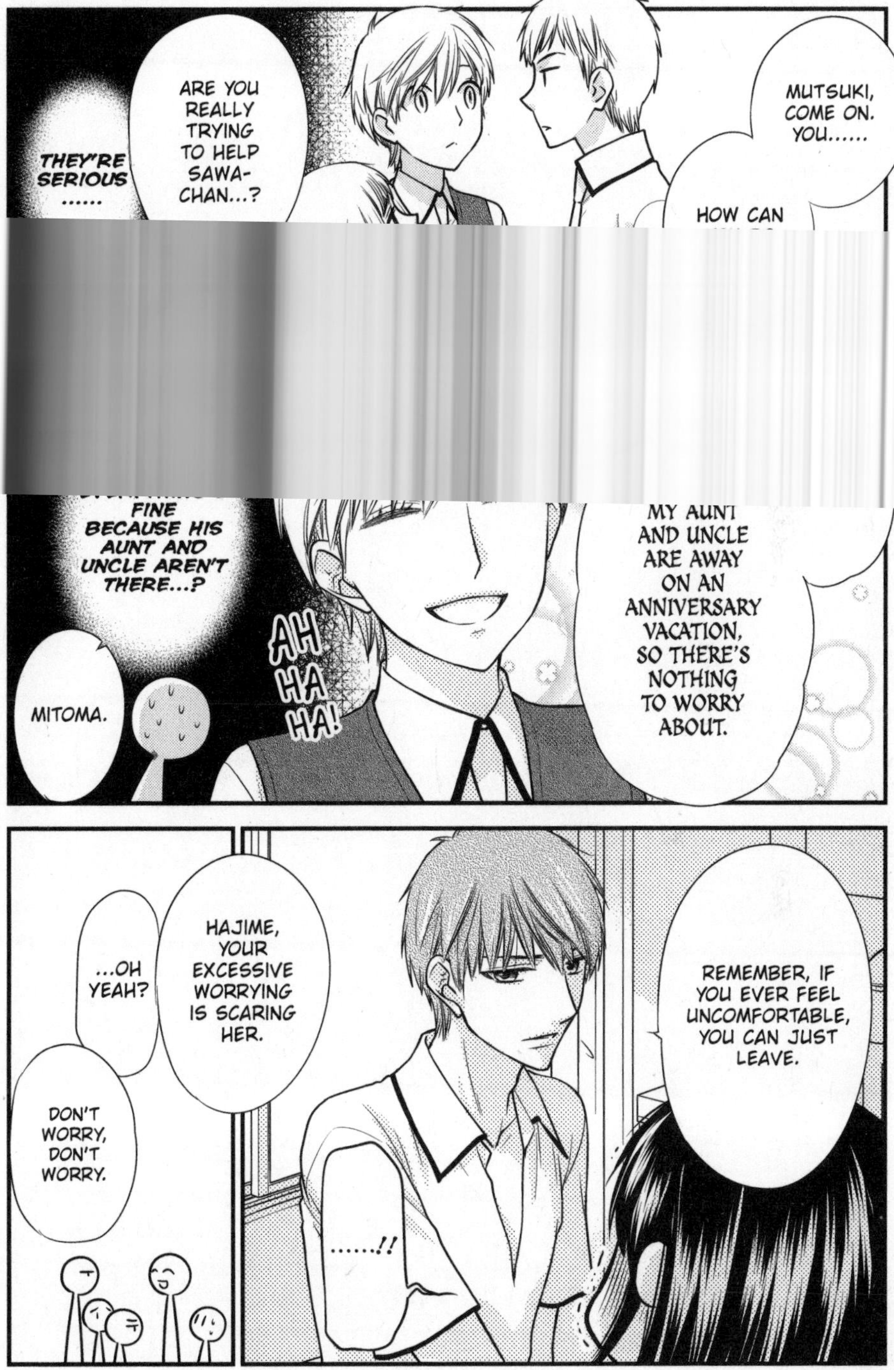
MUTSUKI, COME ON. YOU......
HOW CAN
ARE YOU REALLY TRYING TO HELP SAWA-CHAN...?
THEY'RE SERIOUS ......
MY AUNT AND UNCLE ARE AWAY ON AN ANNIVERSARY VACATION, SO THERE'S NOTHING TO WORRY ABOUT.
AH HA HA!
FINE BECAUSE HIS AUNT AND UNCLE AREN'T THERE...?
MITOMA.
REMEMBER, IF YOU EVER FEEL UNCOMFORTABLE, YOU CAN JUST LEAVE.
......!!
HAJIME, YOUR EXCESSIVE WORRYING IS SCARING HER.
...OH YEAH?
DON'T WORRY, DON'T WORRY.

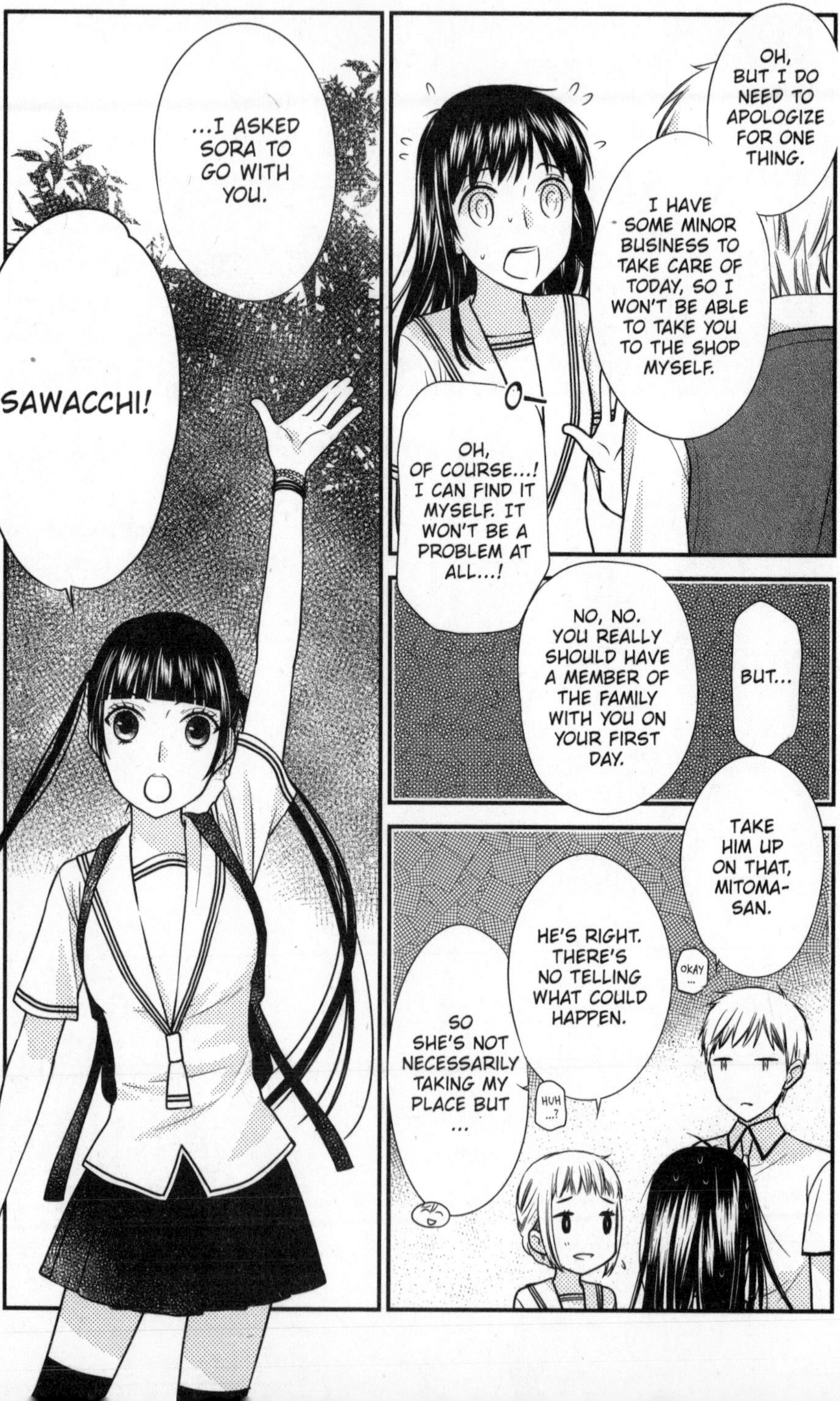
OH, BUT I DO NEED TO APOLOGIZE FOR ONE THING.
I HAVE SOME MINOR BUSINESS TO TAKE CARE OF TODAY, SO I WON'T BE ABLE TO TAKE YOU TO THE SHOP MYSELF.
OH, OF COURSE...! I CAN FIND IT MYSELF. IT WON'T BE A PROBLEM AT ALL...!
BUT...
NO, NO. YOU REALLY SHOULD HAVE A MEMBER OF THE FAMILY WITH YOU ON YOUR FIRST DAY.
TAKE HIM UP ON THAT, MITOMA-SAN.
OKAY...
HE'S RIGHT. THERE'S NO TELLING WHAT COULD HAPPEN.
HUH...?
SO SHE'S NOT NECESSARILY TAKING MY PLACE BUT ...
...I ASKED SORA TO GO WITH YOU.
SAWACCHI!

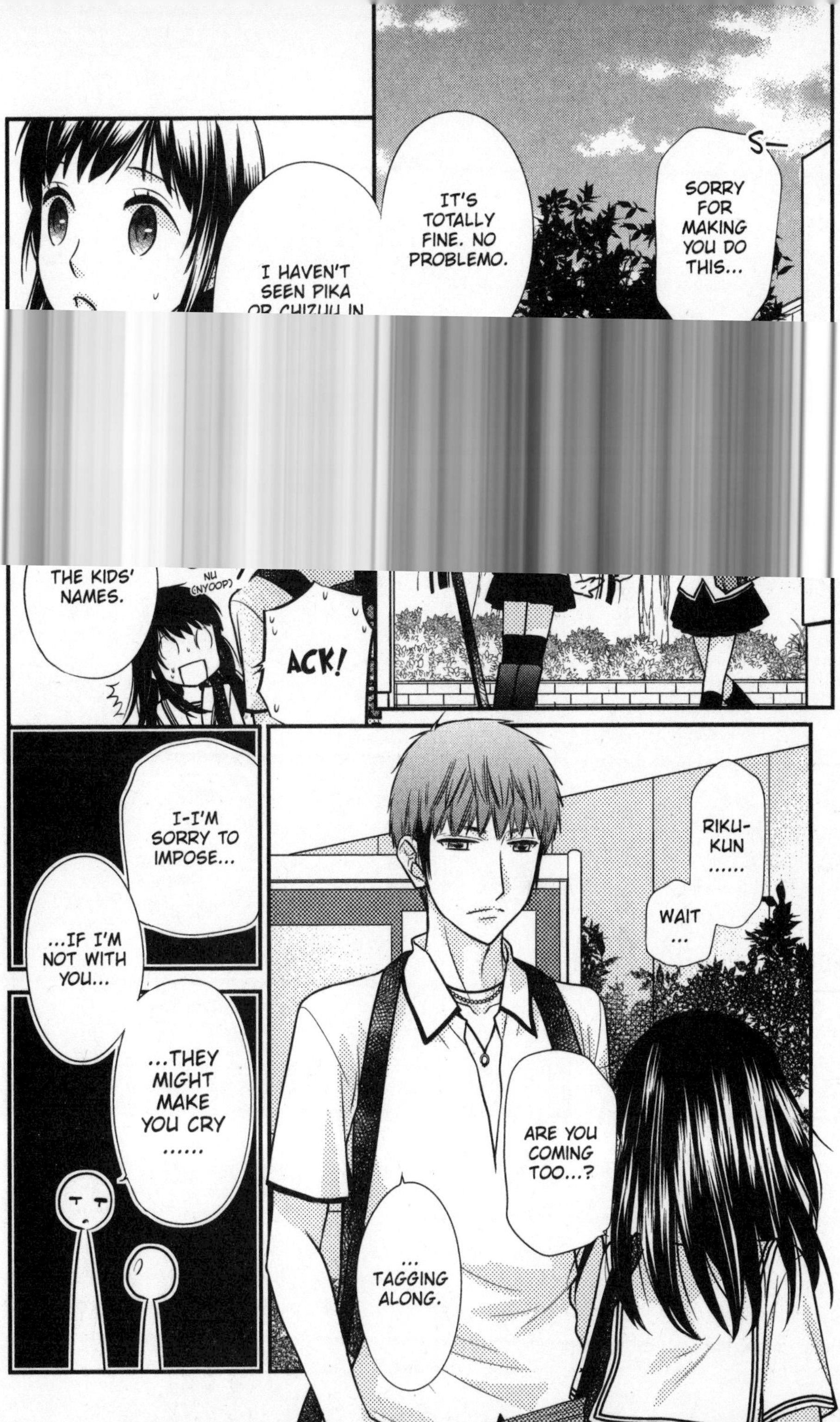
S—
SORRY FOR MAKING YOU DO THIS...
IT'S TOTALLY FINE. NO PROBLEMO.
I HAVEN'T SEEN PIKA
THE KIDS' NAMES.
NU (NYOOP)
ACK!
RIKU-KUN ......
WAIT ...
ARE YOU COMING TOO...?
... TAGGING ALONG.
I-I'M SORRY TO IMPOSE...
...IF I'M NOT WITH YOU...
...THEY MIGHT MAKE YOU CRY ......

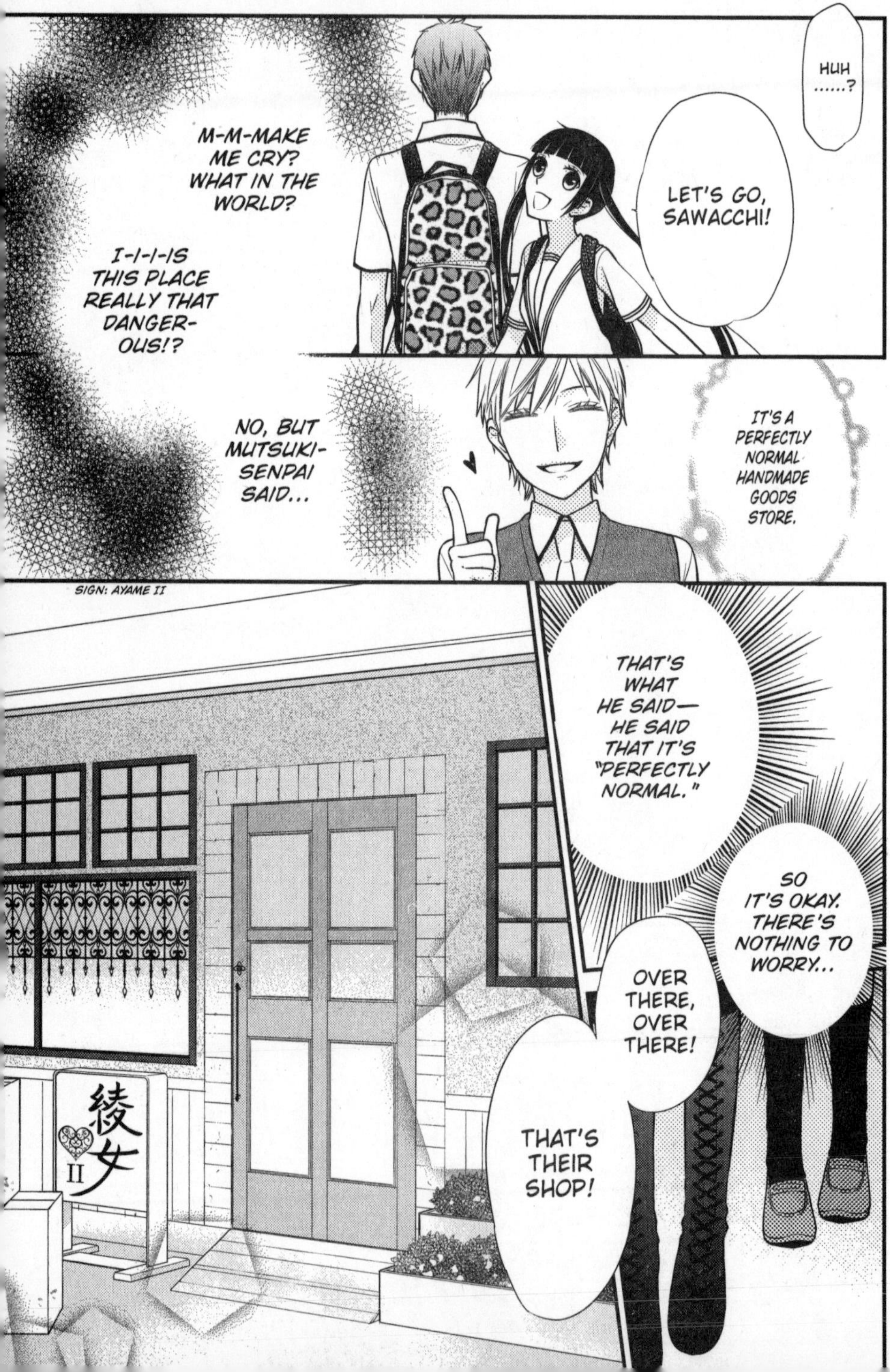
HUH ......?
LET'S GO, SAWACCHI!
M-M-MAKE ME CRY? WHAT IN THE WORLD?
I-I-I-IS THIS PLACE REALLY THAT DANGER-OUS!?
IT'S A PERFECTLY NORMAL HANDMADE GOODS STORE.
NO, BUT MUTSUKI-SENPAI SAID...
THAT'S WHAT HE SAID—HE SAID THAT IT'S "PERFECTLY NORMAL."
SO IT'S OKAY. THERE'S NOTHING TO WORRY...
OVER THERE, OVER THERE!
THAT'S THEIR SHOP!
SIGN: AYAME II
綾女 II

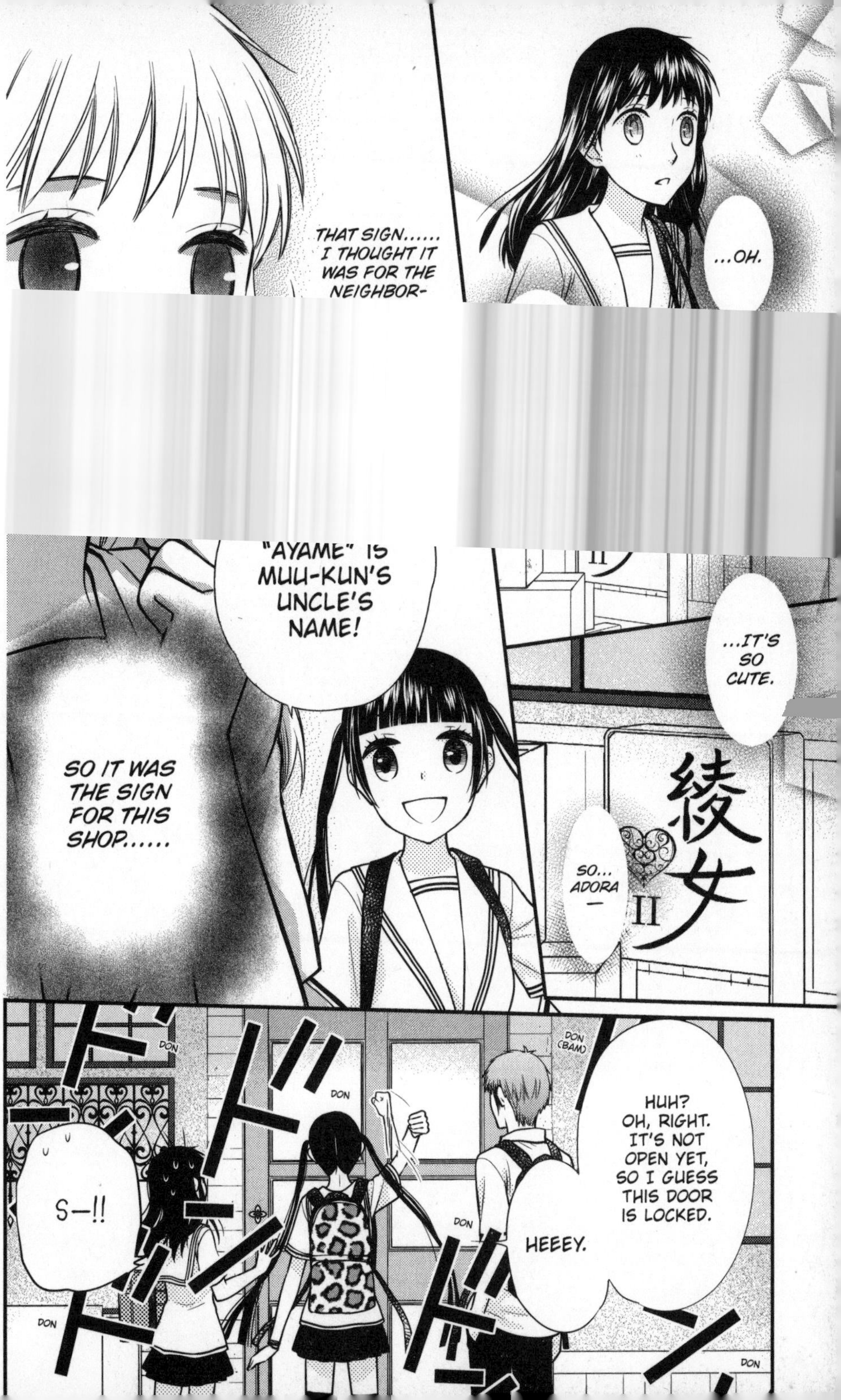
...OH.
THAT SIGN...... I THOUGHT IT WAS FOR THE NEIGHBOR-
...IT'S SO CUTE.
"AYAME" IS MUU-KUN'S UNCLE'S NAME!
SO... ADORA —
SO IT WAS THE SIGN FOR THIS SHOP......
DON (BAM)
HUH? OH, RIGHT. IT'S NOT OPEN YET, SO I GUESS THIS DOOR IS LOCKED.
HEEEY.
DON
DON
DON
S—!!
DON
DON

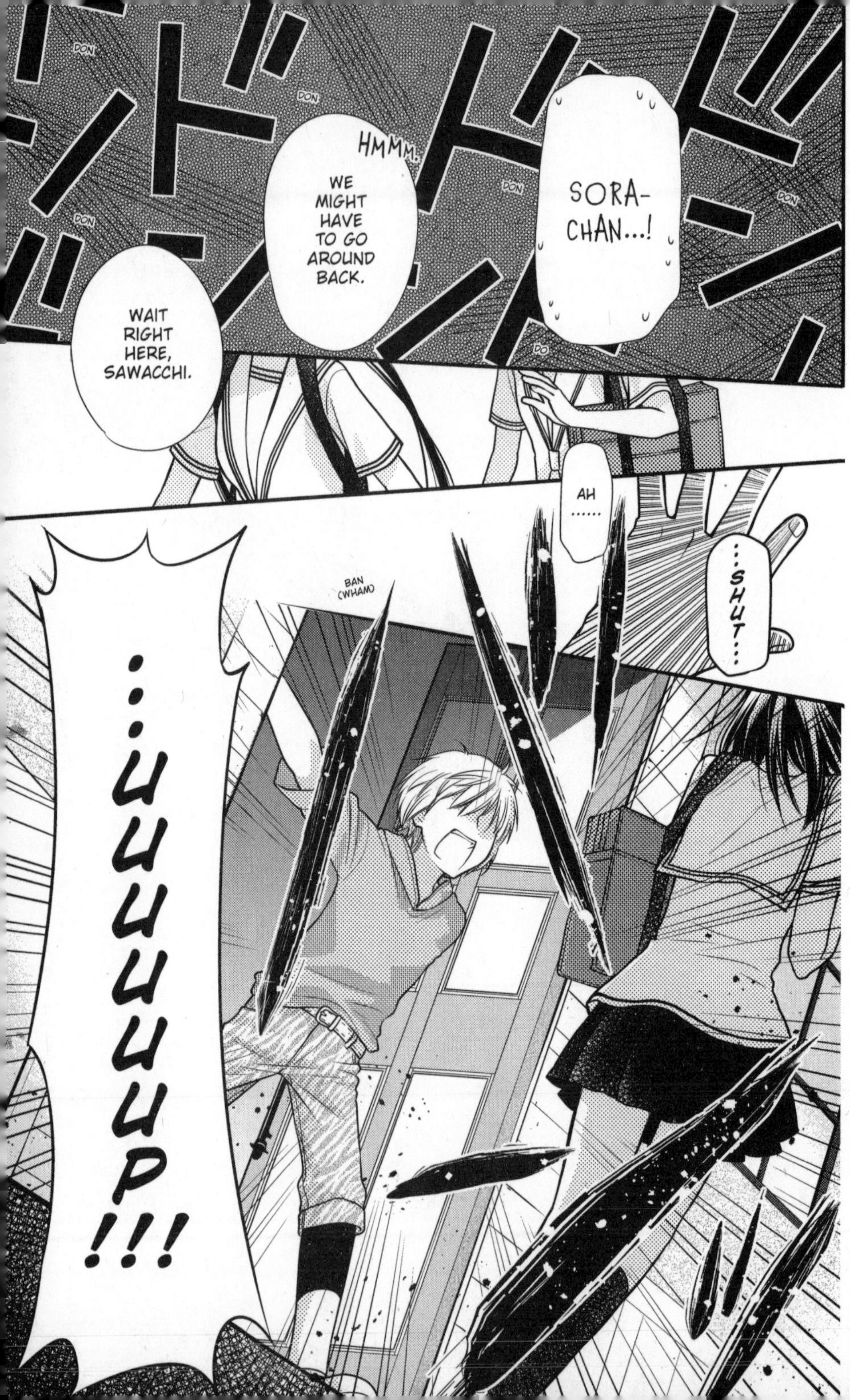
DON
DON
DON
DON
DON
DO
SORA-CHAN...!
HMMM.
WE MIGHT HAVE TO GO AROUND BACK.
WAIT RIGHT HERE, SAWACCHI.
...SHUT...
AH ......
BAN (WHAM)
...UUUUUUP!!!

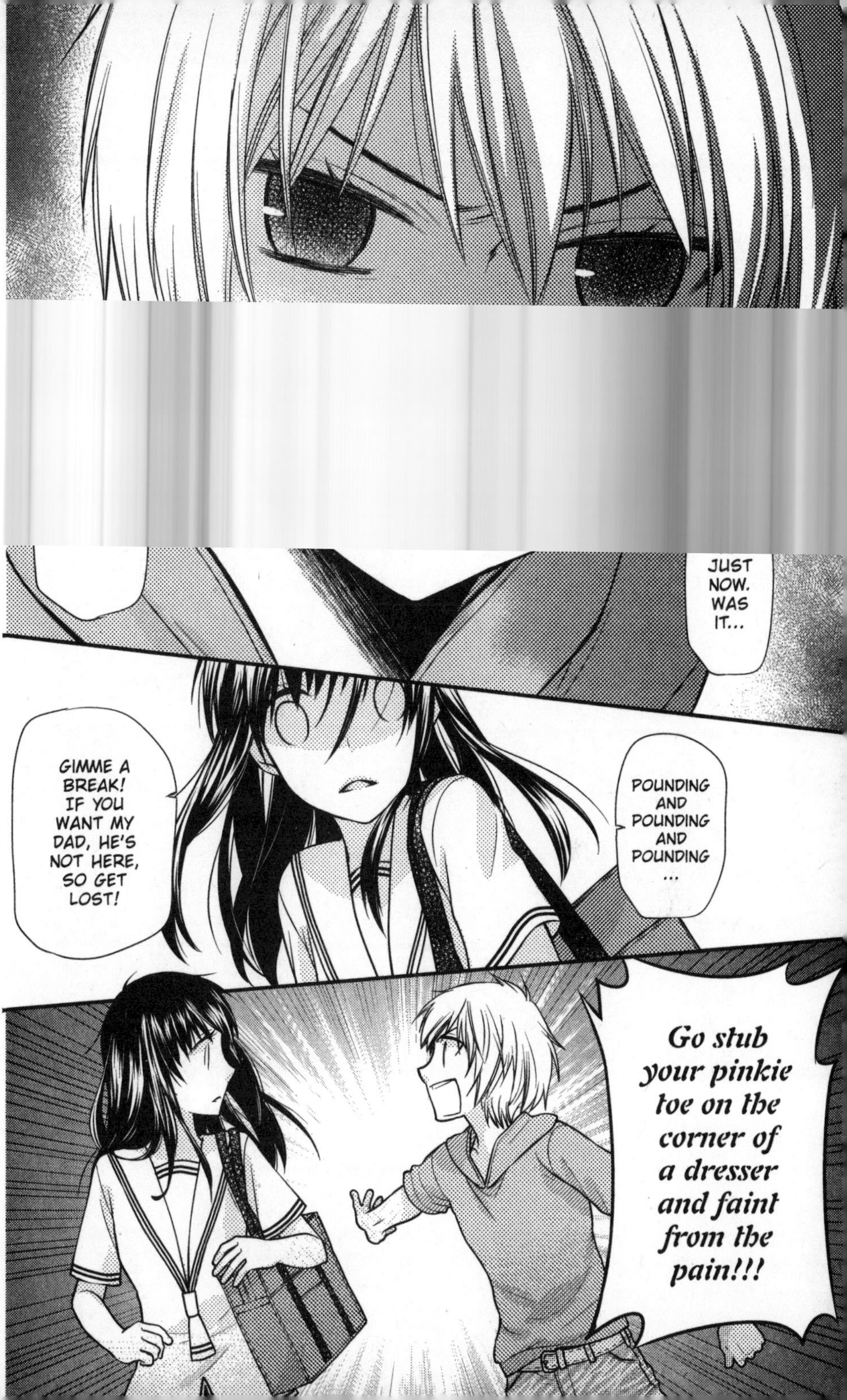
JUST NOW. WAS IT...
POUNDING AND POUNDING AND POUNDING ...
GIMME A BREAK! IF YOU WANT MY DAD, HE'S NOT HERE, SO GET LOST!
Go stub your pinkie toe on the corner of a dresser and faint from the pain!!!

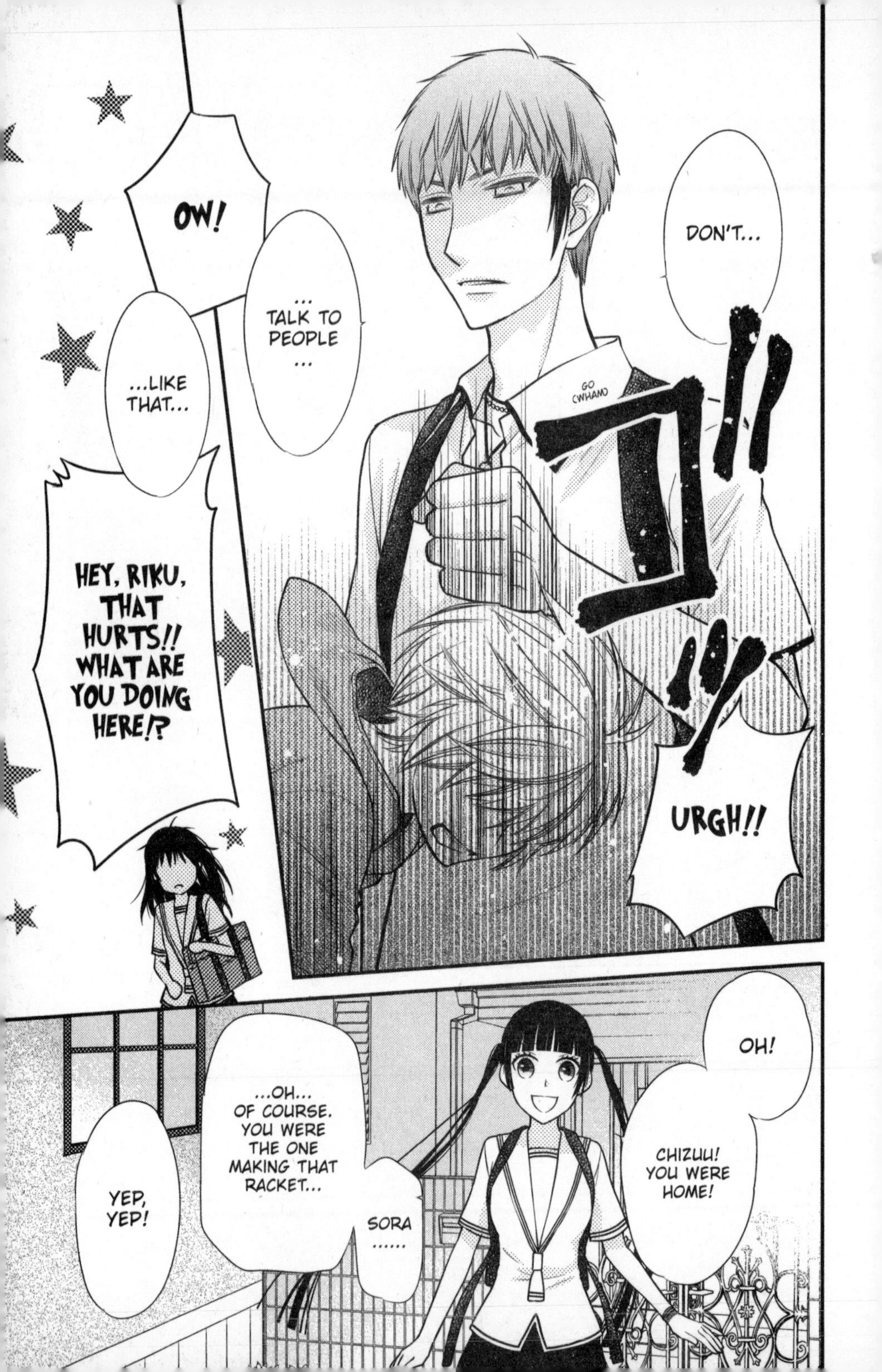
DON'T...
...TALK TO PEOPLE...
...LIKE THAT...
GO (WHAM)
URGH!!
OW!
HEY, RIKU, THAT HURTS!! WHAT ARE YOU DOING HERE!?
OH!
CHIZUU! YOU WERE HOME!
SORA......
...OH... OF COURSE. YOU WERE THE ONE MAKING THAT RACKET...
YEP, YEP!

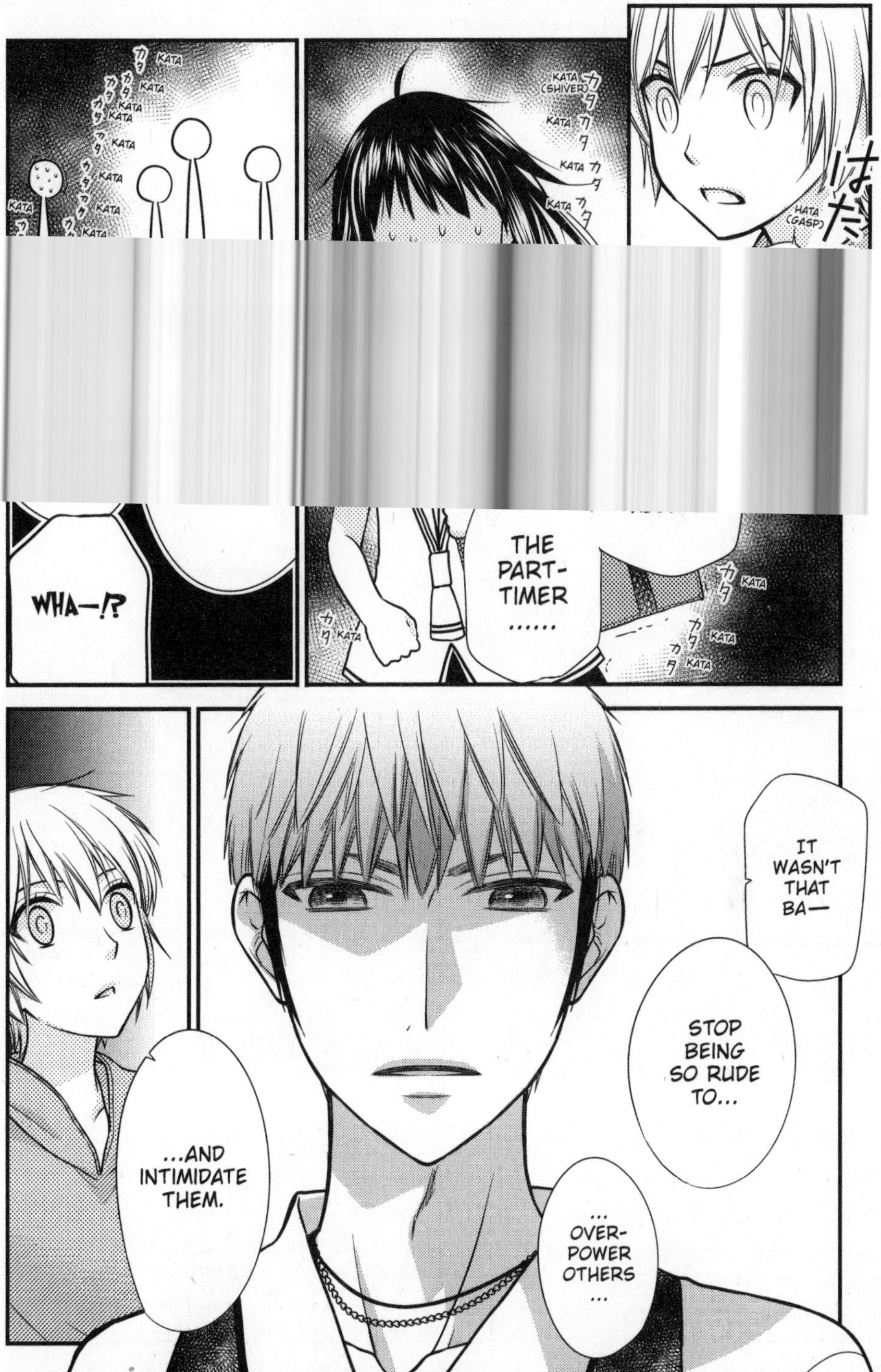

HATA (GASP)
KATA (SHIVER)
KATA
KATA
KATA
KATA
KATA
KATA
KATA
KATA
KATA
KATA
KATA
KATA
THE PART-TIMER ......
KATA
KATA
KATA
KATA
WHA—!?
IT WASN'T THAT BA—
STOP BEING SO RUDE TO...
...OVER-POWER OTHERS...
...AND INTIMIDATE THEM.

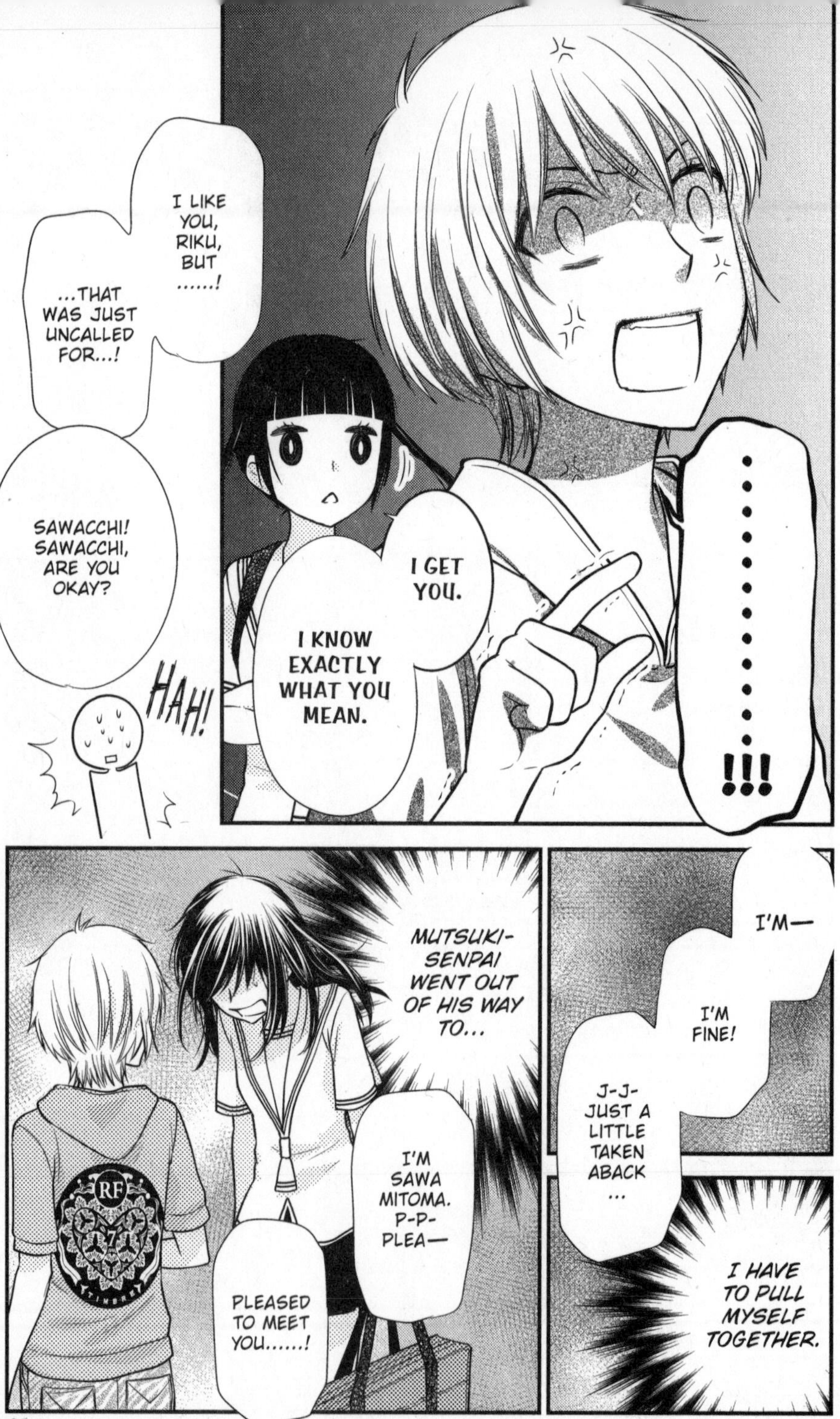

......!!!
I GET YOU.
I KNOW EXACTLY WHAT YOU MEAN.
I LIKE YOU, RIKU, BUT ......!
...THAT WAS JUST UNCALLED FOR...!
SAWACCHI! SAWACCHI, ARE YOU OKAY?
HAH!
I'M—
I'M FINE!
J-J-JUST A LITTLE TAKEN ABACK ...
I HAVE TO PULL MYSELF TOGETHER.
MUTSUKI-SENPAI WENT OUT OF HIS WAY TO...
I'M SAWA MITOMA. P-P-PLEA—
PLEASED TO MEET YOU......!

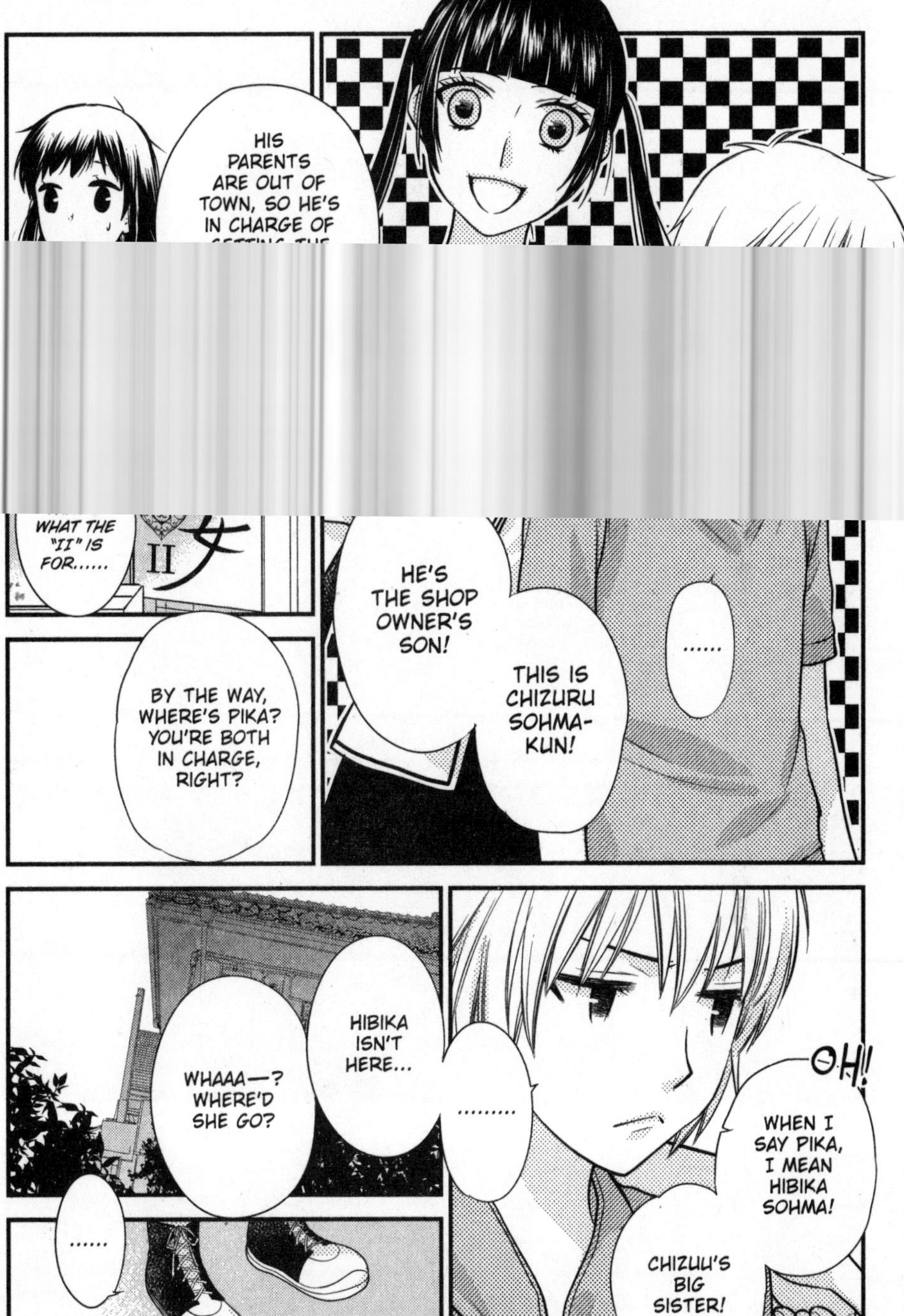
THIS IS CHIZURU SOHMA-KUN!
HE'S THE SHOP OWNER'S SON!
......
HIS PARENTS ARE OUT OF TOWN, SO HE'S IN CHARGE OF
WHAT THE "II" IS FOR......
BY THE WAY, WHERE'S PIKA? YOU'RE BOTH IN CHARGE, RIGHT?
OH!
WHEN I SAY PIKA, I MEAN HIBIKA SOHMA!
CHIZUU'S BIG SISTER!
....
HIBIKA ISN'T HERE...
WHAAA—? WHERE'D SHE GO?
......

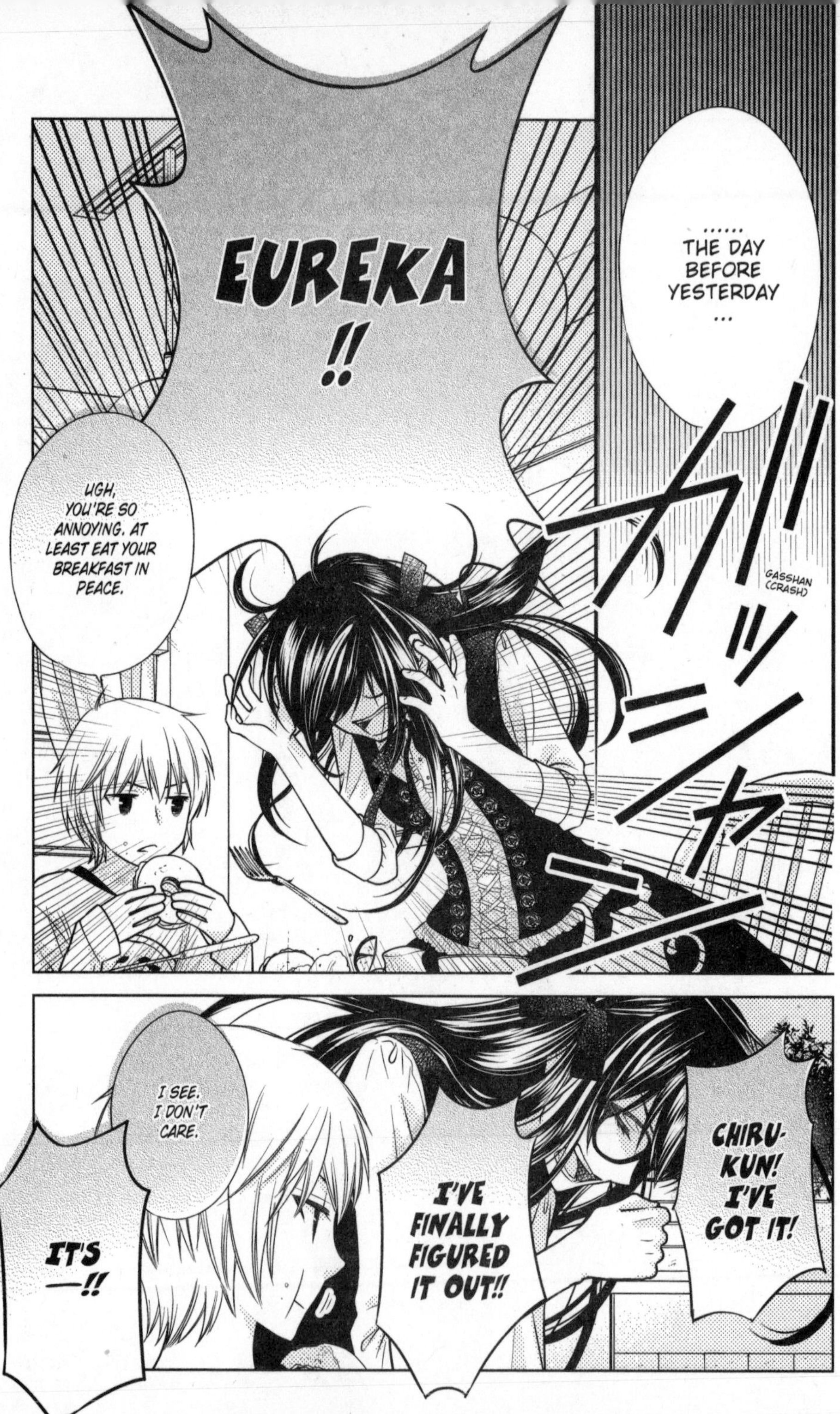

...... THE DAY BEFORE YESTERDAY ...
EUREKA !!
GASSHAN (CRASH)
UGH, YOU'RE SO ANNOYING. AT LEAST EAT YOUR BREAKFAST IN PEACE.
CHIRU-KUN! I'VE GOT IT!
I'VE FINALLY FIGURED IT OUT!!
I SEE. I DON'T CARE.
IT'S —!!

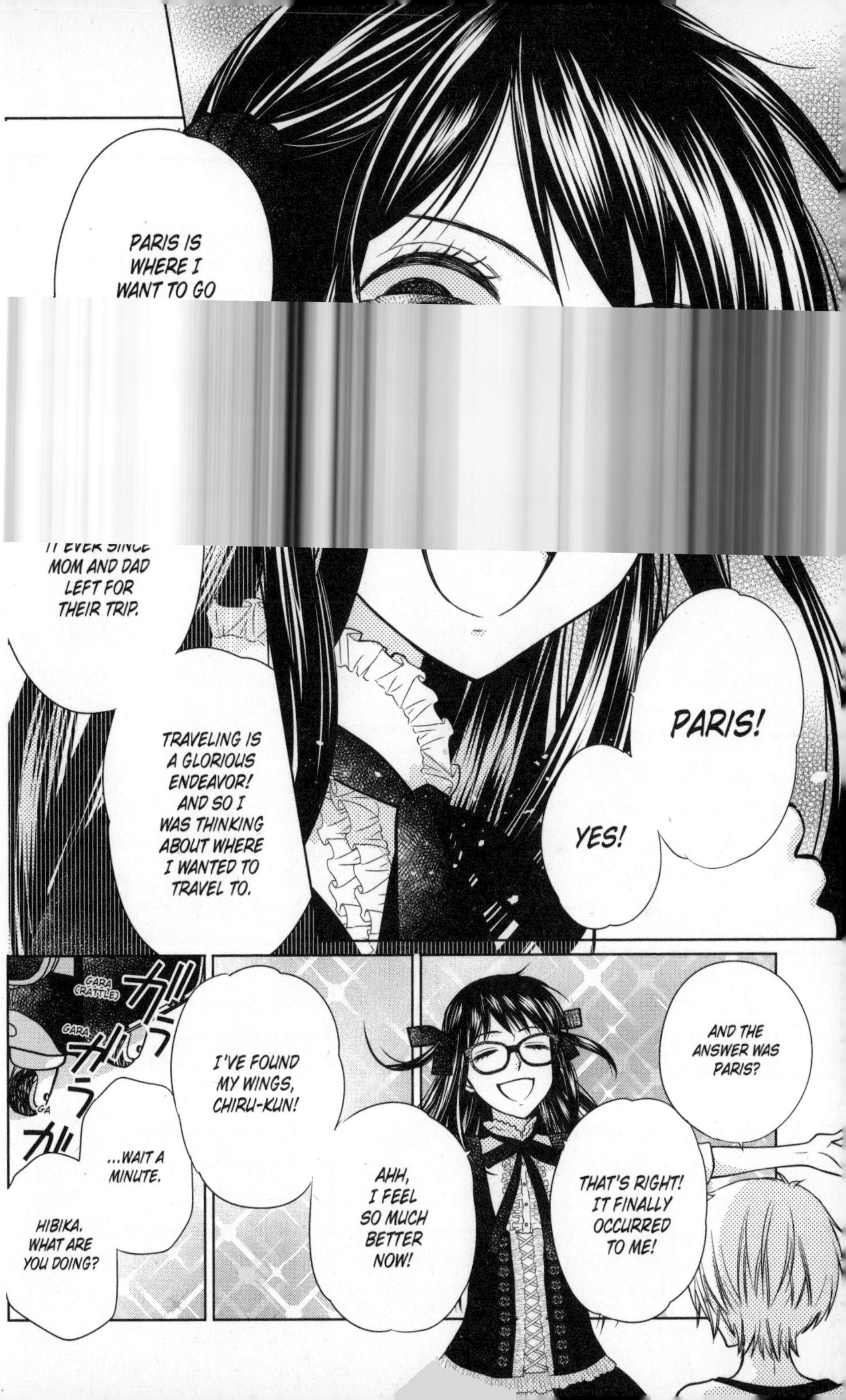
PARIS IS WHERE I WANT TO GO
PARIS!
YES!
IT EVER SINCE MOM AND DAD LEFT FOR THEIR TRIP.
TRAVELING IS A GLORIOUS ENDEAVOR! AND SO I WAS THINKING ABOUT WHERE I WANTED TO TRAVEL TO.
AND THE ANSWER WAS PARIS?
THAT'S RIGHT! IT FINALLY OCCURRED TO ME!
I'VE FOUND MY WINGS, CHIRU-KUN!
AHH, I FEEL SO MUCH BETTER NOW!
GARA (RATTLE)
GARA
GA
...WAIT A MINUTE.
HIBIKA. WHAT ARE YOU DOING?

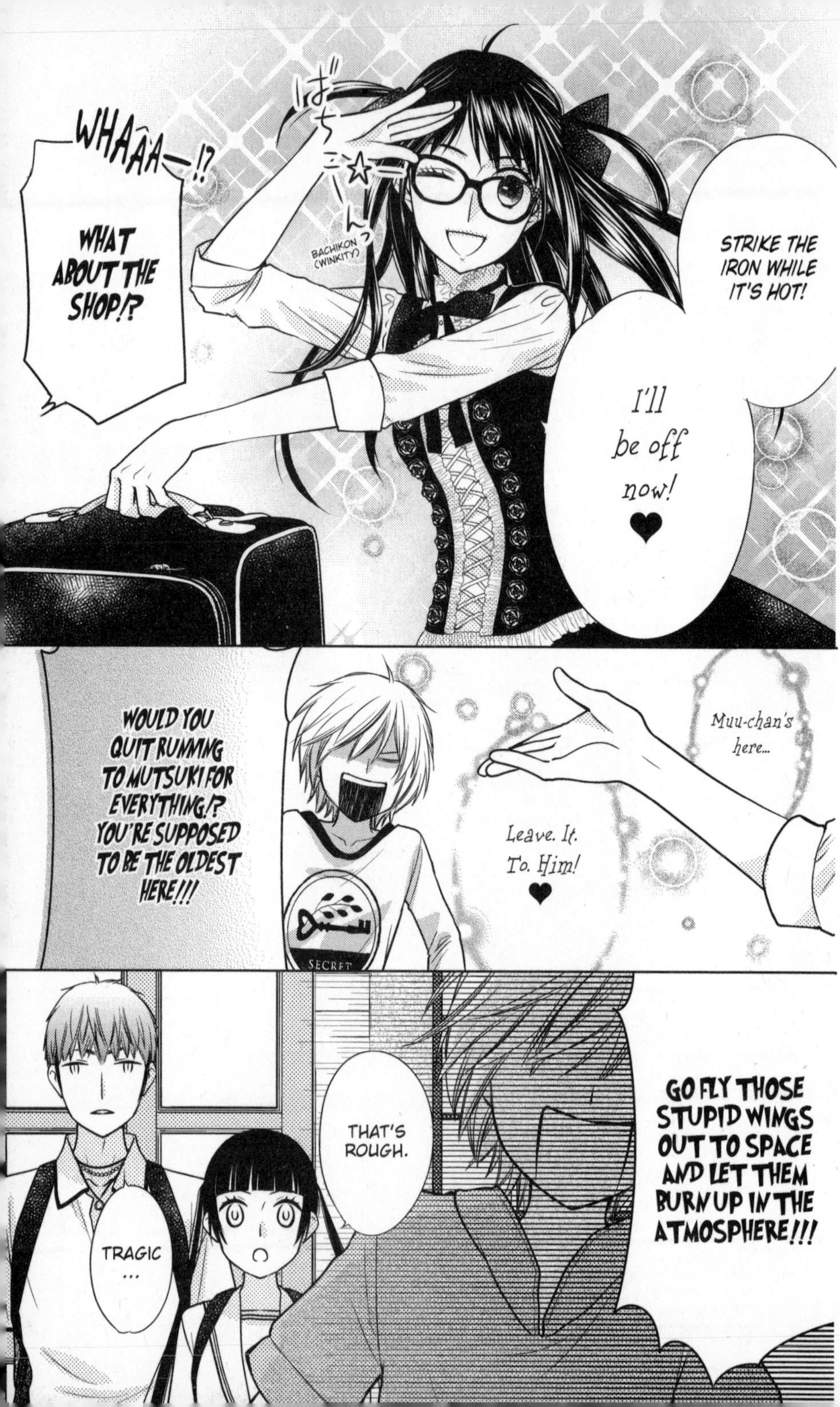
STRIKE THE IRON WHILE IT'S HOT!
I'll be off now! ♥
BACHIKON (WINKITY)
WHAÂÂA—!?
WHAT ABOUT THE SHOP!?
Muu-chan's here...
Leave. It. To. Him! ♥
WOULD YOU QUIT RUNNING TO MUTSUKI FOR EVERYTHING!? YOU'RE SUPPOSED TO BE THE OLDEST HERE!!!
SECRET
GO FLY THOSE STUPID WINGS OUT TO SPACE AND LET THEM BURN UP IN THE ATMOSPHERE!!!
THAT'S ROUGH.
TRAGIC...

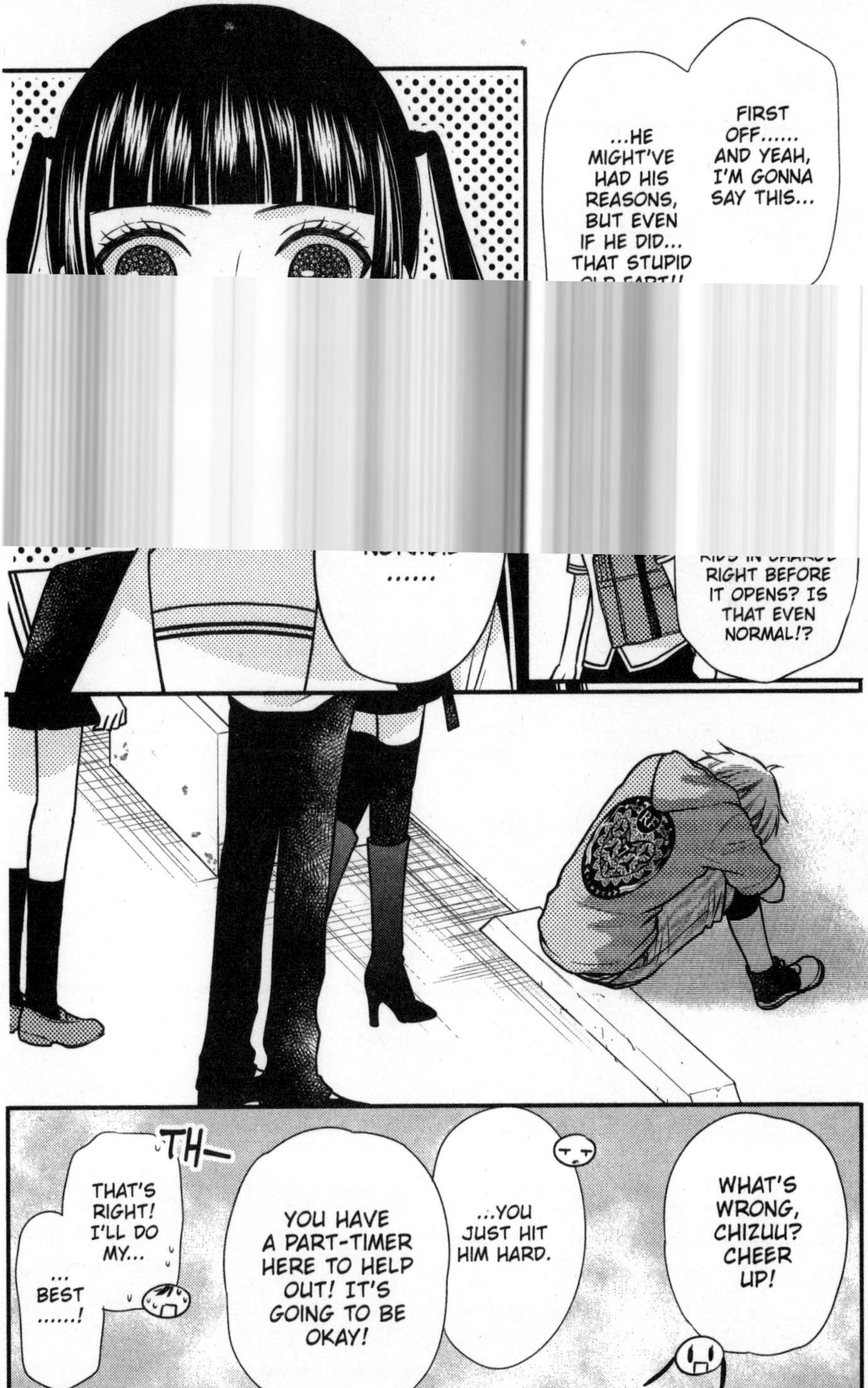
FIRST OFF...... AND YEAH, I'M GONNA SAY THIS...
...HE MIGHT'VE HAD HIS REASONS, BUT EVEN IF HE DID... THAT STUPID
RIGHT BEFORE IT OPENS? IS THAT EVEN NORMAL!?
......
WHAT'S WRONG, CHIZUU? CHEER UP!
...YOU JUST HIT HIM HARD.
YOU HAVE A PART-TIMER HERE TO HELP OUT! IT'S GOING TO BE OKAY!
TH-
THAT'S RIGHT! I'LL DO MY...
...BEST ......!

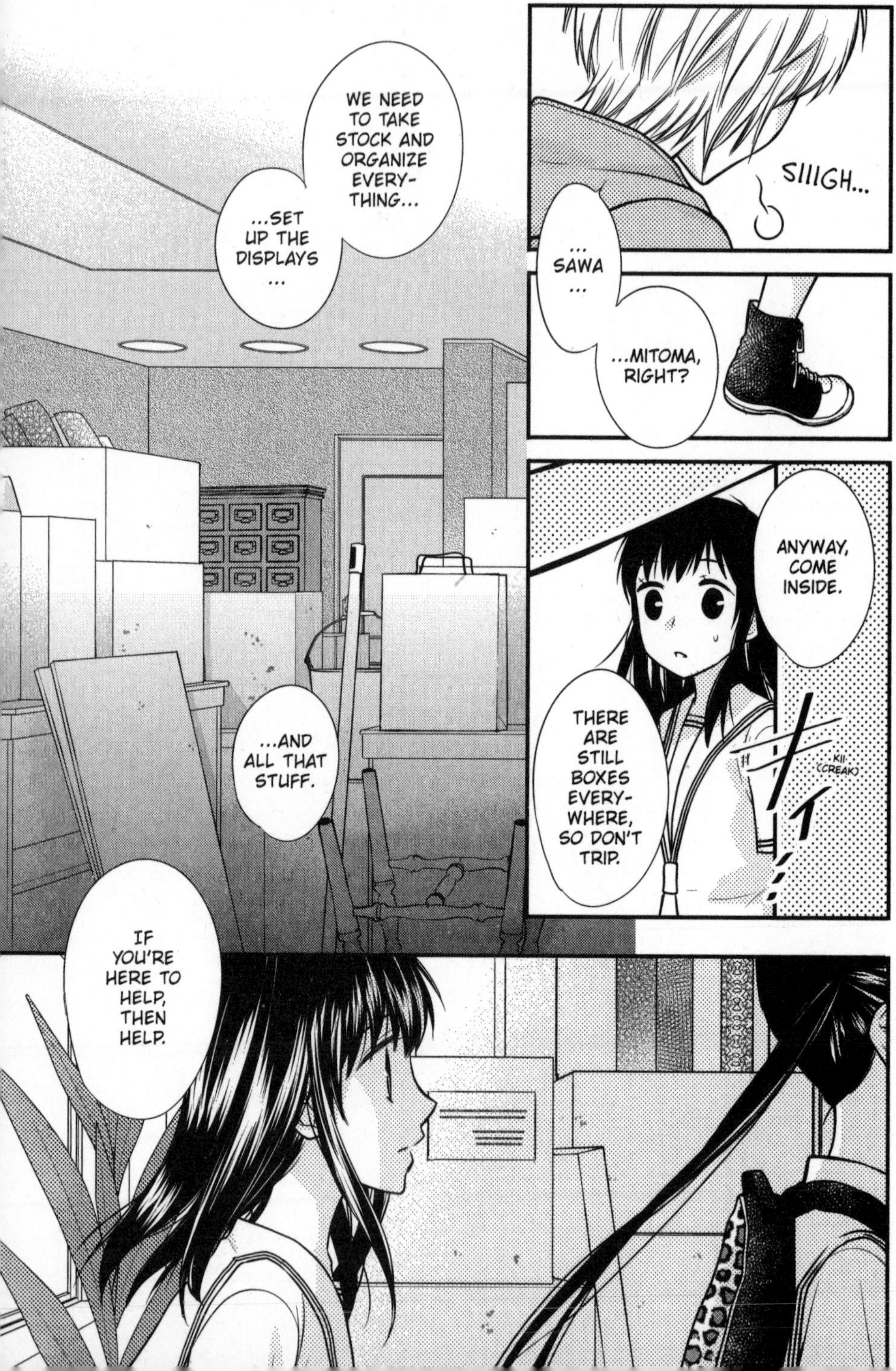
SIIIGH...
...SAWA...
...MITOMA, RIGHT?
ANYWAY, COME INSIDE.
THERE ARE STILL BOXES EVERYWHERE, SO DON'T TRIP.
KII (CREAK)
WE NEED TO TAKE STOCK AND ORGANIZE EVERYTHING...
...SET UP THE DISPLAYS...
...AND ALL THAT STUFF.
IF YOU'RE HERE TO HELP, THEN HELP.

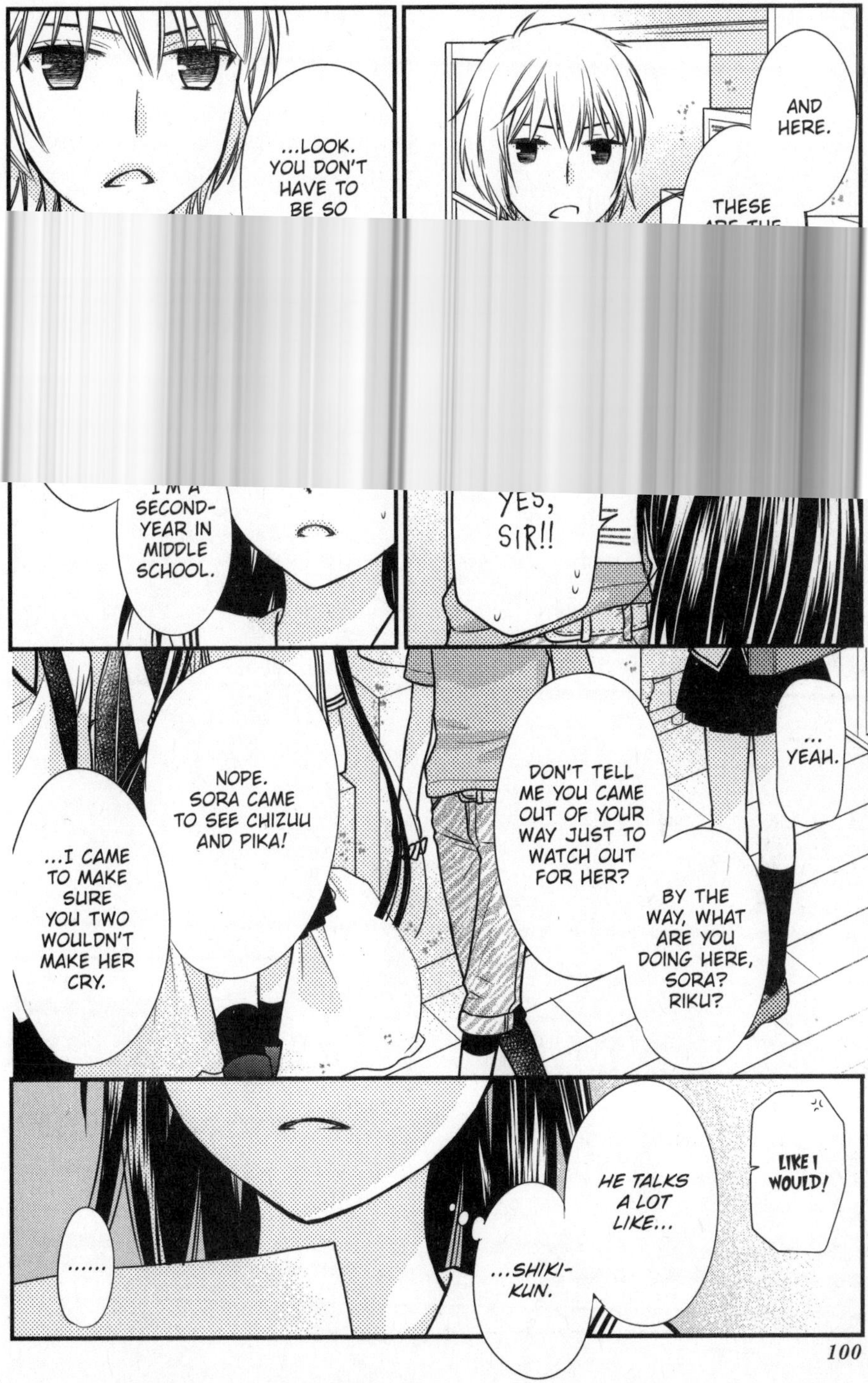
AND HERE.
THESE
...LOOK. YOU DON'T HAVE TO BE SO
YES, SIR!!
I'M A SECOND-YEAR IN MIDDLE SCHOOL.
BY THE WAY, WHAT ARE YOU DOING HERE, SORA? RIKU?
NOPE. SORA CAME TO SEE CHIZUU AND PIKA!
...I CAME TO MAKE SURE YOU TWO WOULDN'T MAKE HER CRY.
DON'T TELL ME YOU CAME OUT OF YOUR WAY JUST TO WATCH OUT FOR HER?
...YEAH.
LIKE I WOULD!
HE TALKS A LOT LIKE...
...SHIKI-KUN.
......

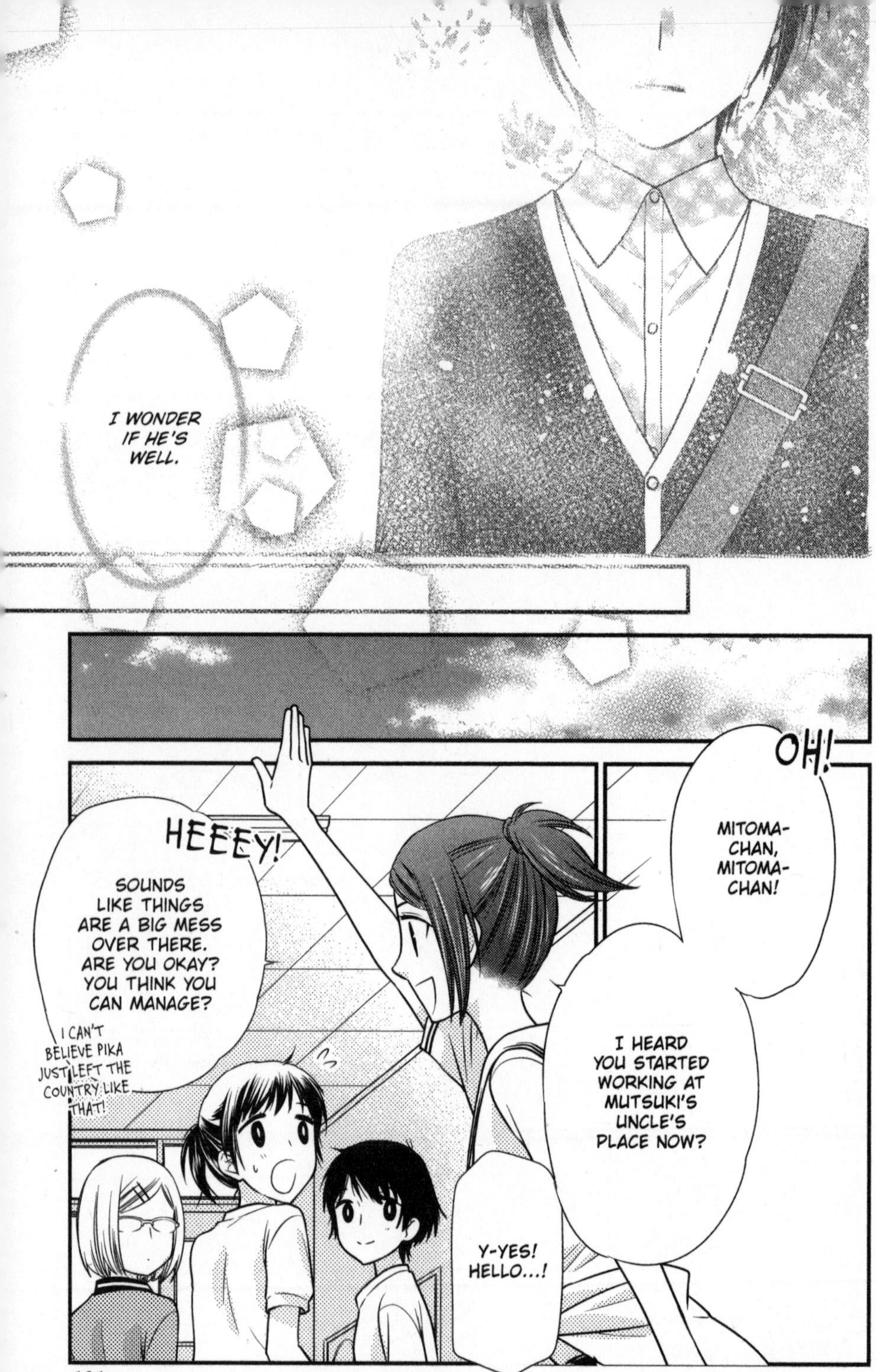
I WONDER IF HE'S WELL.
OH!
MITOMA-CHAN, MITOMA-CHAN!
I HEARD YOU STARTED WORKING AT MUTSUKI'S UNCLE'S PLACE NOW?
HEEEY!
SOUNDS LIKE THINGS ARE A BIG MESS OVER THERE. ARE YOU OKAY? YOU THINK YOU CAN MANAGE?
Y-YES! HELLO...!
I CAN'T BELIEVE PIKA JUST LEFT THE COUNTRY LIKE THAT!

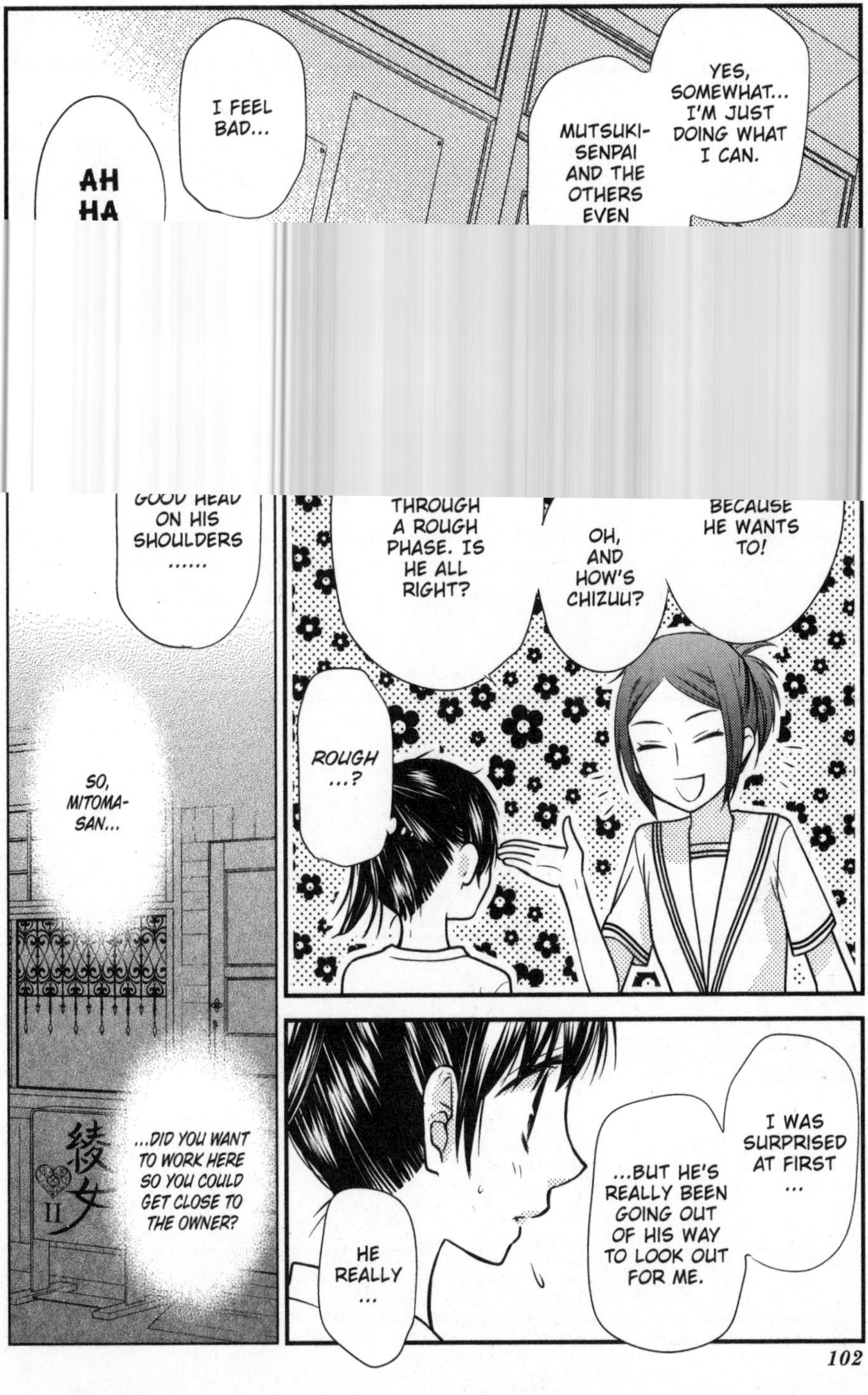
YES, SOMEWHAT... I'M JUST DOING WHAT I CAN.
MUTSUKI-SENPAI AND THE OTHERS EVEN
I FEEL BAD...
AH HA
BECAUSE HE WANTS TO!
OH, AND HOW'S CHIZUU?
THROUGH A ROUGH PHASE. IS HE ALL RIGHT?
ROUGH ...?
I WAS SURPRISED AT FIRST ...
...BUT HE'S REALLY BEEN GOING OUT OF HIS WAY TO LOOK OUT FOR ME.
HE REALLY ...
GOOD HEAD ON HIS SHOULDERS ......
SO, MITOMA-SAN...
...DID YOU WANT TO WORK HERE SO YOU COULD GET CLOSE TO THE OWNER?
綾女 II

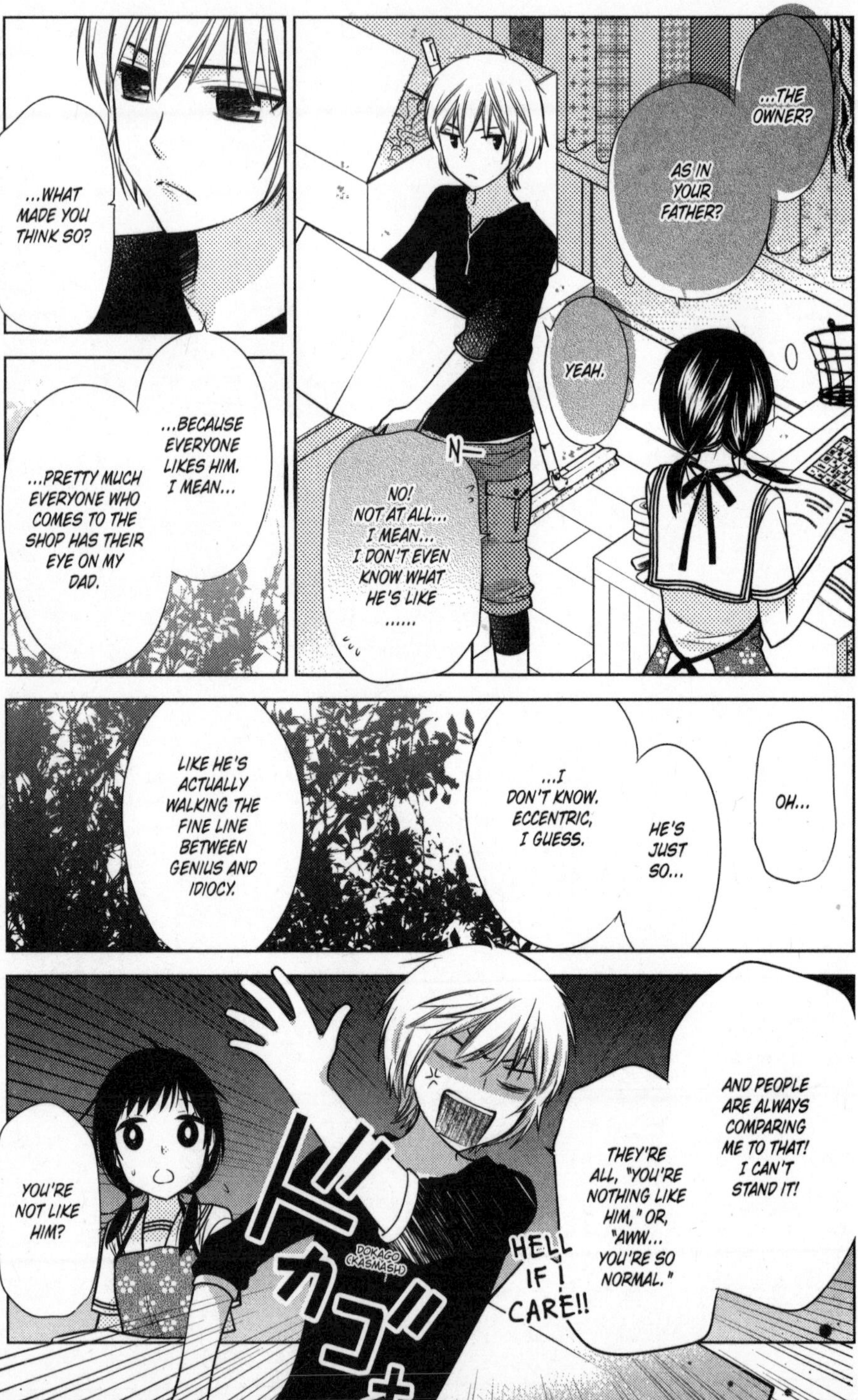
...THE OWNER?
AS IN YOUR FATHER?
YEAH.
N—
NO! NOT AT ALL... I MEAN... I DON'T EVEN KNOW WHAT HE'S LIKE ......
...WHAT MADE YOU THINK SO?
...BECAUSE EVERYONE LIKES HIM. I MEAN...
...PRETTY MUCH EVERYONE WHO COMES TO THE SHOP HAS THEIR EYE ON MY DAD.
OH...
...I DON'T KNOW. ECCENTRIC, I GUESS.
HE'S JUST SO...
LIKE HE'S ACTUALLY WALKING THE FINE LINE BETWEEN GENIUS AND IDIOCY.
AND PEOPLE ARE ALWAYS COMPARING ME TO THAT! I CAN'T STAND IT!
THEY'RE ALL, "YOU'RE NOTHING LIKE HIM," OR, "AWW... YOU'RE SO NORMAL."
HELL IF I CARE!!
DOKAGO (KASMASH)
YOU'RE NOT LIKE HIM?

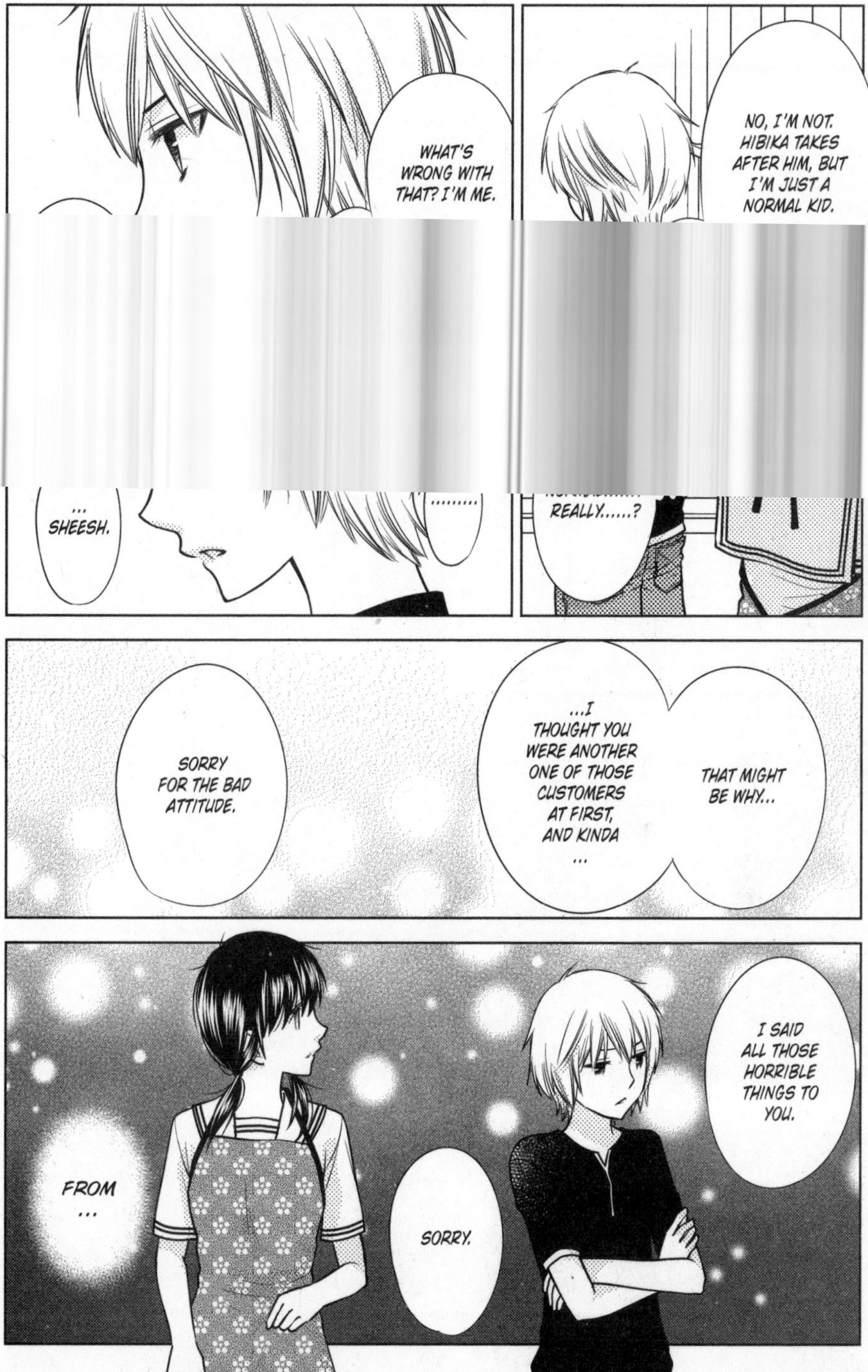
NO, I'M NOT. HIBIKA TAKES AFTER HIM, BUT I'M JUST A NORMAL KID.
WHAT'S WRONG WITH THAT? I'M ME.
REALLY......?
....
... SHEESH.
...I THOUGHT YOU WERE ANOTHER ONE OF THOSE CUSTOMERS AT FIRST, AND KINDA ...
THAT MIGHT BE WHY...
SORRY FOR THE BAD ATTITUDE.
I SAID ALL THOSE HORRIBLE THINGS TO YOU.
SORRY.
FROM ...

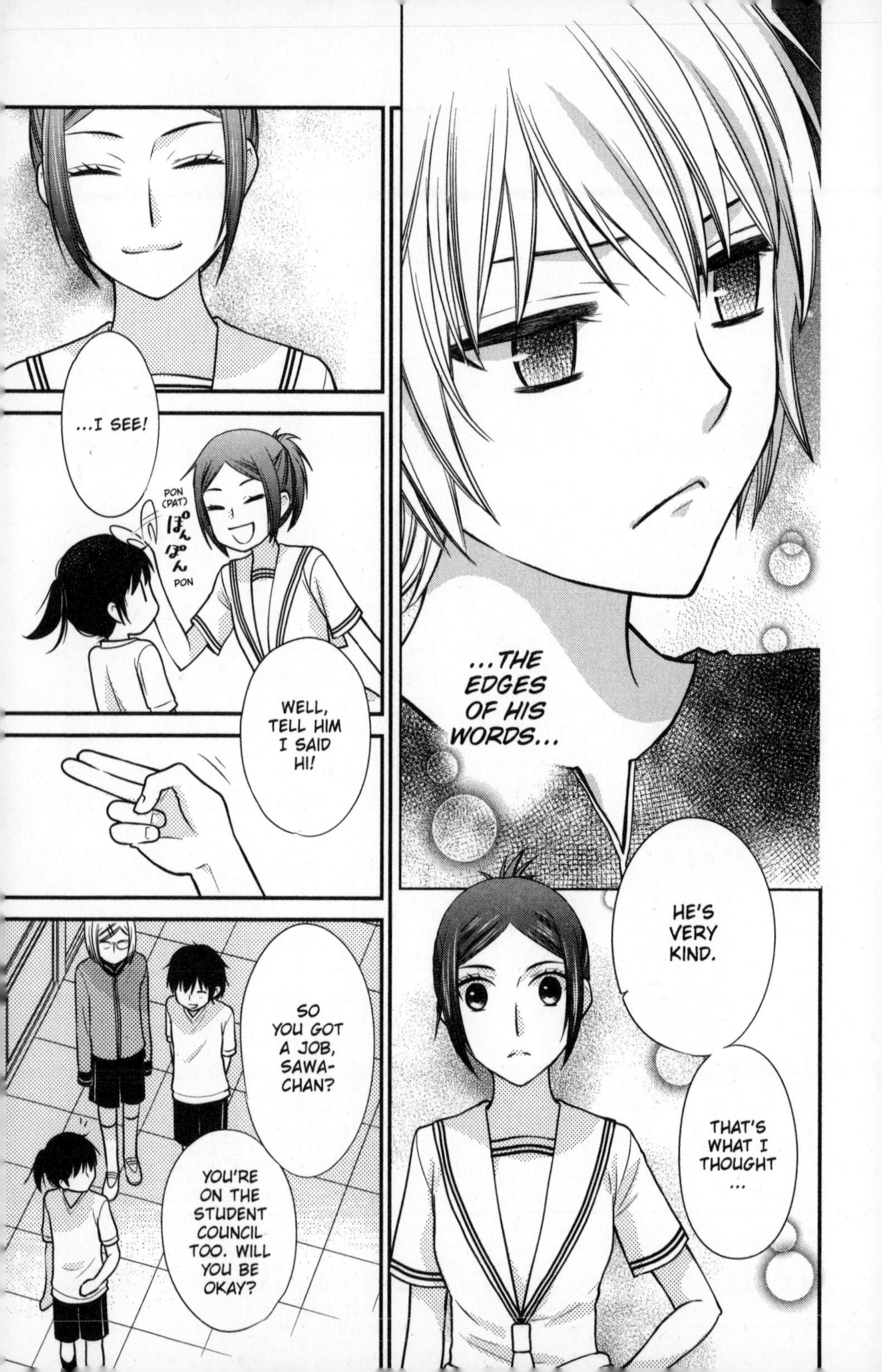
...THE EDGES OF HIS WORDS...
...I SEE!
PON (PAT)
ぽんぽん
PON
WELL, TELL HIM I SAID HI!
HE'S VERY KIND.
THAT'S WHAT I THOUGHT ...
SO YOU GOT A JOB, SAWA-CHAN?
YOU'RE ON THE STUDENT COUNCIL TOO. WILL YOU BE OKAY?

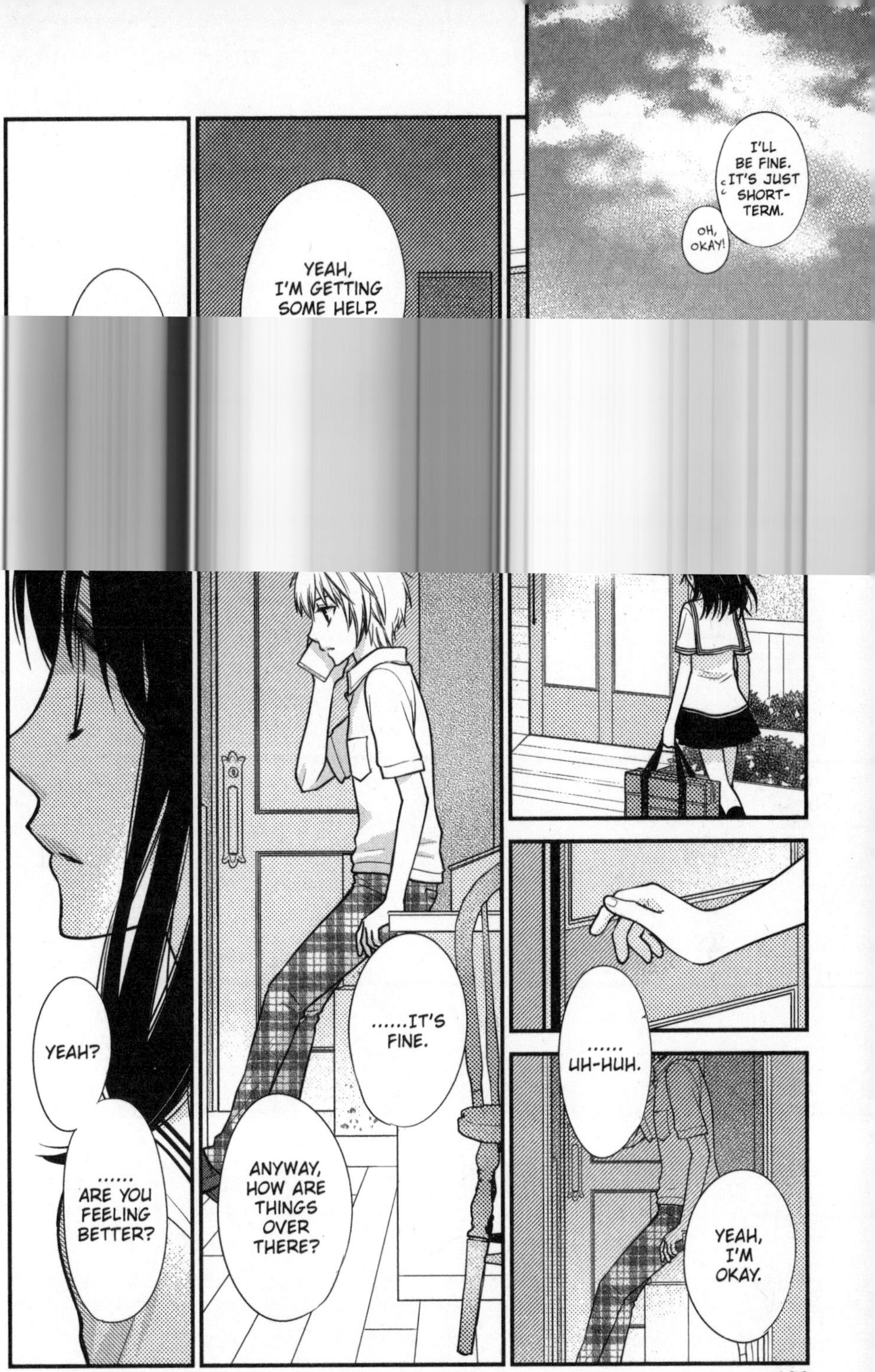
I'LL BE FINE. IT'S JUST SHORT-TERM.
OH, OKAY!
...... UH-HUH.
YEAH, I'M OKAY.
YEAH, I'M GETTING SOME HELP.
......IT'S FINE.
ANYWAY, HOW ARE THINGS OVER THERE?
YEAH?
...... ARE YOU FEELING BETTER?

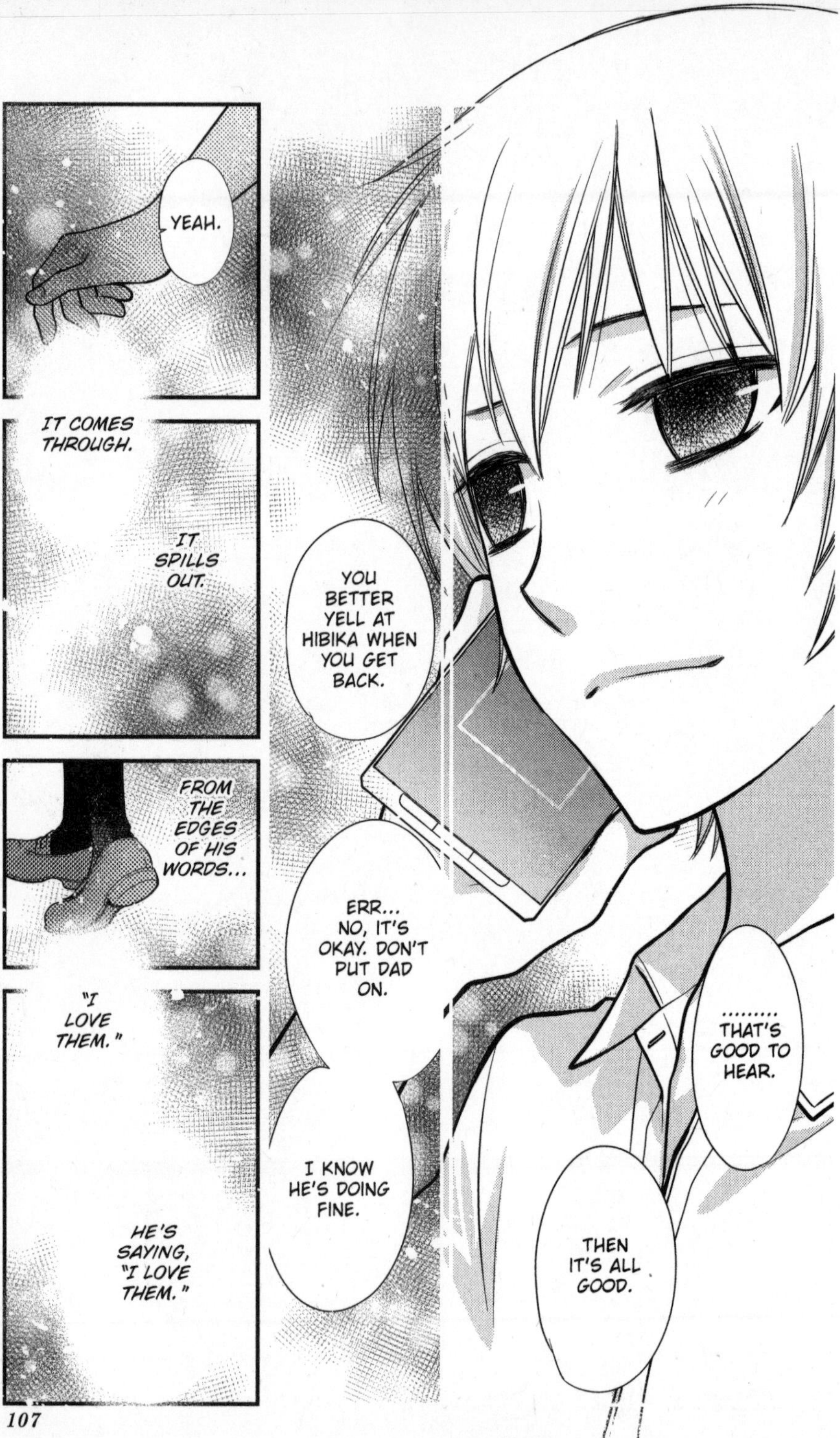
YOU BETTER YELL AT HIBIKA WHEN YOU GET BACK.
ERR... NO, IT'S OKAY. DON'T PUT DAD ON.
I KNOW HE'S DOING FINE.
.... THAT'S GOOD TO HEAR.
THEN IT'S ALL GOOD.
YEAH.
IT COMES THROUGH.
IT SPILLS OUT.
FROM THE EDGES OF HIS WORDS...
"I LOVE THEM."
HE'S SAYING, "I LOVE THEM."

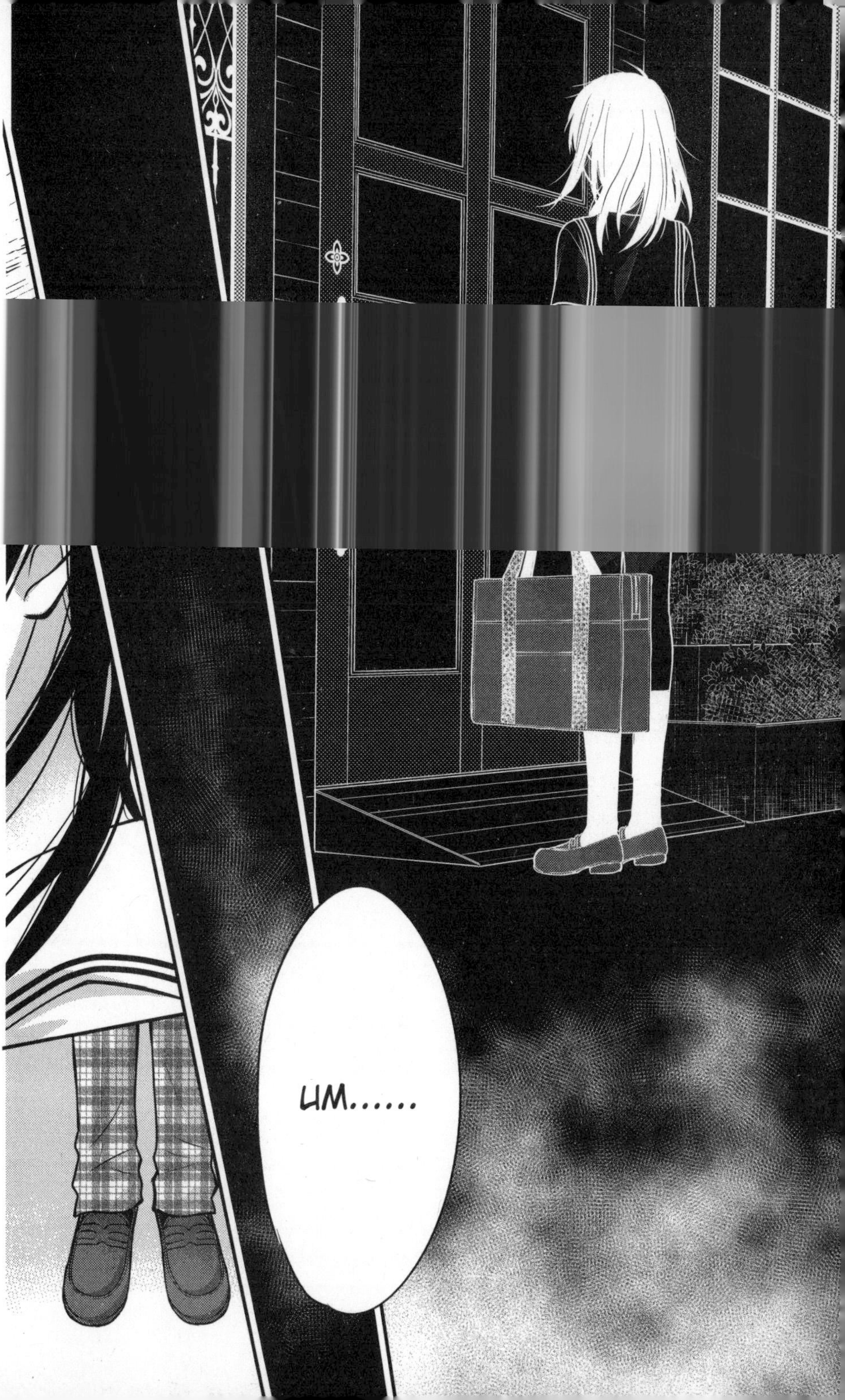
UM......

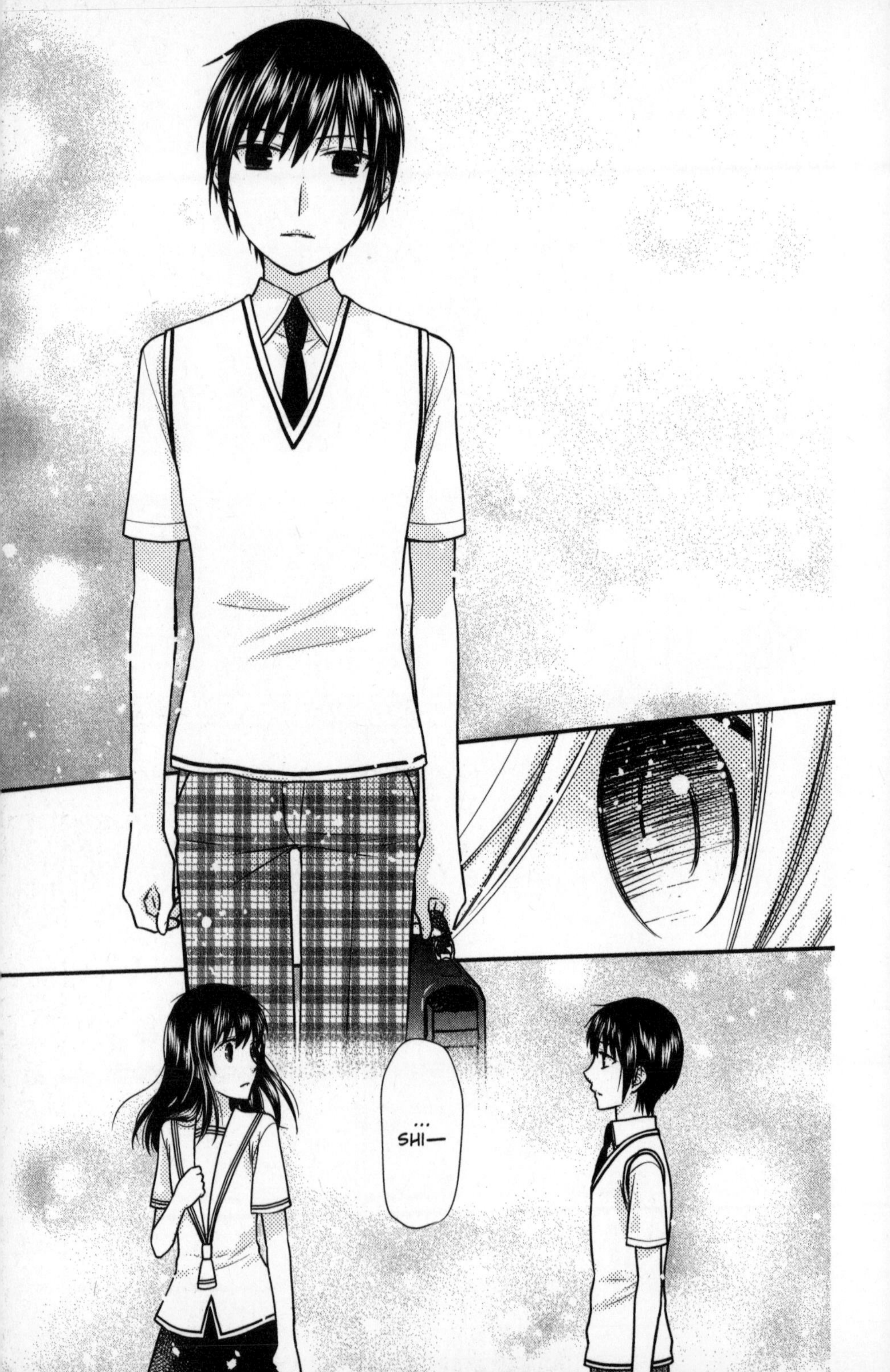
...
SHI—

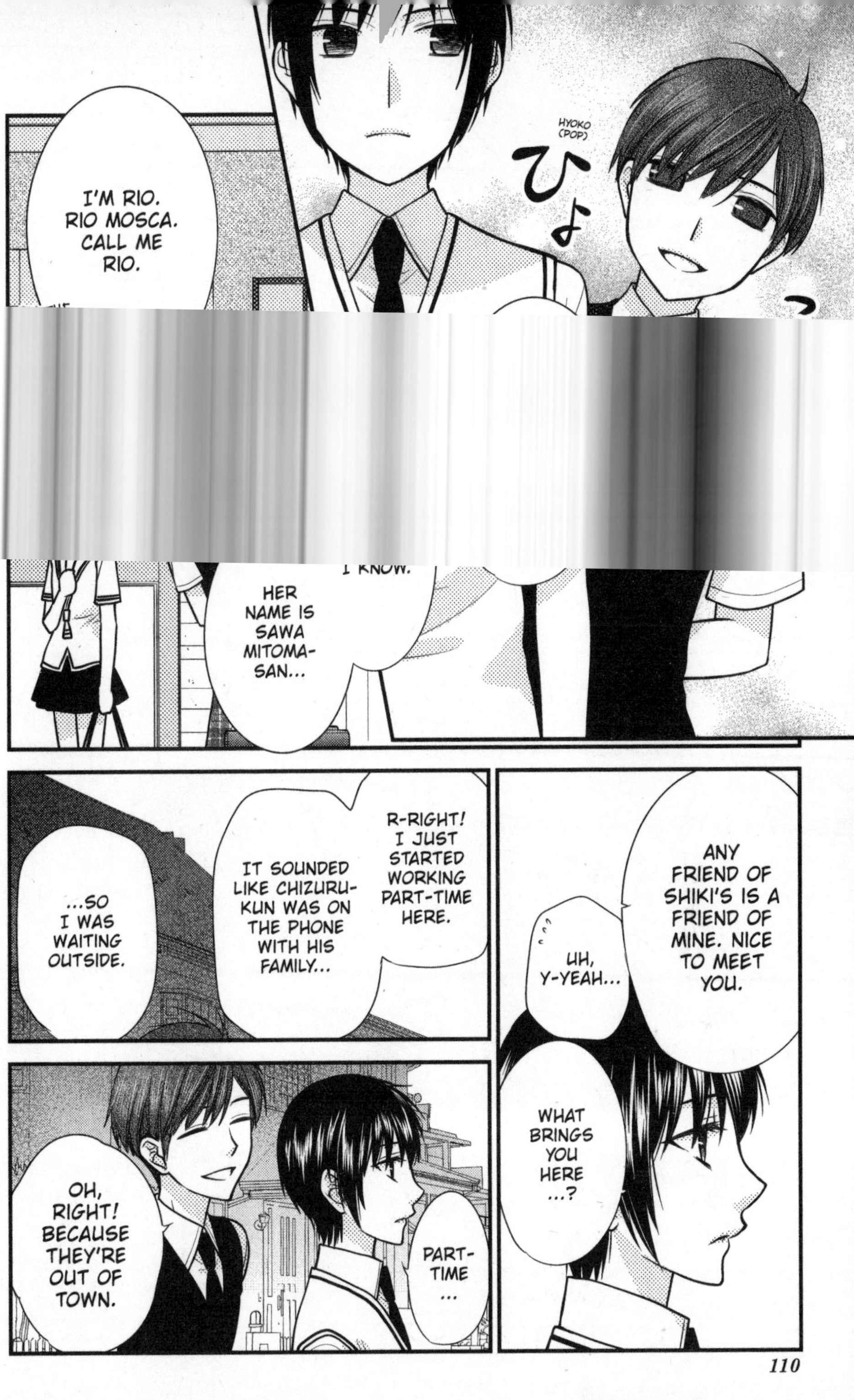
HYOKO (POP)
ひょ
I'M RIO. RIO MOSCA. CALL ME RIO.
I KNOW.
HER NAME IS SAWA MITOMA-SAN...
ANY FRIEND OF SHIKI'S IS A FRIEND OF MINE. NICE TO MEET YOU.
UH, Y-YEAH...
WHAT BRINGS YOU HERE ...?
R-RIGHT! I JUST STARTED WORKING PART-TIME HERE.
IT SOUNDED LIKE CHIZURU-KUN WAS ON THE PHONE WITH HIS FAMILY...
...SO I WAS WAITING OUTSIDE.
PART-TIME ...
OH, RIGHT! BECAUSE THEY'RE OUT OF TOWN.

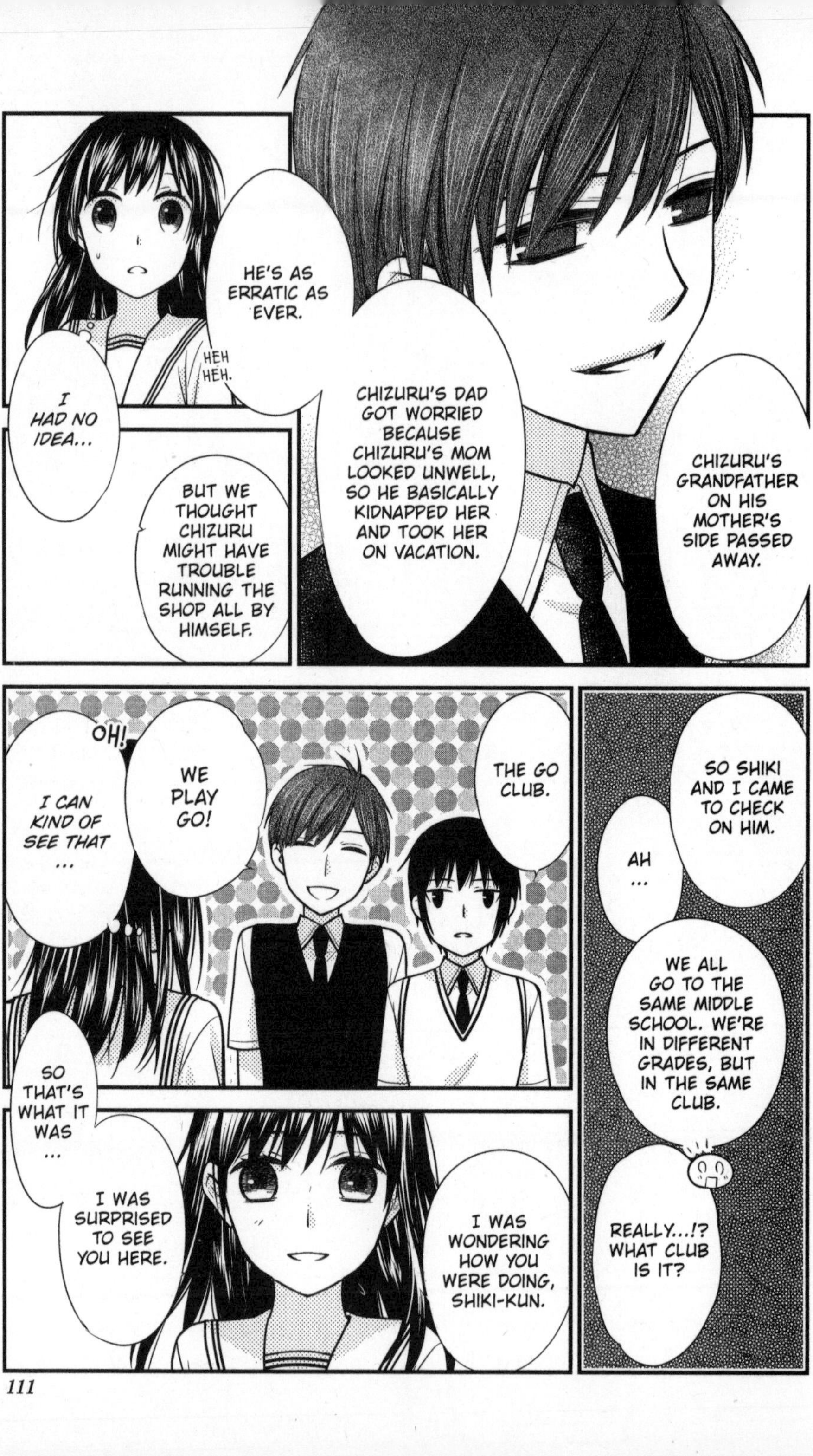
CHIZURU'S GRANDFATHER ON HIS MOTHER'S SIDE PASSED AWAY.
CHIZURU'S DAD GOT WORRIED BECAUSE CHIZURU'S MOM LOOKED UNWELL, SO HE BASICALLY KIDNAPPED HER AND TOOK HER ON VACATION.
HE'S AS ERRATIC AS EVER.
HEH HEH.
I HAD NO IDEA...
BUT WE THOUGHT CHIZURU MIGHT HAVE TROUBLE RUNNING THE SHOP ALL BY HIMSELF.
SO SHIKI AND I CAME TO CHECK ON HIM.
AH ...
WE ALL GO TO THE SAME MIDDLE SCHOOL. WE'RE IN DIFFERENT GRADES, BUT IN THE SAME CLUB.
REALLY...!? WHAT CLUB IS IT?
THE GO CLUB.
WE PLAY GO!
OH!
I CAN KIND OF SEE THAT ...
I WAS WONDERING HOW YOU WERE DOING, SHIKI-KUN.
I WAS SURPRISED TO SEE YOU HERE.
SO THAT'S WHAT IT WAS ...

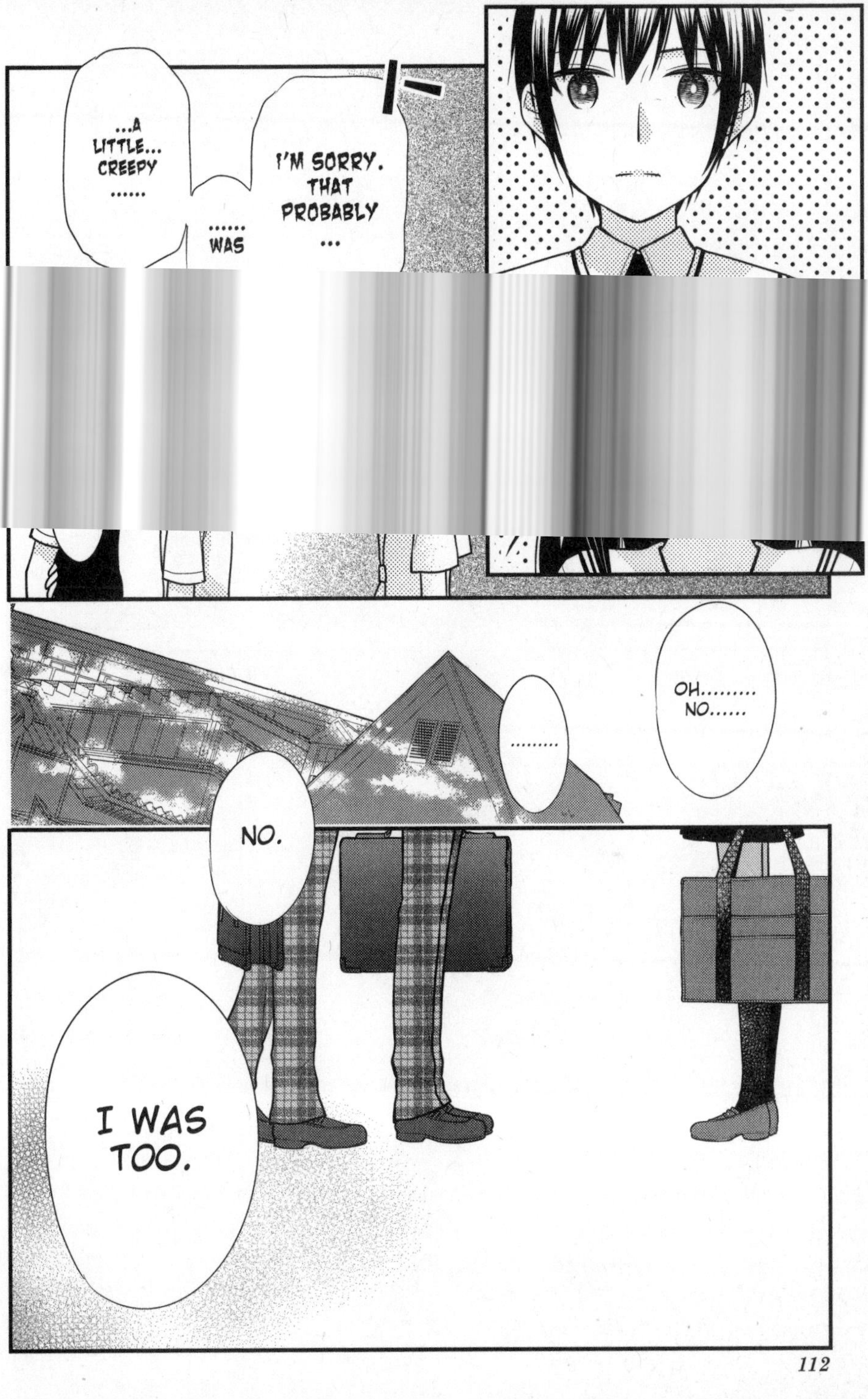
I'M SORRY. THAT PROBABLY ...
...... WAS
...A LITTLE... CREEPY ......
OH......... NO......
....
NO.
I WAS TOO.

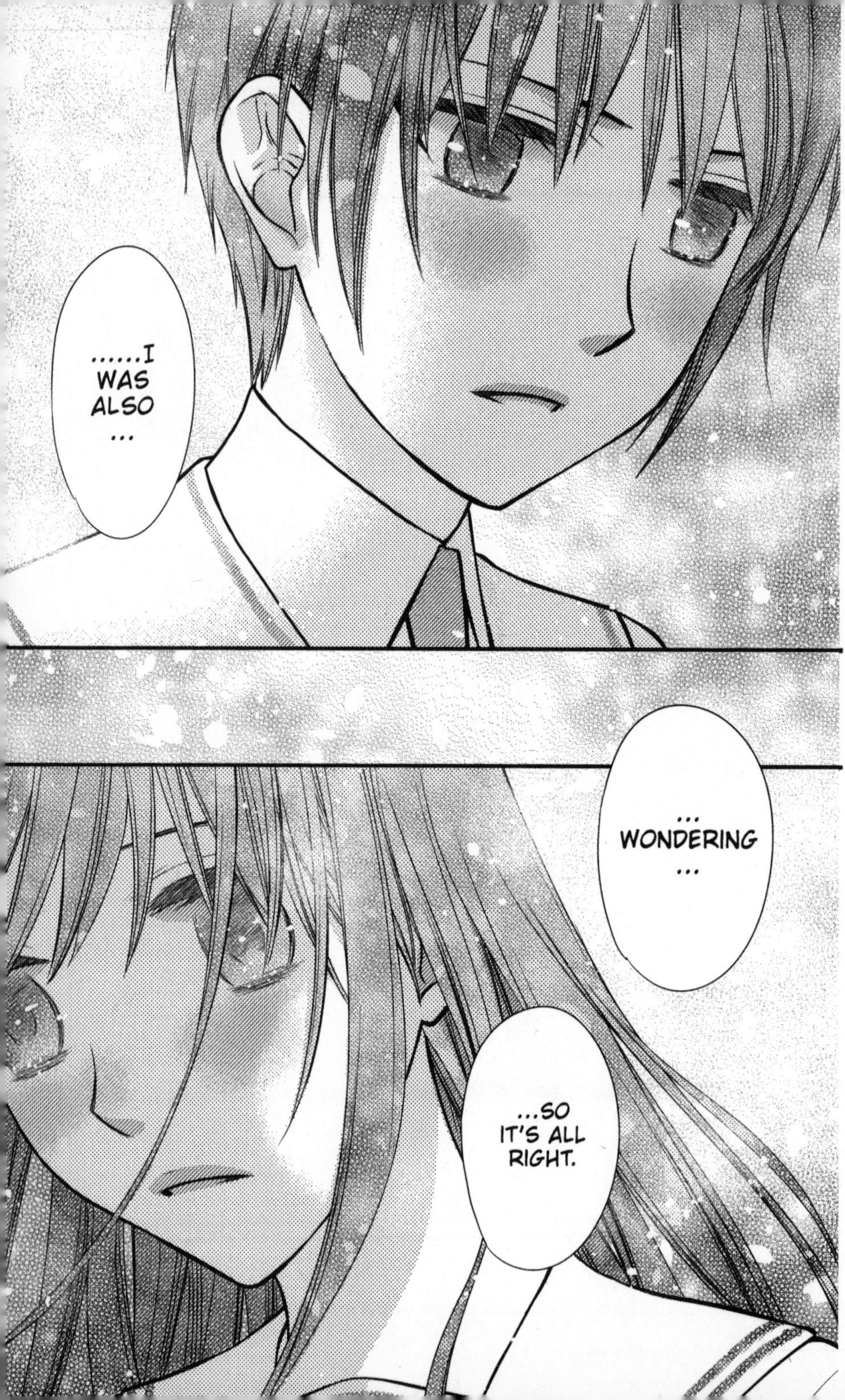
......I WAS ALSO ...
... WONDERING ...
...SO IT'S ALL RIGHT.

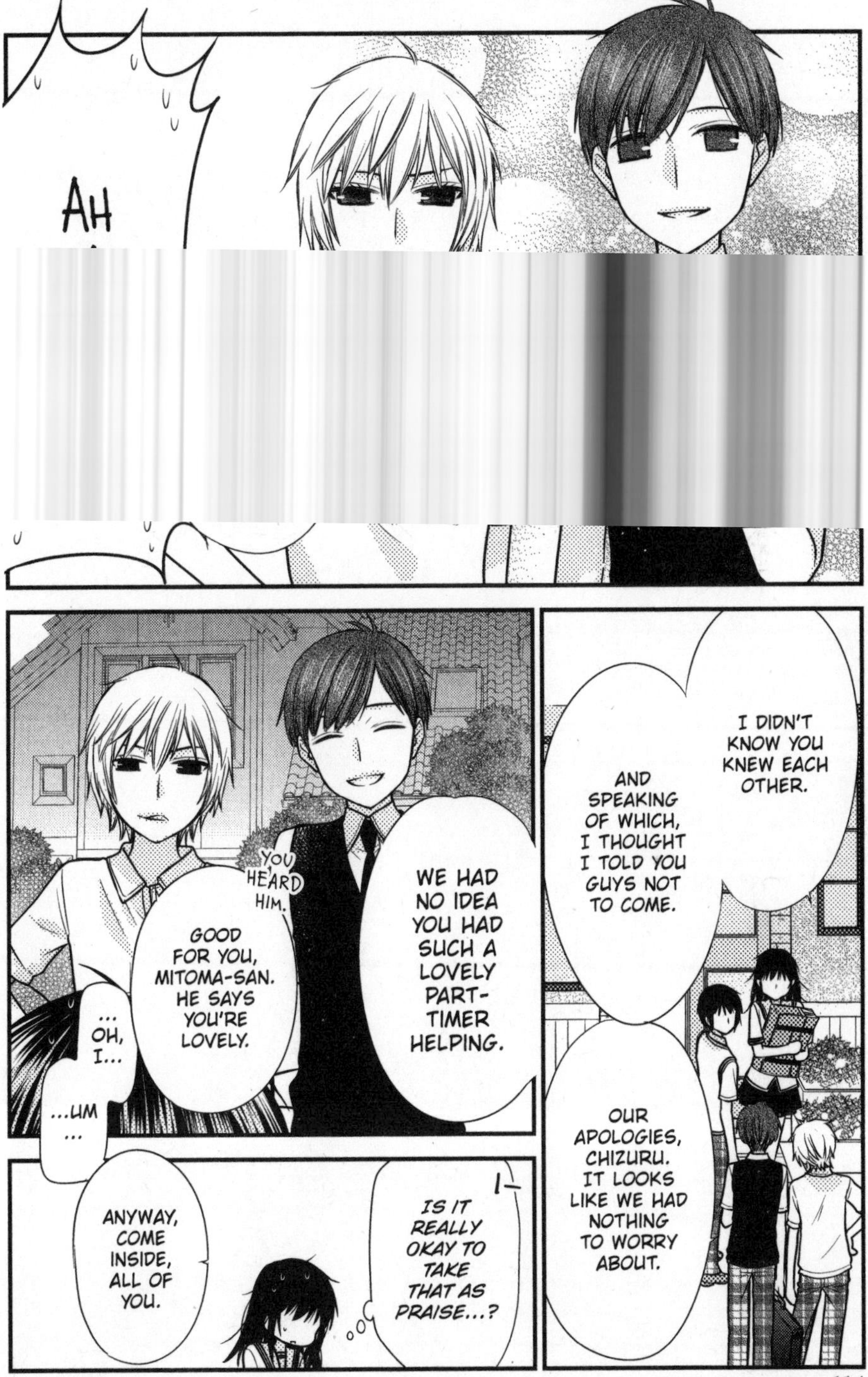
AH
I DIDN'T KNOW YOU KNEW EACH OTHER.
AND SPEAKING OF WHICH, I THOUGHT I TOLD YOU GUYS NOT TO COME.
OUR APOLOGIES, CHIZURU. IT LOOKS LIKE WE HAD NOTHING TO WORRY ABOUT.
WE HAD NO IDEA YOU HAD SUCH A LOVELY PART-TIMER HELPING.
YOU HEARD HIM.
GOOD FOR YOU, MITOMA-SAN. HE SAYS YOU'RE LOVELY.
...OH, I...
...UM ...
I—
IS IT REALLY OKAY TO TAKE THAT AS PRAISE...?
ANYWAY, COME INSIDE, ALL OF YOU.

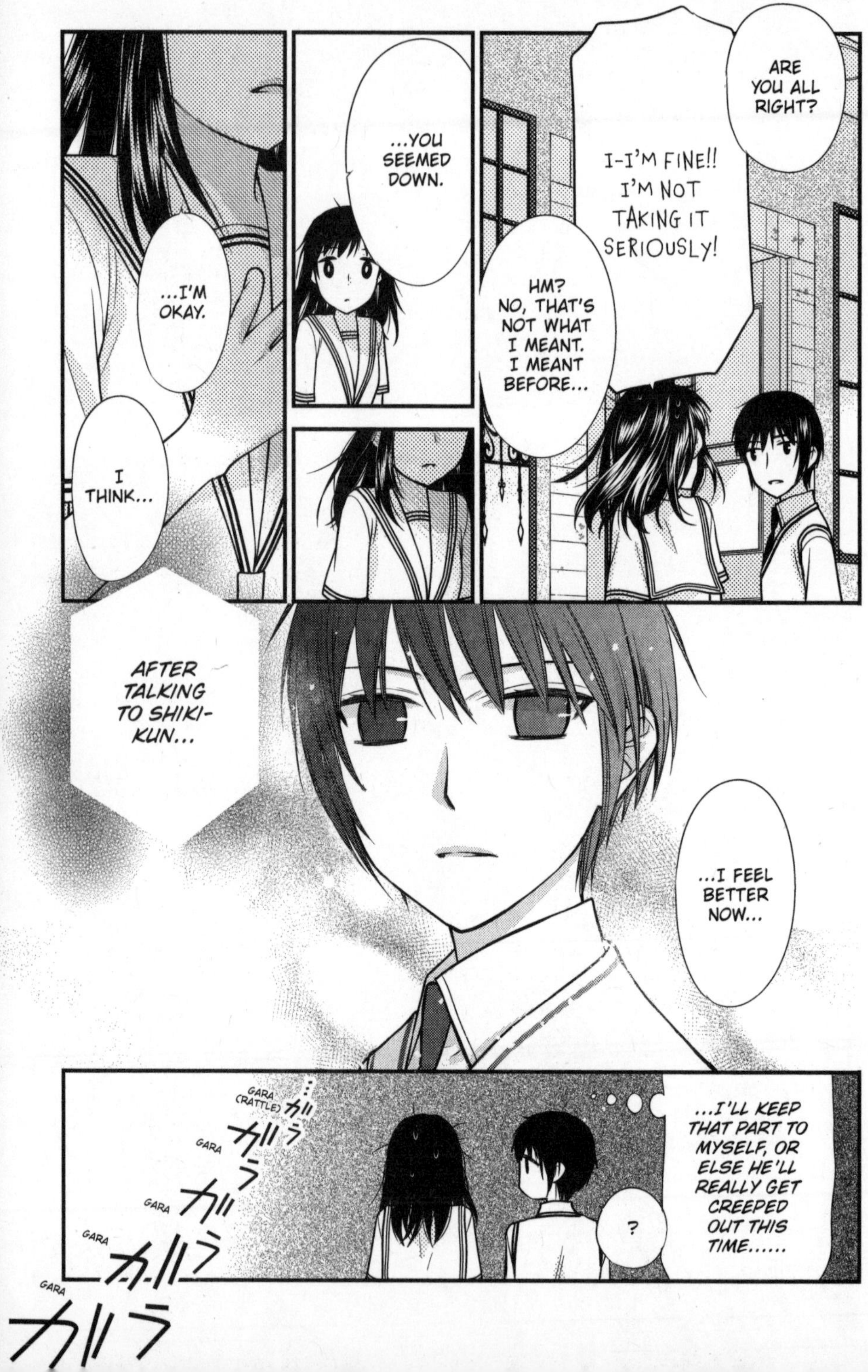
ARE YOU ALL RIGHT?
I-I'M FINE!! I'M NOT TAKING IT SERIOUSLY!
HM? NO, THAT'S NOT WHAT I MEANT. I MEANT BEFORE...
...YOU SEEMED DOWN.
...I'M OKAY.
I THINK...
AFTER TALKING TO SHIKI-KUN...
...I FEEL BETTER NOW...
...I'LL KEEP THAT PART TO MYSELF, OR ELSE HE'LL REALLY GET CREEPED OUT THIS TIME......
?
GARA (RATTLE)
GARA
GARA
GARA
GARA

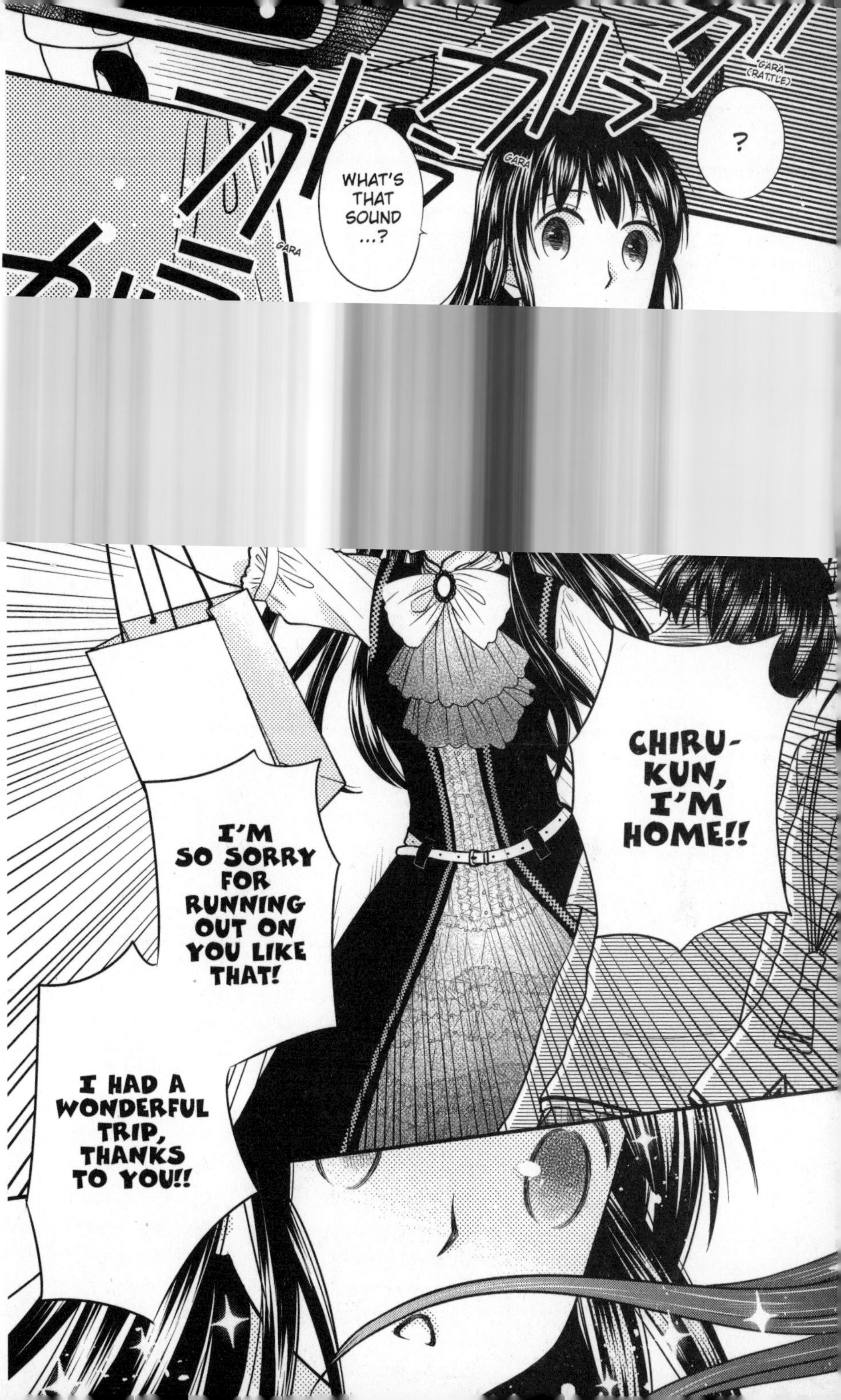
GARA (RATTLE)
?
GARA
WHAT'S THAT SOUND ...?
GARA
CHIRU-KUN, I'M HOME!!
I'M SO SORRY FOR RUNNING OUT ON YOU LIKE THAT!
I HAD A WONDERFUL TRIP, THANKS TO YOU!!

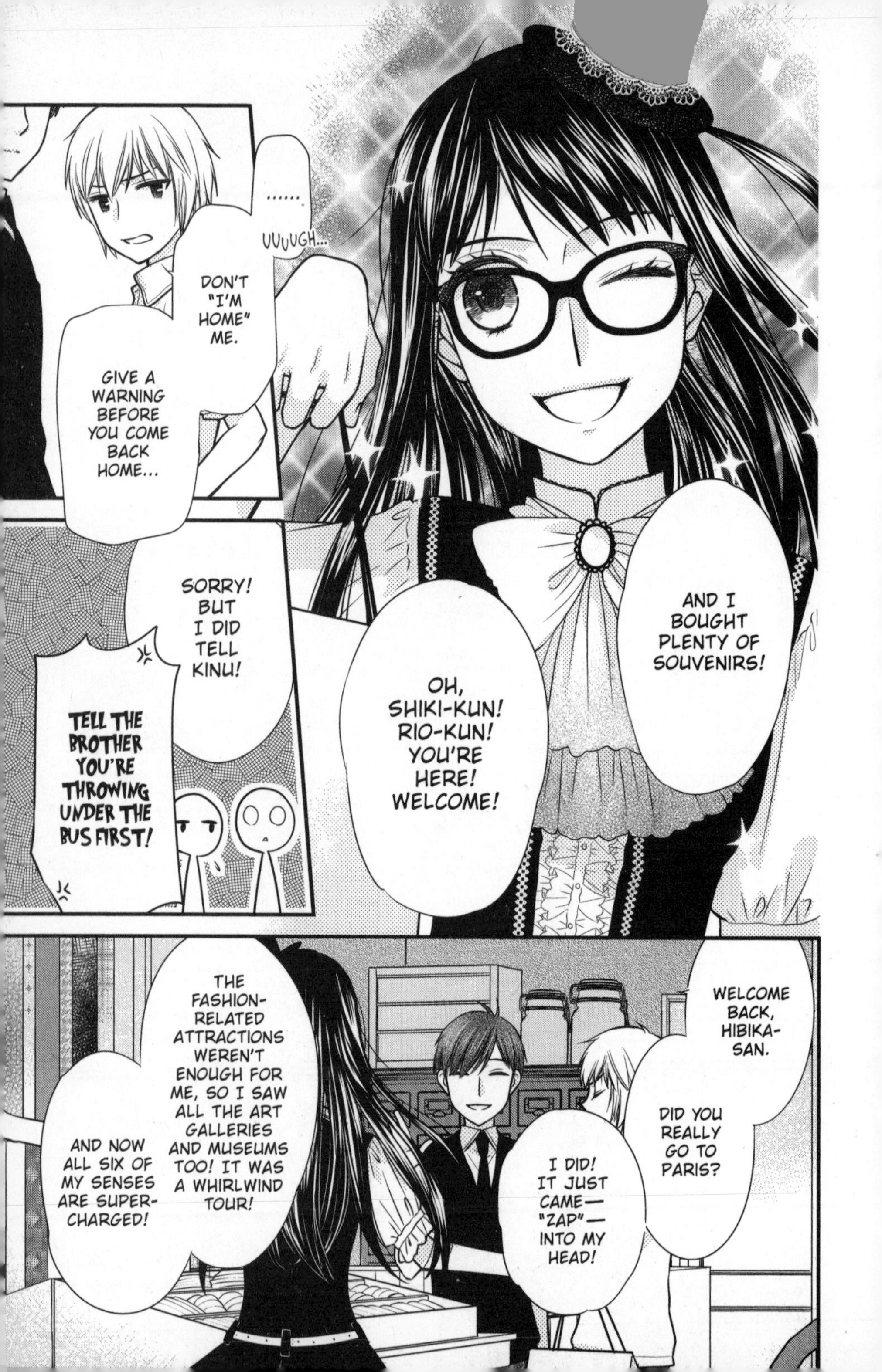
OH, SHIKI-KUN! RIO-KUN! YOU'RE HERE! WELCOME!
AND I BOUGHT PLENTY OF SOUVENIRS!
......
UUUUGH...
DON'T "I'M HOME" ME.
GIVE A WARNING BEFORE YOU COME BACK HOME...
SORRY! BUT I DID TELL KINU!
TELL THE BROTHER YOU'RE THROWING UNDER THE BUS FIRST!
WELCOME BACK, HIBIKA-SAN.
DID YOU REALLY GO TO PARIS?
I DID! IT JUST CAME—"ZAP"—INTO MY HEAD!
THE FASHION-RELATED ATTRACTIONS WEREN'T ENOUGH FOR ME, SO I SAW ALL THE ART GALLERIES AND MUSEUMS TOO! IT WAS A WHIRLWIND TOUR!
AND NOW ALL SIX OF MY SENSES ARE SUPER-CHARGED!

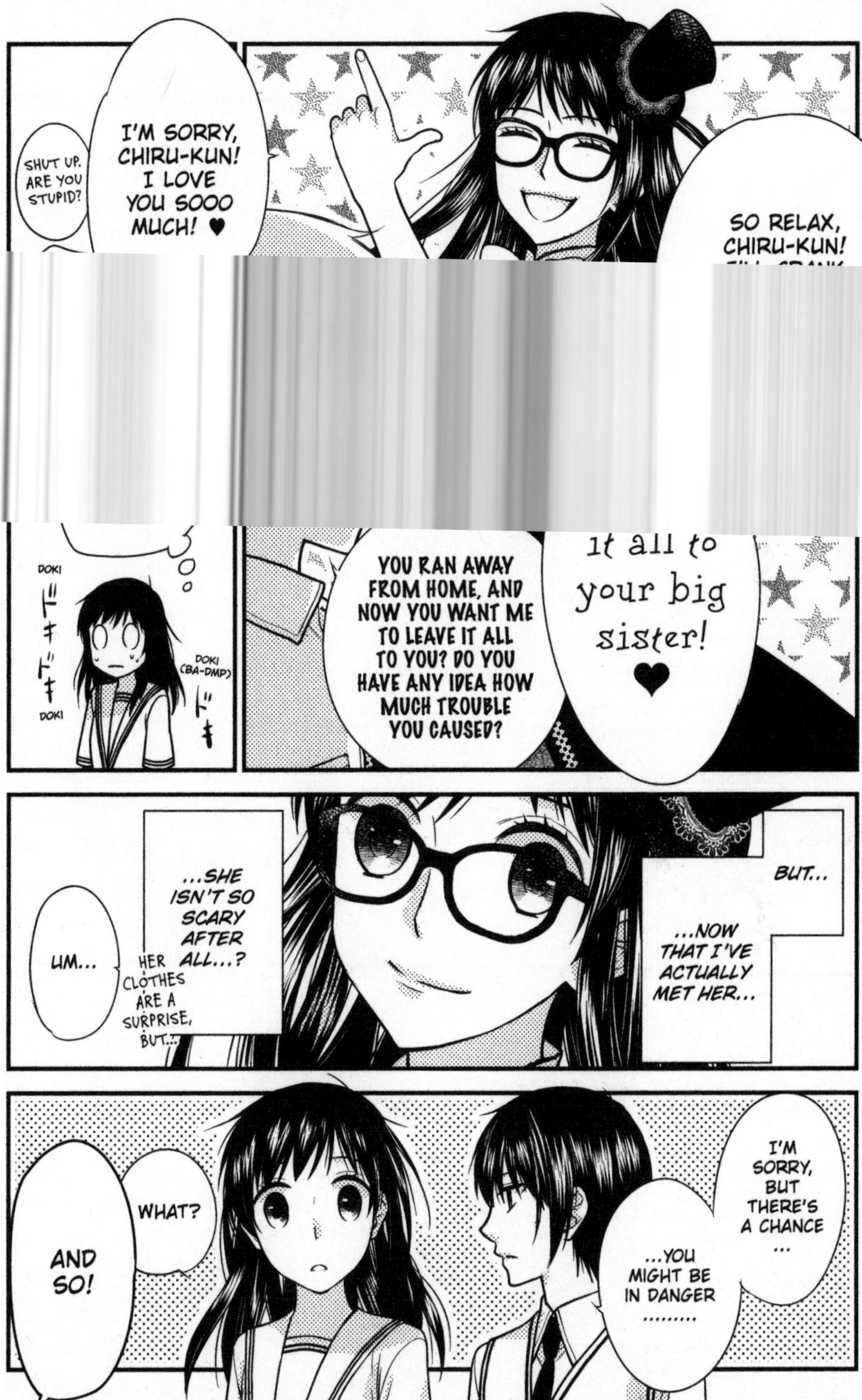
SO RELAX, CHIRU-KUN!
it all to your big sister! ♥
YOU RAN AWAY FROM HOME, AND NOW YOU WANT ME TO LEAVE IT ALL TO YOU? DO YOU HAVE ANY IDEA HOW MUCH TROUBLE YOU CAUSED?
I'M SORRY, CHIRU-KUN! I LOVE YOU SOOO MUCH! ♥
SHUT UP. ARE YOU STUPID?
DOKI ドキドキ DOKI
DOKI (BA-DMP) ドキ
BUT...
...NOW THAT I'VE ACTUALLY MET HER...
...SHE ISN'T SO SCARY AFTER ALL...?
HER CLOTHES ARE A SURPRISE, BUT...
UM...
I'M SORRY, BUT THERE'S A CHANCE ...
...YOU MIGHT BE IN DANGER ....
WHAT?
AND SO!

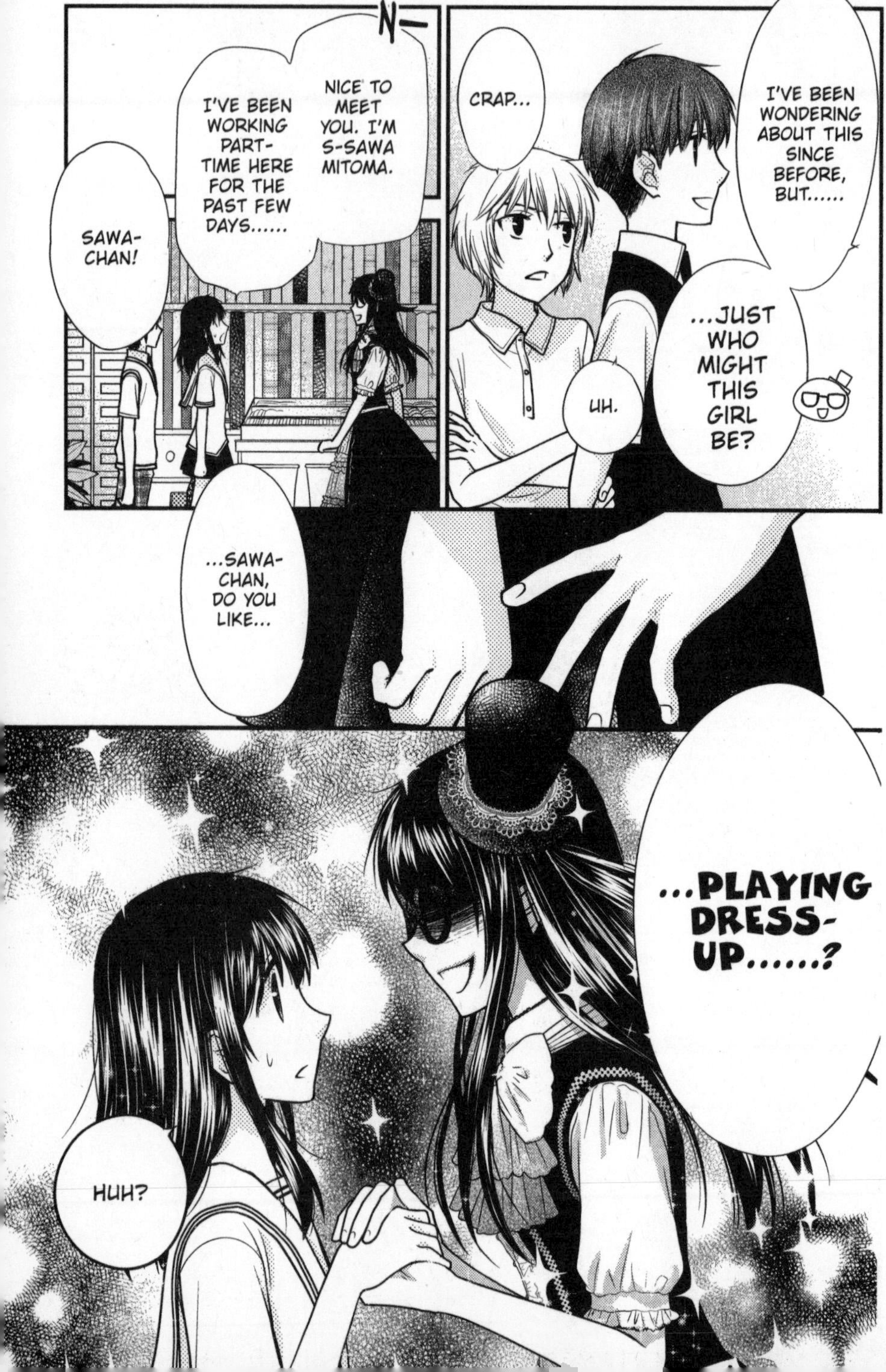
I'VE BEEN WONDERING ABOUT THIS SINCE BEFORE, BUT......
CRAP...
...JUST WHO MIGHT THIS GIRL BE?
UH.
N—
NICE TO MEET YOU. I'M S-SAWA MITOMA.
I'VE BEEN WORKING PART-TIME HERE FOR THE PAST FEW DAYS......
SAWA-CHAN!
...SAWA-CHAN, DO YOU LIKE...
...PLAYING DRESS-UP......?
HUH?

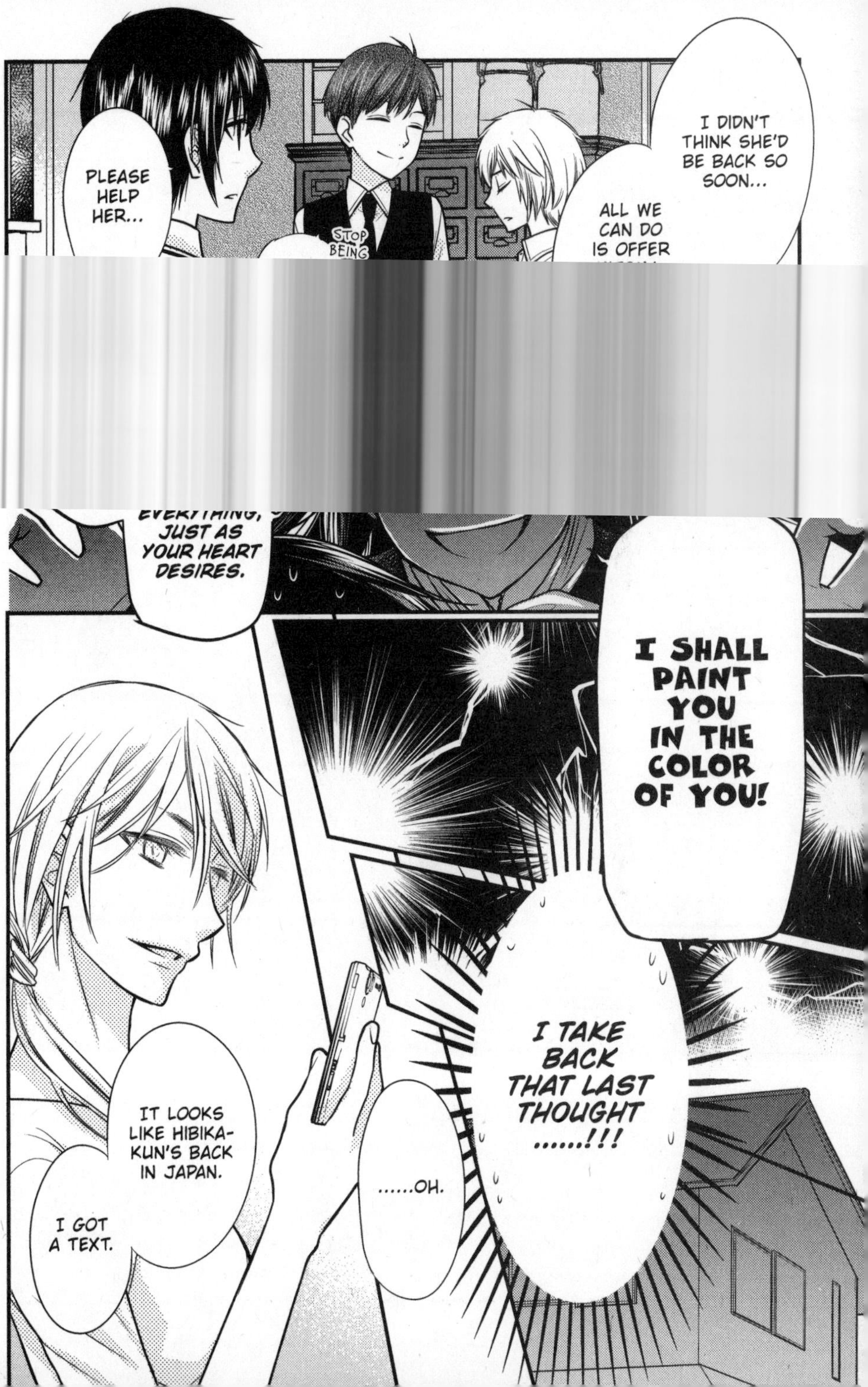
I DIDN'T THINK SHE'D BE BACK SO SOON...
ALL WE CAN DO IS OFFER
STOP BEING
PLEASE HELP HER...
JUST AS YOUR HEART DESIRES.
I SHALL PAINT YOU IN THE COLOR OF YOU!
I TAKE BACK THAT LAST THOUGHT ......!!!
......OH.
IT LOOKS LIKE HIBIKA-KUN'S BACK IN JAPAN.
I GOT A TEXT.

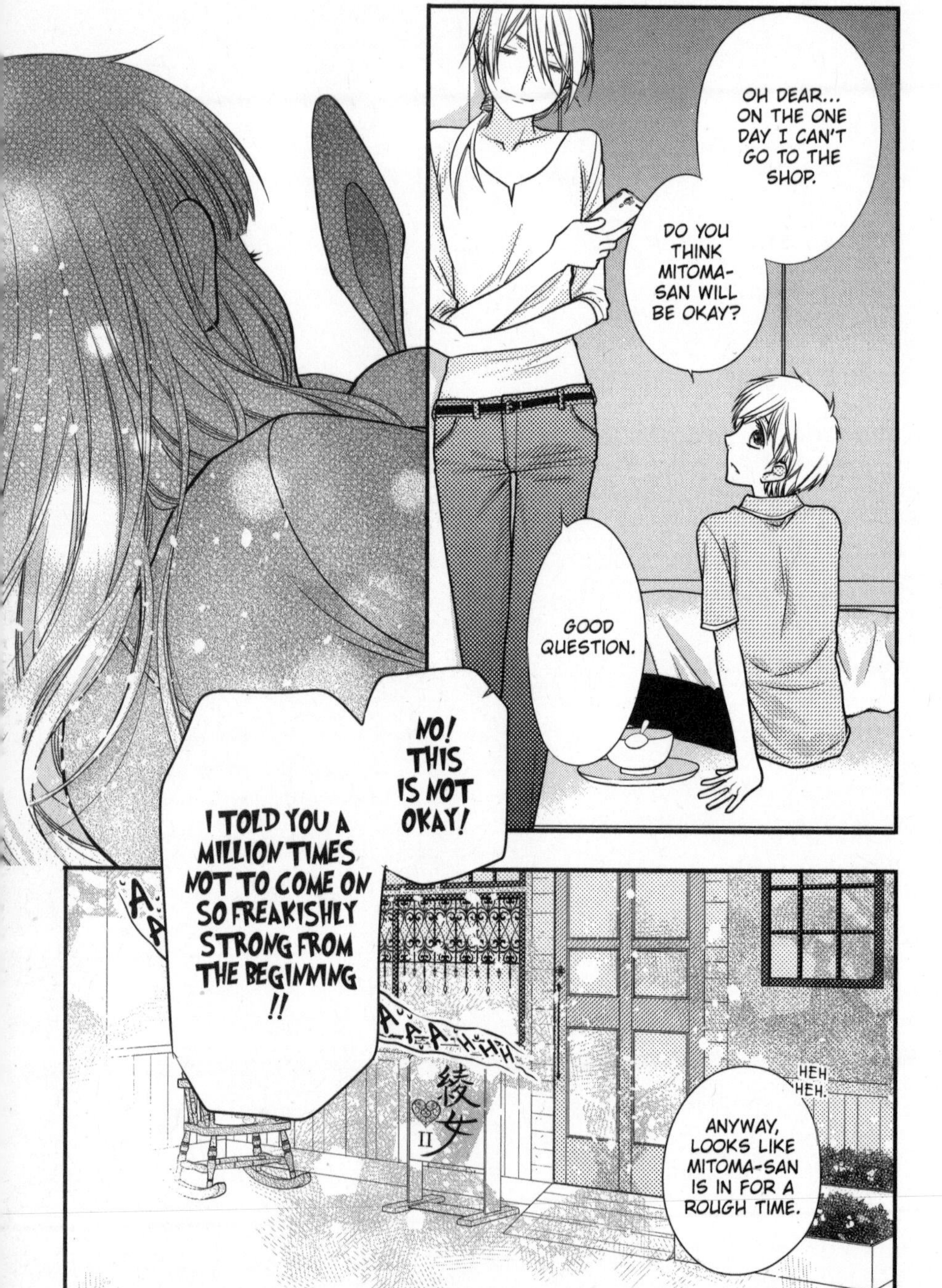
OH DEAR... ON THE ONE DAY I CAN'T GO TO THE SHOP.
DO YOU THINK MITOMA-SAN WILL BE OKAY?
GOOD QUESTION.
NO! THIS IS NOT OKAY!
I TOLD YOU A MILLION TIMES NOT TO COME ON SO FREAKISHLY STRONG FROM THE BEGINNING!!
A-A-A-A-A-H-H-H
綾女 II
HEH HEH.
ANYWAY, LOOKS LIKE MITOMA-SAN IS IN FOR A ROUGH TIME.

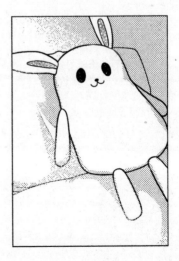

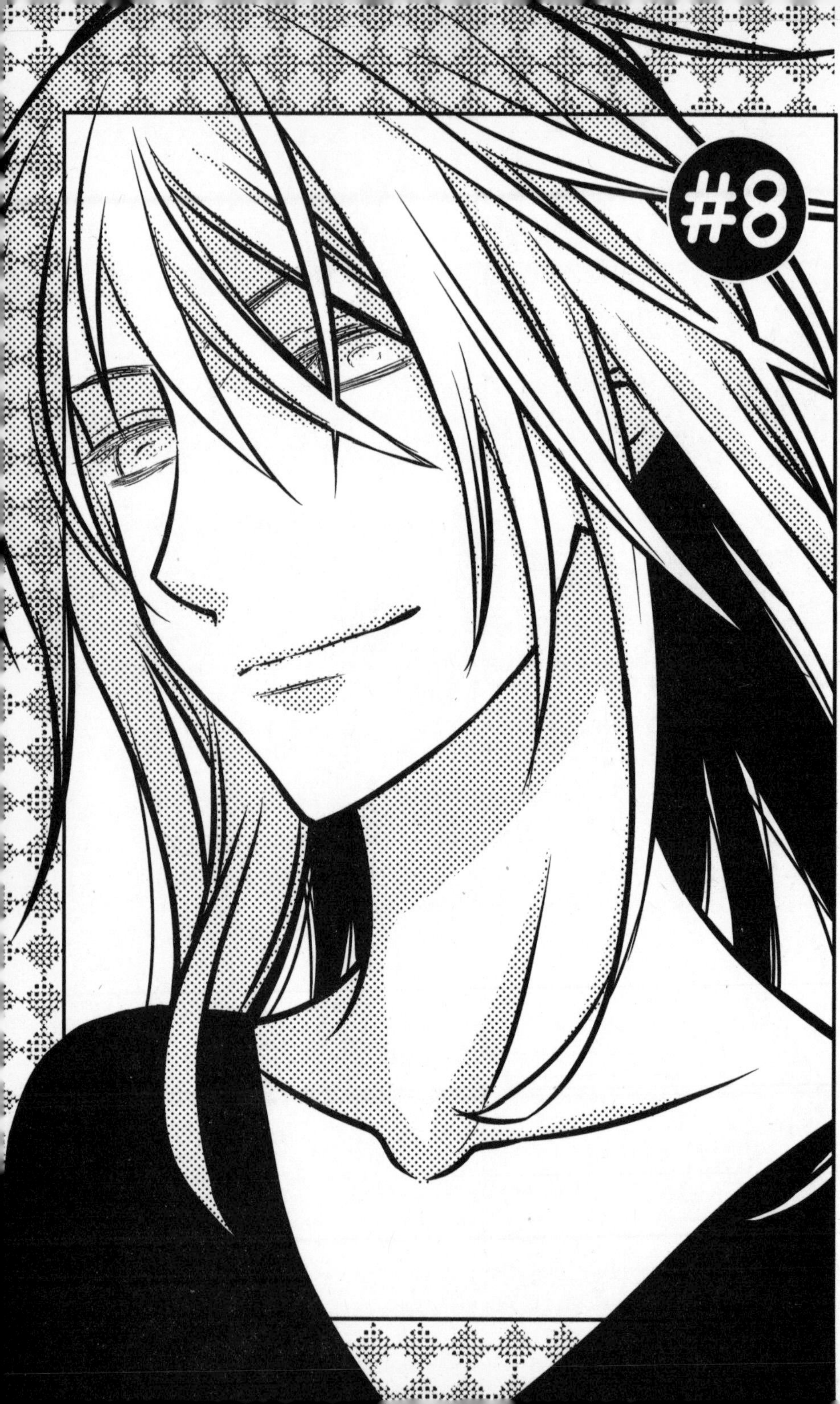
#8

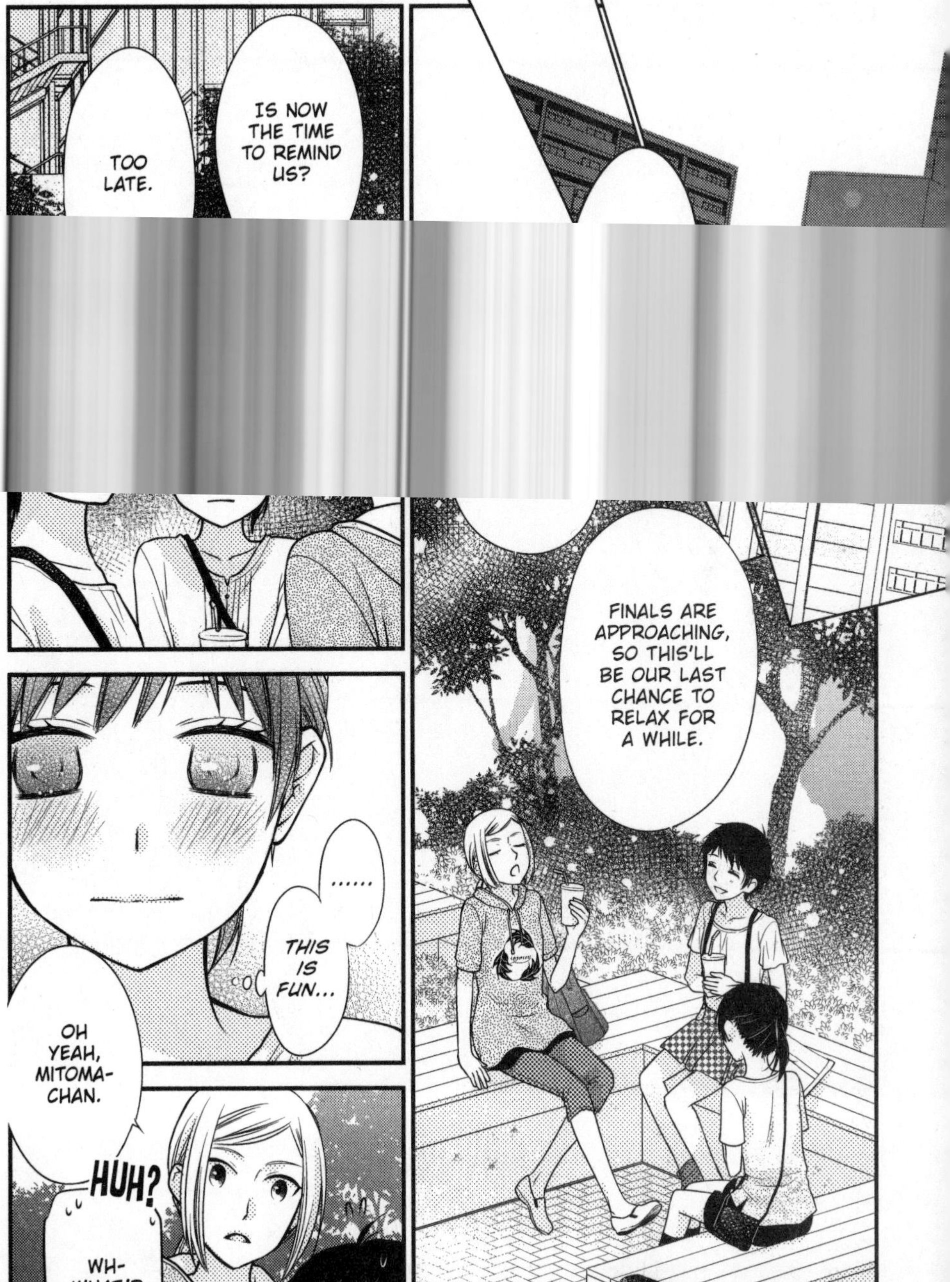
FINALS ARE APPROACHING, SO THIS'LL BE OUR LAST CHANCE TO RELAX FOR A WHILE.
IS NOW THE TIME TO REMIND US?
TOO LATE.
......
THIS IS FUN...
OH YEAH, MITOMA-CHAN.
HUH?
WH-WHAT!?

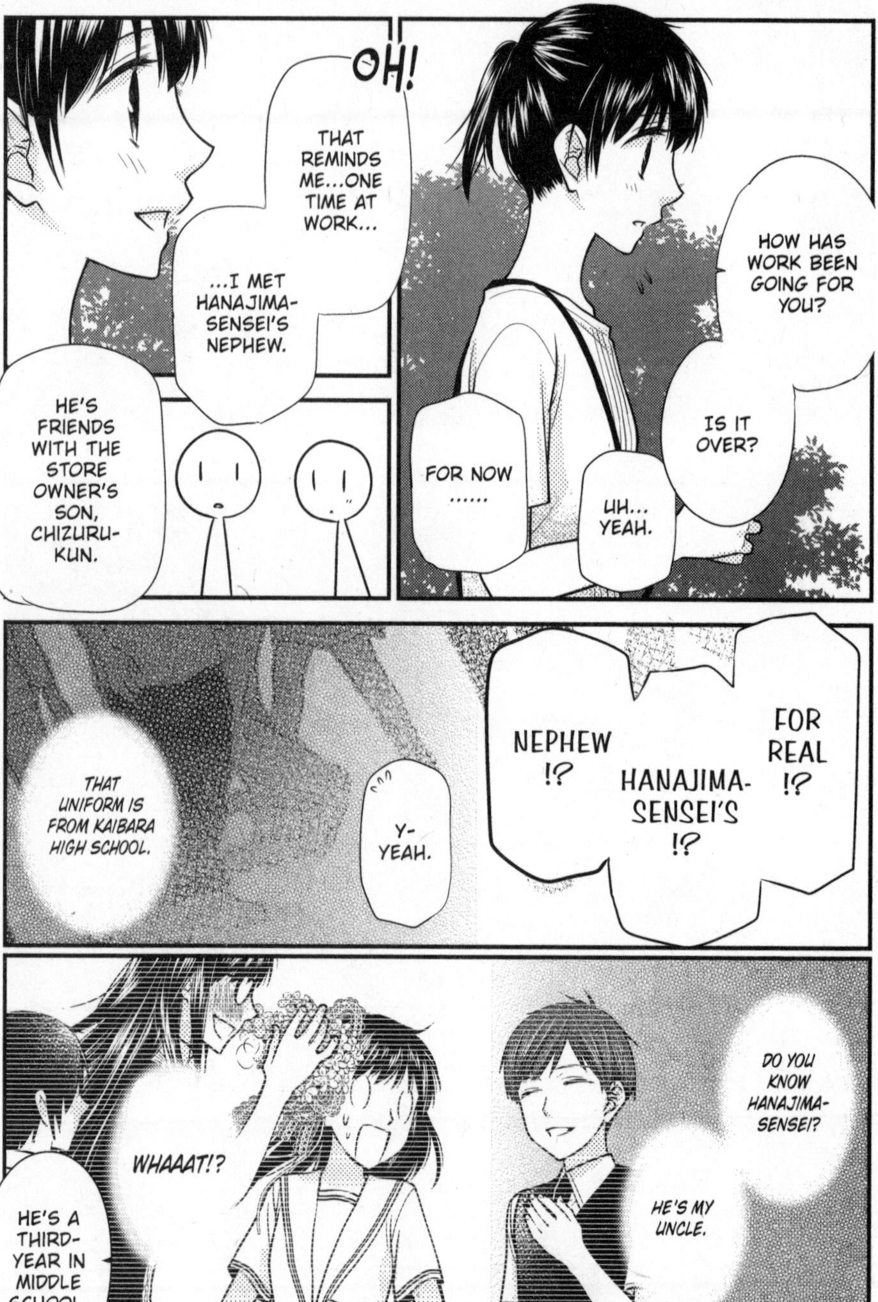
HOW HAS WORK BEEN GOING FOR YOU?
IS IT OVER?
UH... YEAH.
FOR NOW ......
OH!
THAT REMINDS ME...ONE TIME AT WORK...
...I MET HANAJIMA-SENSEI'S NEPHEW.
HE'S FRIENDS WITH THE STORE OWNER'S SON, CHIZURU-KUN.
FOR REAL!?
HANAJIMA-SENSEI'S!?
NEPHEW!?
Y-YEAH.
THAT UNIFORM IS FROM KAIBARA HIGH SCHOOL.
DO YOU KNOW HANAJIMA-SENSEI?
HE'S MY UNCLE.
WHAAAT!?
HE'S A THIRD-YEAR IN MIDDLE SCHOOL.

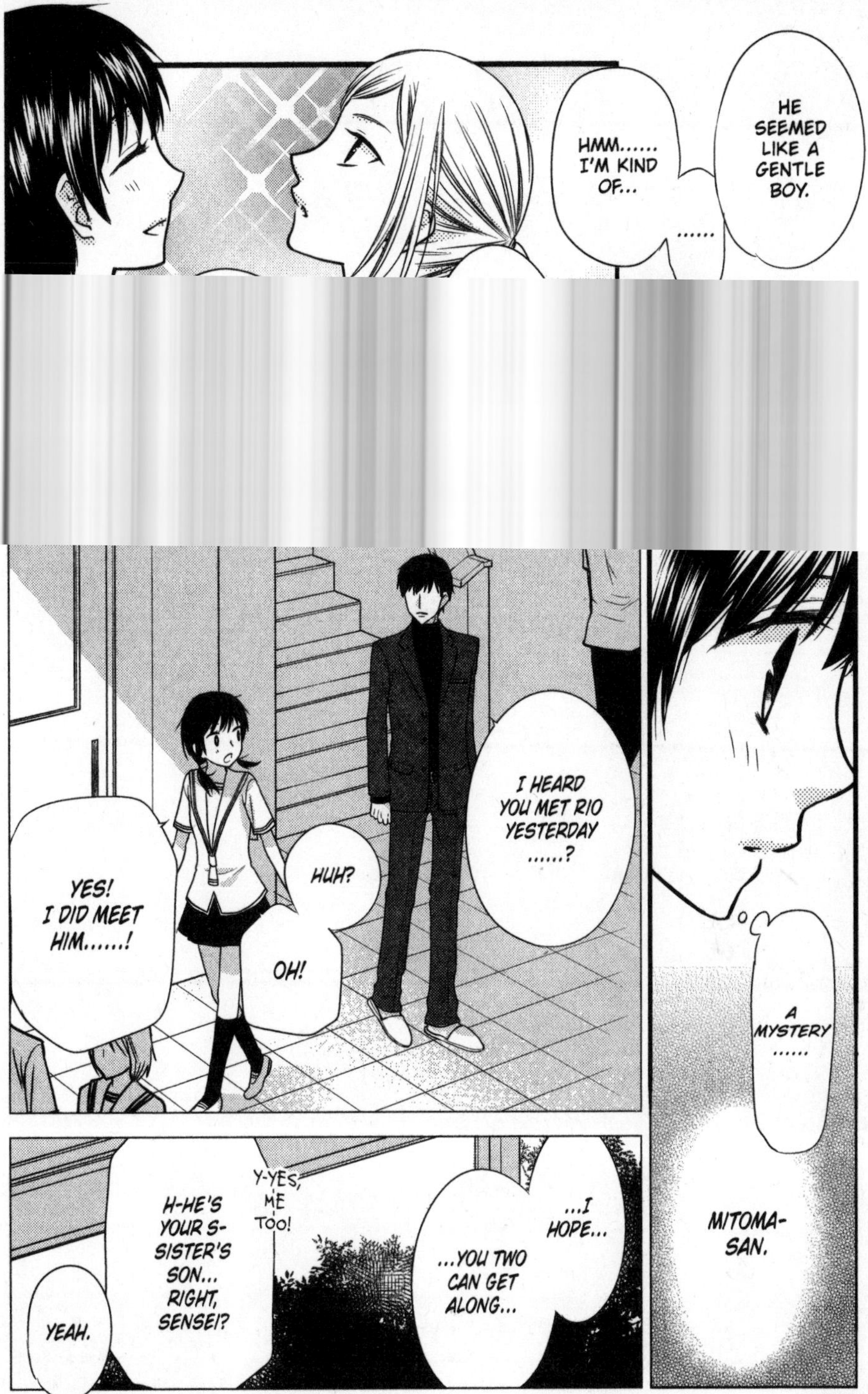
HE SEEMED LIKE A GENTLE BOY.
......
HMM...... I'M KIND OF...
A MYSTERY ......
MITOMA-SAN.
I HEARD YOU MET RIO YESTERDAY ......?
HUH?
OH!
YES! I DID MEET HIM......!
...I HOPE...
...YOU TWO CAN GET ALONG...
Y-YES, ME TOO!
H-HE'S YOUR S-SISTER'S SON... RIGHT, SENSEI?
YEAH.

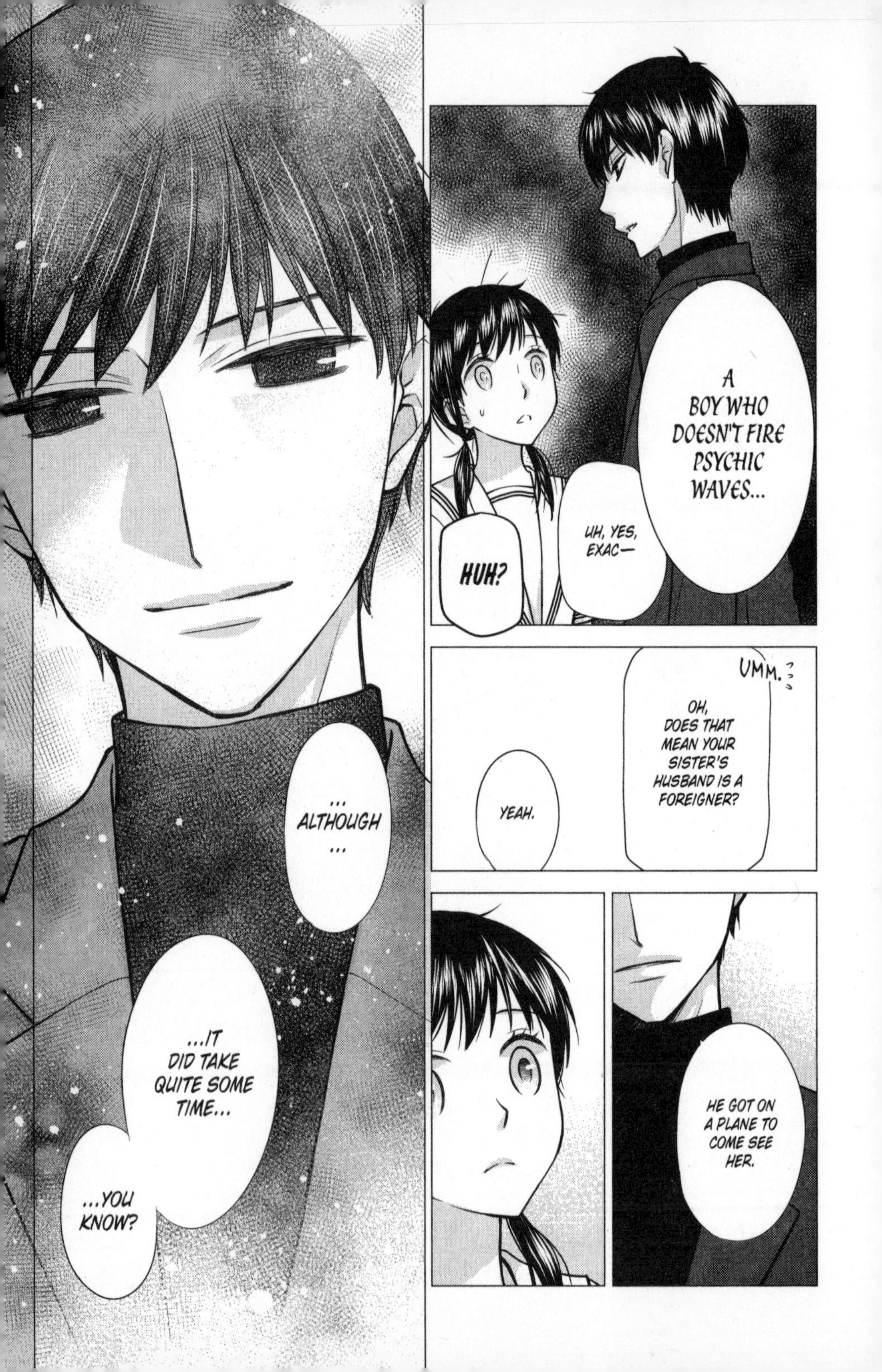
A BOY WHO DOESN'T FIRE PSYCHIC WAVES...
UH, YES, EXAC—
HUH?
UMM.
OH, DOES THAT MEAN YOUR SISTER'S HUSBAND IS A FOREIGNER?
YEAH.
HE GOT ON A PLANE TO COME SEE HER.
...ALTHOUGH...
...IT DID TAKE QUITE SOME TIME...
...YOU KNOW?

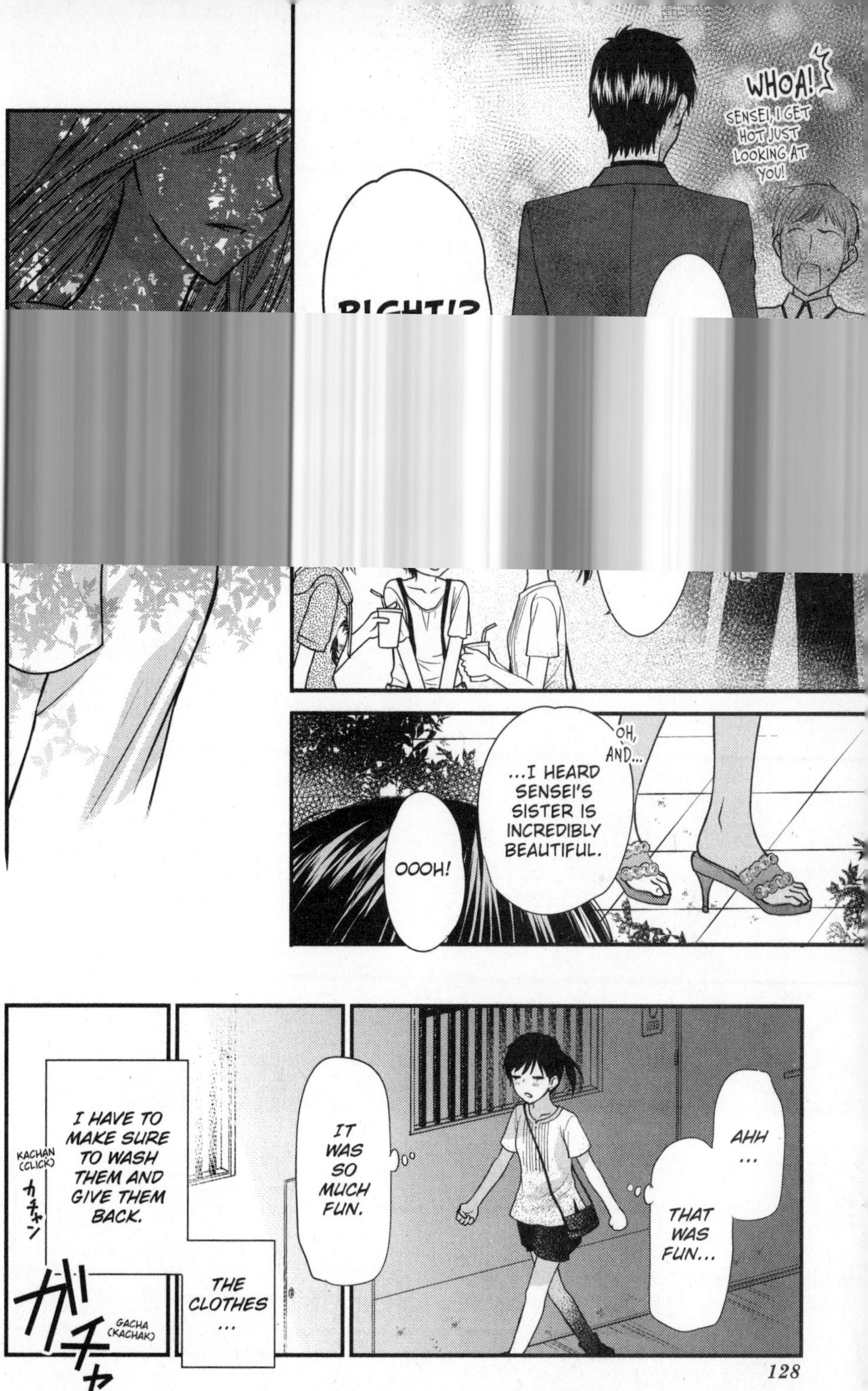
WHOA!
SENSEI, I GET HOT JUST LOOKING AT YOU!
OH, AND...
...I HEARD SENSEI'S SISTER IS INCREDIBLY BEAUTIFUL.
OOOH!
AHH...
THAT WAS FUN...
IT WAS SO MUCH FUN.
I HAVE TO MAKE SURE TO WASH THEM AND GIVE THEM BACK.
THE CLOTHES...
KACHAN (CLICK)
カチャン
GACHA (KACHAK)
ガチャ

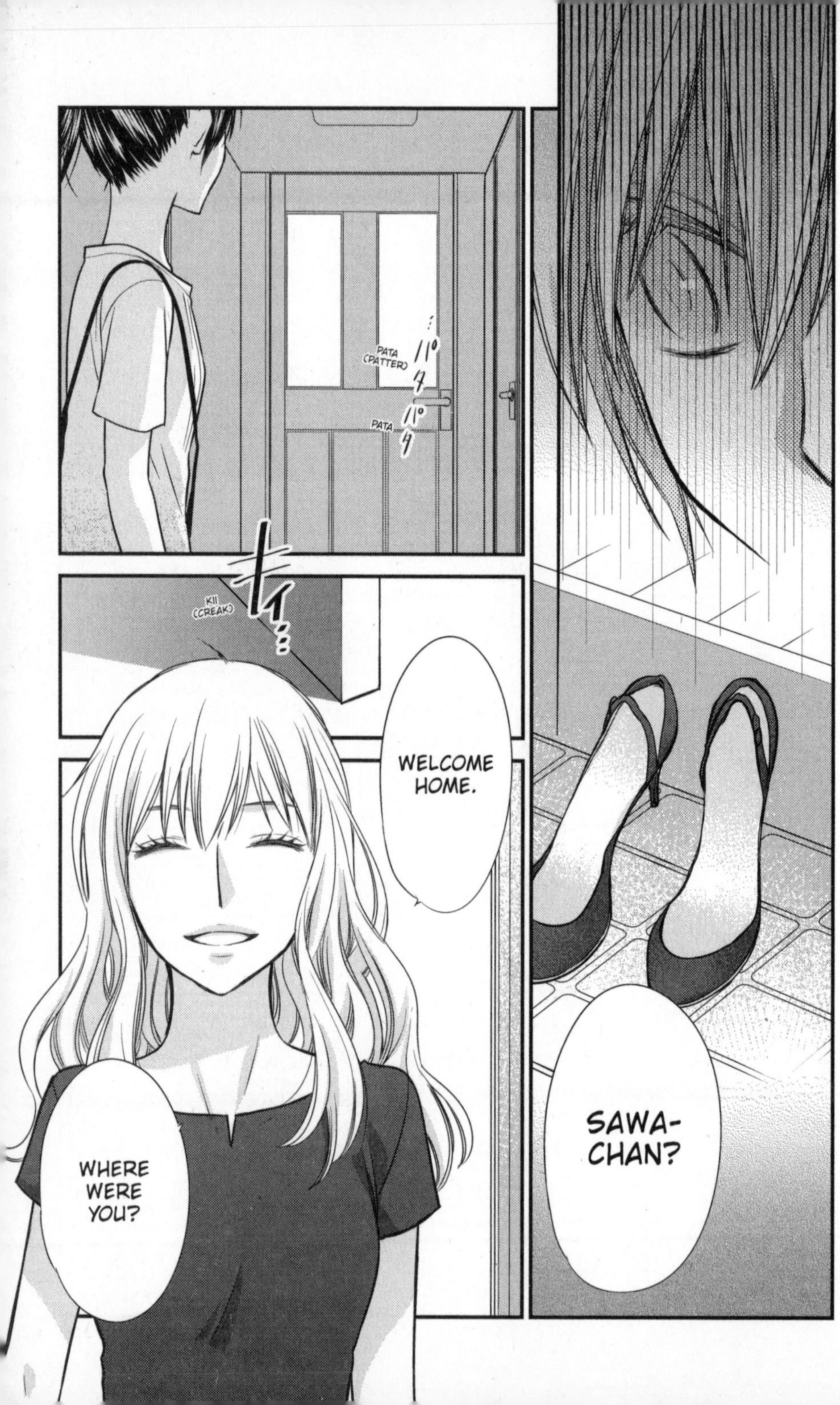
SAWA-CHAN?
PATA (PATTER)
PATA
KII (CREAK)
WELCOME HOME.
WHERE WERE YOU?

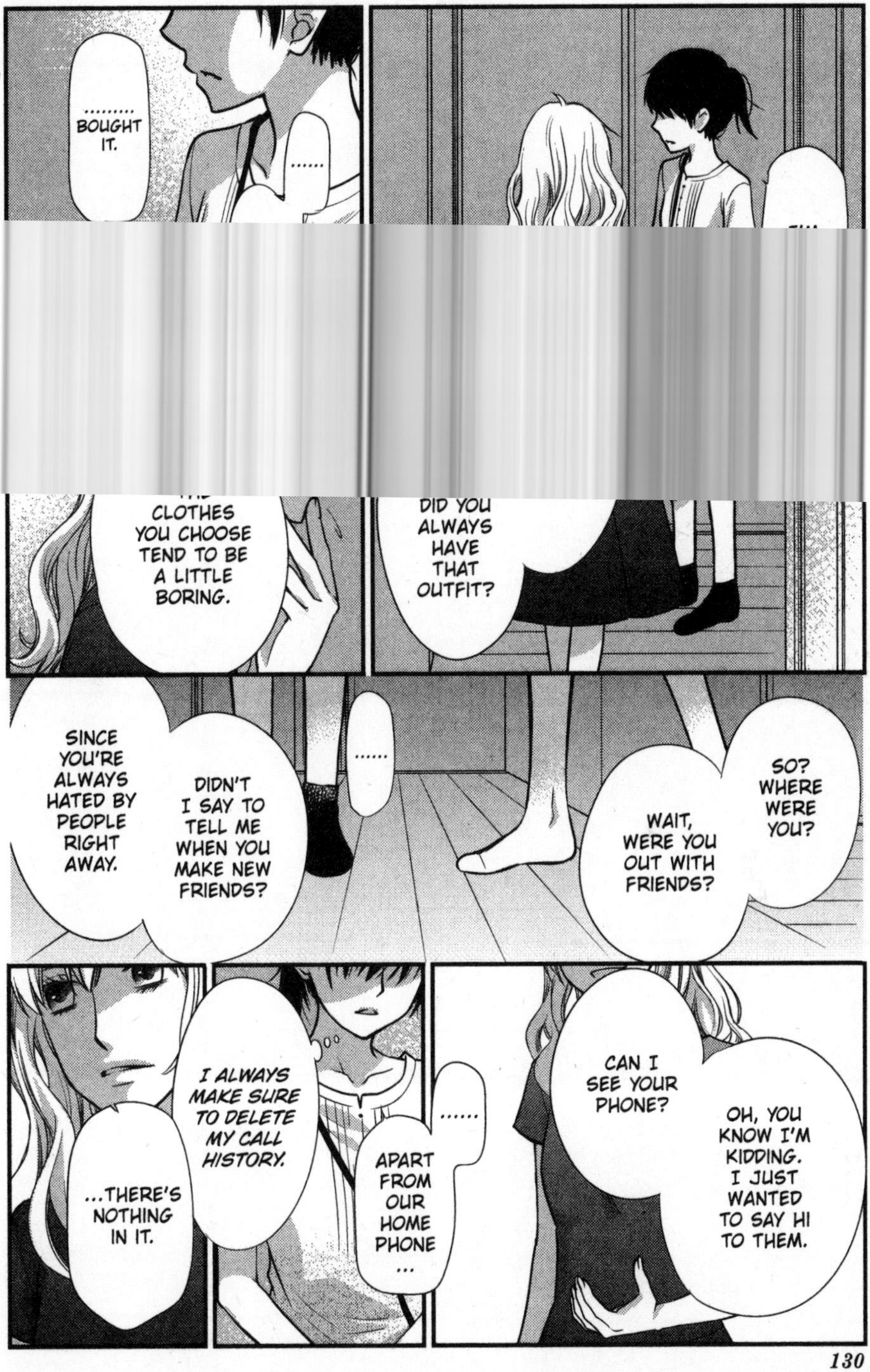
DID YOU ALWAYS HAVE THAT OUTFIT?
.... BOUGHT IT.
......
CLOTHES YOU CHOOSE TEND TO BE A LITTLE BORING.
SO? WHERE WERE YOU?
WAIT, WERE YOU OUT WITH FRIENDS?
......
DIDN'T I SAY TO TELL ME WHEN YOU MAKE NEW FRIENDS?
SINCE YOU'RE ALWAYS HATED BY PEOPLE RIGHT AWAY.
CAN I SEE YOUR PHONE?
OH, YOU KNOW I'M KIDDING. I JUST WANTED TO SAY HI TO THEM.
......
APART FROM OUR HOME PHONE ...
I ALWAYS MAKE SURE TO DELETE MY CALL HISTORY.
...THERE'S NOTHING IN IT.

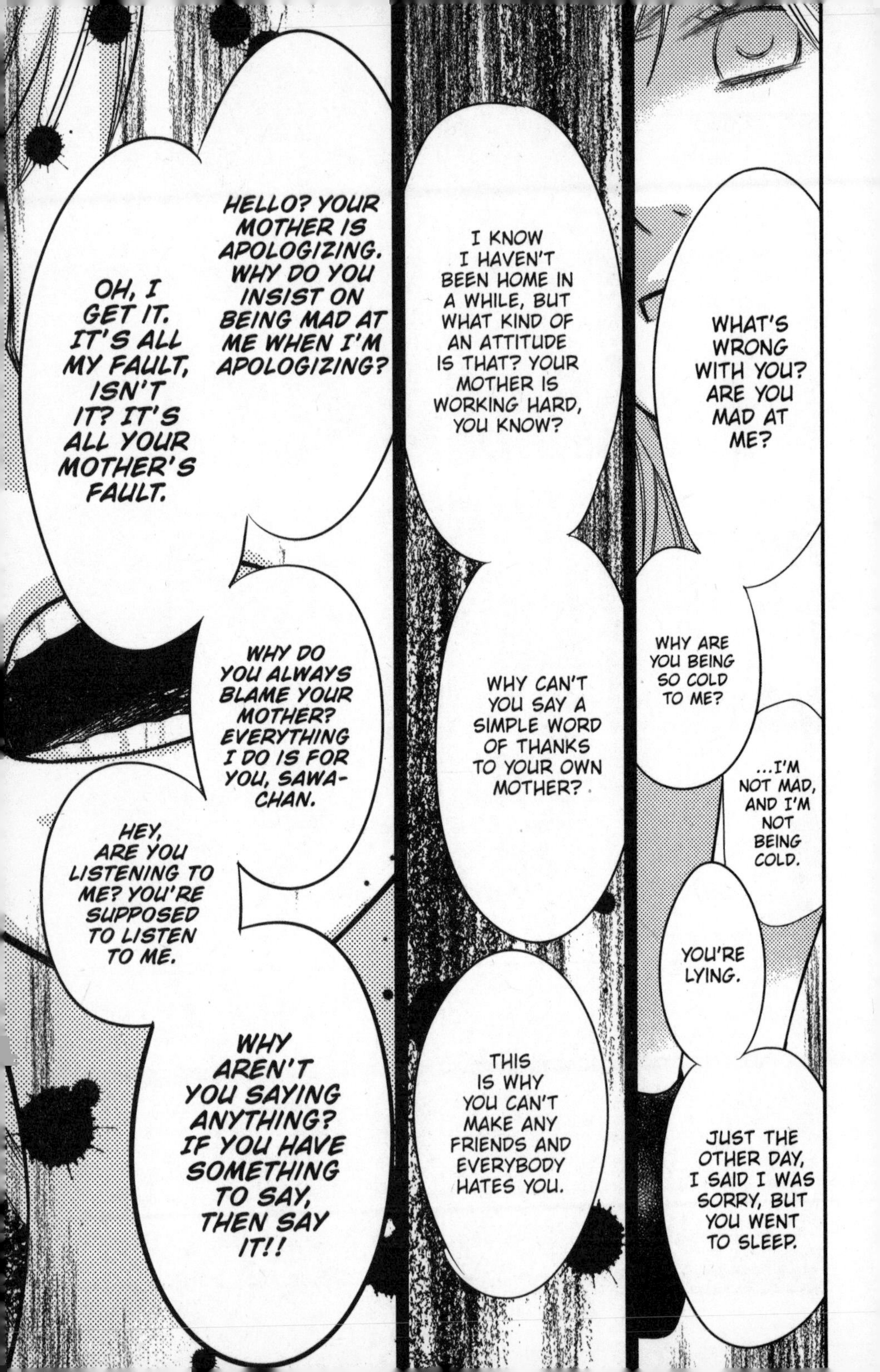
WHAT'S WRONG WITH YOU? ARE YOU MAD AT ME?
WHY ARE YOU BEING SO COLD TO ME?
...I'M NOT MAD, AND I'M NOT BEING COLD.
YOU'RE LYING.
JUST THE OTHER DAY, I SAID I WAS SORRY, BUT YOU WENT TO SLEEP.
I KNOW I HAVEN'T BEEN HOME IN A WHILE, BUT WHAT KIND OF AN ATTITUDE IS THAT? YOUR MOTHER IS WORKING HARD, YOU KNOW?
WHY CAN'T YOU SAY A SIMPLE WORD OF THANKS TO YOUR OWN MOTHER?
THIS IS WHY YOU CAN'T MAKE ANY FRIENDS AND EVERYBODY HATES YOU.
HELLO? YOUR MOTHER IS APOLOGIZING. WHY DO YOU INSIST ON BEING MAD AT ME WHEN I'M APOLOGIZING?
OH, I GET IT. IT'S ALL MY FAULT, ISN'T IT? IT'S ALL YOUR MOTHER'S FAULT.
WHY DO YOU ALWAYS BLAME YOUR MOTHER? EVERYTHING I DO IS FOR YOU, SAWA-CHAN.
HEY, ARE YOU LISTENING TO ME? YOU'RE SUPPOSED TO LISTEN TO ME.
WHY AREN'T YOU SAYING ANYTHING? IF YOU HAVE SOMETHING TO SAY, THEN SAY IT!!

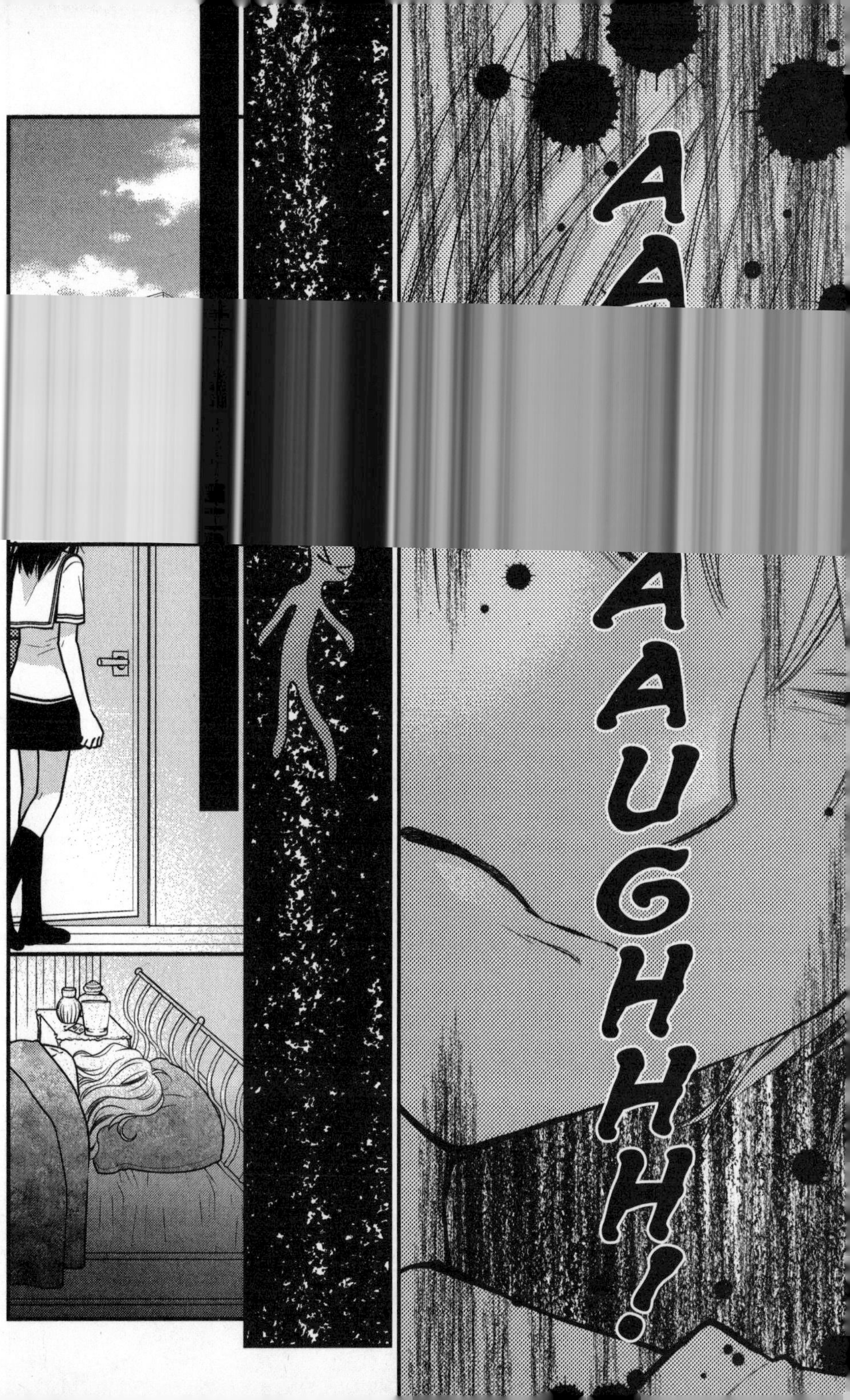
AA
AAUGHHH!

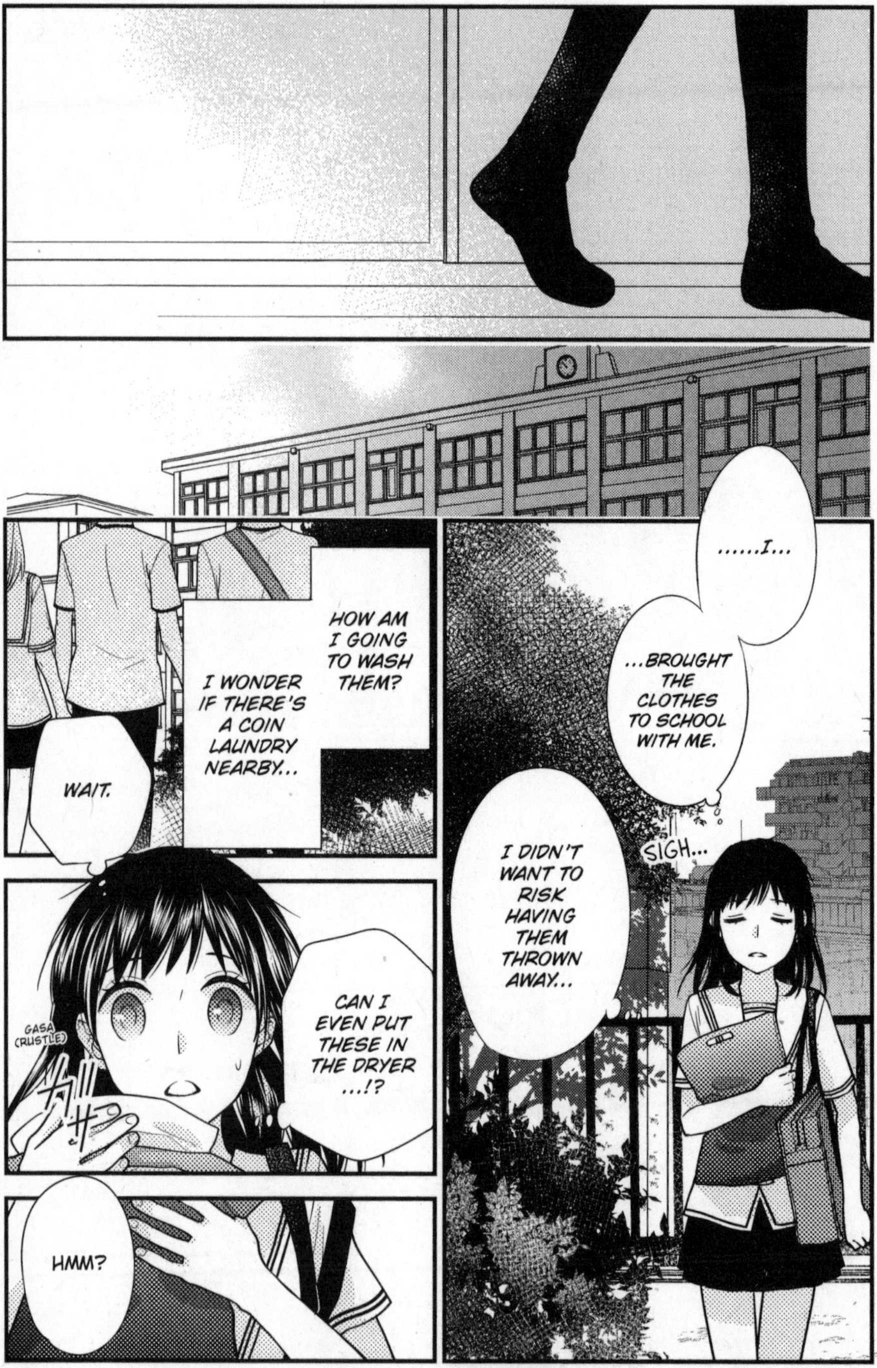
......I...
...BROUGHT THE CLOTHES TO SCHOOL WITH ME.
SIGH...
I DIDN'T WANT TO RISK HAVING THEM THROWN AWAY...
HOW AM I GOING TO WASH THEM?
I WONDER IF THERE'S A COIN LAUNDRY NEARBY...
WAIT.
CAN I EVEN PUT THESE IN THE DRYER ...!?
GASA (RUSTLE)
HMM?

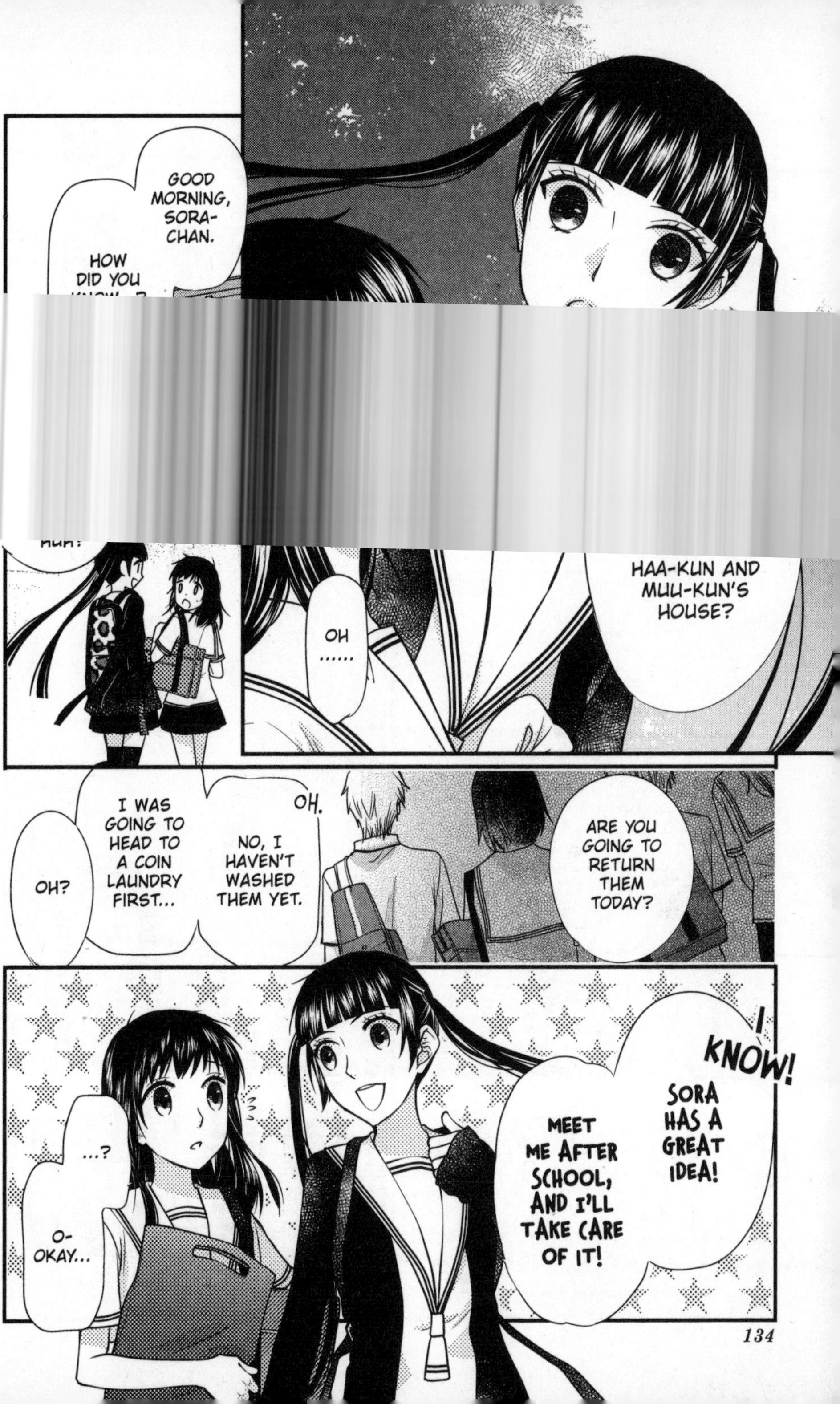
GOOD MORNING, SORA-CHAN.
HOW DID YOU
HAA-KUN AND MUU-KUN'S HOUSE?
OH ......
ARE YOU GOING TO RETURN THEM TODAY?
OH.
NO, I HAVEN'T WASHED THEM YET.
I WAS GOING TO HEAD TO A COIN LAUNDRY FIRST...
OH?
I KNOW!
SORA HAS A GREAT IDEA!
MEET ME AFTER SCHOOL, AND I'LL TAKE CARE OF IT!
...?
O-OKAY...

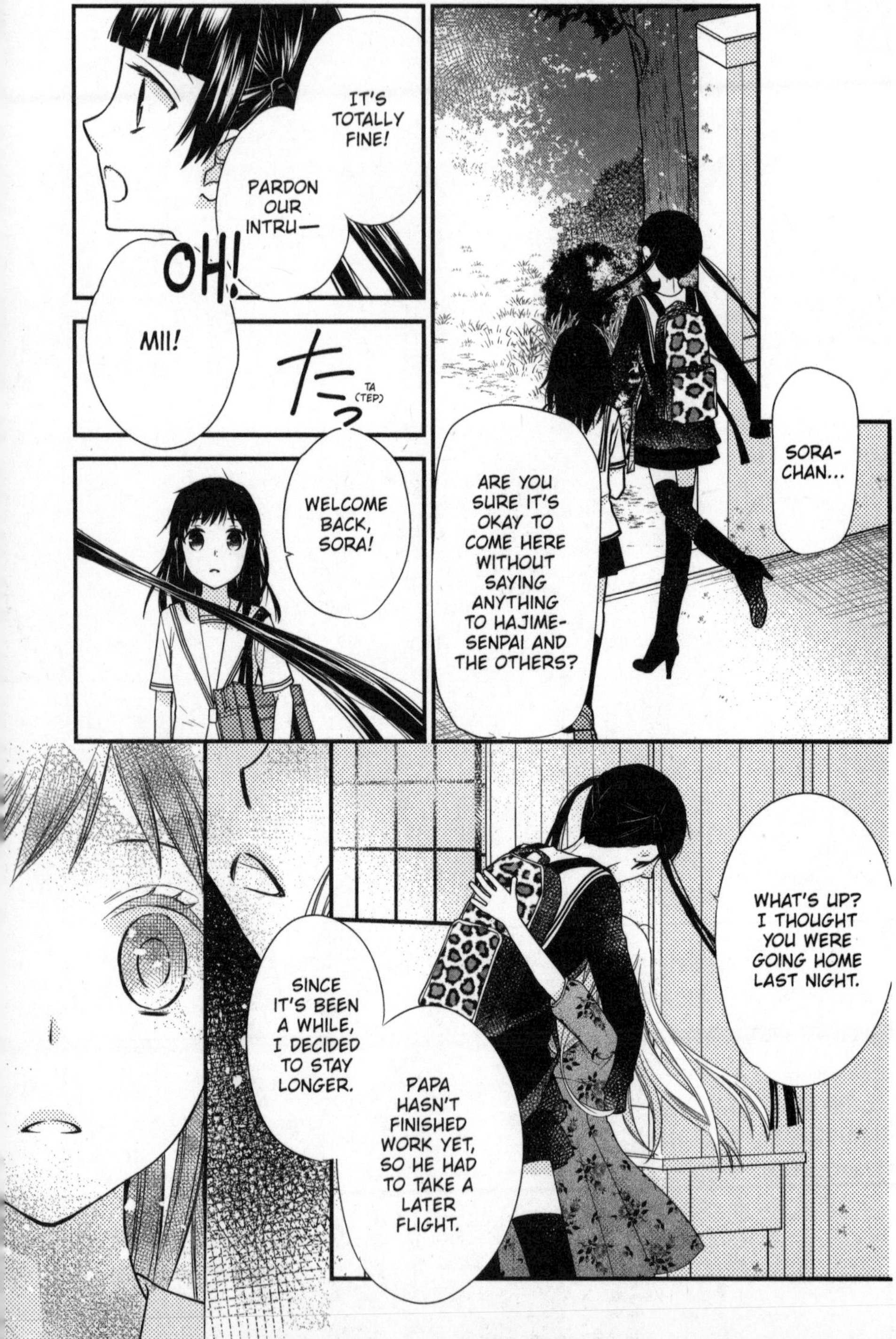
SORA-CHAN...
ARE YOU SURE IT'S OKAY TO COME HERE WITHOUT SAYING ANYTHING TO HAJIME-SENPAI AND THE OTHERS?
IT'S TOTALLY FINE!
PARDON OUR INTRU—
OH!
MII!
たっ
TA (TEP)
WELCOME BACK, SORA!
WHAT'S UP? I THOUGHT YOU WERE GOING HOME LAST NIGHT.
SINCE IT'S BEEN A WHILE, I DECIDED TO STAY LONGER.
PAPA HASN'T FINISHED WORK YET, SO HE HAD TO TAKE A LATER FLIGHT.

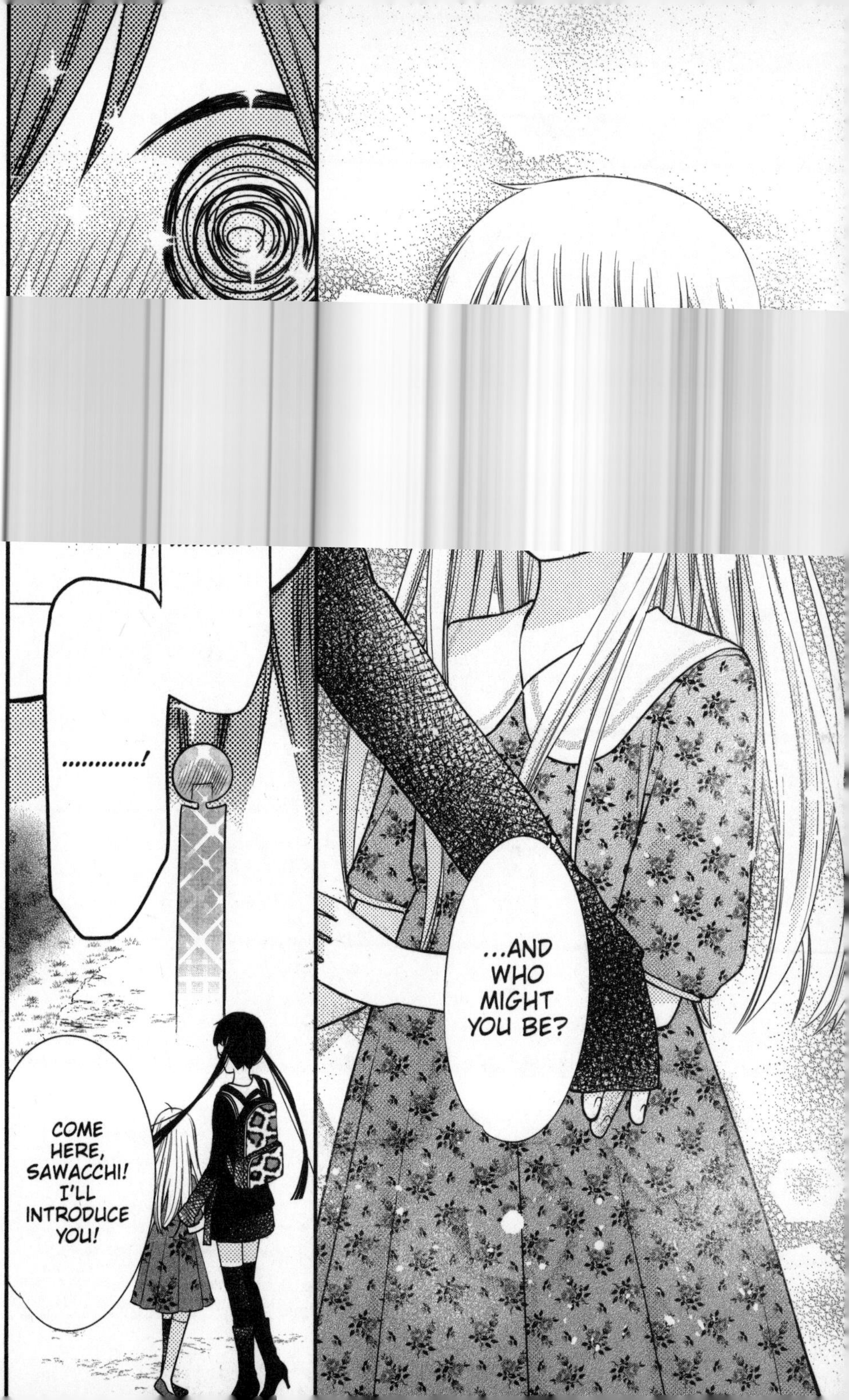
...AND WHO MIGHT YOU BE?
............!
COME HERE, SAWACCHI! I'LL INTRODUCE YOU!

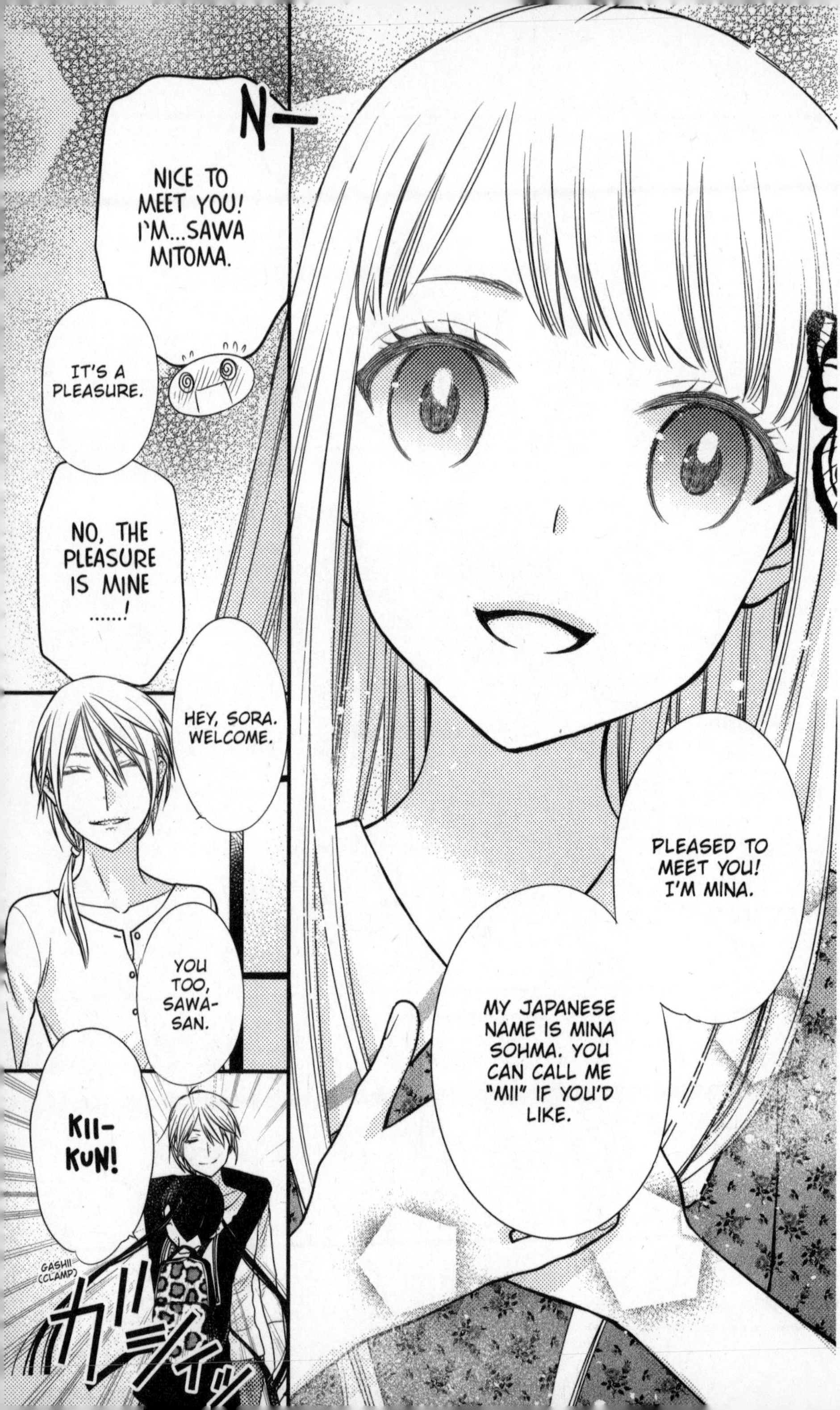
PLEASED TO MEET YOU! I'M MINA.
MY JAPANESE NAME IS MINA SOHMA. YOU CAN CALL ME "MII" IF YOU'D LIKE.
N—
NICE TO MEET YOU! I'M...SAWA MITOMA.
IT'S A PLEASURE.
NO, THE PLEASURE IS MINE ......!
HEY, SORA. WELCOME.
YOU TOO, SAWA-SAN.
KII-KUN!
GASHII (CLAMP)

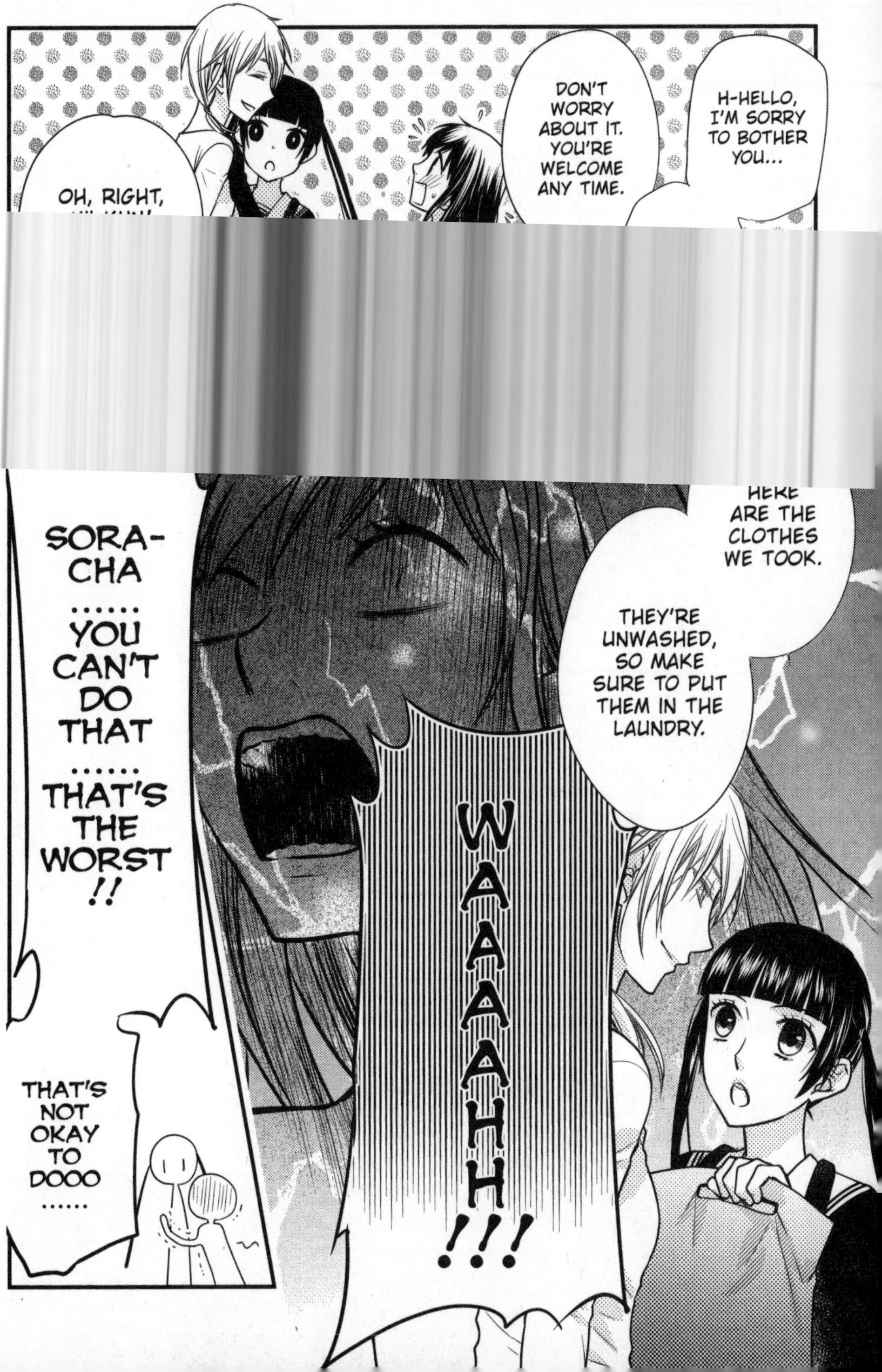
H-HELLO, I'M SORRY TO BOTHER YOU...
DON'T WORRY ABOUT IT. YOU'RE WELCOME ANY TIME.
OH, RIGHT,
HERE ARE THE CLOTHES WE TOOK.
THEY'RE UNWASHED, SO MAKE SURE TO PUT THEM IN THE LAUNDRY.
WAAAAAH!!!
SORA-CHA...... YOU CAN'T DO THAT...... THAT'S THE WORST!!
THAT'S NOT OKAY TO DOOO......

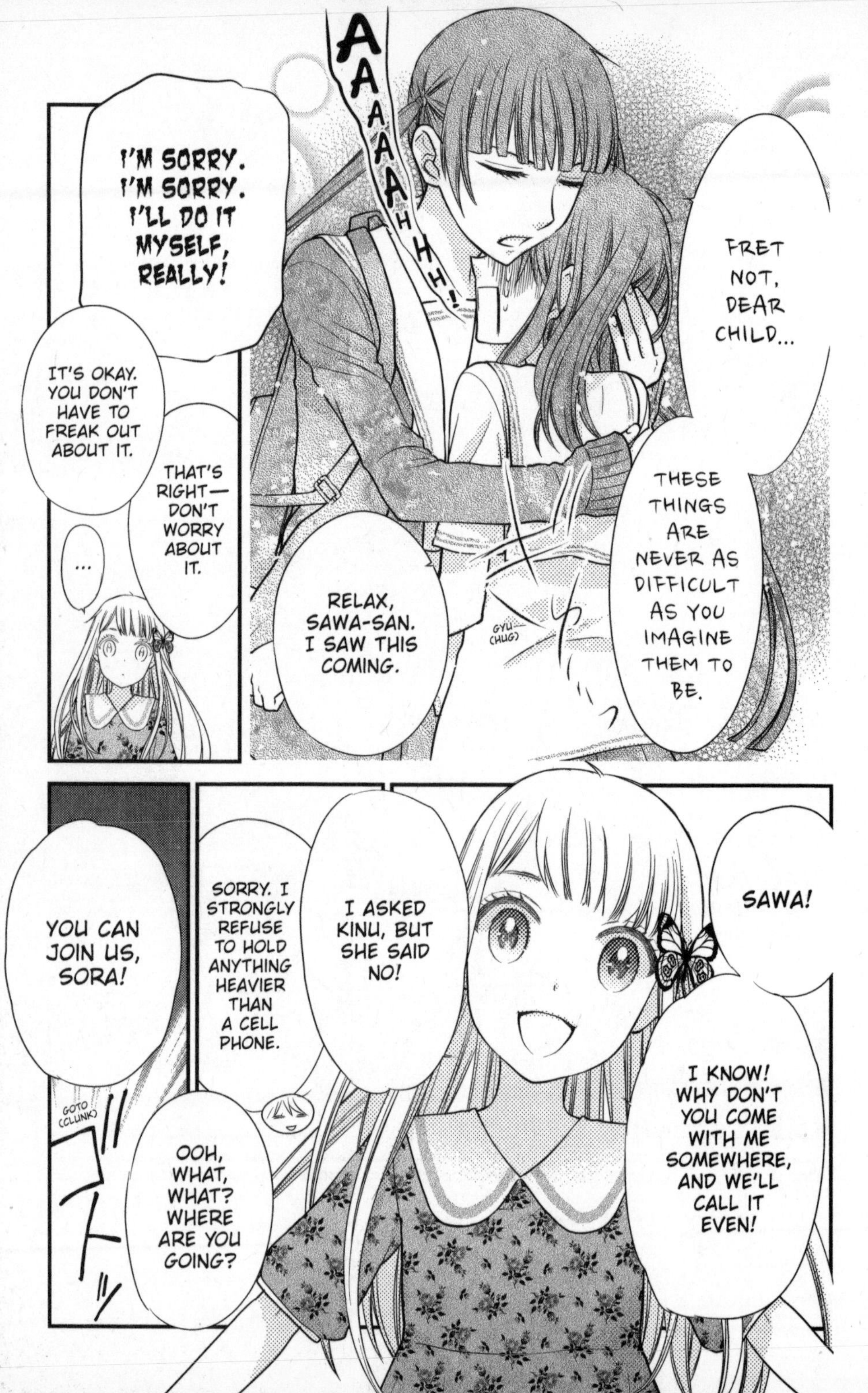
I'M SORRY. I'M SORRY. I'LL DO IT MYSELF, REALLY!
AAAAAAHHH!
FRET NOT, DEAR CHILD...
THESE THINGS ARE NEVER AS DIFFICULT AS YOU IMAGINE THEM TO BE.
GYU (HUG)
RELAX, SAWA-SAN. I SAW THIS COMING.
IT'S OKAY. YOU DON'T HAVE TO FREAK OUT ABOUT IT.
THAT'S RIGHT—DON'T WORRY ABOUT IT.
...
SAWA!
I KNOW! WHY DON'T YOU COME WITH ME SOMEWHERE, AND WE'LL CALL IT EVEN!
OOH, WHAT, WHAT? WHERE ARE YOU GOING?
I ASKED KINU, BUT SHE SAID NO!
SORRY. I STRONGLY REFUSE TO HOLD ANYTHING HEAVIER THAN A CELL PHONE.
YOU CAN JOIN US, SORA!
GOTO (CLUNK)

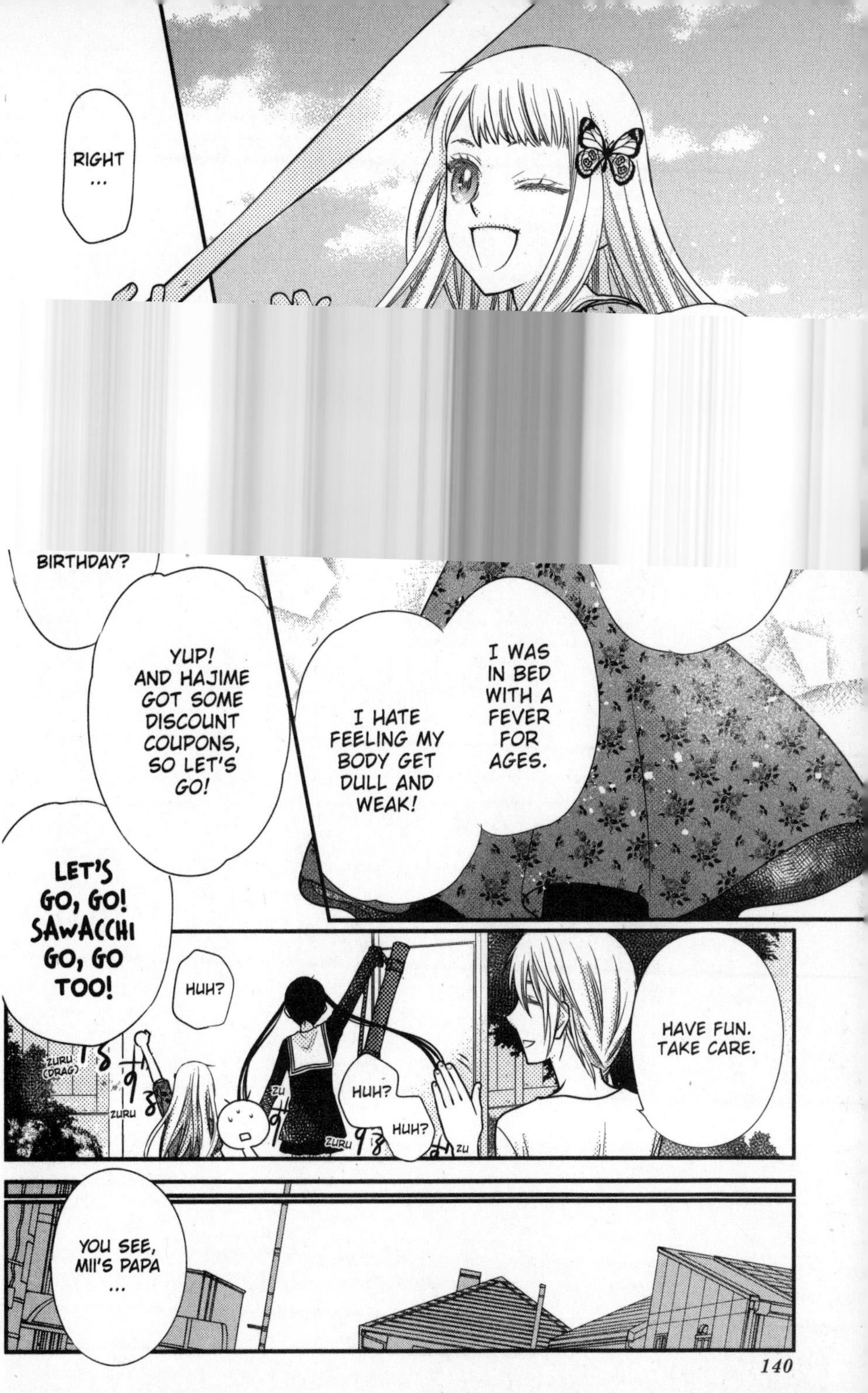
RIGHT ...
I WAS IN BED WITH A FEVER FOR AGES.
I HATE FEELING MY BODY GET DULL AND WEAK!
BIRTHDAY?
YUP! AND HAJIME GOT SOME DISCOUNT COUPONS, SO LET'S GO!
LET'S GO, GO! SAWACCHI GO, GO TOO!
HAVE FUN. TAKE CARE.
ZU
HUH?
HUH?
ZURU
ZU
HUH?
ZURU (DRAG)
ZURU
YOU SEE, MII'S PAPA ...

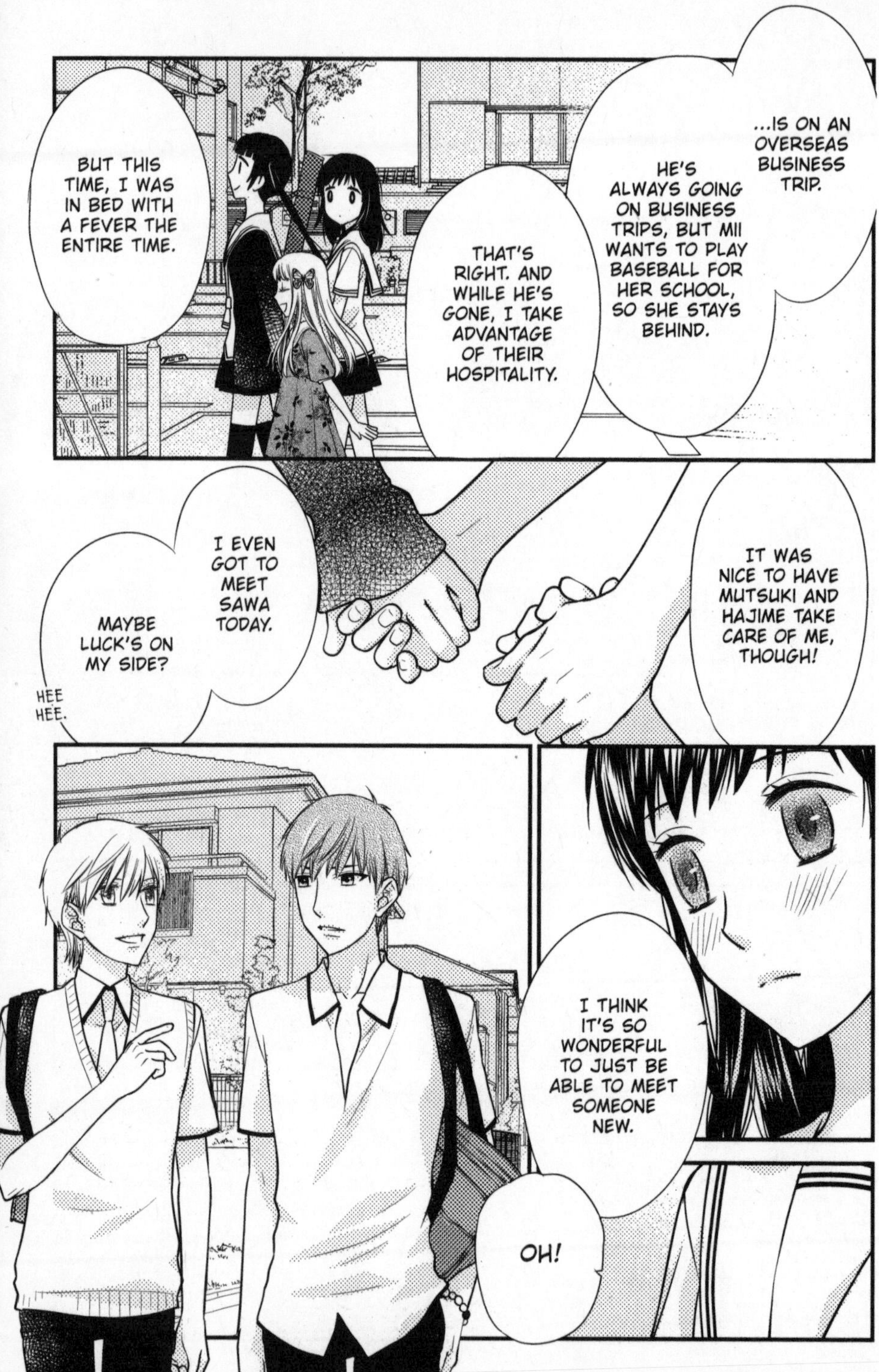
...IS ON AN OVERSEAS BUSINESS TRIP.
HE'S ALWAYS GOING ON BUSINESS TRIPS, BUT MII WANTS TO PLAY BASEBALL FOR HER SCHOOL, SO SHE STAYS BEHIND.
THAT'S RIGHT. AND WHILE HE'S GONE, I TAKE ADVANTAGE OF THEIR HOSPITALITY.
BUT THIS TIME, I WAS IN BED WITH A FEVER THE ENTIRE TIME.
IT WAS NICE TO HAVE MUTSUKI AND HAJIME TAKE CARE OF ME, THOUGH!
I EVEN GOT TO MEET SAWA TODAY.
MAYBE LUCK'S ON MY SIDE?
HEE HEE.
I THINK IT'S SO WONDERFUL TO JUST BE ABLE TO MEET SOMEONE NEW.
OH!

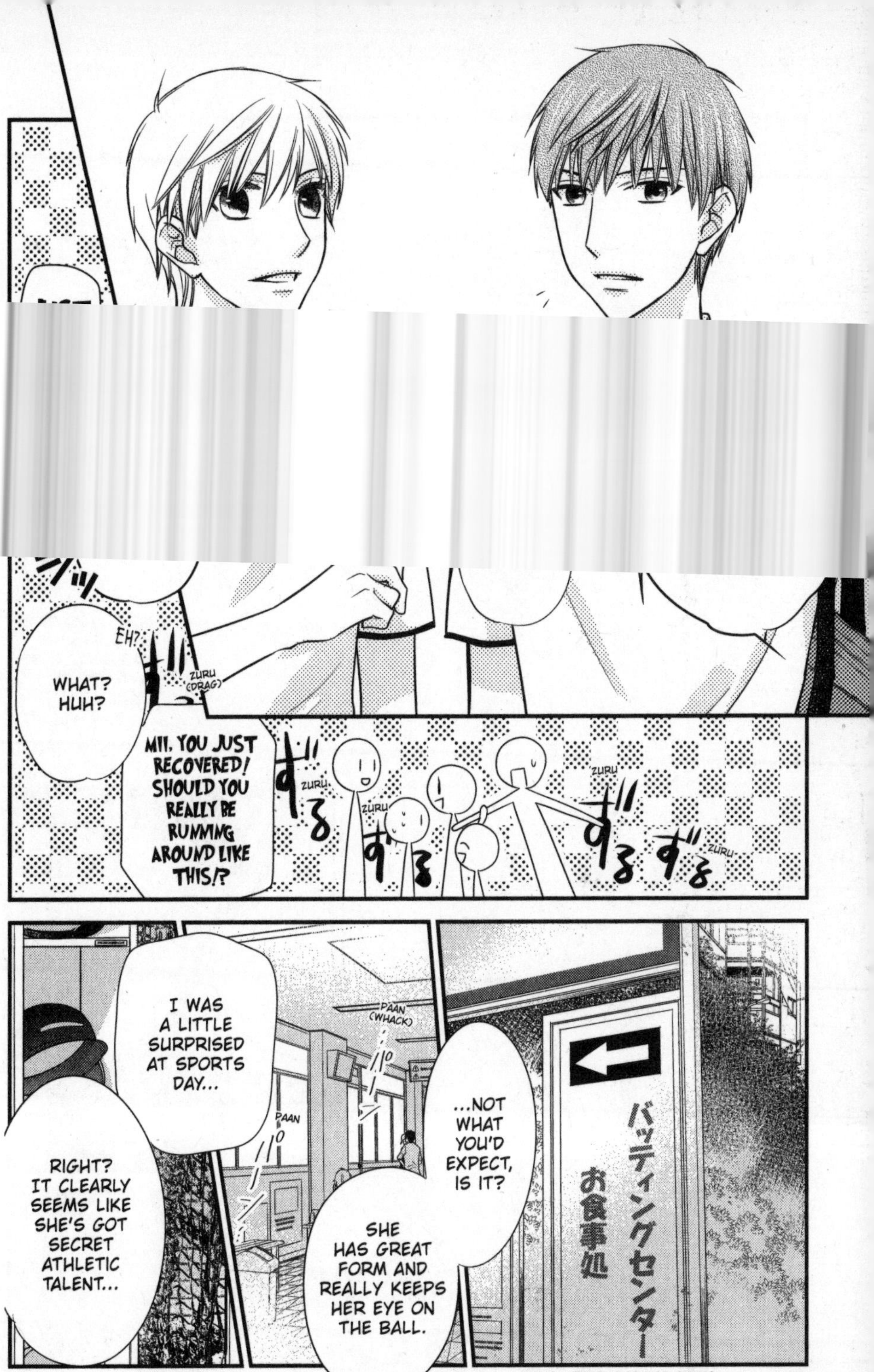
EH?
WHAT? HUH?
ZURU (DRAG)
MII, YOU JUST RECOVERED! SHOULD YOU REALLY BE RUNNING AROUND LIKE THIS!?
ZURU
ZURU
ZURU
ZURU
バッティングセンター
お食事処
...NOT WHAT YOU'D EXPECT, IS IT?
PAAN (WHACK)
PAAN
I WAS A LITTLE SURPRISED AT SPORTS DAY...
SHE HAS GREAT FORM AND REALLY KEEPS HER EYE ON THE BALL.
RIGHT? IT CLEARLY SEEMS LIKE SHE'S GOT SECRET ATHLETIC TALENT...

SIGN: BATTING CENTER, DINING

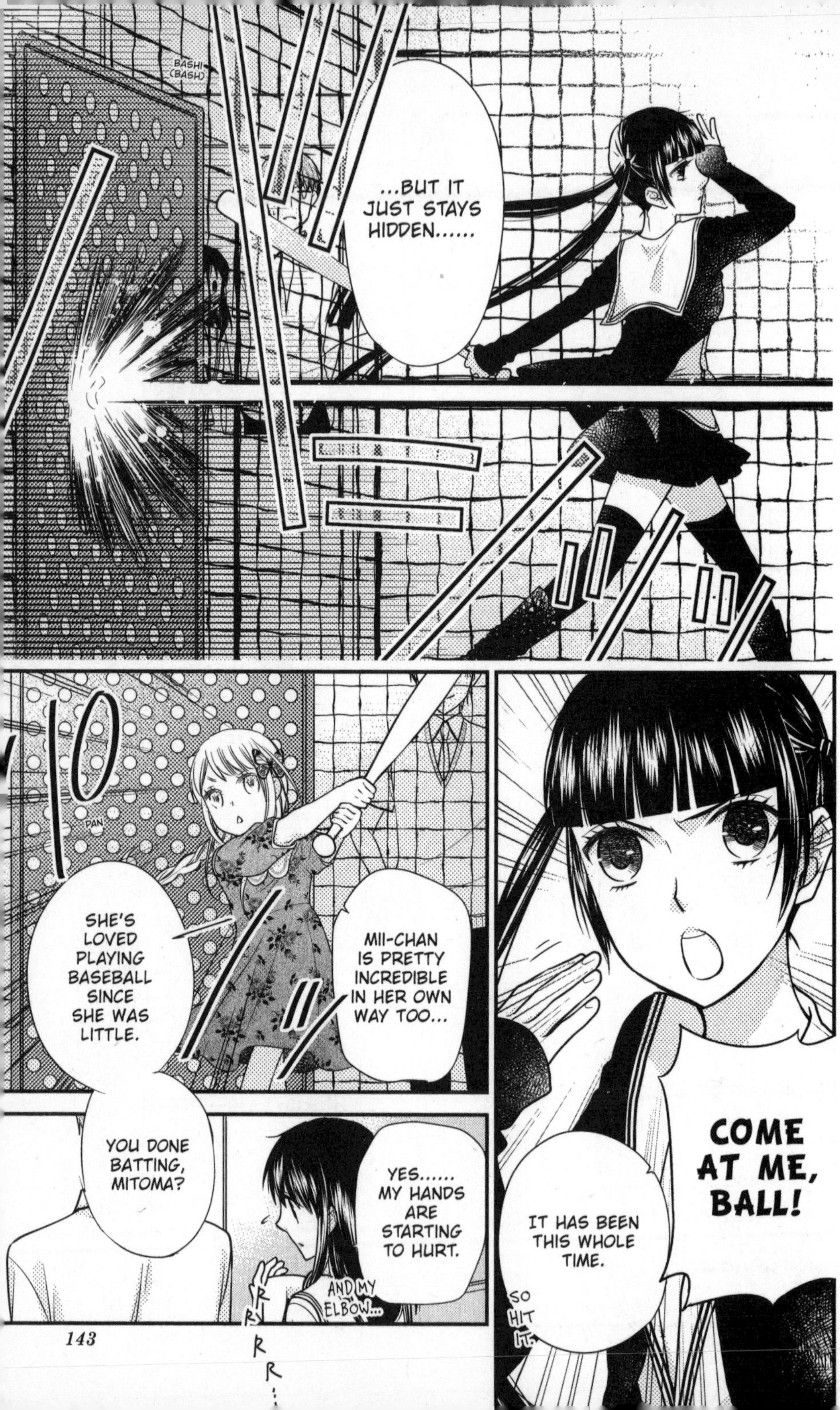
BASHI (BASH)
...BUT IT JUST STAYS HIDDEN......
COME AT ME, BALL!
IT HAS BEEN THIS WHOLE TIME.
SO HIT IT.
PAN
MII-CHAN IS PRETTY INCREDIBLE IN HER OWN WAY TOO...
SHE'S LOVED PLAYING BASEBALL SINCE SHE WAS LITTLE.
YOU DONE BATTING, MITOMA?
YES...... MY HANDS ARE STARTING TO HURT.
AND MY ELBOW...
R R R R

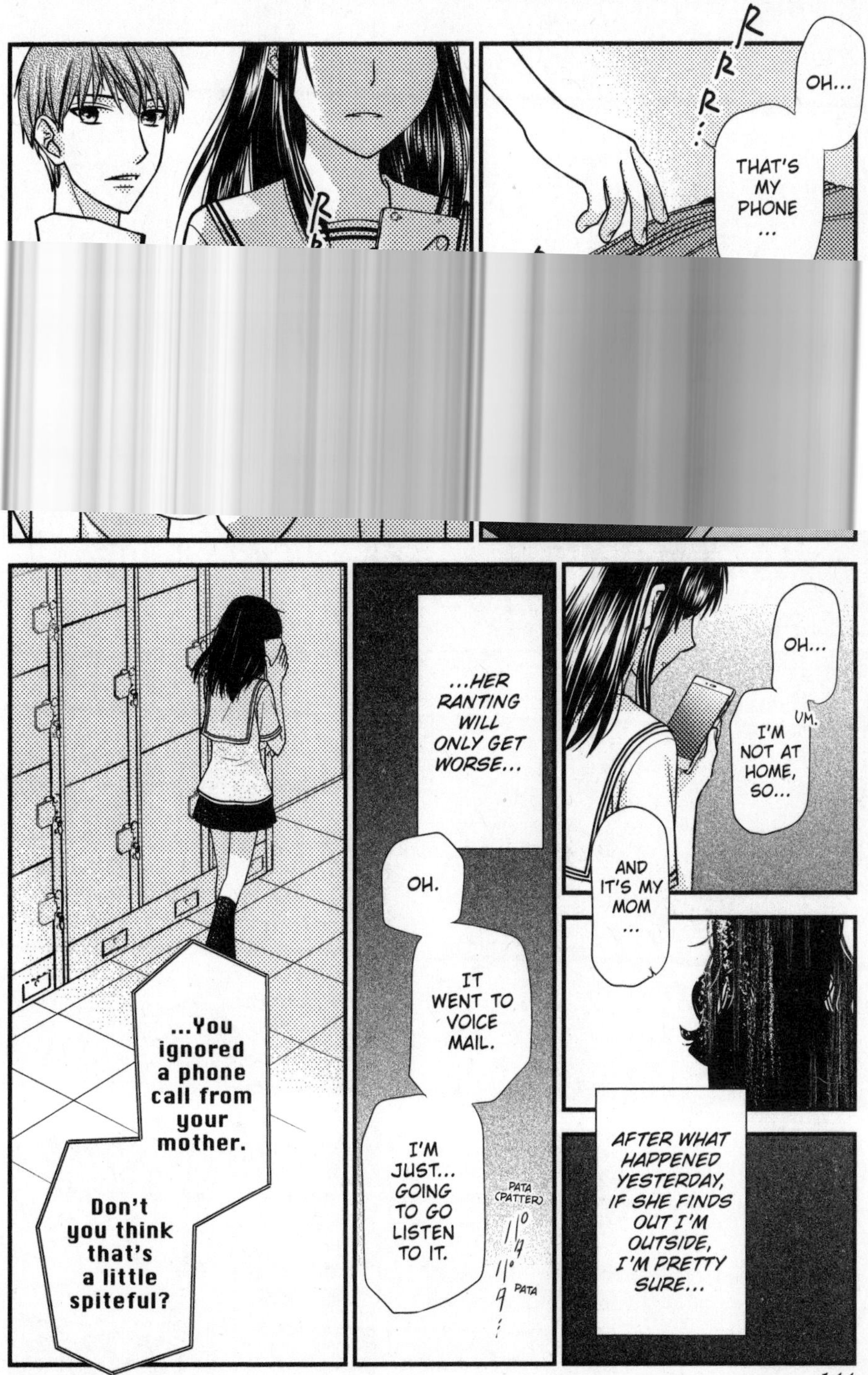
RRR...
OH...
THAT'S MY PHONE ...
R
OH...
UM.
I'M NOT AT HOME, SO...
AND IT'S MY MOM ...
AFTER WHAT HAPPENED YESTERDAY, IF SHE FINDS OUT I'M OUTSIDE, I'M PRETTY SURE...
...HER RANTING WILL ONLY GET WORSE...
OH.
IT WENT TO VOICE MAIL.
I'M JUST... GOING TO GO LISTEN TO IT.
PATA (PATTER)
PATA
...You ignored a phone call from your mother.
Don't you think that's a little spiteful?

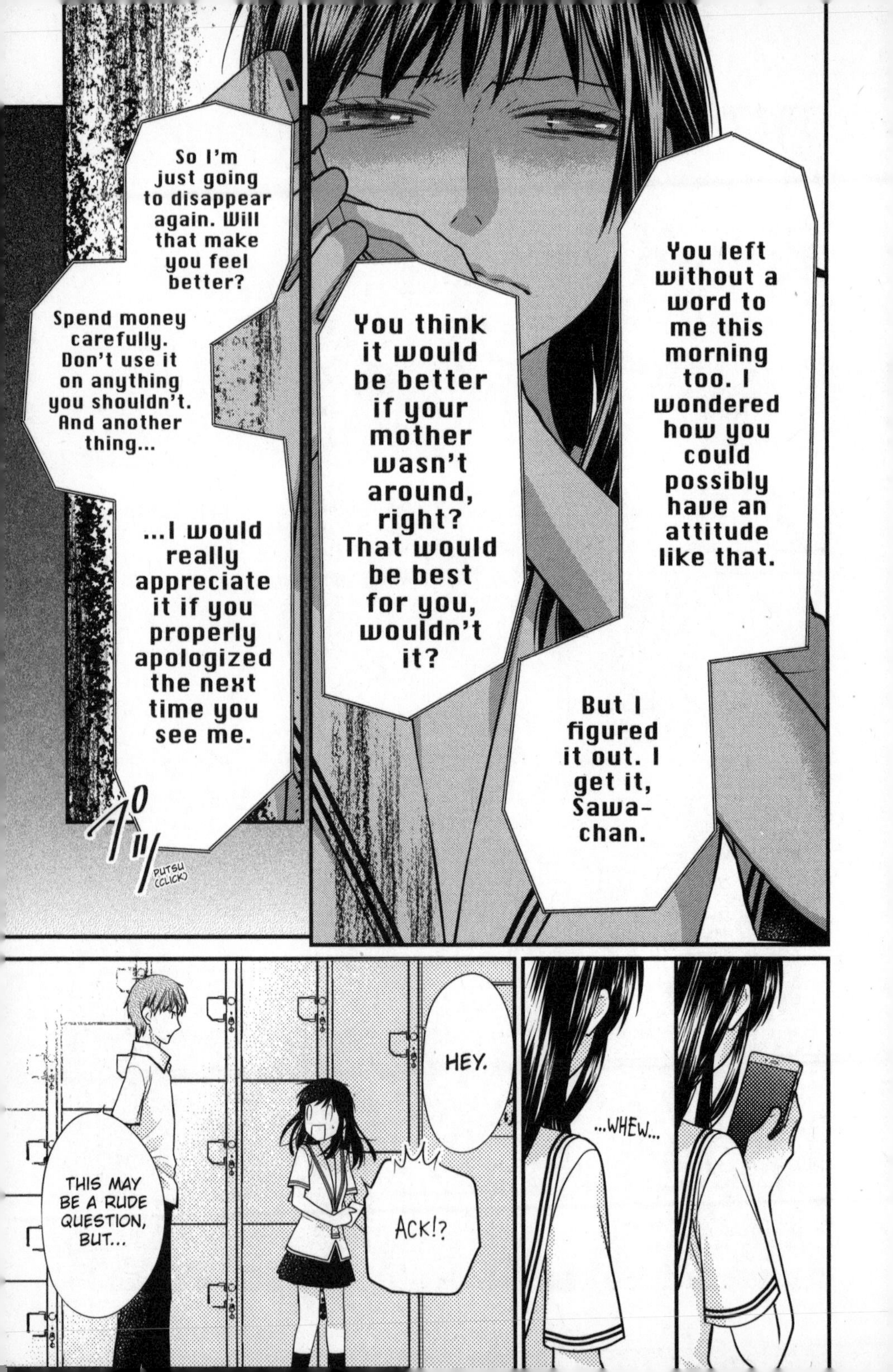
You left without a word to me this morning too. I wondered how you could possibly have an attitude like that.
But I figured it out. I get it, Sawa-chan.
You think it would be better if your mother wasn't around, right? That would be best for you, wouldn't it?
So I'm just going to disappear again. Will that make you feel better?
Spend money carefully. Don't use it on anything you shouldn't. And another thing...
...I would really appreciate it if you properly apologized the next time you see me.
PUTSU (CLICK)
...WHEW...
HEY.
ACK!?
THIS MAY BE A RUDE QUESTION, BUT...

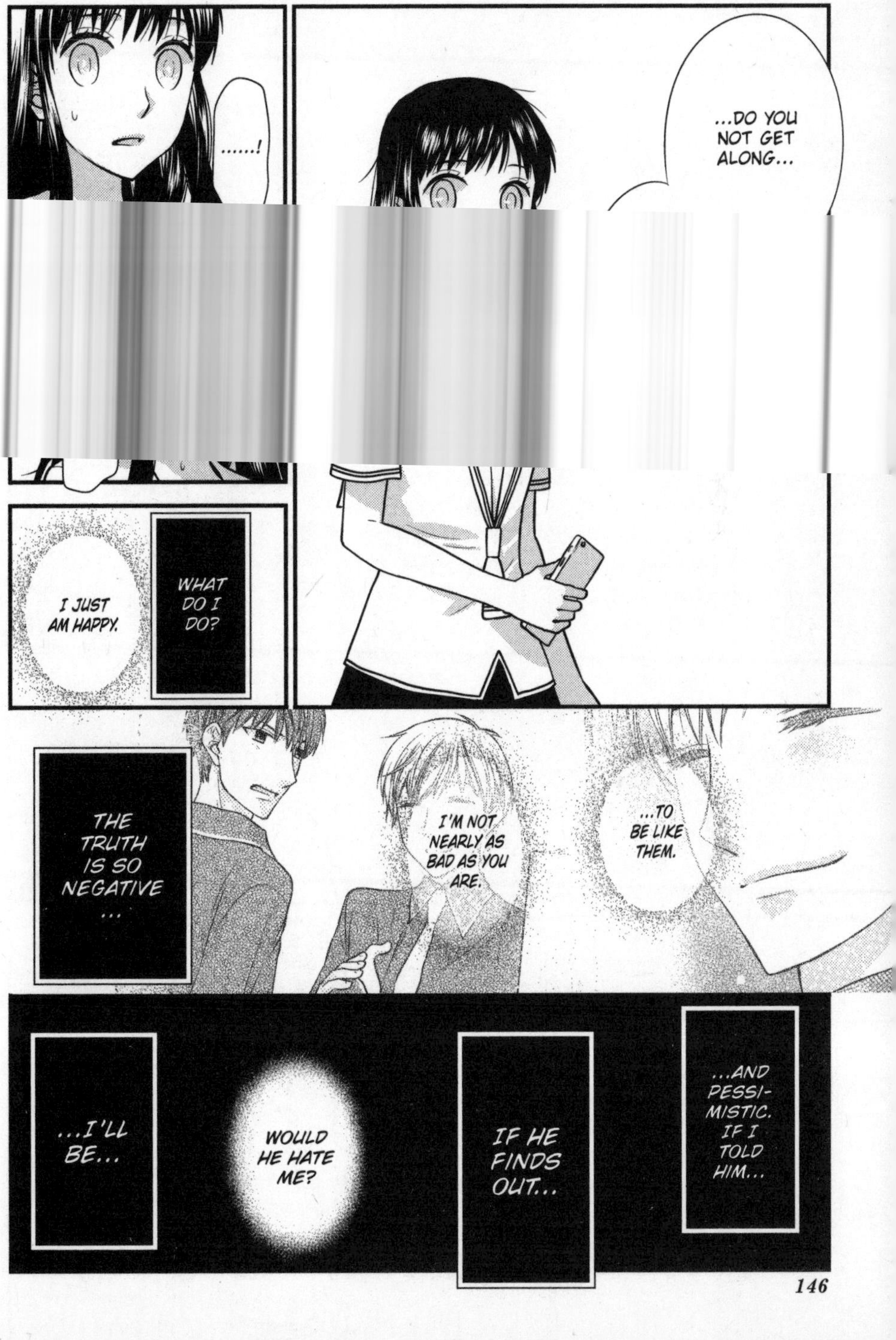
...DO YOU NOT GET ALONG...
......!
WHAT DO I DO?
I JUST AM HAPPY.
...TO BE LIKE THEM.
I'M NOT NEARLY AS BAD AS YOU ARE.
THE TRUTH IS SO NEGATIVE...
...AND PESSI-MISTIC. IF I TOLD HIM...
IF HE FINDS OUT...
WOULD HE HATE ME?
...I'LL BE...

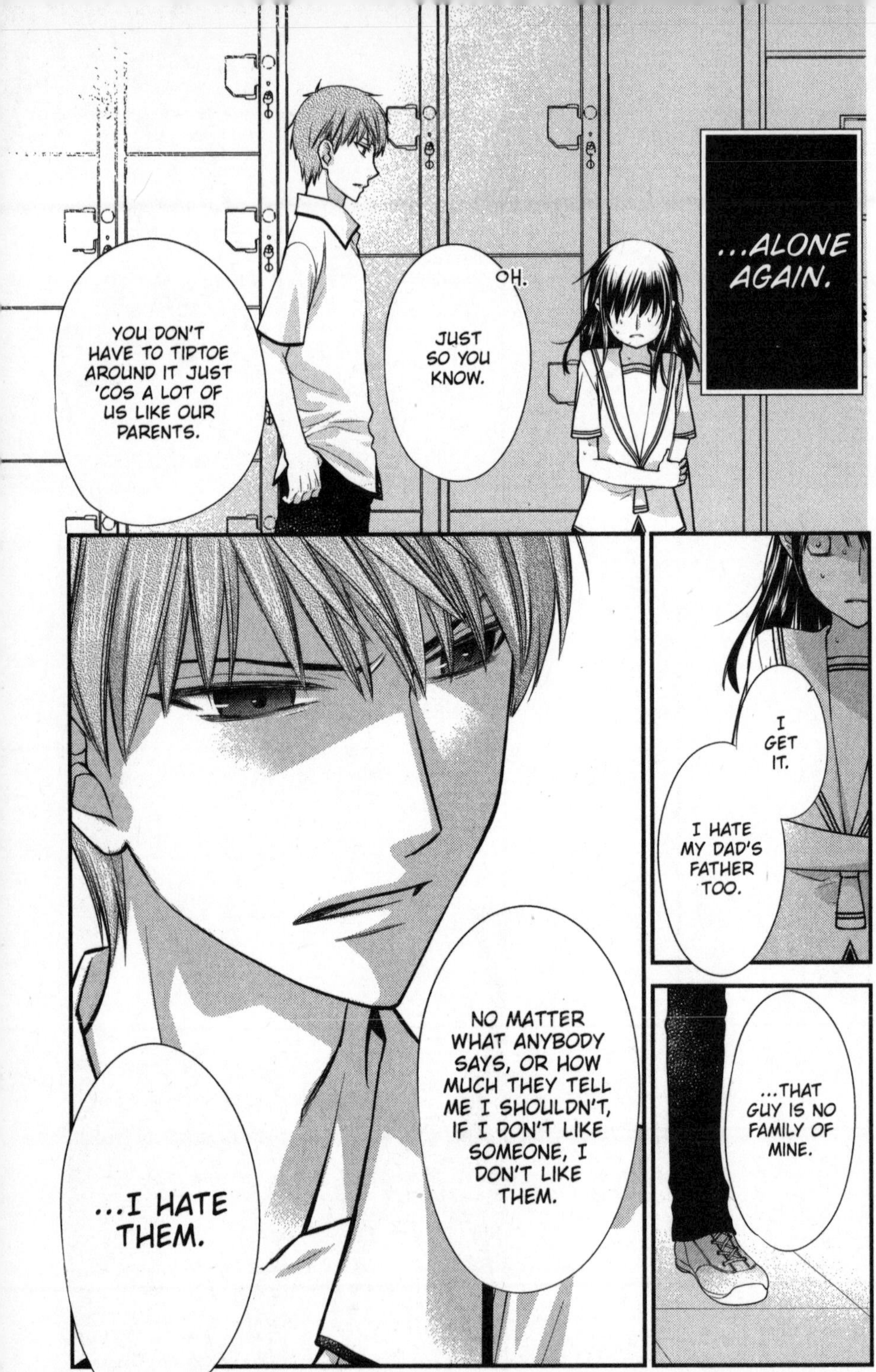

...ALONE AGAIN.
OH.
JUST SO YOU KNOW.
YOU DON'T HAVE TO TIPTOE AROUND IT JUST 'COS A LOT OF US LIKE OUR PARENTS.
I GET IT.
I HATE MY DAD'S FATHER TOO.
...THAT GUY IS NO FAMILY OF MINE.
NO MATTER WHAT ANYBODY SAYS, OR HOW MUCH THEY TELL ME I SHOULDN'T, IF I DON'T LIKE SOMEONE, I DON'T LIKE THEM.
...I HATE THEM.

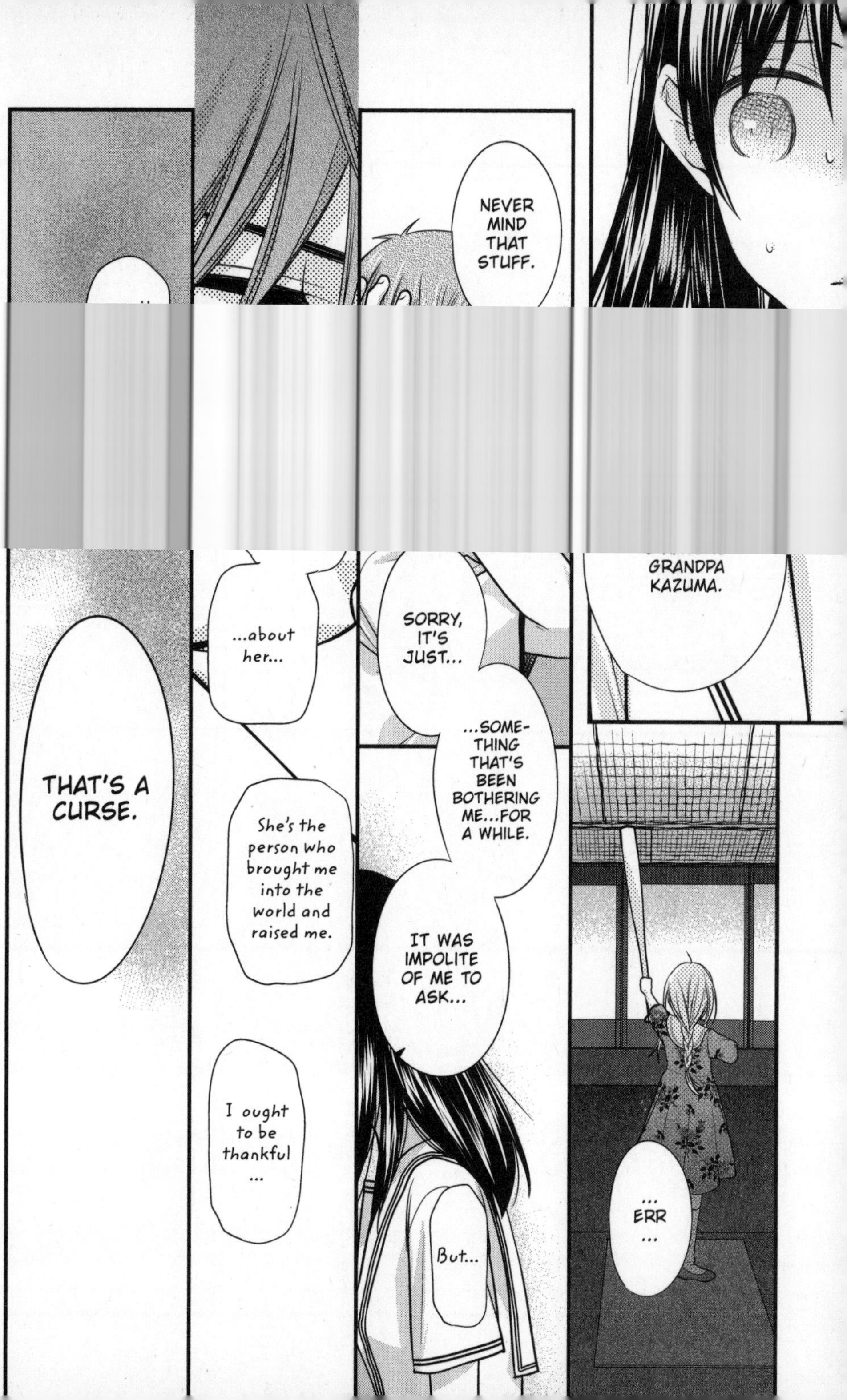
GRANDPA KAZUMA.
...
ERR
...
NEVER MIND THAT STUFF.
SORRY, IT'S JUST...
...SOME-THING THAT'S BEEN BOTHERING ME...FOR A WHILE.
IT WAS IMPOLITE OF ME TO ASK...
But...
...about her...
She's the person who brought me into the world and raised me.
I ought to be thankful ...
THAT'S A CURSE.

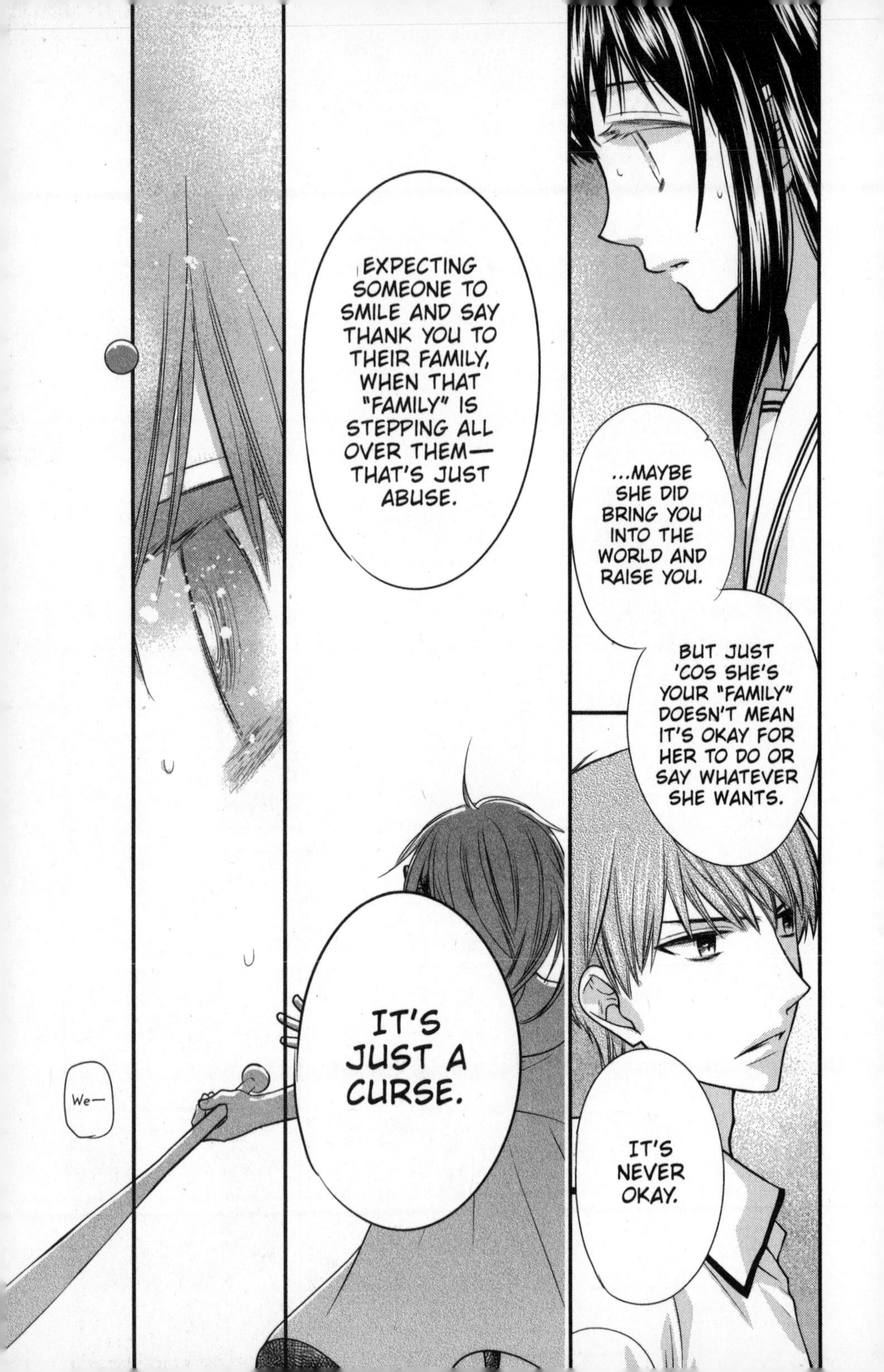
...MAYBE SHE DID BRING YOU INTO THE WORLD AND RAISE YOU.
BUT JUST 'COS SHE'S YOUR "FAMILY" DOESN'T MEAN IT'S OKAY FOR HER TO DO OR SAY WHATEVER SHE WANTS.
IT'S NEVER OKAY.
EXPECTING SOMEONE TO SMILE AND SAY THANK YOU TO THEIR FAMILY, WHEN THAT "FAMILY" IS STEPPING ALL OVER THEM—THAT'S JUST ABUSE.
IT'S JUST A CURSE.
We—

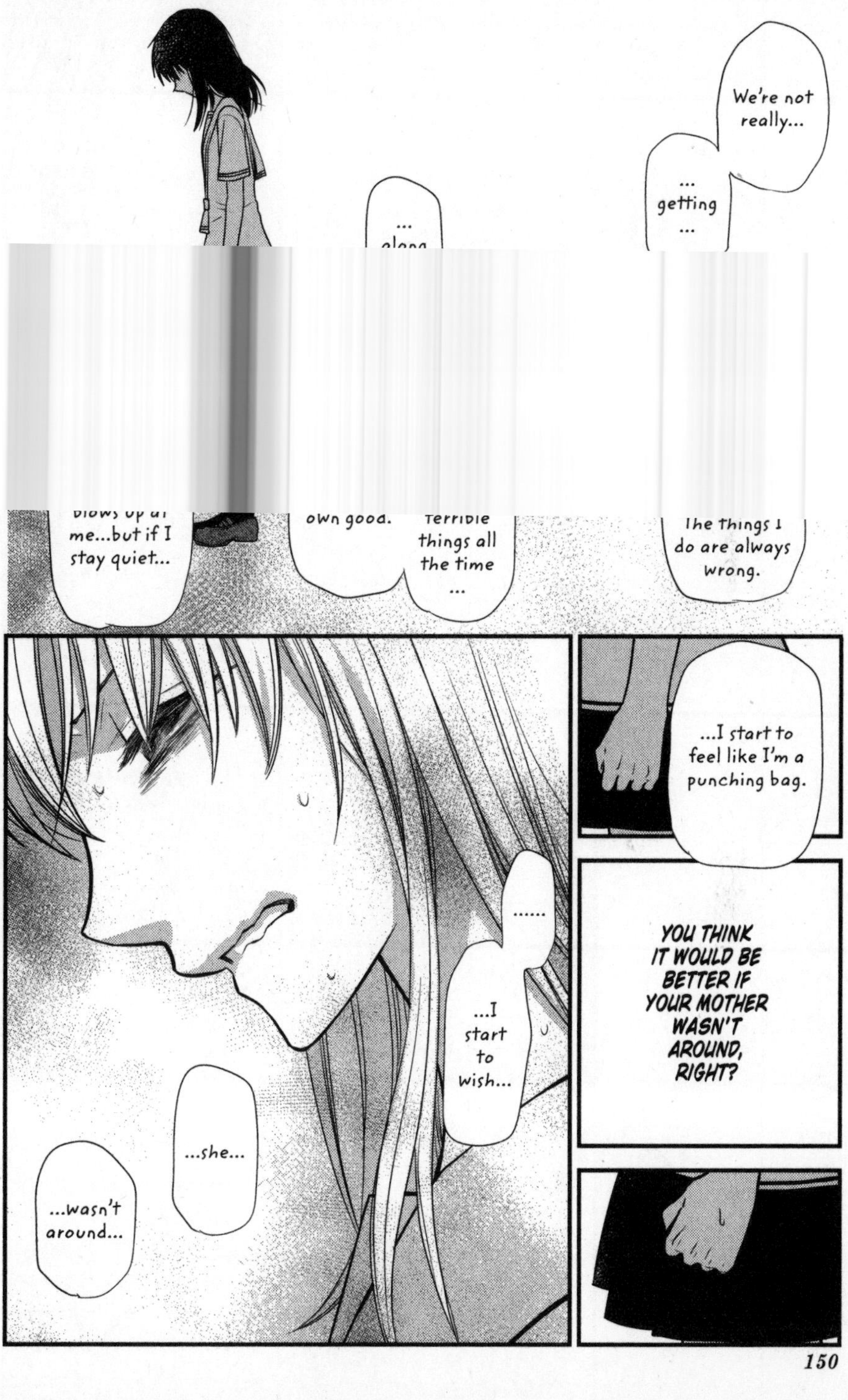
We're not really...
...getting...
do are always wrong.
things all the time ...
own good.
me...but if I stay quiet...
...I start to feel like I'm a punching bag.
YOU THINK IT WOULD BE BETTER IF YOUR MOTHER WASN'T AROUND, RIGHT?
......
...I start to wish...
...she...
...wasn't around...

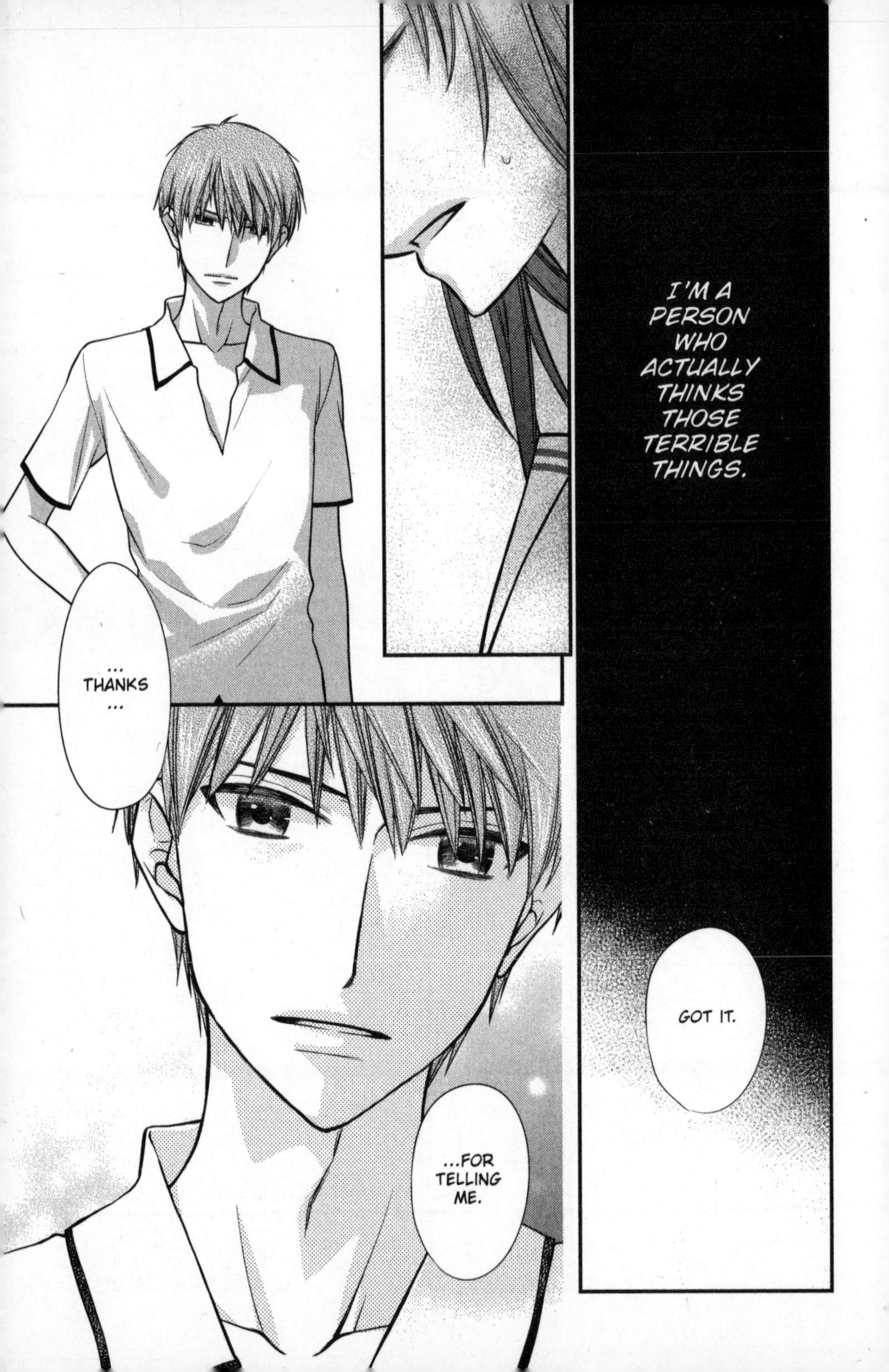
I'M A PERSON WHO ACTUALLY THINKS THOSE TERRIBLE THINGS.
GOT IT.
...THANKS...
...FOR TELLING ME.

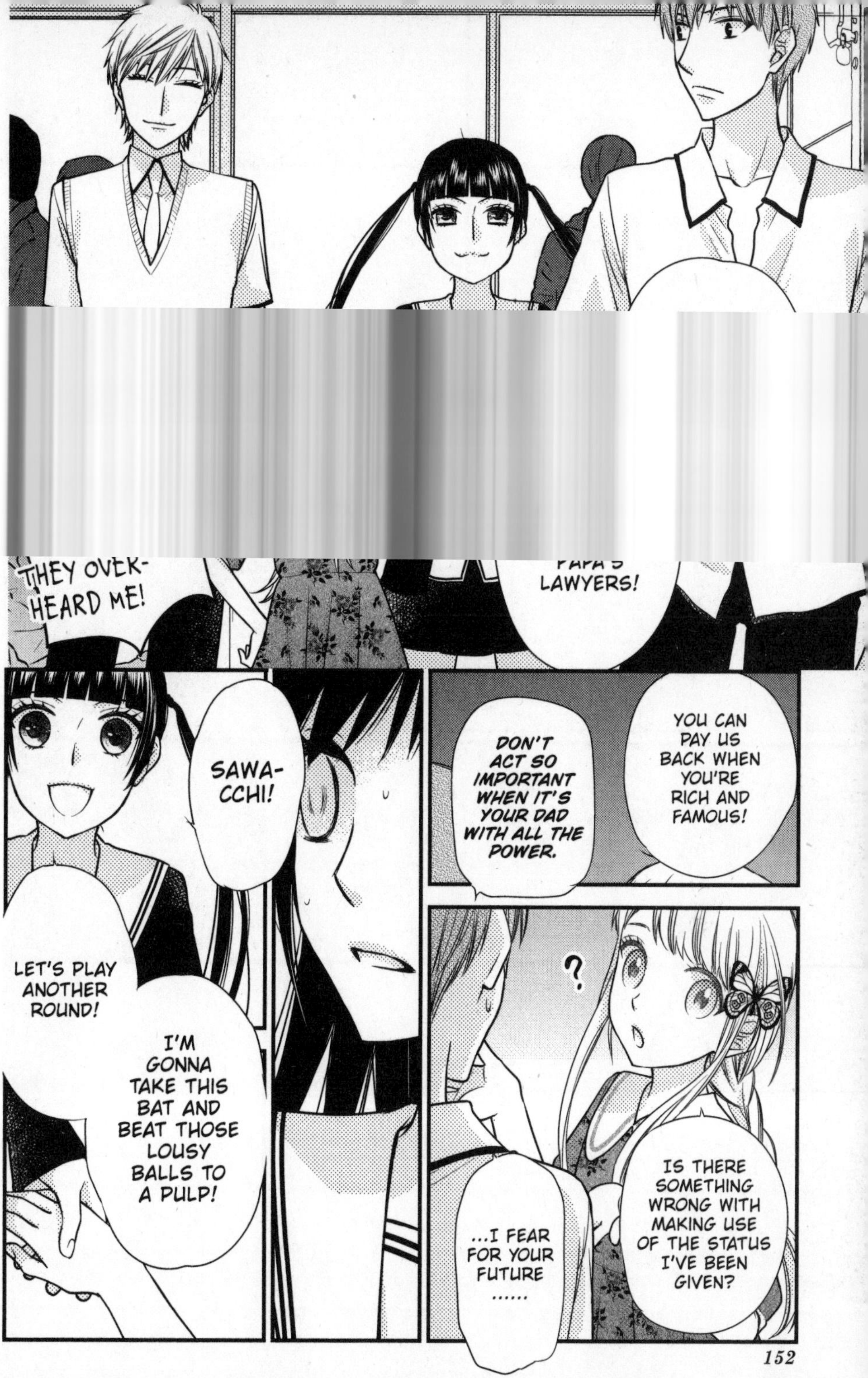
PAPA'S LAWYERS!
THEY OVER-HEARD ME!
YOU CAN PAY US BACK WHEN YOU'RE RICH AND FAMOUS!
DON'T ACT SO IMPORTANT WHEN IT'S YOUR DAD WITH ALL THE POWER.
?
IS THERE SOMETHING WRONG WITH MAKING USE OF THE STATUS I'VE BEEN GIVEN?
...I FEAR FOR YOUR FUTURE ......
SAWA-CCHI!
LET'S PLAY ANOTHER ROUND!
I'M GONNA TAKE THIS BAT AND BEAT THOSE LOUSY BALLS TO A PULP!

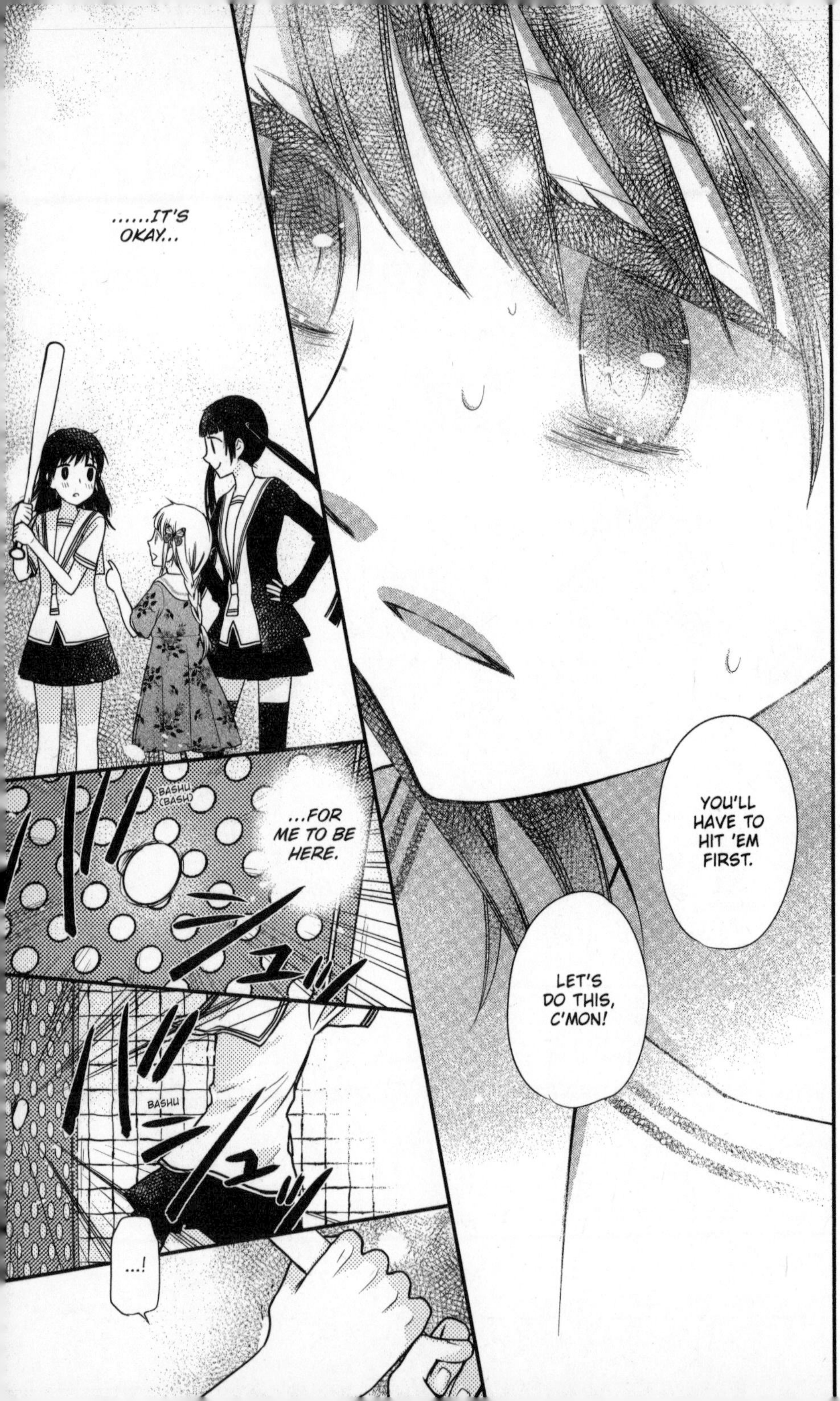
YOU'LL HAVE TO HIT 'EM FIRST.
LET'S DO THIS, C'MON!
......IT'S OKAY...
BASHU (BASH)
...FOR ME TO BE HERE.
BASHU
...!

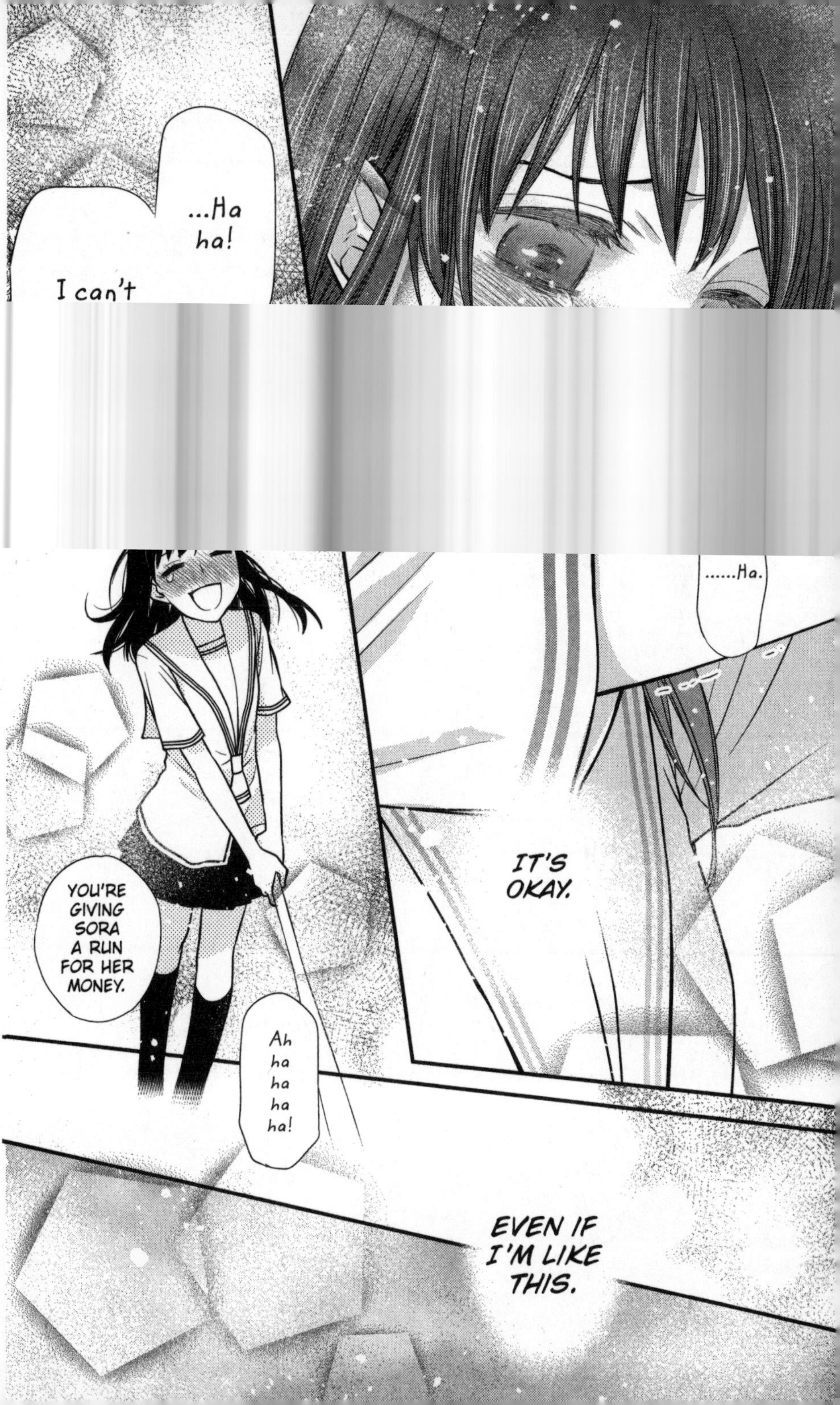
...Ha ha!
I can't
......Ha.
IT'S OKAY.
YOU'RE GIVING SORA A RUN FOR HER MONEY.
Ah ha ha ha ha!
EVEN IF I'M LIKE THIS.

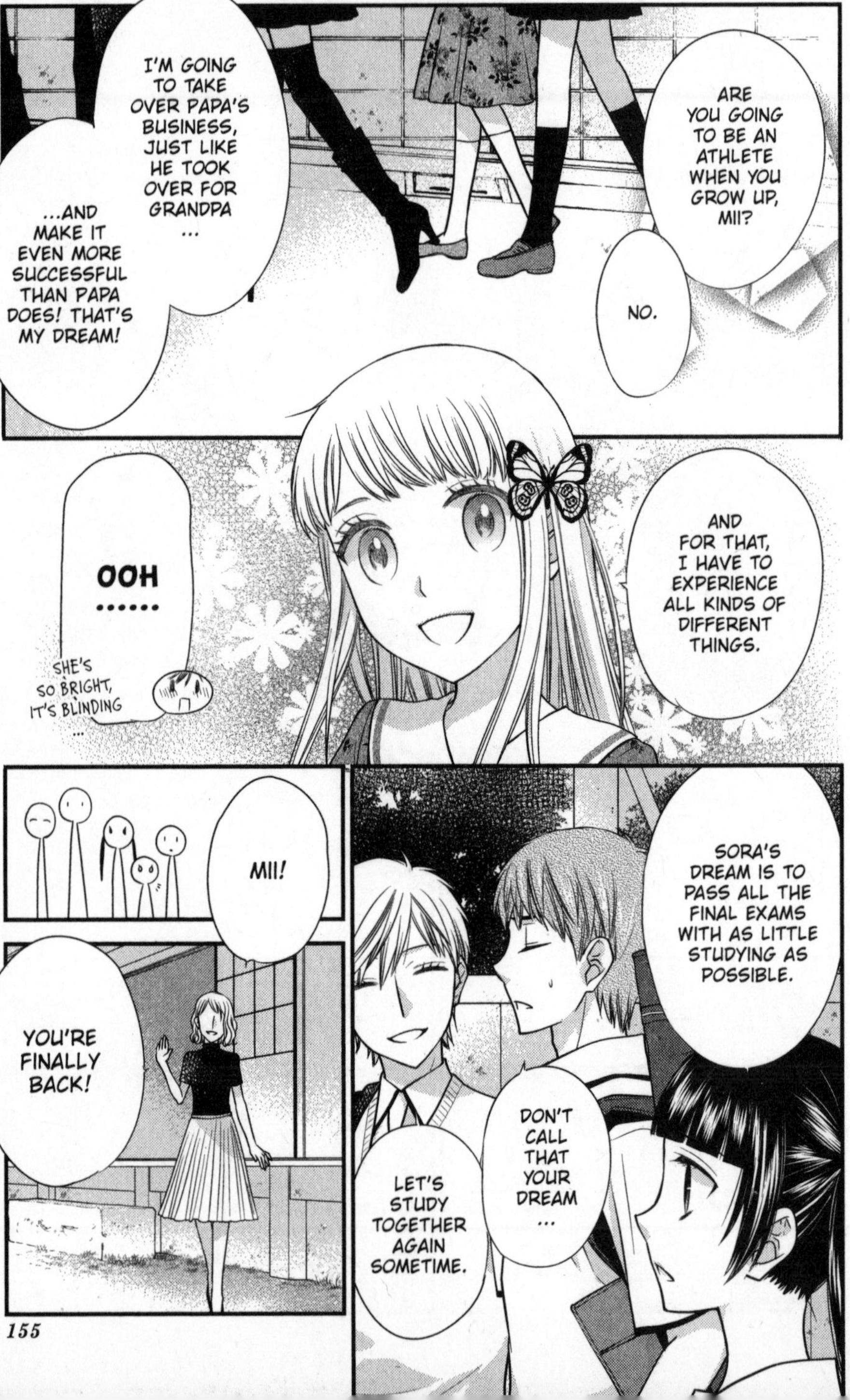
ARE YOU GOING TO BE AN ATHLETE WHEN YOU GROW UP, MII?
NO.
I'M GOING TO TAKE OVER PAPA'S BUSINESS, JUST LIKE HE TOOK OVER FOR GRANDPA...
...AND MAKE IT EVEN MORE SUCCESSFUL THAN PAPA DOES! THAT'S MY DREAM!
AND FOR THAT, I HAVE TO EXPERIENCE ALL KINDS OF DIFFERENT THINGS.
OOH......
SHE'S SO BRIGHT, IT'S BLINDING...
SORA'S DREAM IS TO PASS ALL THE FINAL EXAMS WITH AS LITTLE STUDYING AS POSSIBLE.
DON'T CALL THAT YOUR DREAM...
LET'S STUDY TOGETHER AGAIN SOMETIME.
MII!
YOU'RE FINALLY BACK!

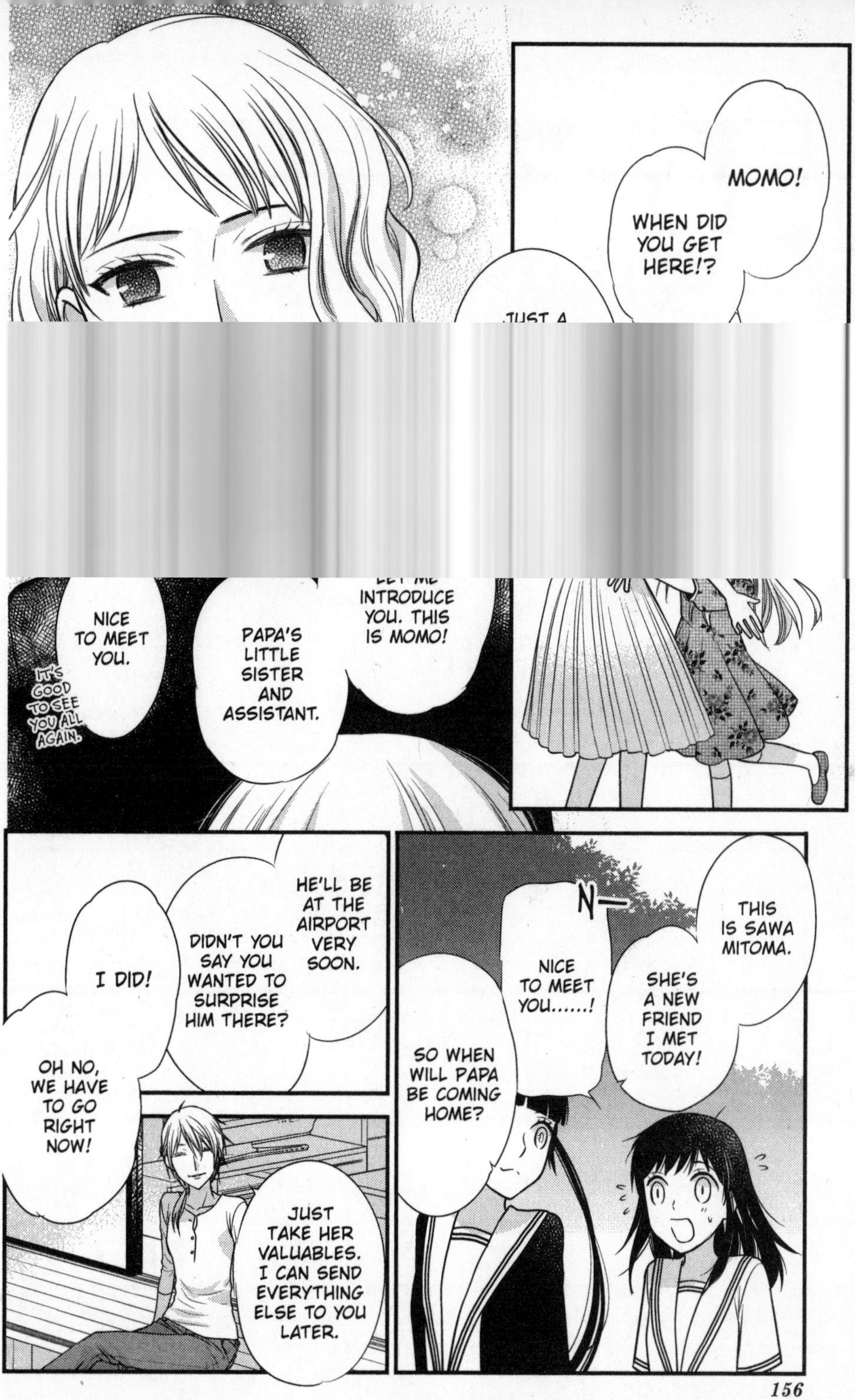
MOMO!
WHEN DID YOU GET HERE!?
INTRODUCE YOU. THIS IS MOMO!
PAPA'S LITTLE SISTER AND ASSISTANT.
NICE TO MEET YOU.
IT'S GOOD TO SEE YOU ALL AGAIN.
THIS IS SAWA MITOMA.
SHE'S A NEW FRIEND I MET TODAY!
N—
NICE TO MEET YOU......!
SO WHEN WILL PAPA BE COMING HOME?
HE'LL BE AT THE AIRPORT VERY SOON.
DIDN'T YOU SAY YOU WANTED TO SURPRISE HIM THERE?
I DID!
OH NO, WE HAVE TO GO RIGHT NOW!
JUST TAKE HER VALUABLES. I CAN SEND EVERYTHING ELSE TO YOU LATER.

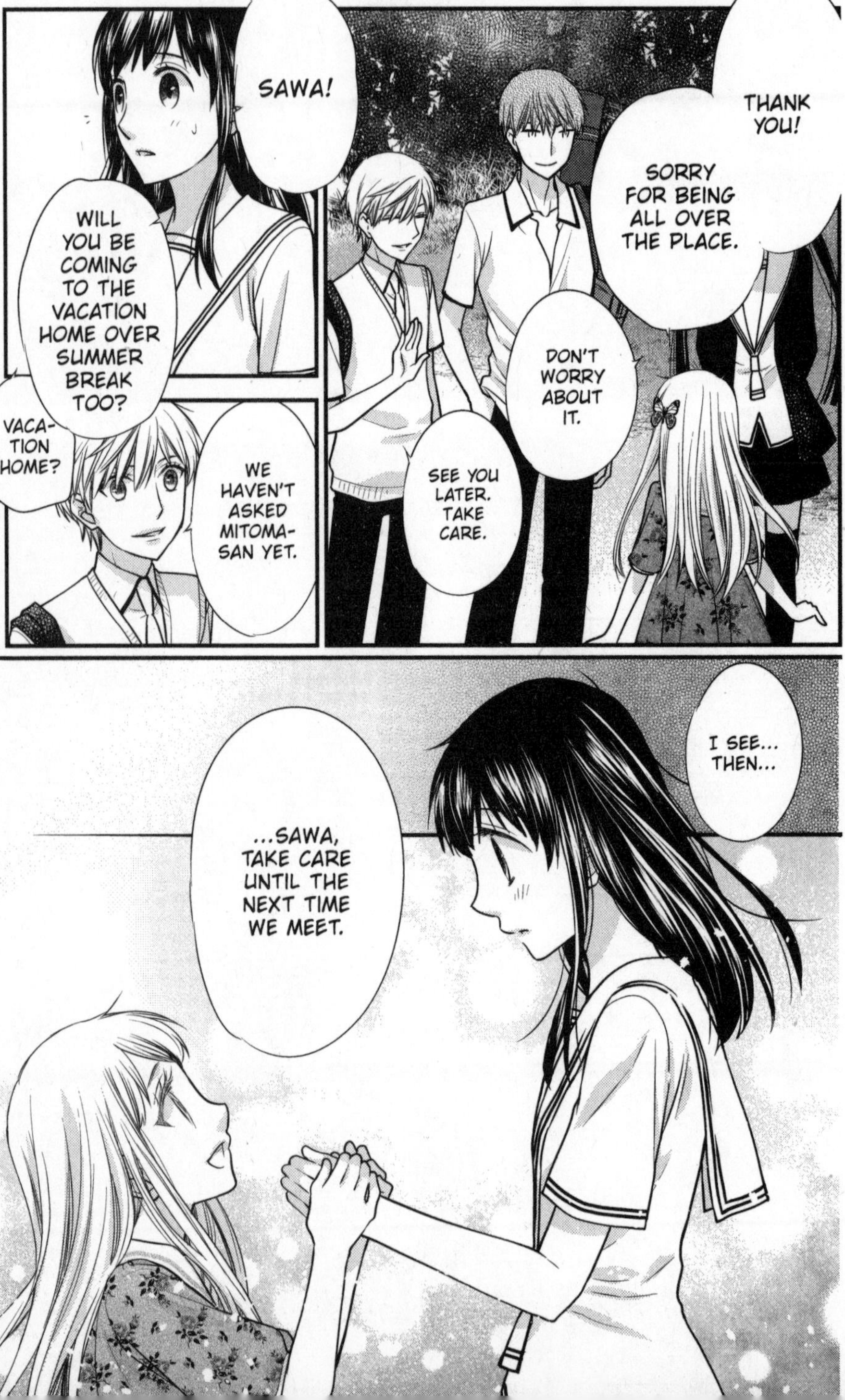
THANK YOU!
SORRY FOR BEING ALL OVER THE PLACE.
DON'T WORRY ABOUT IT.
SEE YOU LATER. TAKE CARE.
SAWA!
WILL YOU BE COMING TO THE VACATION HOME OVER SUMMER BREAK TOO?
VACA-TION HOME?
WE HAVEN'T ASKED MITOMA-SAN YET.
I SEE... THEN...
...SAWA, TAKE CARE UNTIL THE NEXT TIME WE MEET.

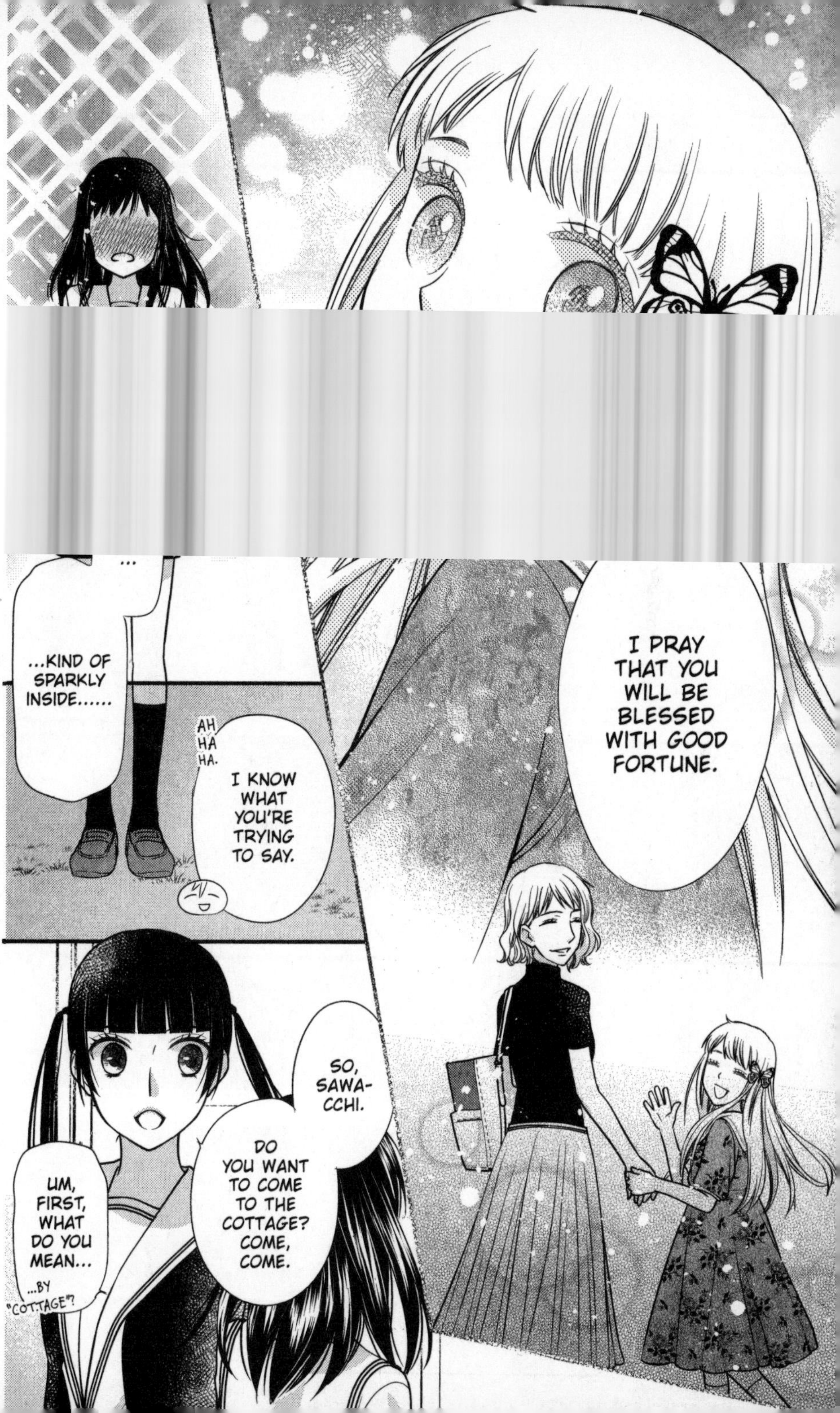
I PRAY THAT YOU WILL BE BLESSED WITH GOOD FORTUNE.
...
...KIND OF SPARKLY INSIDE......
AH HA HA.
I KNOW WHAT YOU'RE TRYING TO SAY.
SO, SAWACCHI.
DO YOU WANT TO COME TO THE COTTAGE? COME, COME.
UM, FIRST, WHAT DO YOU MEAN...
...BY "COTTAGE"?

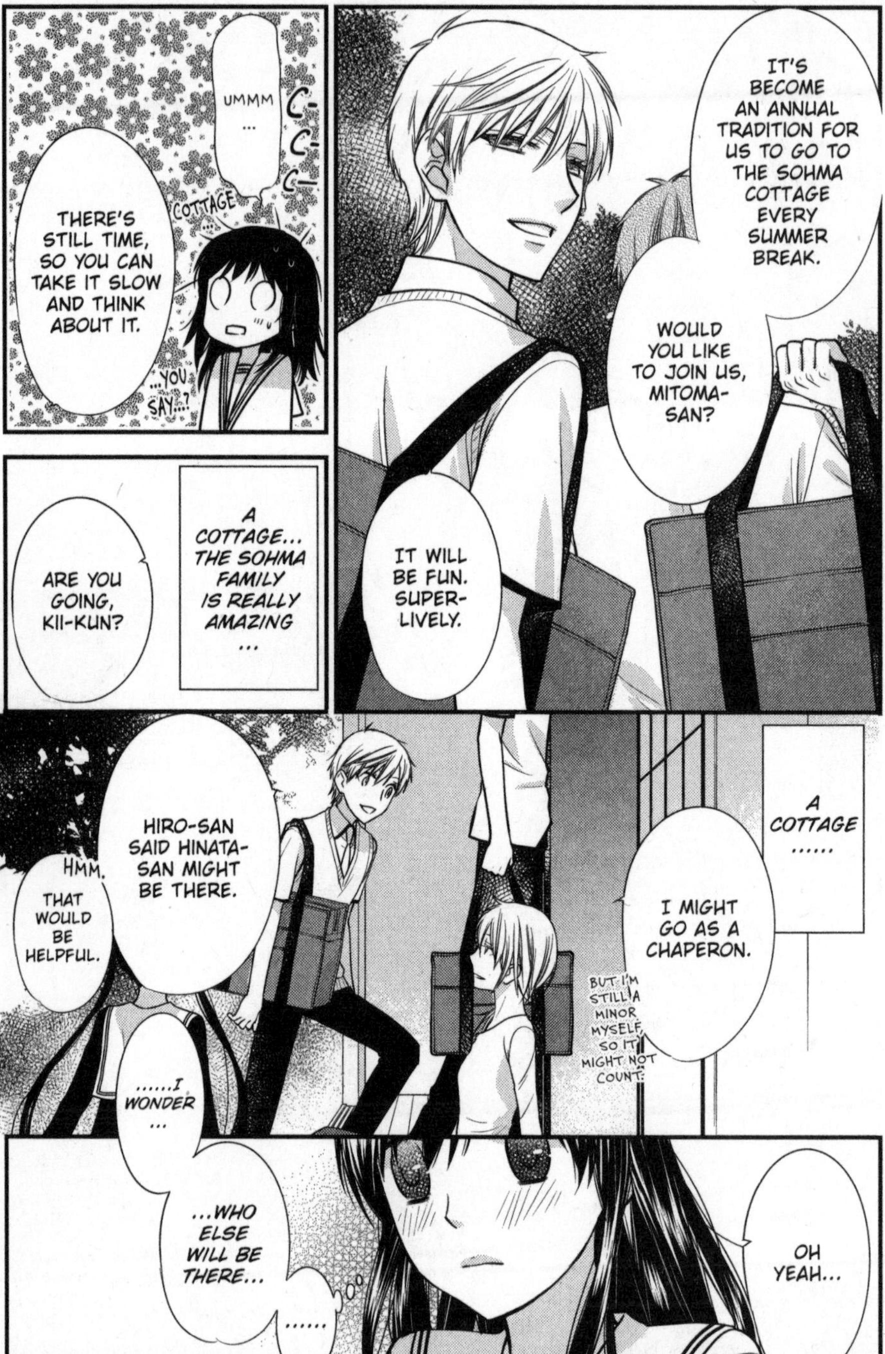
IT'S BECOME AN ANNUAL TRADITION FOR US TO GO TO THE SOHMA COTTAGE EVERY SUMMER BREAK.
WOULD YOU LIKE TO JOIN US, MITOMA-SAN?
IT WILL BE FUN. SUPER-LIVELY.
UMMM ...
C- C- C-
COTTAGE ...
...YOU SAY...?
THERE'S STILL TIME, SO YOU CAN TAKE IT SLOW AND THINK ABOUT IT.
A COTTAGE... THE SOHMA FAMILY IS REALLY AMAZING ...
ARE YOU GOING, KII-KUN?
A COTTAGE ......
I MIGHT GO AS A CHAPERON.
BUT I'M STILL A MINOR MYSELF, SO IT MIGHT NOT COUNT.
HIRO-SAN SAID HINATA-SAN MIGHT BE THERE.
HMM.
THAT WOULD BE HELPFUL.
......I WONDER ...
OH YEAH...
...WHO ELSE WILL BE THERE...
......

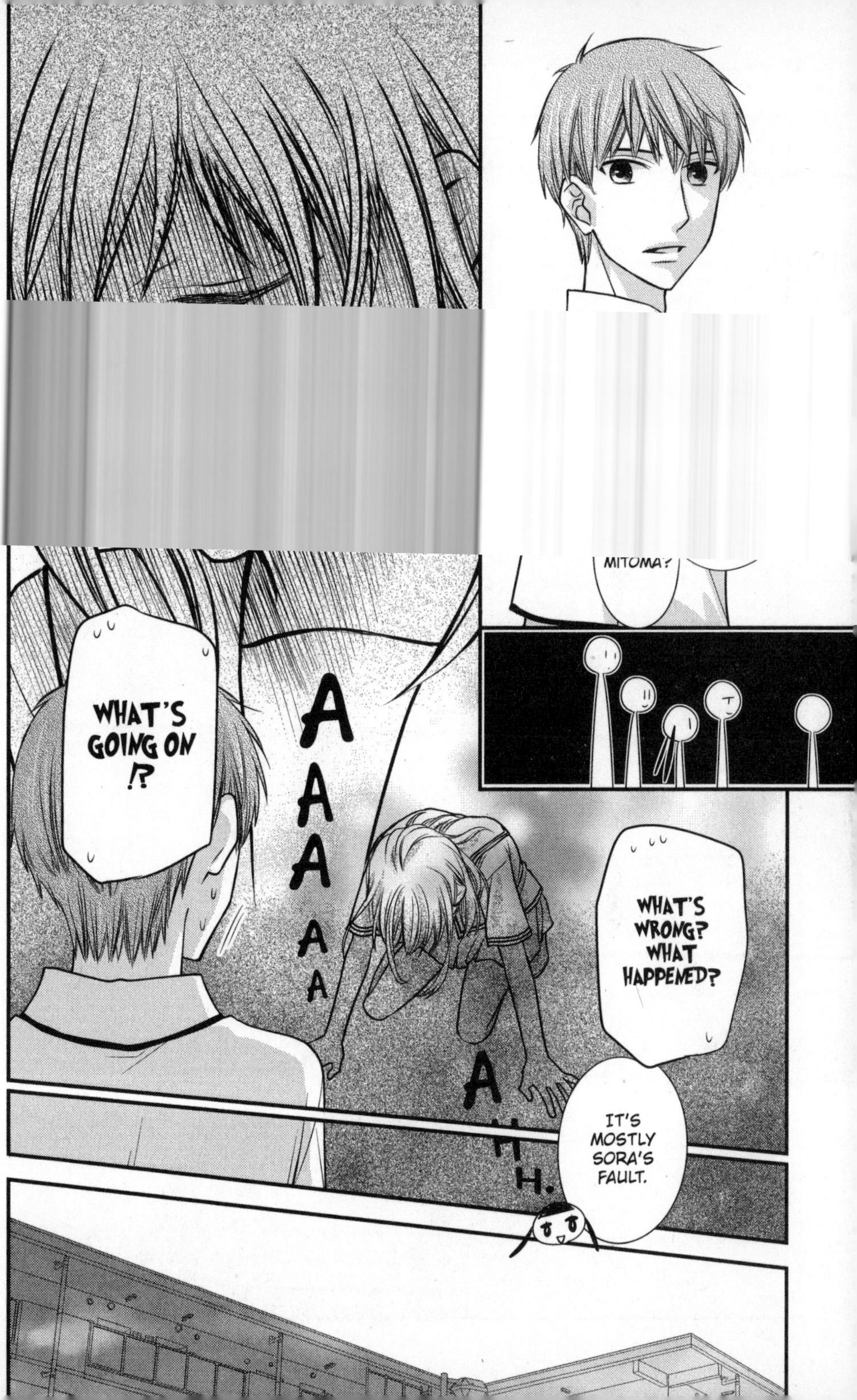
MITOMA?
WHAT'S WRONG? WHAT HAPPENED?
WHAT'S GOING ON !?
AAAAAAAAHH.
IT'S MOSTLY SORA'S FAULT.

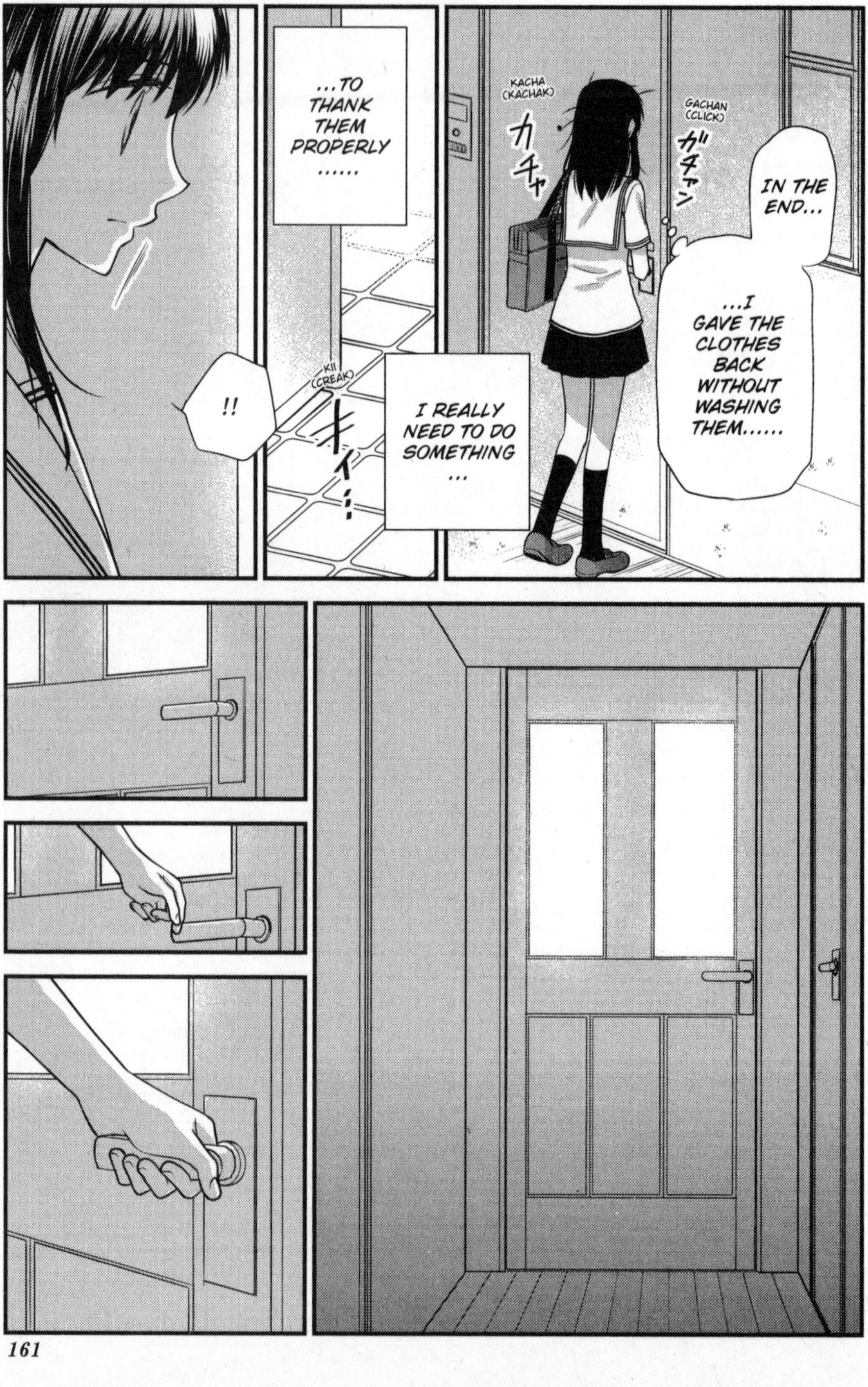
GACHAN (CLICK)
ガチャン
KACHA (KACHAK)
カチャ
IN THE END...
...I GAVE THE CLOTHES BACK WITHOUT WASHING THEM......
...TO THANK THEM PROPERLY ......
I REALLY NEED TO DO SOMETHING ...
KII (CREAK)
!!

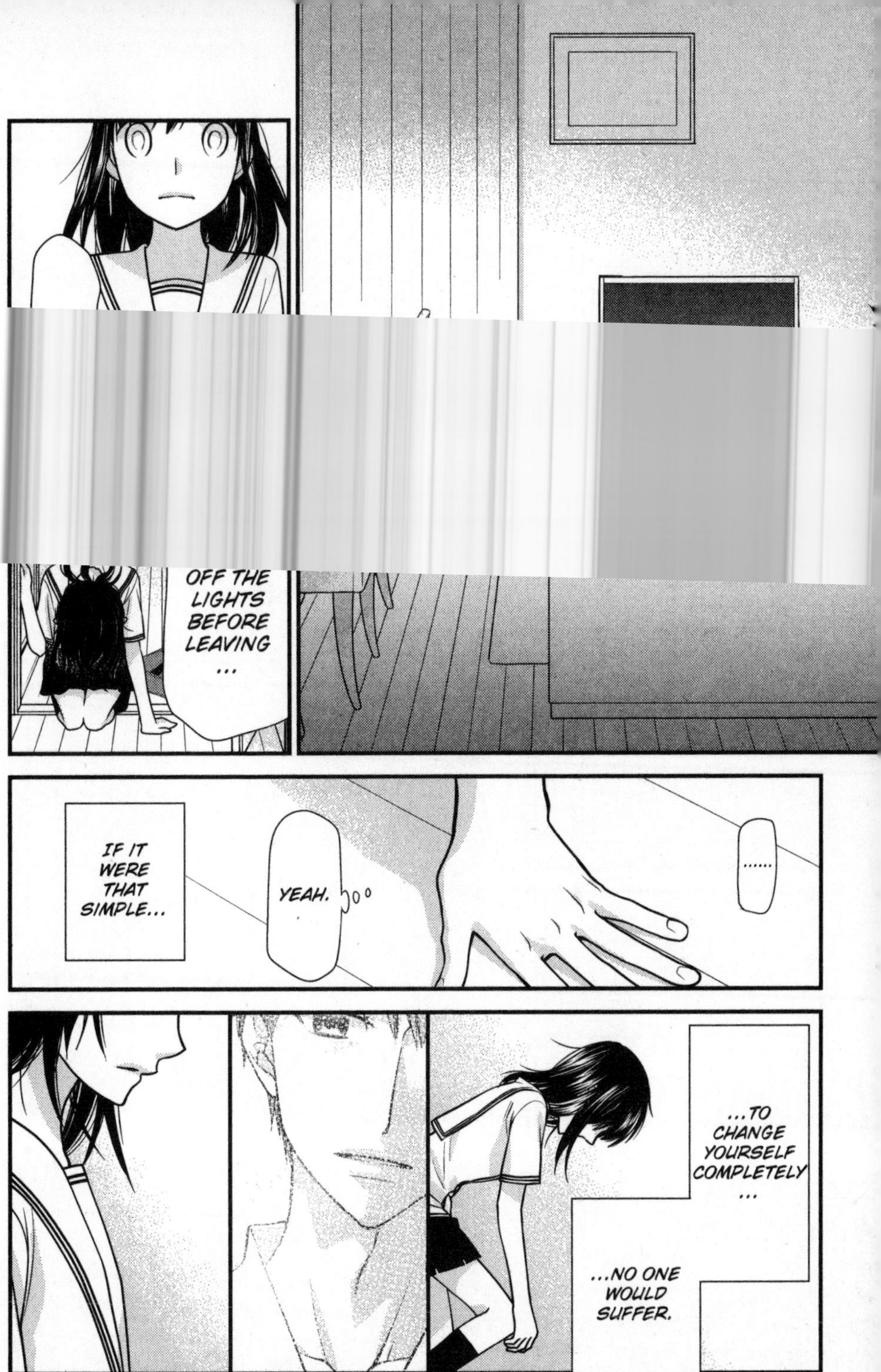
OFF THE LIGHTS BEFORE LEAVING ...
......
YEAH.
IF IT WERE THAT SIMPLE...
...TO CHANGE YOURSELF COMPLETELY ...
...NO ONE WOULD SUFFER.

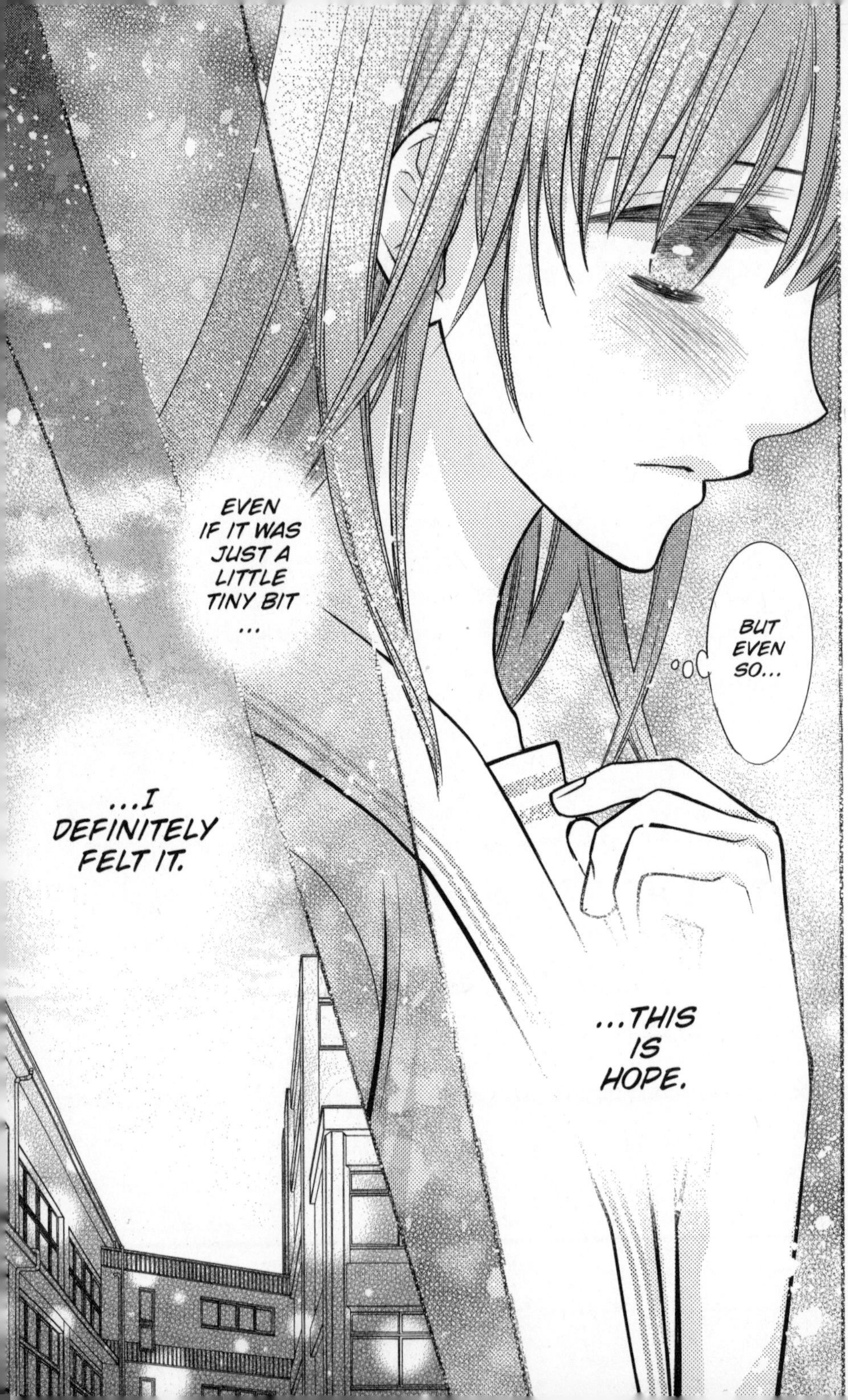
BUT EVEN SO...
EVEN IF IT WAS JUST A LITTLE TINY BIT ...
...I DEFINITELY FELT IT.
...THIS IS HOPE.

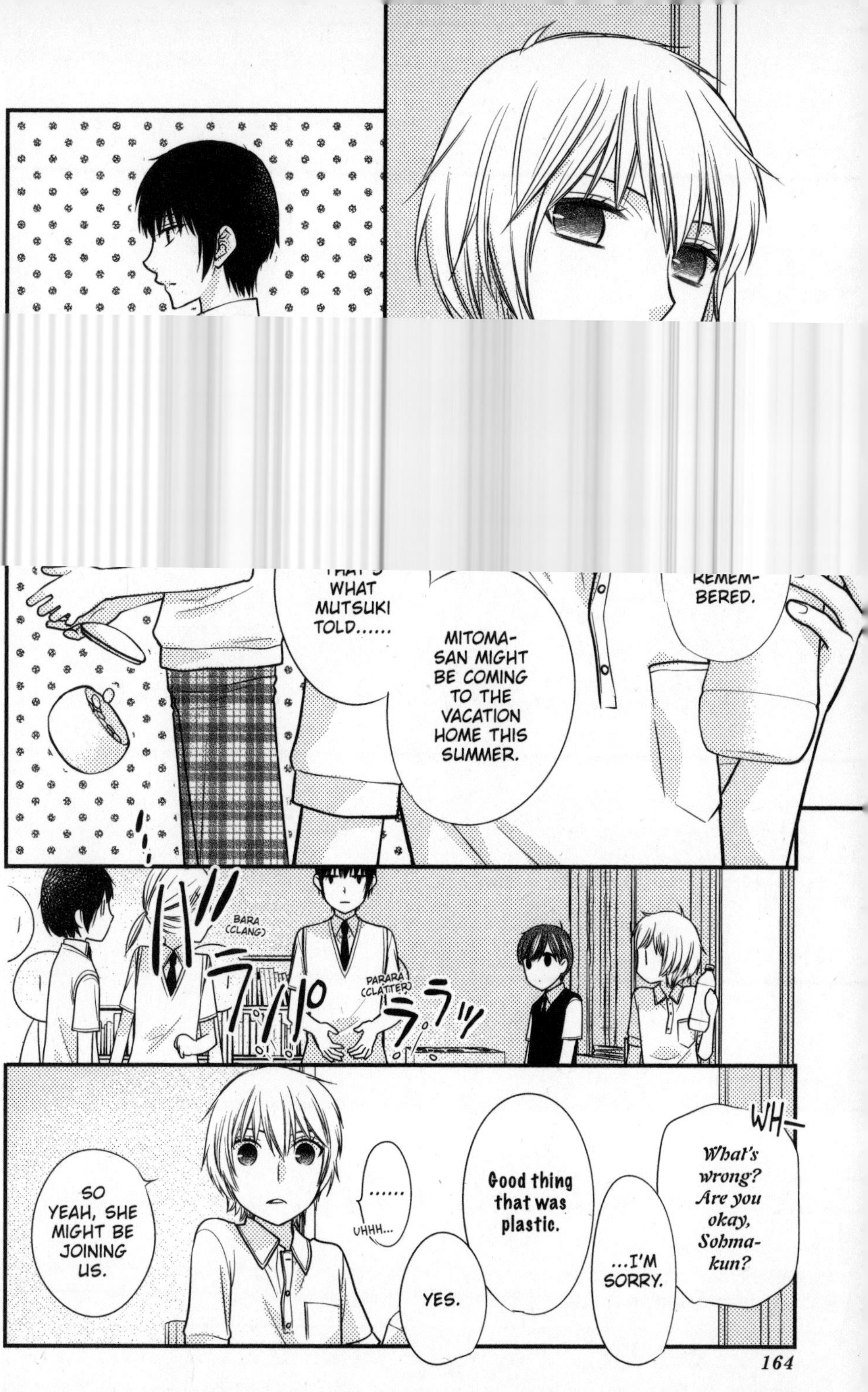
REMEM-BERED.
WHAT MUTSUKI TOLD......
MITOMA-SAN MIGHT BE COMING TO THE VACATION HOME THIS SUMMER.
BARA (CLANG)
PARARA (CLATTER)
WH–
What's wrong? Are you okay, Sohma-kun?
...I'M SORRY.
Good thing that was plastic.
YES.
......
UHHH...
SO YEAH, SHE MIGHT BE JOINING US.

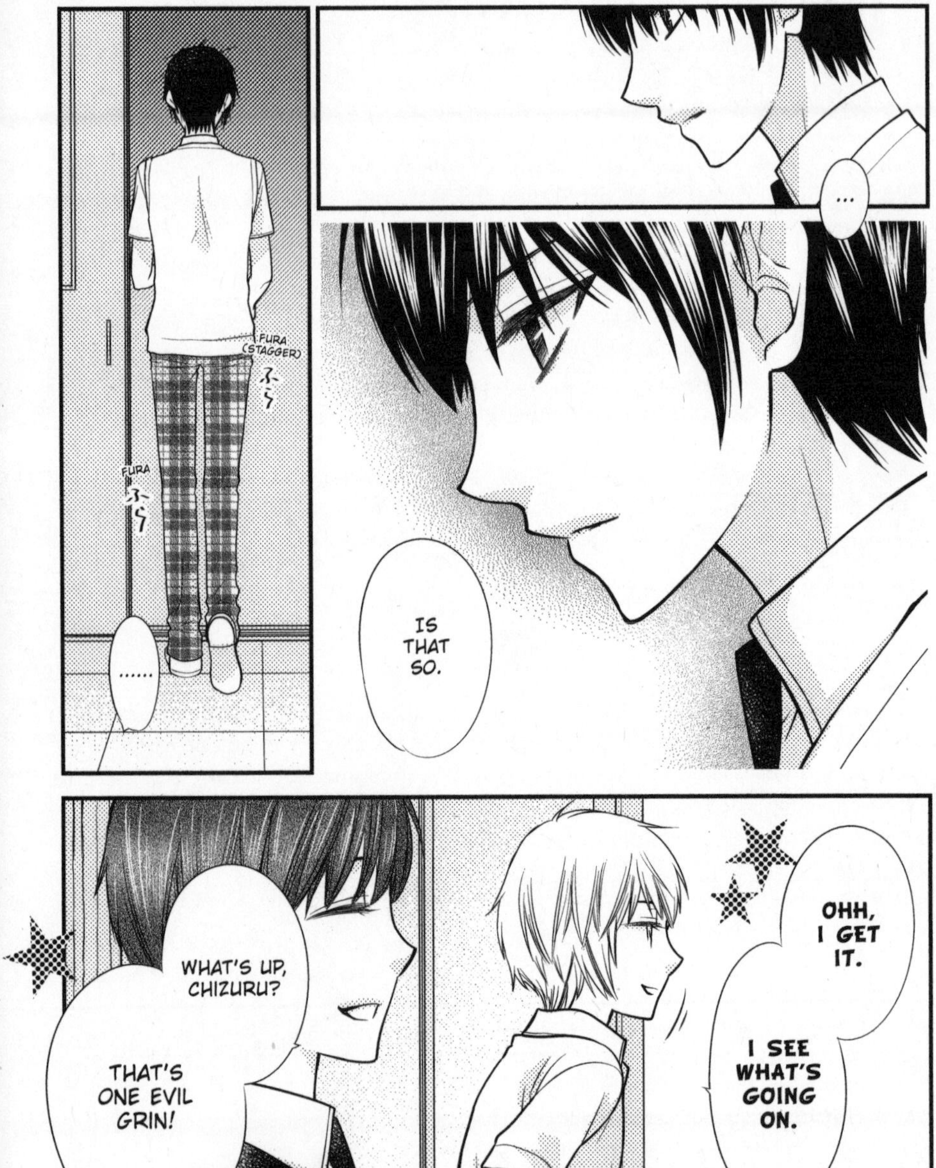
...
IS THAT SO.
FURA (STAGGER) ふら
FURA ふら
......
OHH, I GET IT.
I SEE WHAT'S GOING ON.
WHAT'S UP, CHIZURU?
THAT'S ONE EVIL GRIN!

TRANSLATION NOTES

COMMON HONORIFICS

no honorific: Indicates familiarity or closeness; if used without permission or reason, addressing someone in this manner would constitute an insult.

-san: The Japanese equivalent of Mr./Mrs./Miss. If a situation calls for politeness, this is the fail-safe honorific.

[illegible]

-kouhai: A suffix used to address underclassmen or less experienced coworkers.

-sensei: A respectful term for teachers, artists, or high-level professionals.

Page 111

Go: Go is a strategy board game that is similar to Othello but not quite the same. Two players take turns placing stones of their color (black or white) on the board, with the goal of accumulating the most territory and surrounding as many of their opponent's stones as they can.

Page 159

Still a minor: In Japan, the age of adulthood is twenty, so although Kinu is a college student, she's still legally a minor.

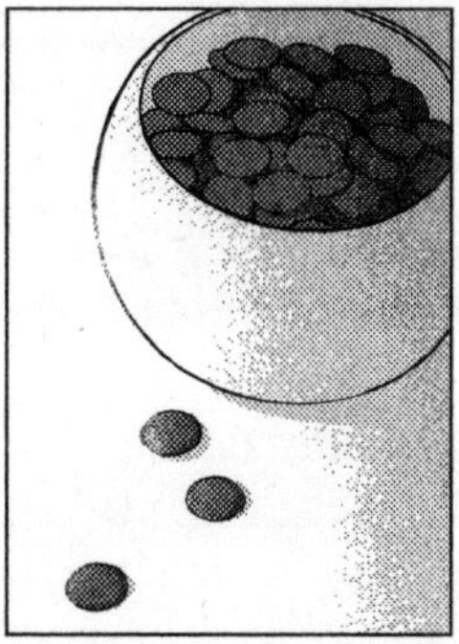

Page 181

Bon Festival: A festival usually held in August. It is believed that the spirit world is closer to the world of the living and that ancestors come to visit their families during this festival. That being the case, it is usually a time for families to come together.

Page 182

Jason the bear: A character originally based on a fictional character by the same name from an American horror series, *Friday the 13th*. In *Fruits Basket*, Shigure pretends Jason is actually a dangerous breed of bear to scare Yuki, Kyo, and Tohru.

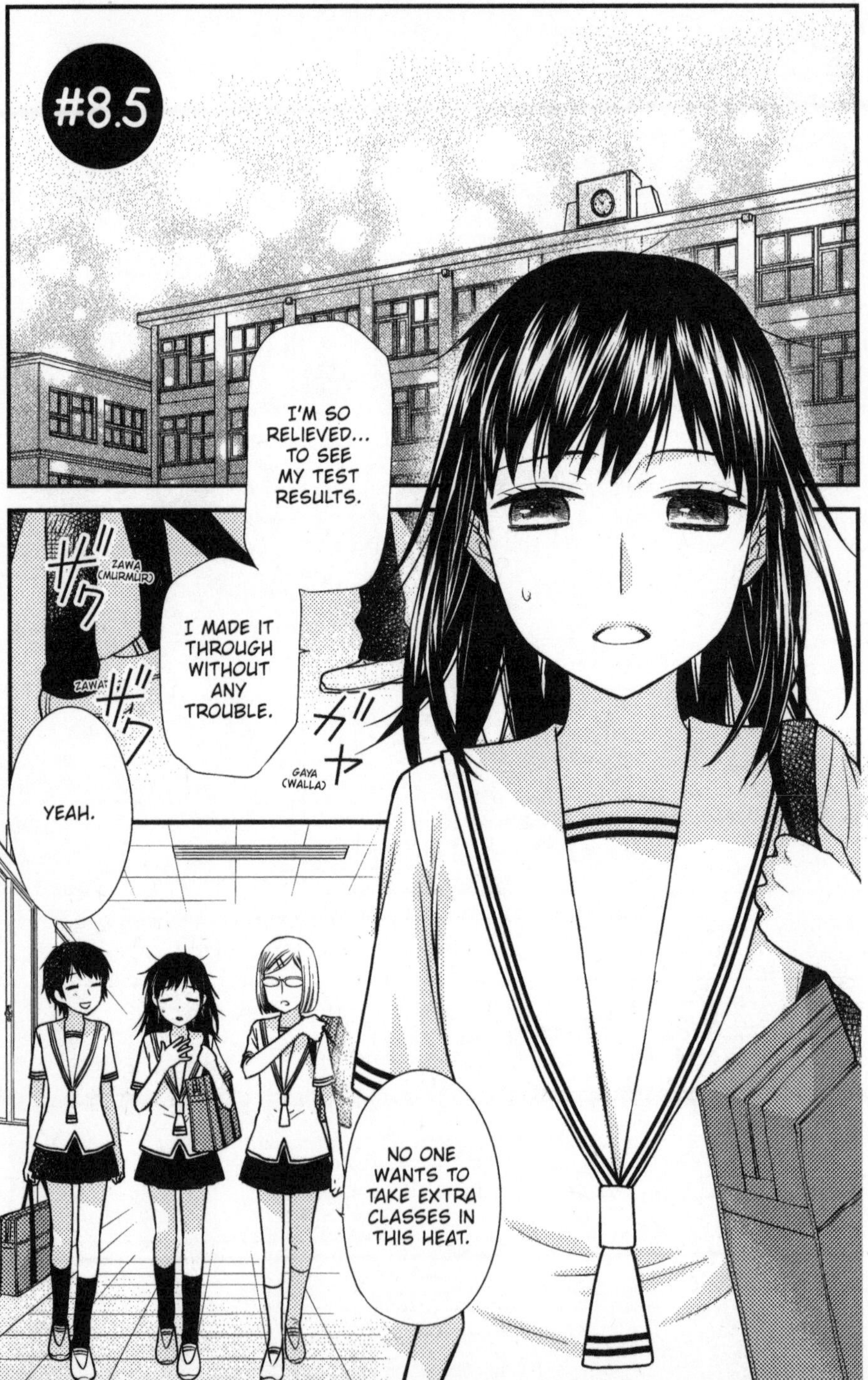
#8.5
I'M SO RELIEVED... TO SEE MY TEST RESULTS.
GAYA (WALLA)
I MADE IT THROUGH WITHOUT ANY TROUBLE.
ZAWA (MURMUR)
ZAWA
NO ONE WANTS TO TAKE EXTRA CLASSES IN THIS HEAT.
YEAH.

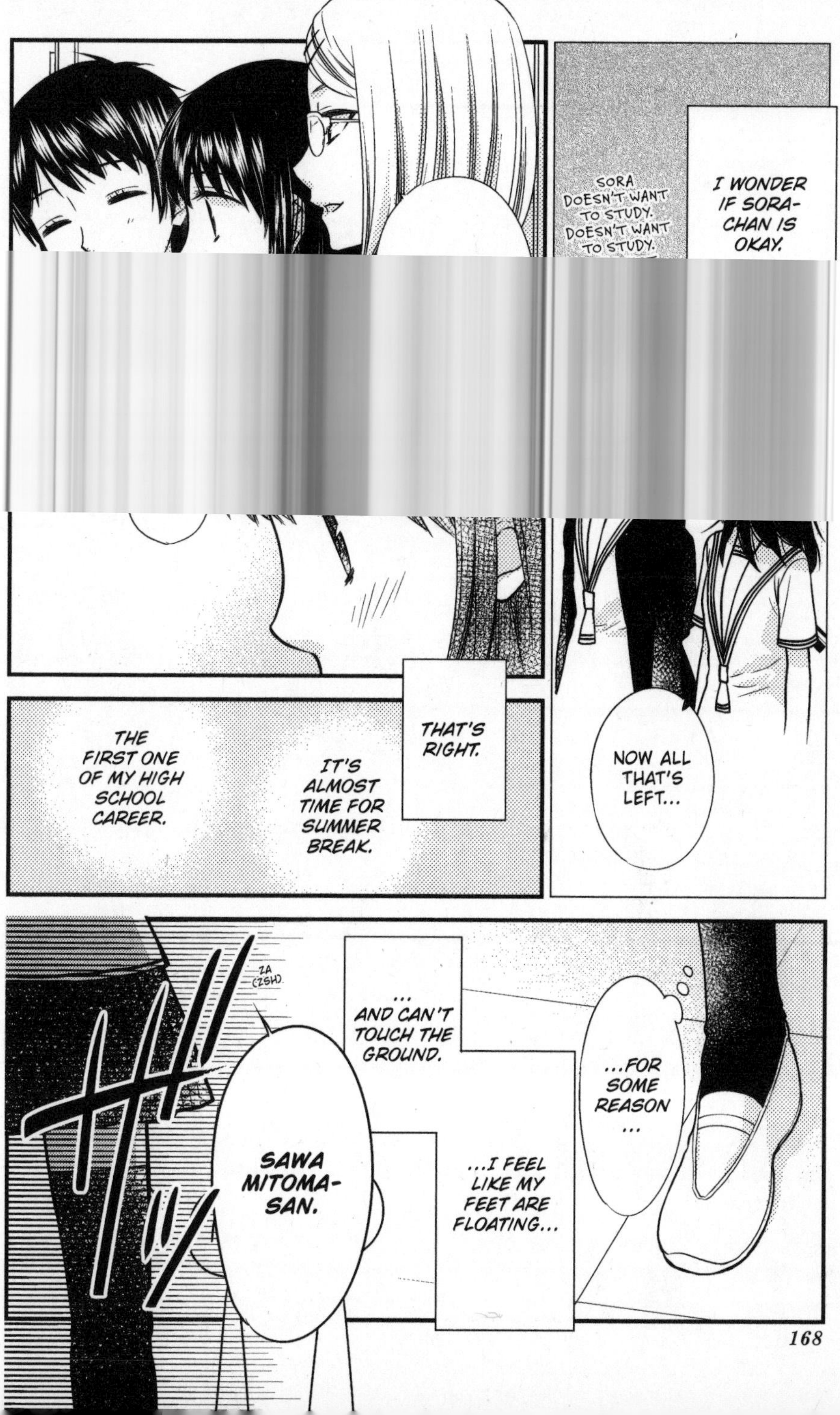
I WONDER IF SORA-CHAN IS OKAY.
SORA DOESN'T WANT TO STUDY. DOESN'T WANT TO STUDY.
NOW ALL THAT'S LEFT...
THAT'S RIGHT.
IT'S ALMOST TIME FOR SUMMER BREAK.
THE FIRST ONE OF MY HIGH SCHOOL CAREER.
...FOR SOME REASON...
...I FEEL LIKE MY FEET ARE FLOATING...
...AND CAN'T TOUCH THE GROUND.
ZA (ZSH)
SAWA MITOMA-SAN.

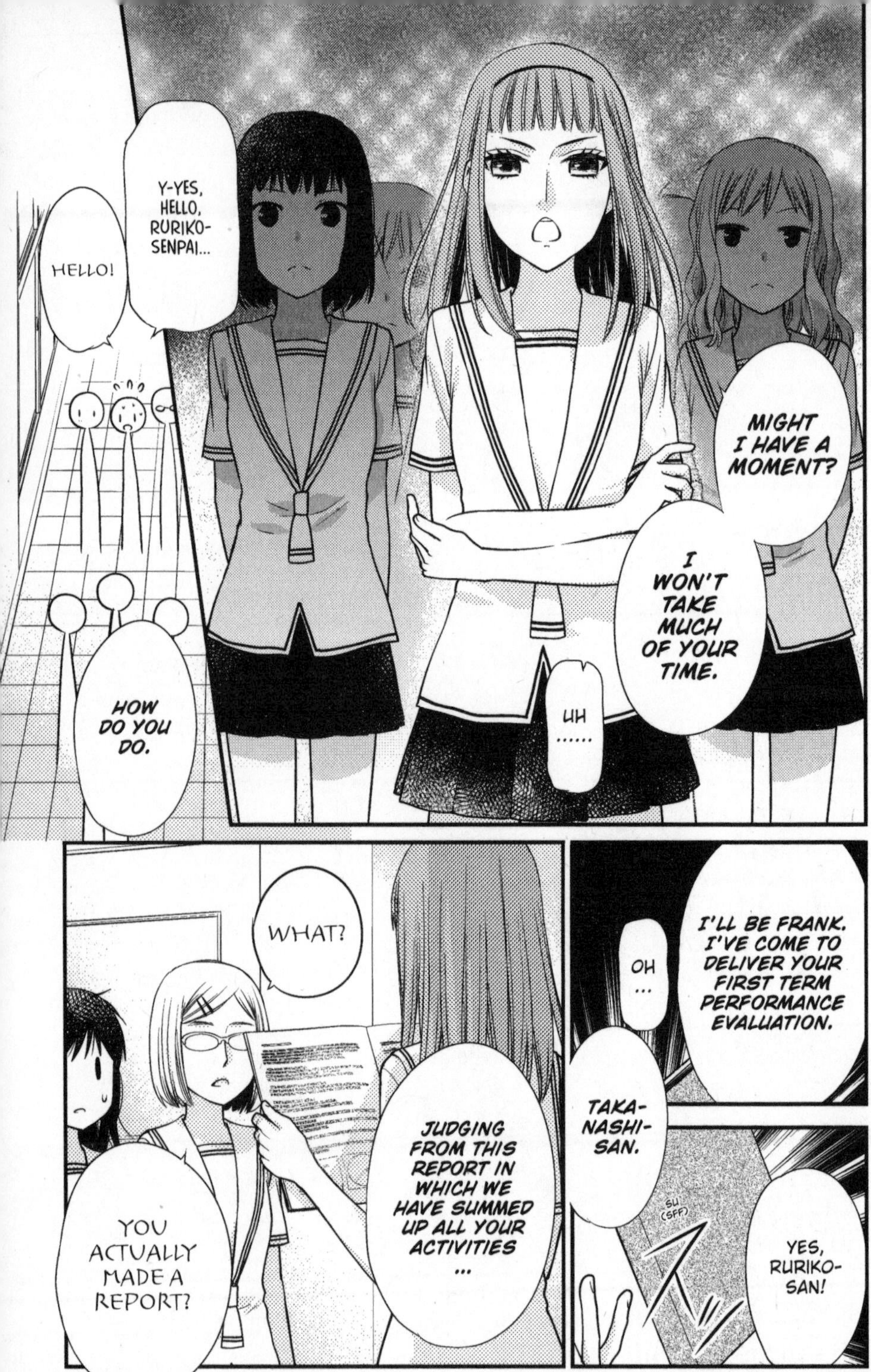
MIGHT I HAVE A MOMENT?
I WON'T TAKE MUCH OF YOUR TIME.
UH ......
Y-YES, HELLO, RURIKO-SENPAI...
HELLO!
HOW DO YOU DO.
I'LL BE FRANK. I'VE COME TO DELIVER YOUR FIRST TERM PERFORMANCE EVALUATION.
TAKA-NASHI-SAN.
OH ...
SU (SFF)
YES, RURIKO-SAN!
JUDGING FROM THIS REPORT IN WHICH WE HAVE SUMMED UP ALL YOUR ACTIVITIES ...
WHAT?
YOU ACTUALLY MADE A REPORT?

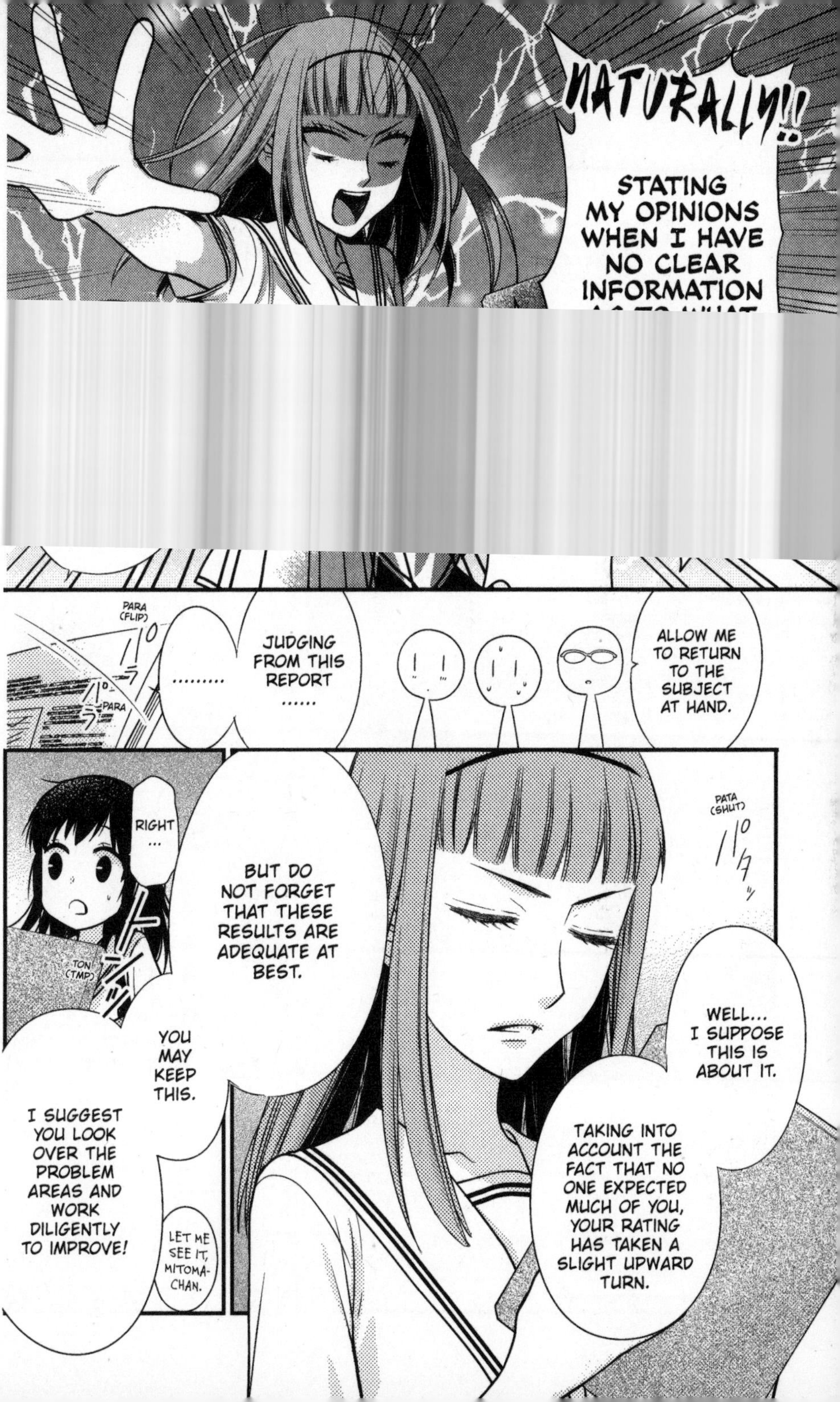
NATURALLY!!
STATING MY OPINIONS WHEN I HAVE NO CLEAR INFORMATION
ALLOW ME TO RETURN TO THE SUBJECT AT HAND.
JUDGING FROM THIS REPORT ......
....
PARA (FLIP)
PARA
PATA (SHUT)
WELL... I SUPPOSE THIS IS ABOUT IT.
TAKING INTO ACCOUNT THE FACT THAT NO ONE EXPECTED MUCH OF YOU, YOUR RATING HAS TAKEN A SLIGHT UPWARD TURN.
BUT DO NOT FORGET THAT THESE RESULTS ARE ADEQUATE AT BEST.
YOU MAY KEEP THIS.
I SUGGEST YOU LOOK OVER THE PROBLEM AREAS AND WORK DILIGENTLY TO IMPROVE!
RIGHT ...
TON (TMP)
LET ME SEE IT, MITOMA-CHAN.

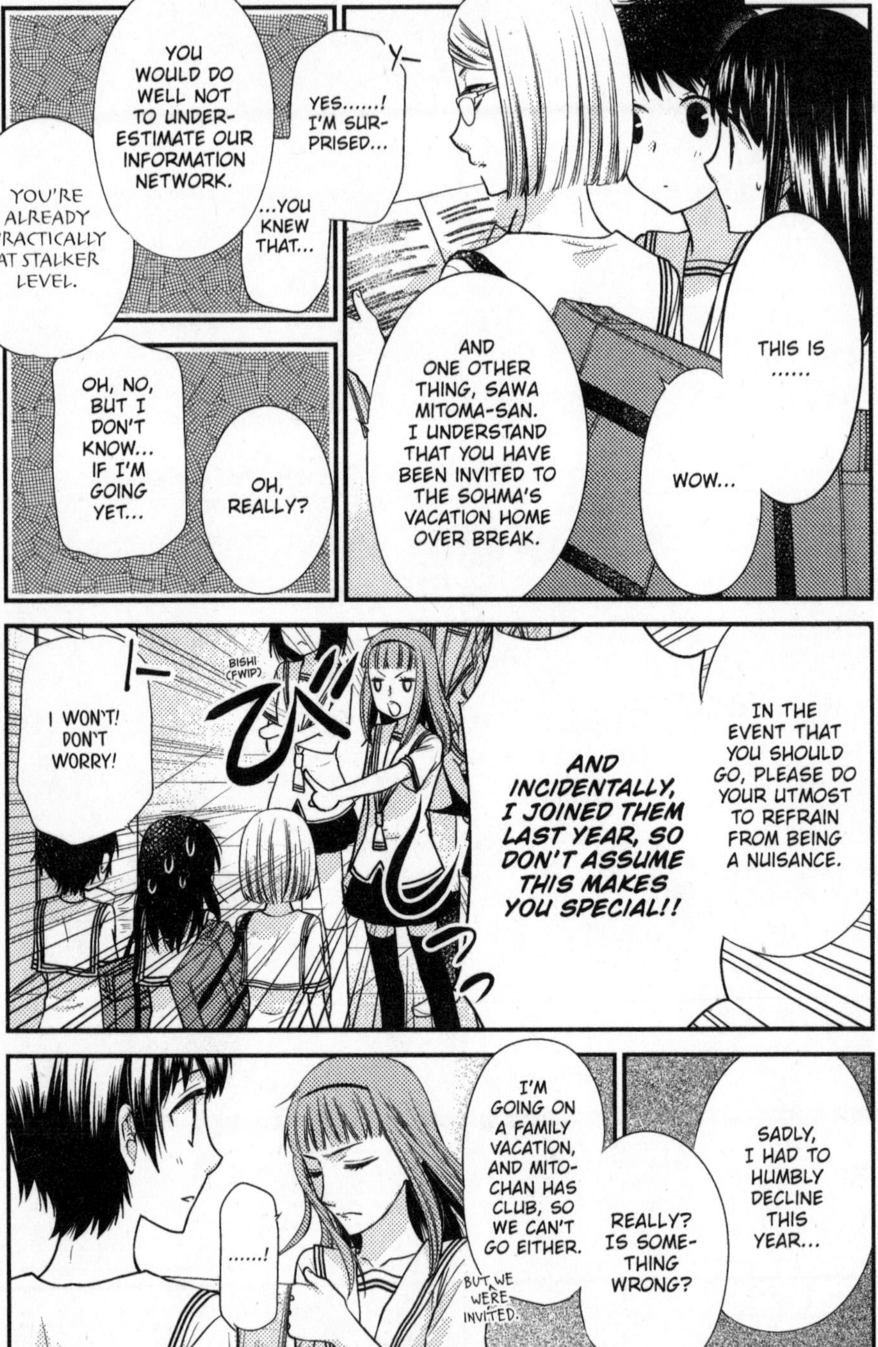
THIS IS ......
WOW...
AND ONE OTHER THING, SAWA MITOMA-SAN. I UNDERSTAND THAT YOU HAVE BEEN INVITED TO THE SOHMA'S VACATION HOME OVER BREAK.
Y—
YES......! I'M SURPRISED...
...YOU KNEW THAT...
YOU WOULD DO WELL NOT TO UNDERESTIMATE OUR INFORMATION NETWORK.
YOU'RE ALREADY PRACTICALLY AT STALKER LEVEL.
OH, REALLY?
OH, NO, BUT I DON'T KNOW... IF I'M GOING YET...
IN THE EVENT THAT YOU SHOULD GO, PLEASE DO YOUR UTMOST TO REFRAIN FROM BEING A NUISANCE.
AND INCIDENTALLY, I JOINED THEM LAST YEAR, SO DON'T ASSUME THIS MAKES YOU SPECIAL!!
BISHI (FWIP)
I WON'T! DON'T WORRY!
SADLY, I HAD TO HUMBLY DECLINE THIS YEAR...
REALLY? IS SOMETHING WRONG?
I'M GOING ON A FAMILY VACATION, AND MITO-CHAN HAS CLUB, SO WE CAN'T GO EITHER.
BUT WE WERE INVITED.
......!

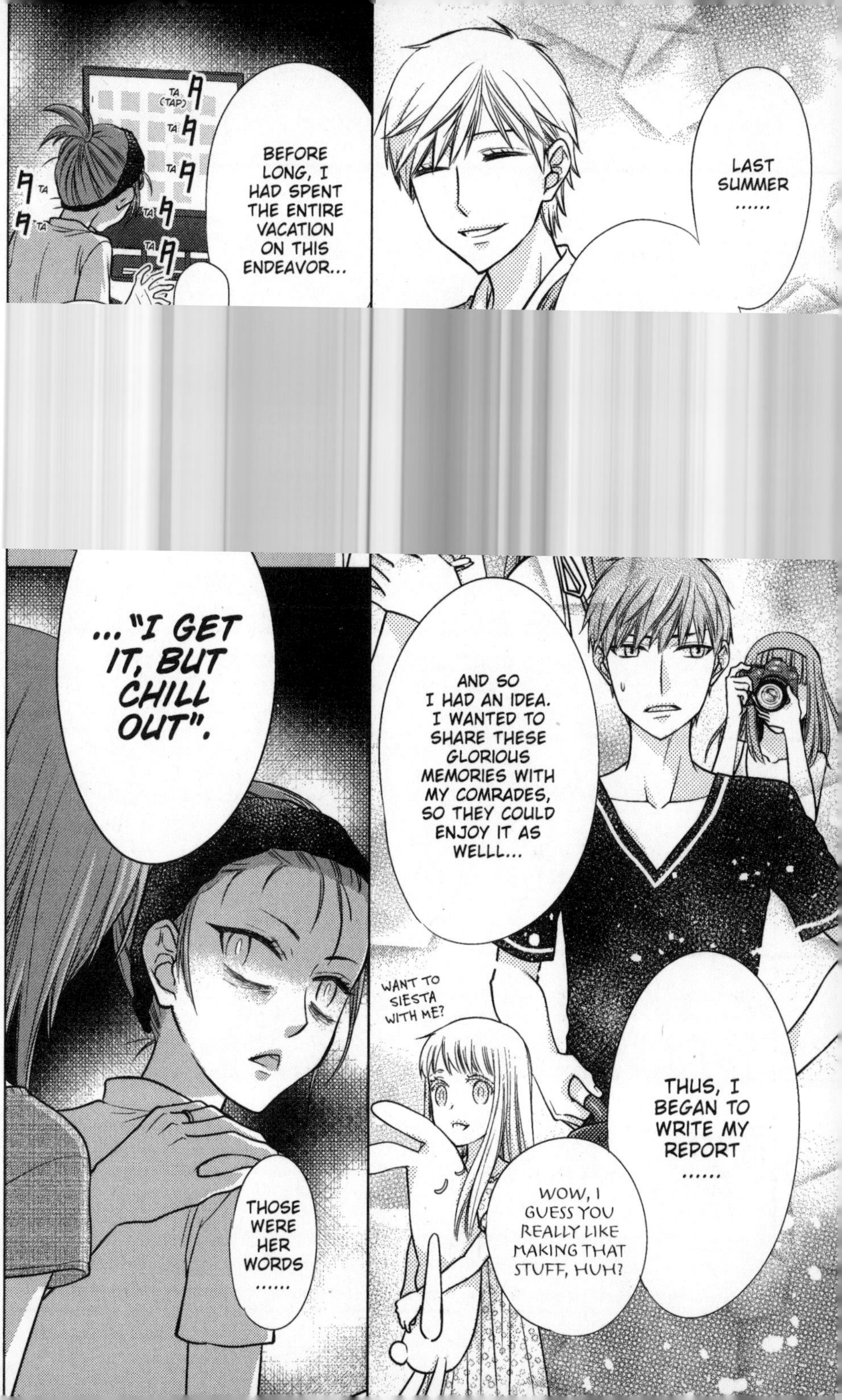
LAST SUMMER ......
TA (TAP)
TA
TA
TA
TA
TA
BEFORE LONG, I HAD SPENT THE ENTIRE VACATION ON THIS ENDEAVOR...
AND SO I HAD AN IDEA. I WANTED TO SHARE THESE GLORIOUS MEMORIES WITH MY COMRADES, SO THEY COULD ENJOY IT AS WELLL...
THUS, I BEGAN TO WRITE MY REPORT ......
WANT TO SIESTA WITH ME?
WOW, I GUESS YOU REALLY LIKE MAKING THAT STUFF, HUH?
..."I GET IT, BUT CHILL OUT".
THOSE WERE HER WORDS ......

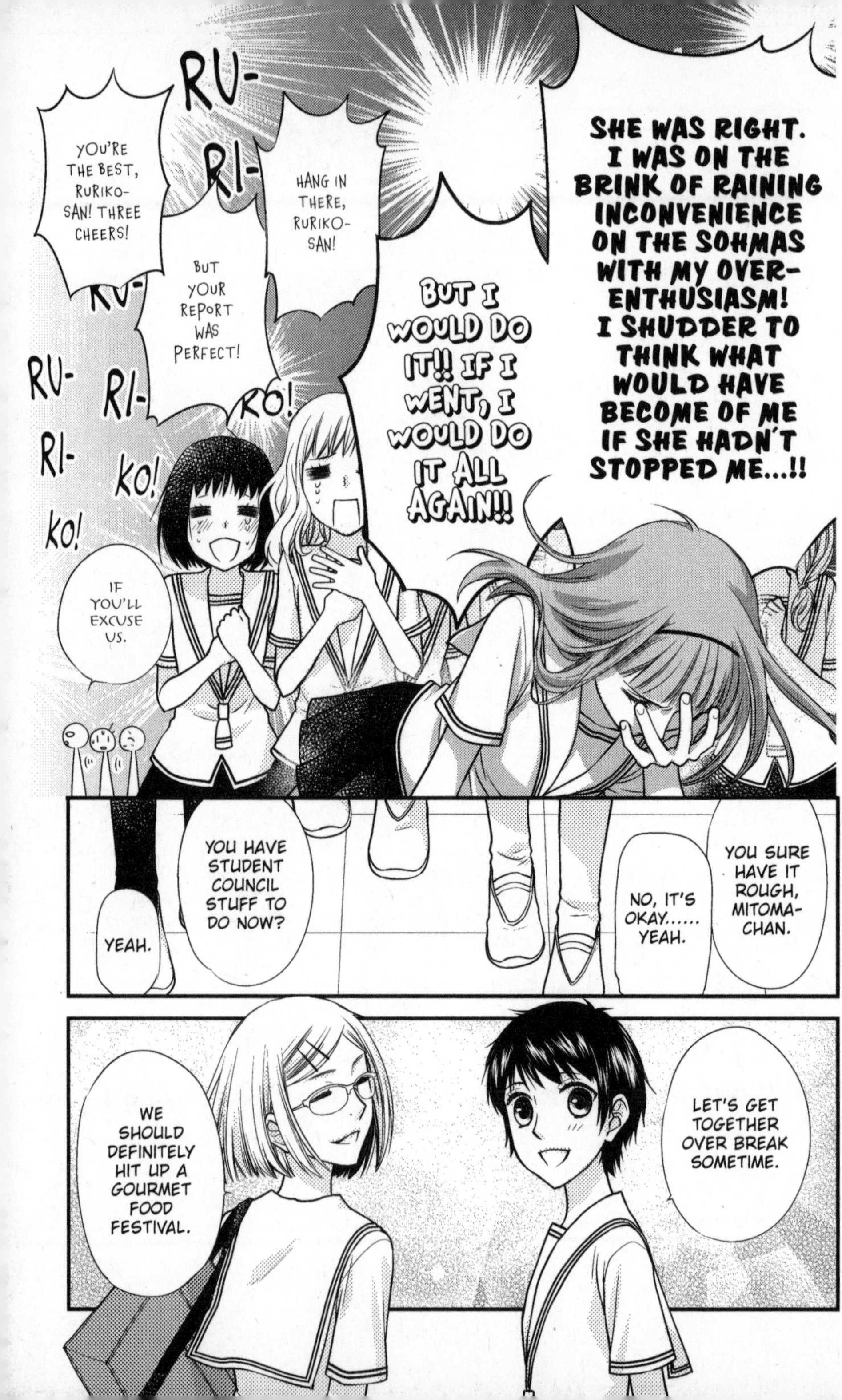

SHE WAS RIGHT. I WAS ON THE BRINK OF RAINING INCONVENIENCE ON THE SOHMAS WITH MY OVER-ENTHUSIASM! I SHUDDER TO THINK WHAT WOULD HAVE BECOME OF ME IF SHE HADN'T STOPPED ME...!!
BUT I WOULD DO IT!! IF I WENT, I WOULD DO IT ALL AGAIN!!
RU-RI-KO!
HANG IN THERE, RURIKO-SAN!
YOU'RE THE BEST, RURIKO-SAN! THREE CHEERS!
BUT YOUR REPORT WAS PERFECT!
RU-RI-KO!
RU-RI-KO!
IF YOU'LL EXCUSE US.
YOU SURE HAVE IT ROUGH, MITOMA-CHAN.
NO, IT'S OKAY...... YEAH.
YOU HAVE STUDENT COUNCIL STUFF TO DO NOW?
YEAH.
LET'S GET TOGETHER OVER BREAK SOMETIME.
WE SHOULD DEFINITELY HIT UP A GOURMET FOOD FESTIVAL.

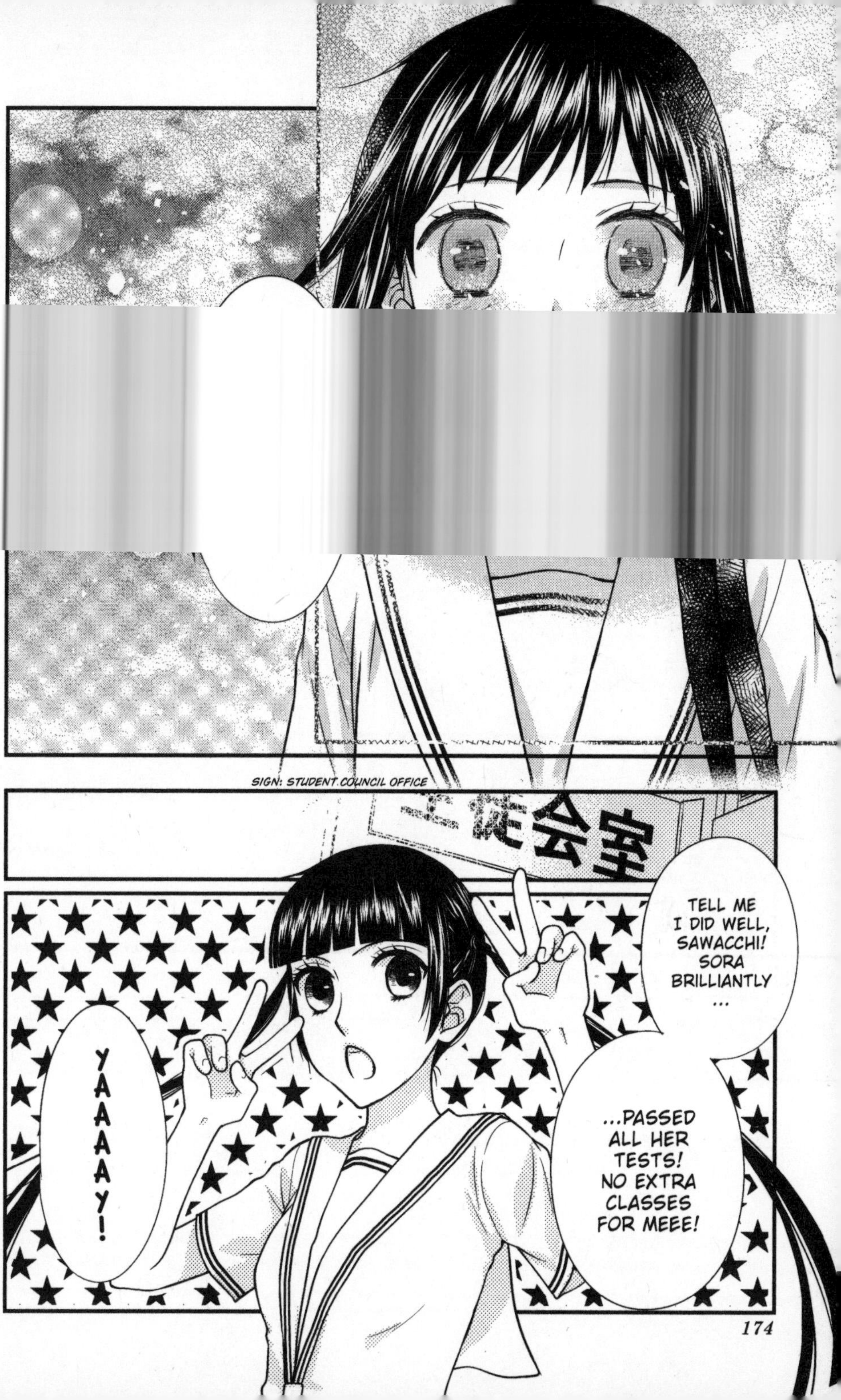
SIGN: STUDENT COUNCIL OFFICE
TELL ME I DID WELL, SAWACCHI! SORA BRILLIANTLY ...
...PASSED ALL HER TESTS! NO EXTRA CLASSES FOR MEEE!
YAAAAAY!

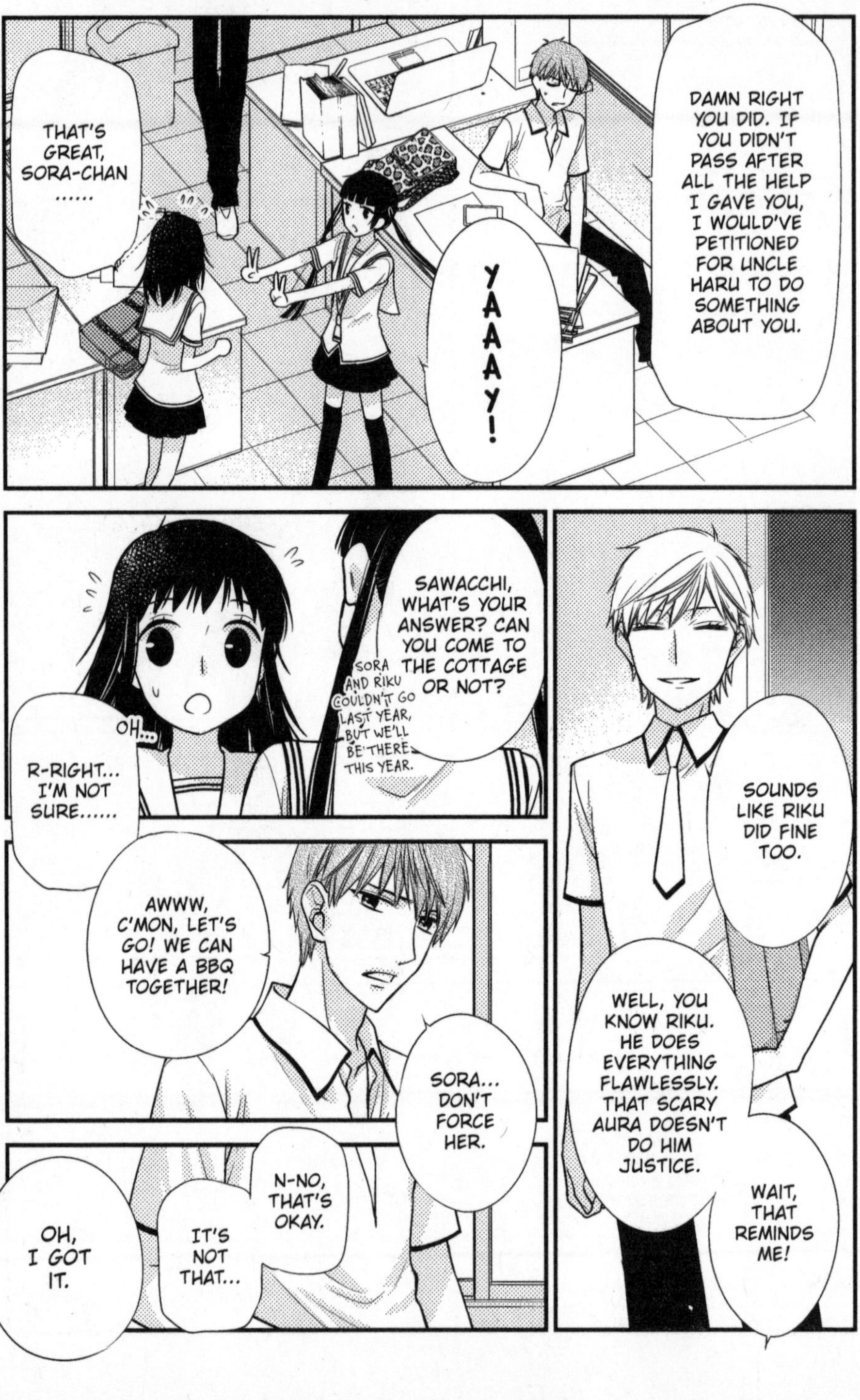
DAMN RIGHT YOU DID. IF YOU DIDN'T PASS AFTER ALL THE HELP I GAVE YOU, I WOULD'VE PETITIONED FOR UNCLE HARU TO DO SOMETHING ABOUT YOU.
YAAAAY!
THAT'S GREAT, SORA-CHAN......
SOUNDS LIKE RIKU DID FINE TOO.
WELL, YOU KNOW RIKU. HE DOES EVERYTHING FLAWLESSLY. THAT SCARY AURA DOESN'T DO HIM JUSTICE.
WAIT, THAT REMINDS ME!
SAWACCHI, WHAT'S YOUR ANSWER? CAN YOU COME TO THE COTTAGE OR NOT?
SORA AND RIKU COULDN'T GO LAST YEAR, BUT WE'LL BE THERE THIS YEAR.
OH...
R-RIGHT... I'M NOT SURE......
AWWW, C'MON, LET'S GO! WE CAN HAVE A BBQ TOGETHER!
SORA... DON'T FORCE HER.
N-NO, THAT'S OKAY.
IT'S NOT THAT...
OH, I GOT IT.

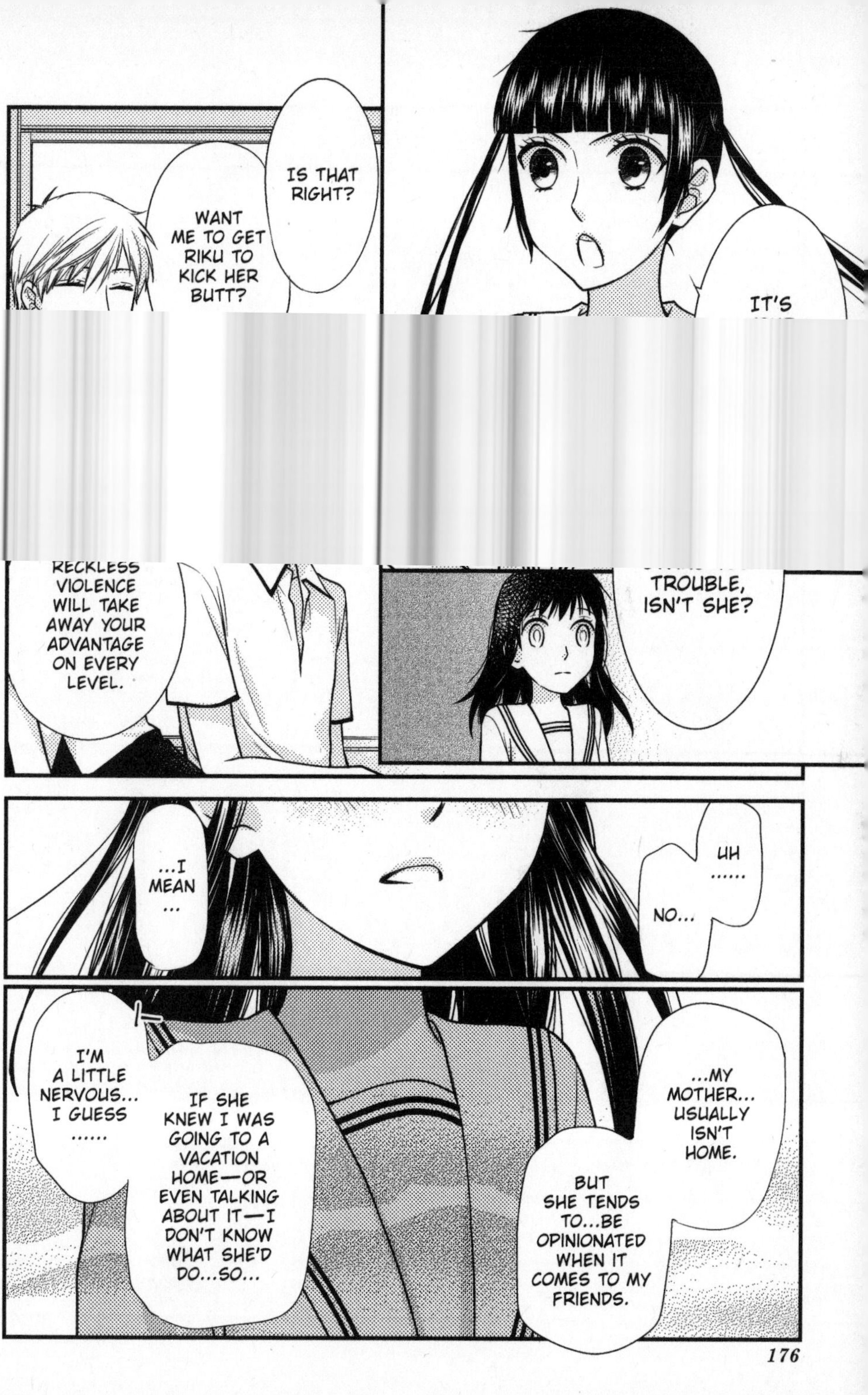
IT'S
IS THAT RIGHT?
WANT ME TO GET RIKU TO KICK HER BUTT?
TROUBLE, ISN'T SHE?
RECKLESS VIOLENCE WILL TAKE AWAY YOUR ADVANTAGE ON EVERY LEVEL.
UH ...... NO...
...I MEAN ...
...MY MOTHER... USUALLY ISN'T HOME.
BUT SHE TENDS TO...BE OPINIONATED WHEN IT COMES TO MY FRIENDS.
IF SHE KNEW I WAS GOING TO A VACATION HOME—OR EVEN TALKING ABOUT IT—I DON'T KNOW WHAT SHE'D DO...SO...
I'M A LITTLE NERVOUS... I GUESS ......

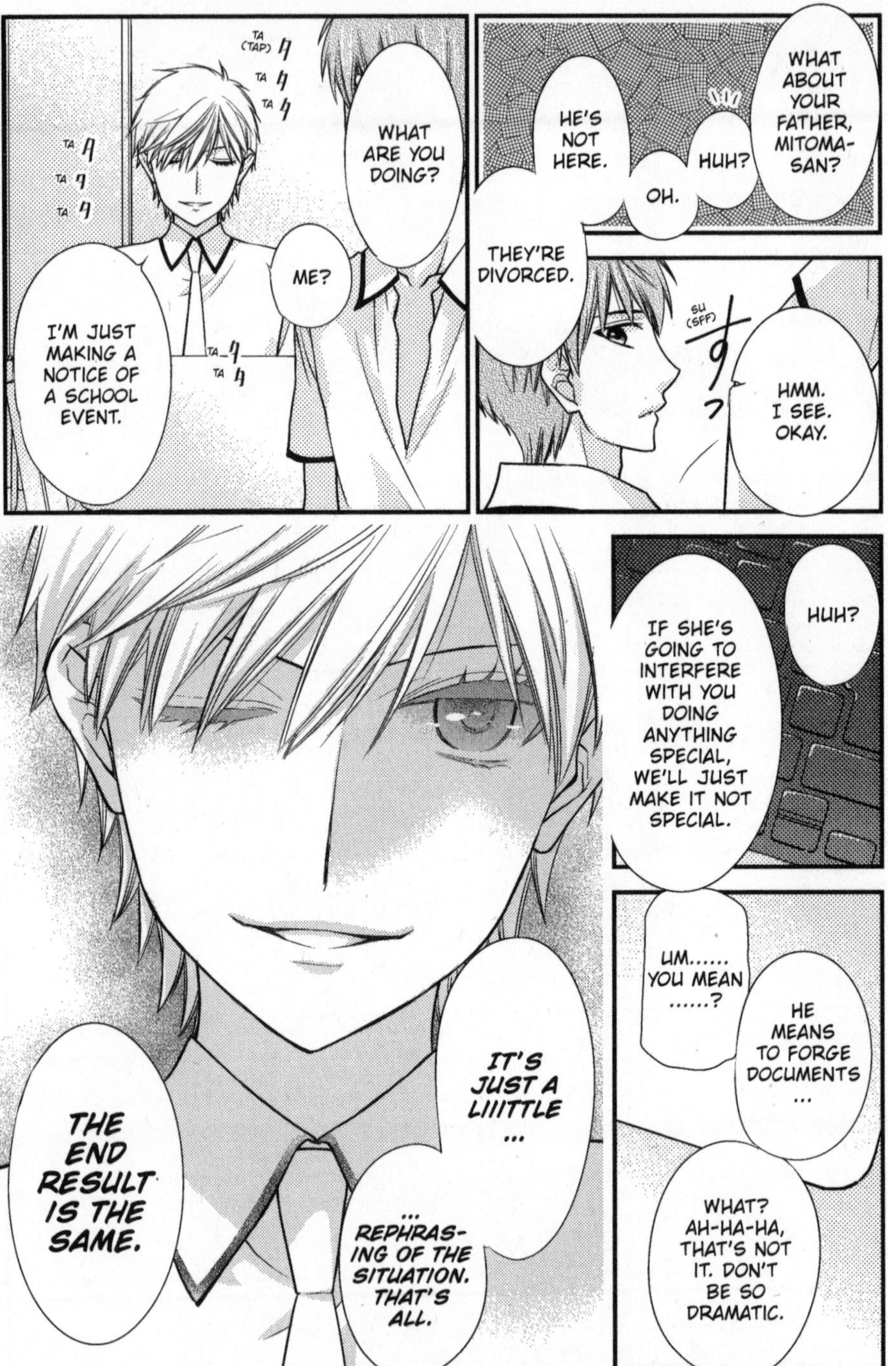
WHAT ABOUT YOUR FATHER, MITOMA-SAN?
HUH?
OH.
HE'S NOT HERE.
THEY'RE DIVORCED.
SU (SFF)
HMM. I SEE. OKAY.
TA (TAP)
TA
TA
TA
TA
TA
WHAT ARE YOU DOING?
ME?
TA
TA
I'M JUST MAKING A NOTICE OF A SCHOOL EVENT.
HUH?
IF SHE'S GOING TO INTERFERE WITH YOU DOING ANYTHING SPECIAL, WE'LL JUST MAKE IT NOT SPECIAL.
UM...... YOU MEAN ......?
HE MEANS TO FORGE DOCUMENTS ...
WHAT? AH-HA-HA, THAT'S NOT IT. DON'T BE SO DRAMATIC.
IT'S JUST A LIIITTLE ...
... REPHRASING OF THE SITUATION. THAT'S ALL.
THE END RESULT IS THE SAME.

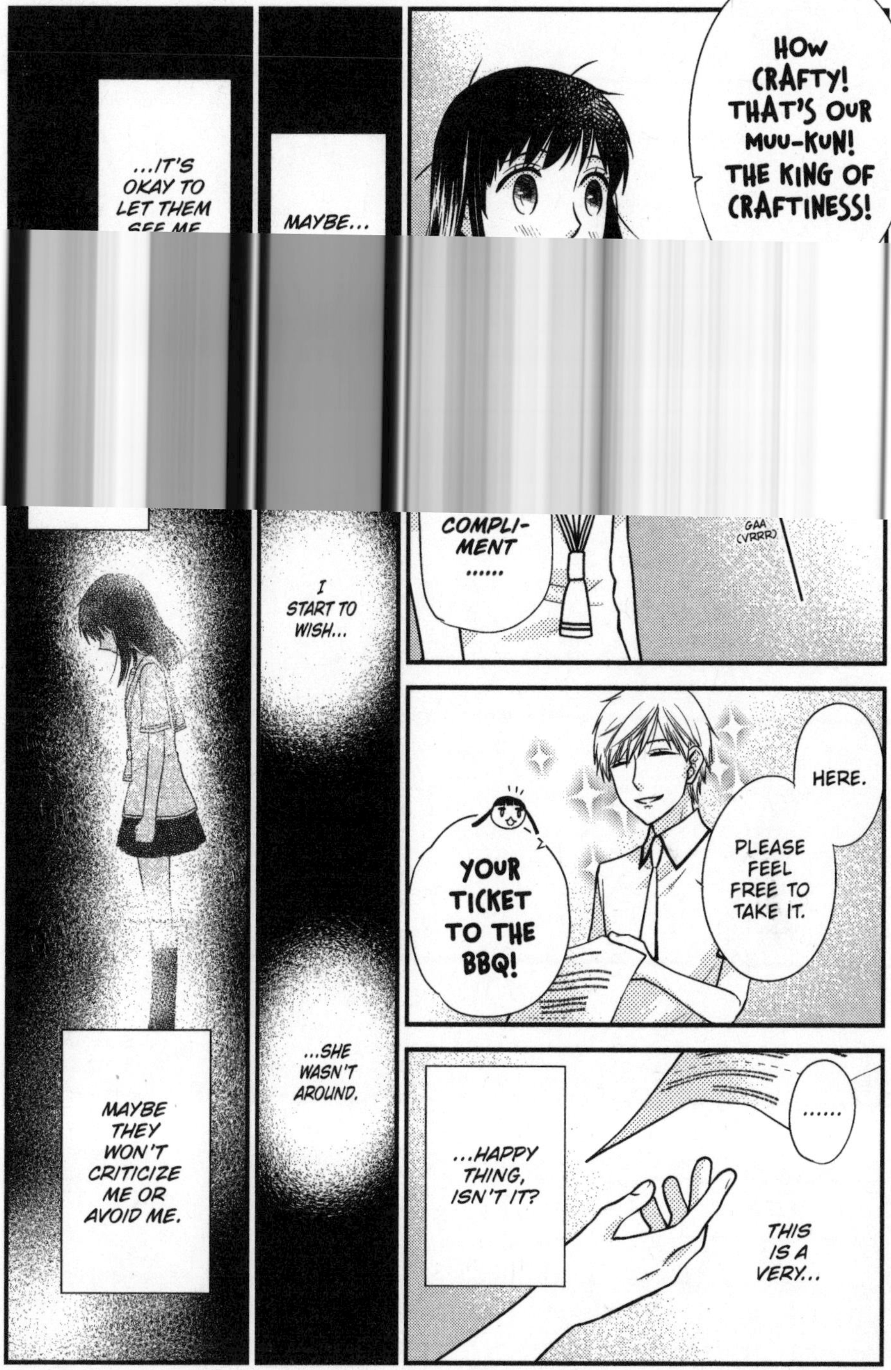
HOW CRAFTY! THAT'S OUR MUU-KUN! THE KING OF CRAFTINESS!
COMPLI-MENT ......
GAA (VRRR)
HERE.
PLEASE FEEL FREE TO TAKE IT.
YOUR TICKET TO THE BBQ!
......
THIS IS A VERY...
...HAPPY THING, ISN'T IT?
MAYBE...
I START TO WISH...
...SHE WASN'T AROUND.
...IT'S OKAY TO LET THEM
MAYBE THEY WON'T CRITICIZE ME OR AVOID ME.

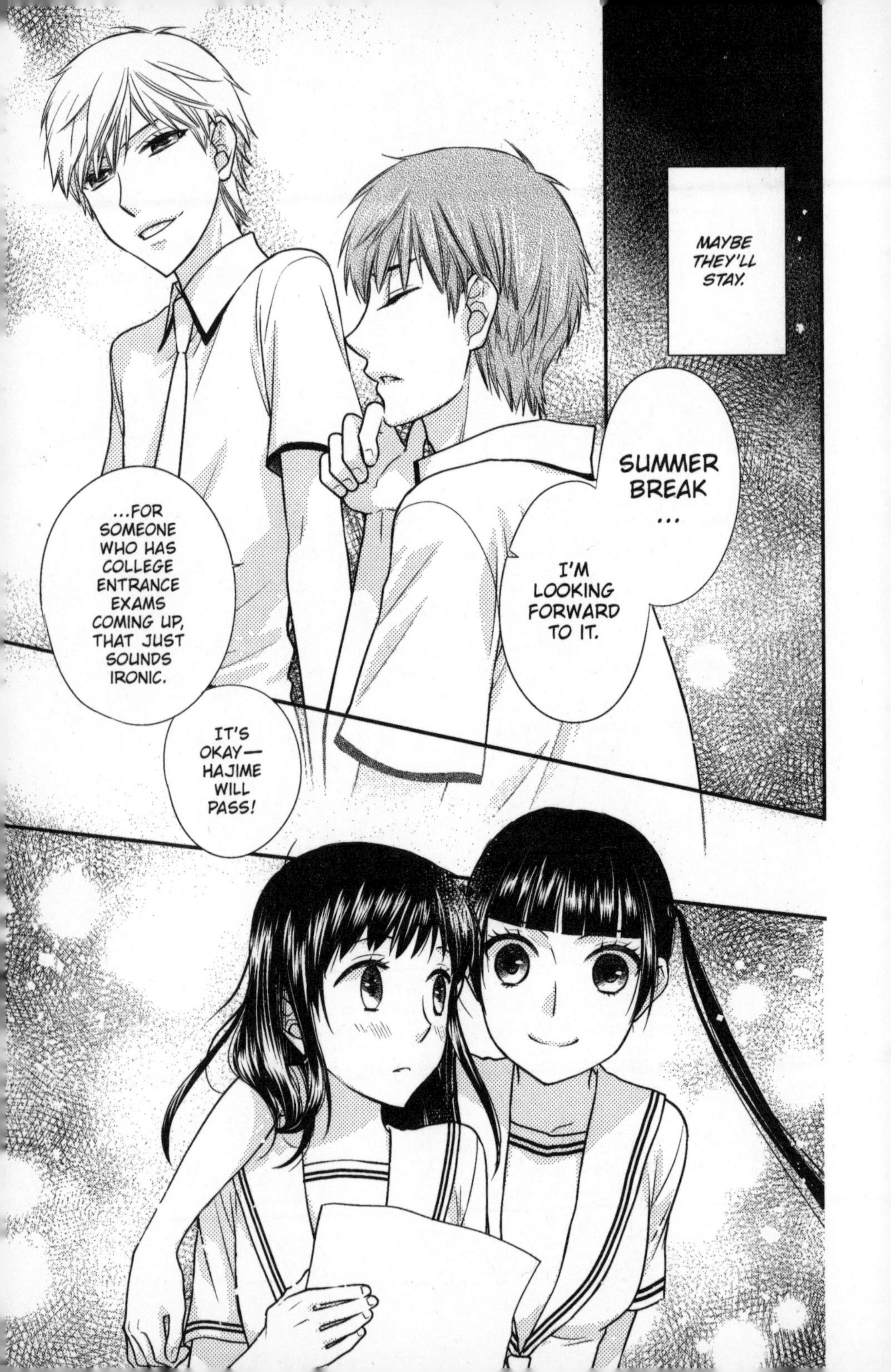
MAYBE THEY'LL STAY.
SUMMER BREAK...
I'M LOOKING FORWARD TO IT.
...FOR SOMEONE WHO HAS COLLEGE ENTRANCE EXAMS COMING UP, THAT JUST SOUNDS IRONIC.
IT'S OKAY—HAJIME WILL PASS!

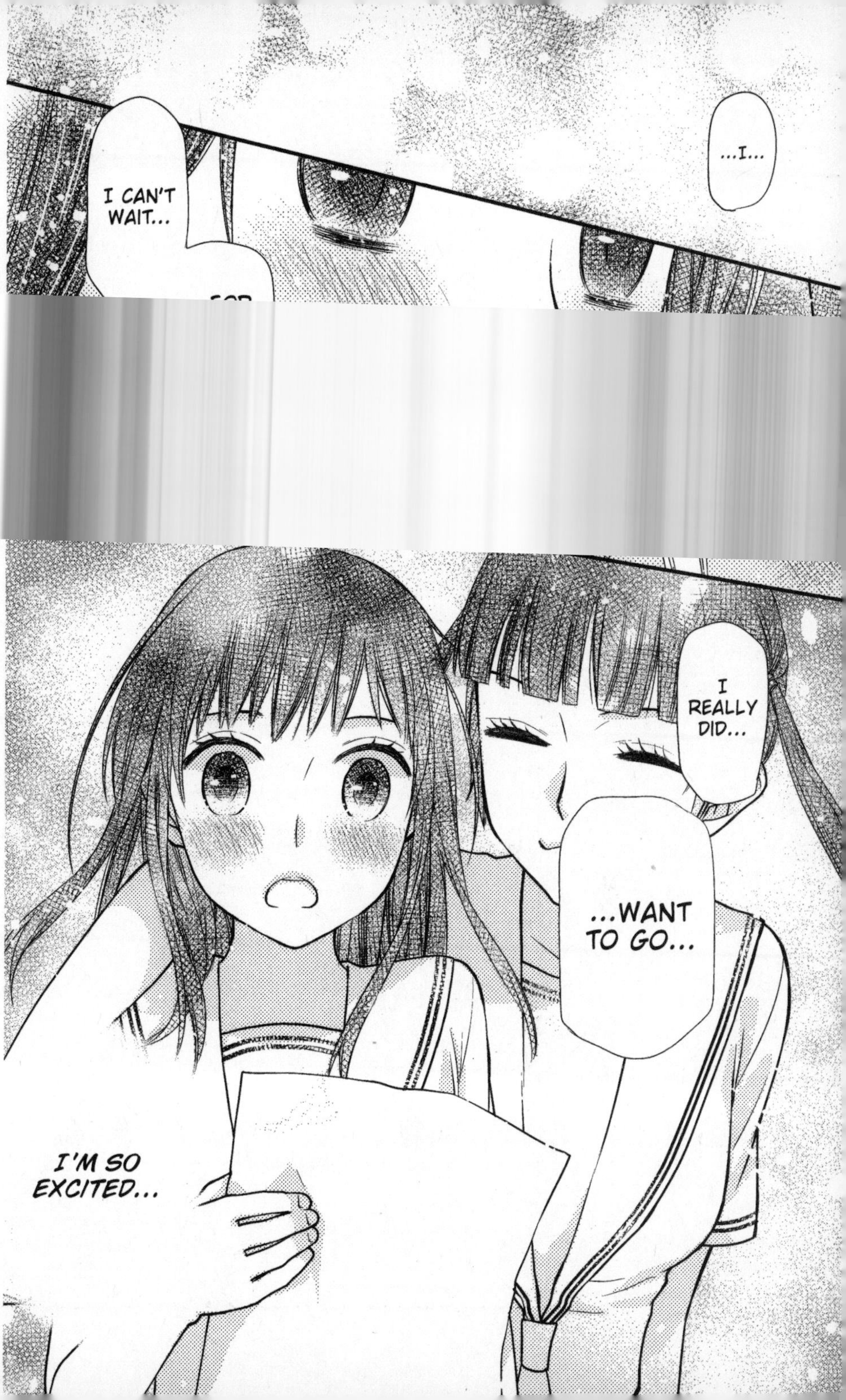
...I...
I CAN'T WAIT...
I REALLY DID...
...WANT TO GO...
I'M SO EXCITED...

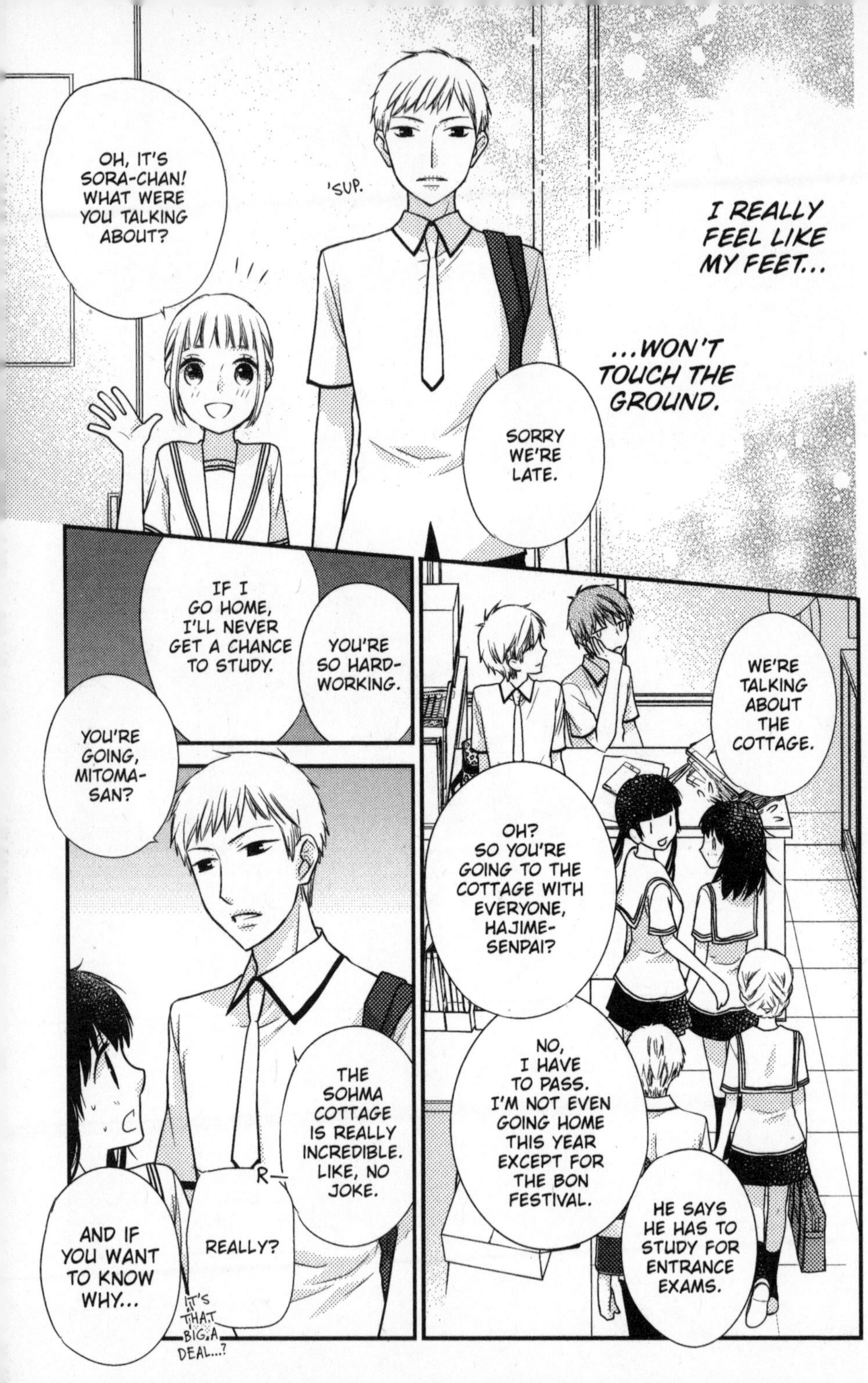
I REALLY FEEL LIKE MY FEET...
...WON'T TOUCH THE GROUND.
SORRY WE'RE LATE.
'SUP.
OH, IT'S SORA-CHAN! WHAT WERE YOU TALKING ABOUT?
WE'RE TALKING ABOUT THE COTTAGE.
OH? SO YOU'RE GOING TO THE COTTAGE WITH EVERYONE, HAJIME-SENPAI?
NO, I HAVE TO PASS. I'M NOT EVEN GOING HOME THIS YEAR EXCEPT FOR THE BON FESTIVAL.
HE SAYS HE HAS TO STUDY FOR ENTRANCE EXAMS.
YOU'RE SO HARD-WORKING.
IF I GO HOME, I'LL NEVER GET A CHANCE TO STUDY.
YOU'RE GOING, MITOMA-SAN?
THE SOHMA COTTAGE IS REALLY INCREDIBLE. LIKE, NO JOKE.
R—
REALLY?
IT'S THAT BIG A DEAL...?
AND IF YOU WANT TO KNOW WHY...

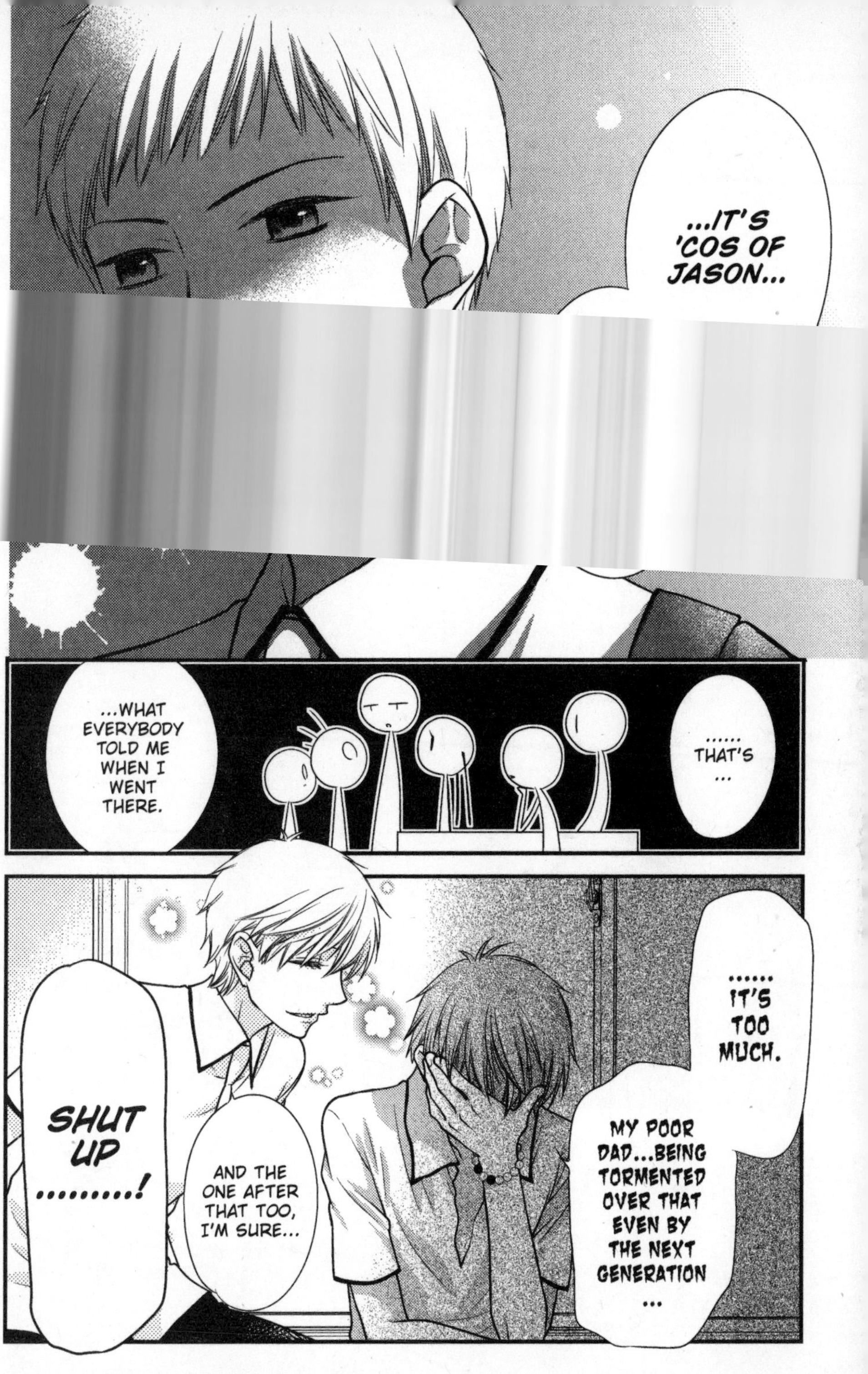
...IT'S 'COS OF JASON...
...... THAT'S ...
...WHAT EVERYBODY TOLD ME WHEN I WENT THERE.
...... IT'S TOO MUCH.
MY POOR DAD...BEING TORMENTED OVER THAT EVEN BY THE NEXT GENERATION ...
AND THE ONE AFTER THAT TOO, I'M SURE...
SHUT UP ....!

FRUITS BASKET ANOTHER 2 THE END

BONUS MANGA

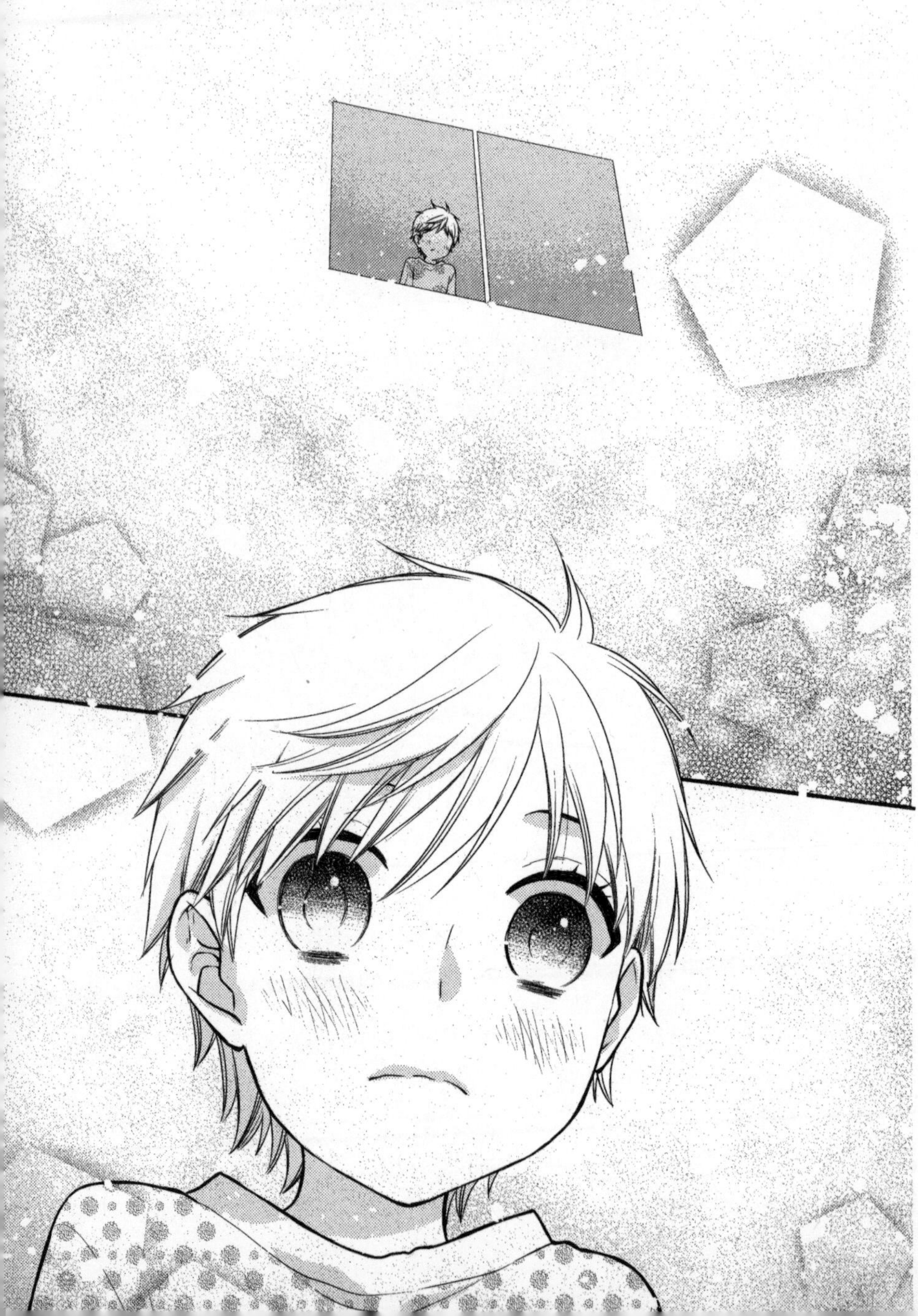

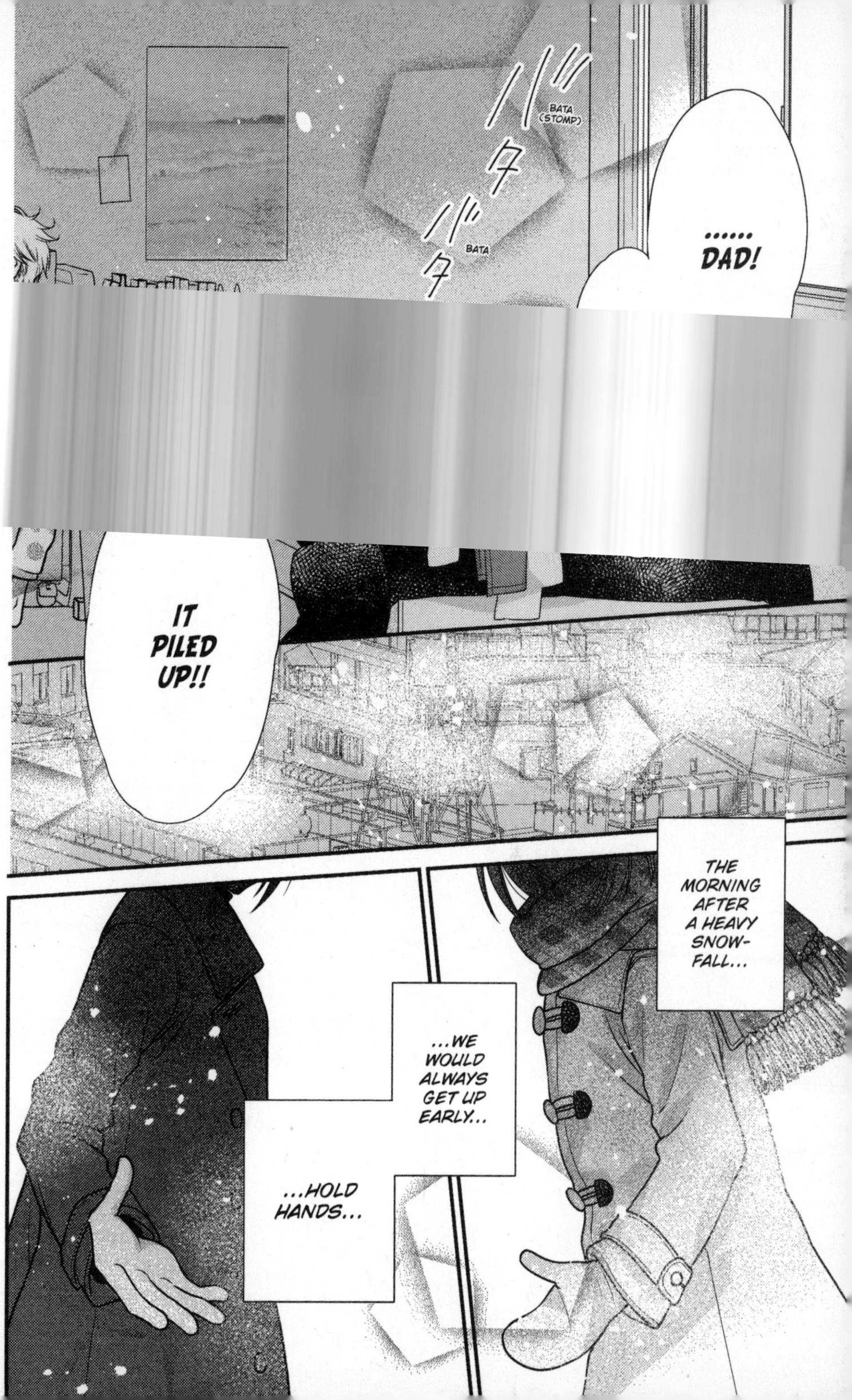
BATA (STOMP)
BATA
...... DAD!
IT PILED UP!!
THE MORNING AFTER A HEAVY SNOW-FALL...
...WE WOULD ALWAYS GET UP EARLY...
...HOLD HANDS...

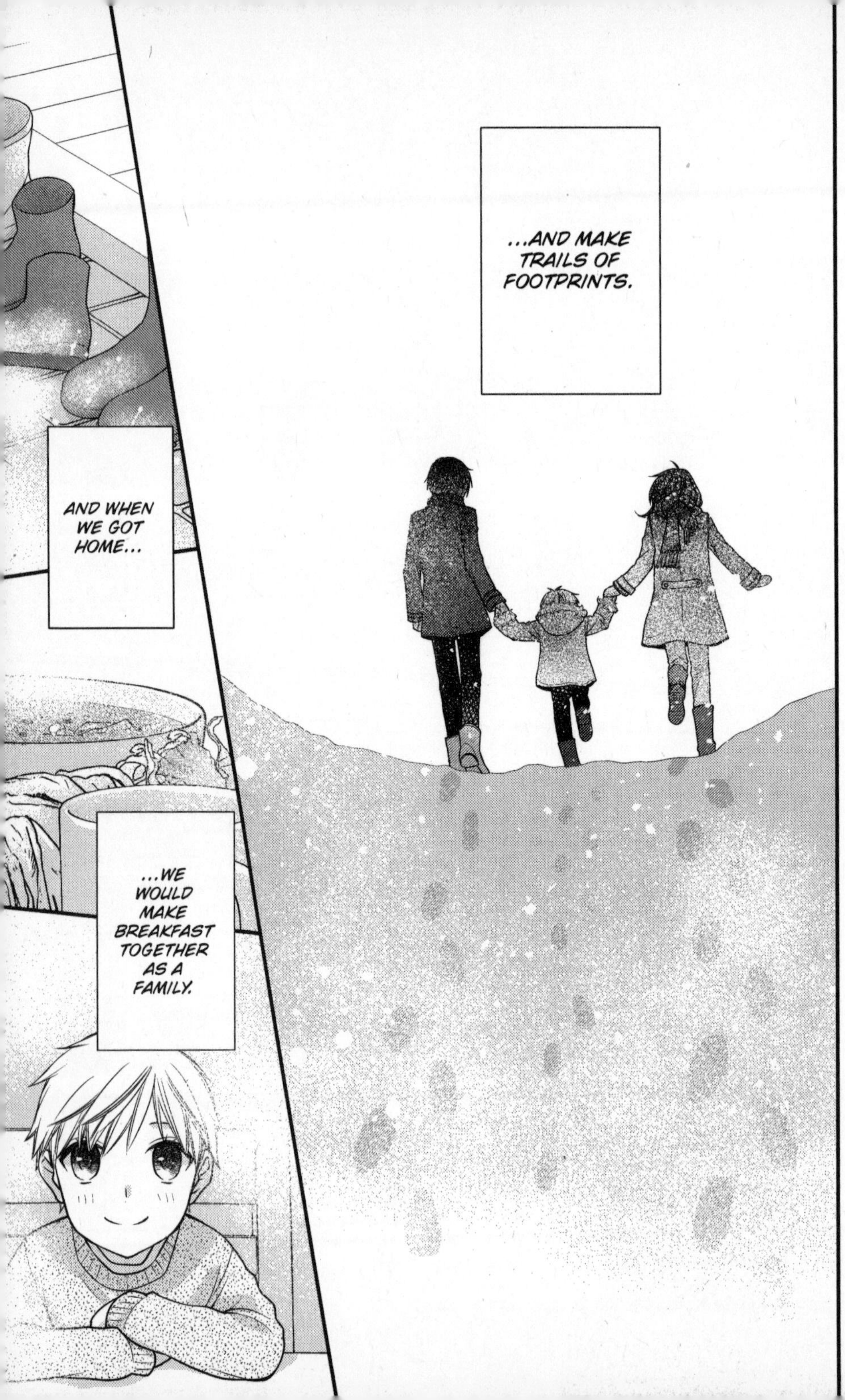
...AND MAKE TRAILS OF FOOTPRINTS.
AND WHEN WE GOT HOME...
...WE WOULD MAKE BREAKFAST TOGETHER AS A FAMILY.

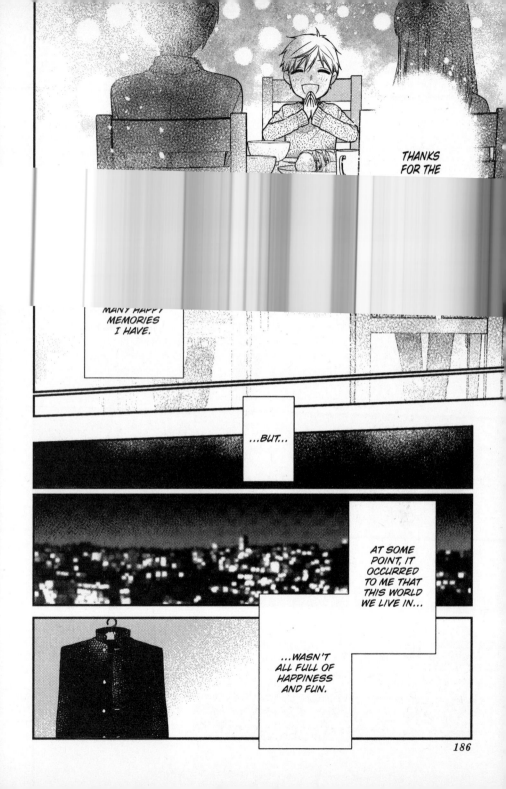

THANKS FOR THE

MANY HAPPY MEMORIES I HAVE.

...BUT...

AT SOME POINT, IT OCCURRED TO ME THAT THIS WORLD WE LIVE IN...

...WASN'T ALL FULL OF HAPPINESS AND FUN.

186

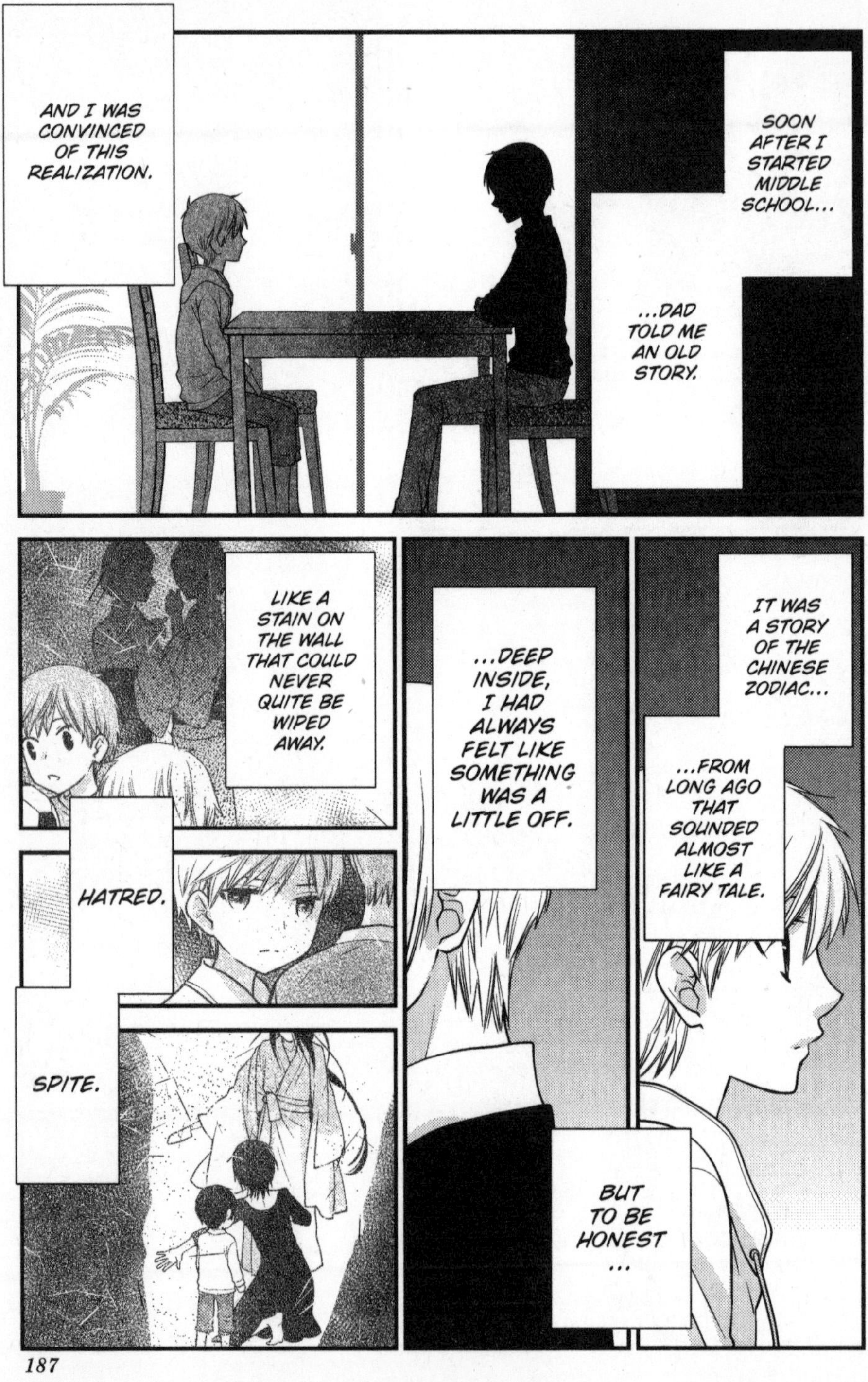
AND I WAS CONVINCED OF THIS REALIZATION.
SOON AFTER I STARTED MIDDLE SCHOOL...
...DAD TOLD ME AN OLD STORY.
IT WAS A STORY OF THE CHINESE ZODIAC...
...FROM LONG AGO THAT SOUNDED ALMOST LIKE A FAIRY TALE.
BUT TO BE HONEST ...
...DEEP INSIDE, I HAD ALWAYS FELT LIKE SOMETHING WAS A LITTLE OFF.
LIKE A STAIN ON THE WALL THAT COULD NEVER QUITE BE WIPED AWAY.
HATRED.
SPITE.

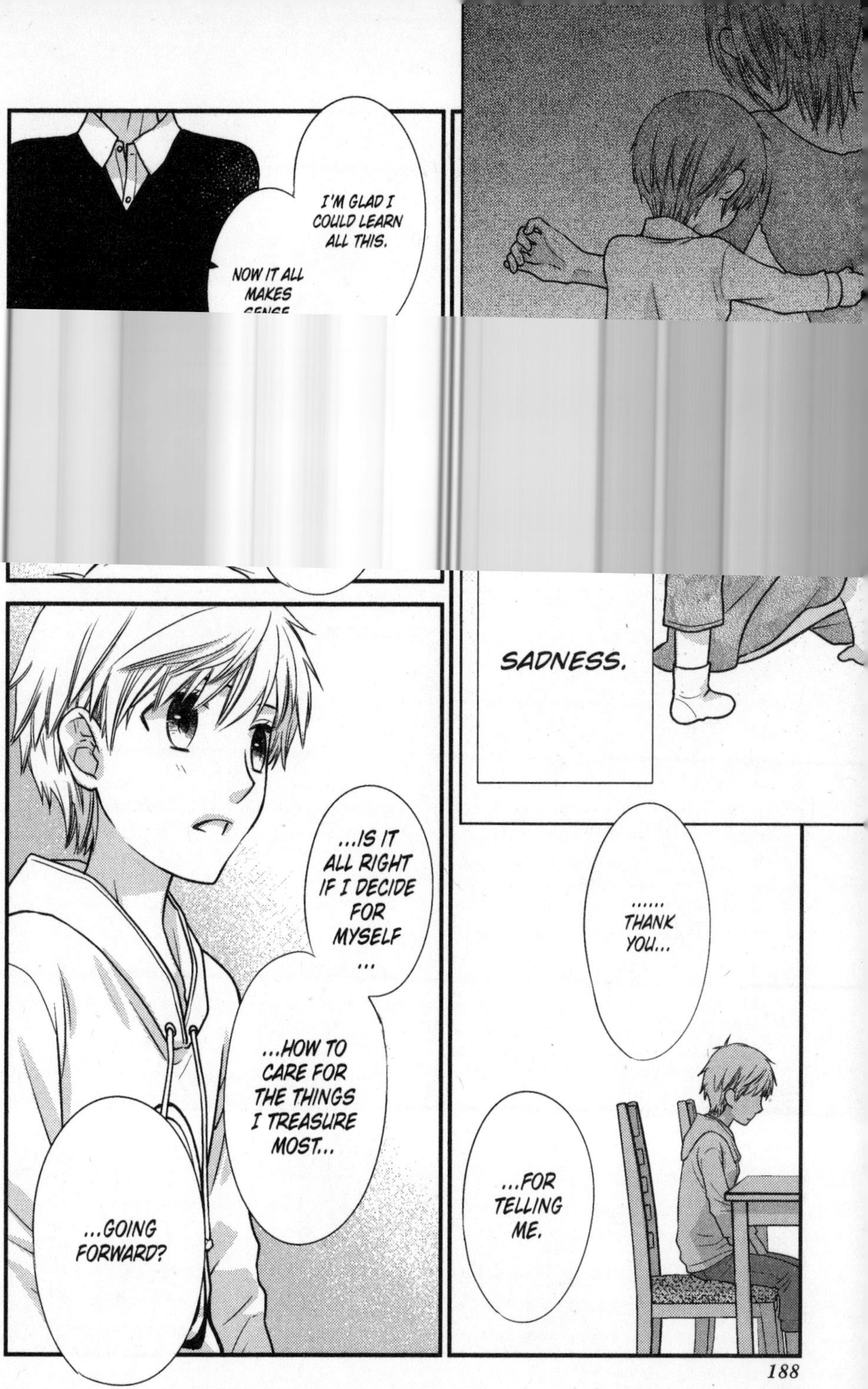
SADNESS.
I'M GLAD I COULD LEARN ALL THIS.
NOW IT ALL MAKES
...... THANK YOU...
...FOR TELLING ME.
...IS IT ALL RIGHT IF I DECIDE FOR MYSELF ...
...HOW TO CARE FOR THE THINGS I TREASURE MOST...
...GOING FORWARD?

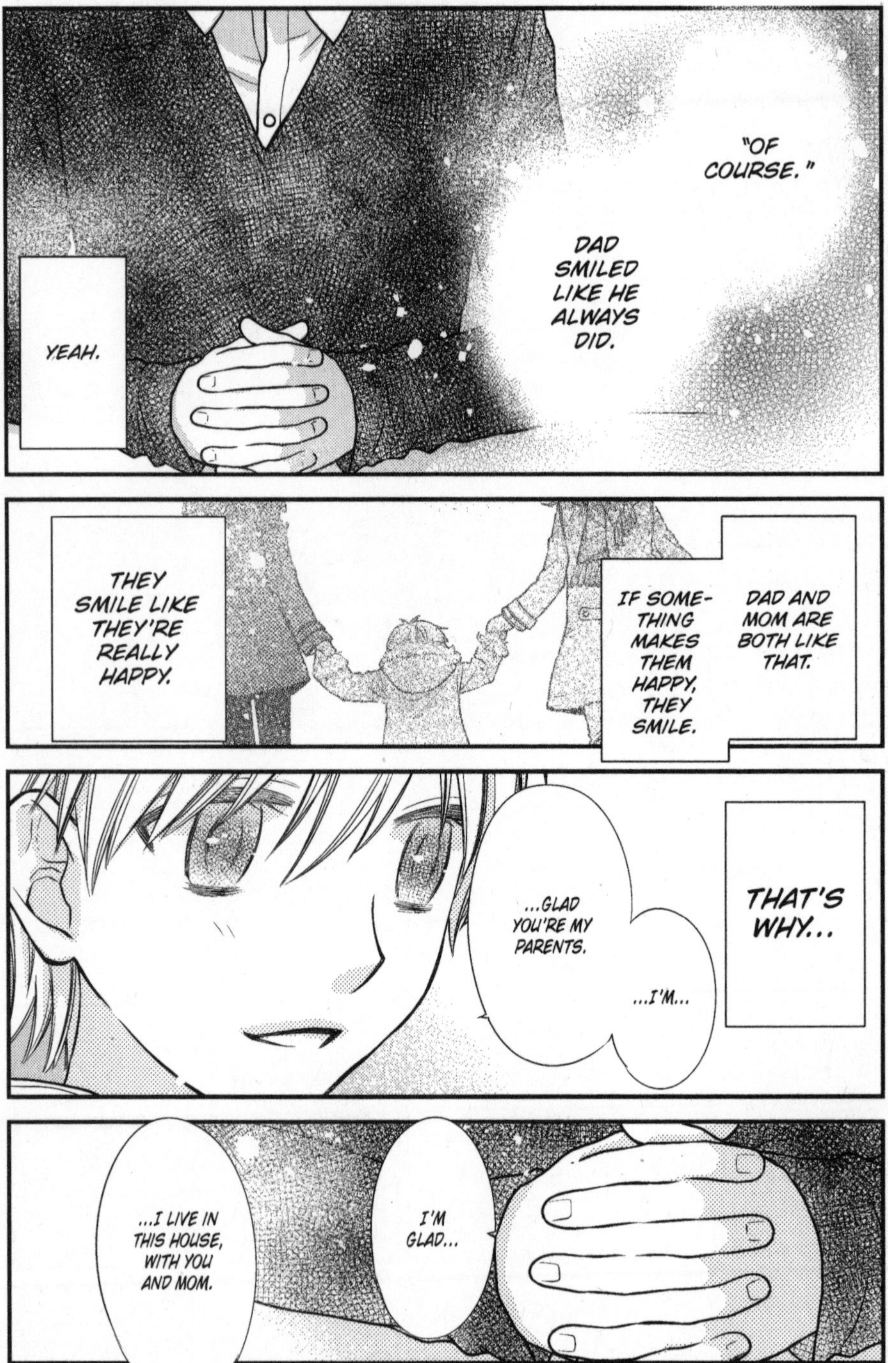

"OF COURSE."
DAD SMILED LIKE HE ALWAYS DID.
YEAH.
DAD AND MOM ARE BOTH LIKE THAT.
IF SOMETHING MAKES THEM HAPPY, THEY SMILE.
THEY SMILE LIKE THEY'RE REALLY HAPPY.
THAT'S WHY...
...I'M...
...GLAD YOU'RE MY PARENTS.
I'M GLAD...
...I LIVE IN THIS HOUSE, WITH YOU AND MOM.

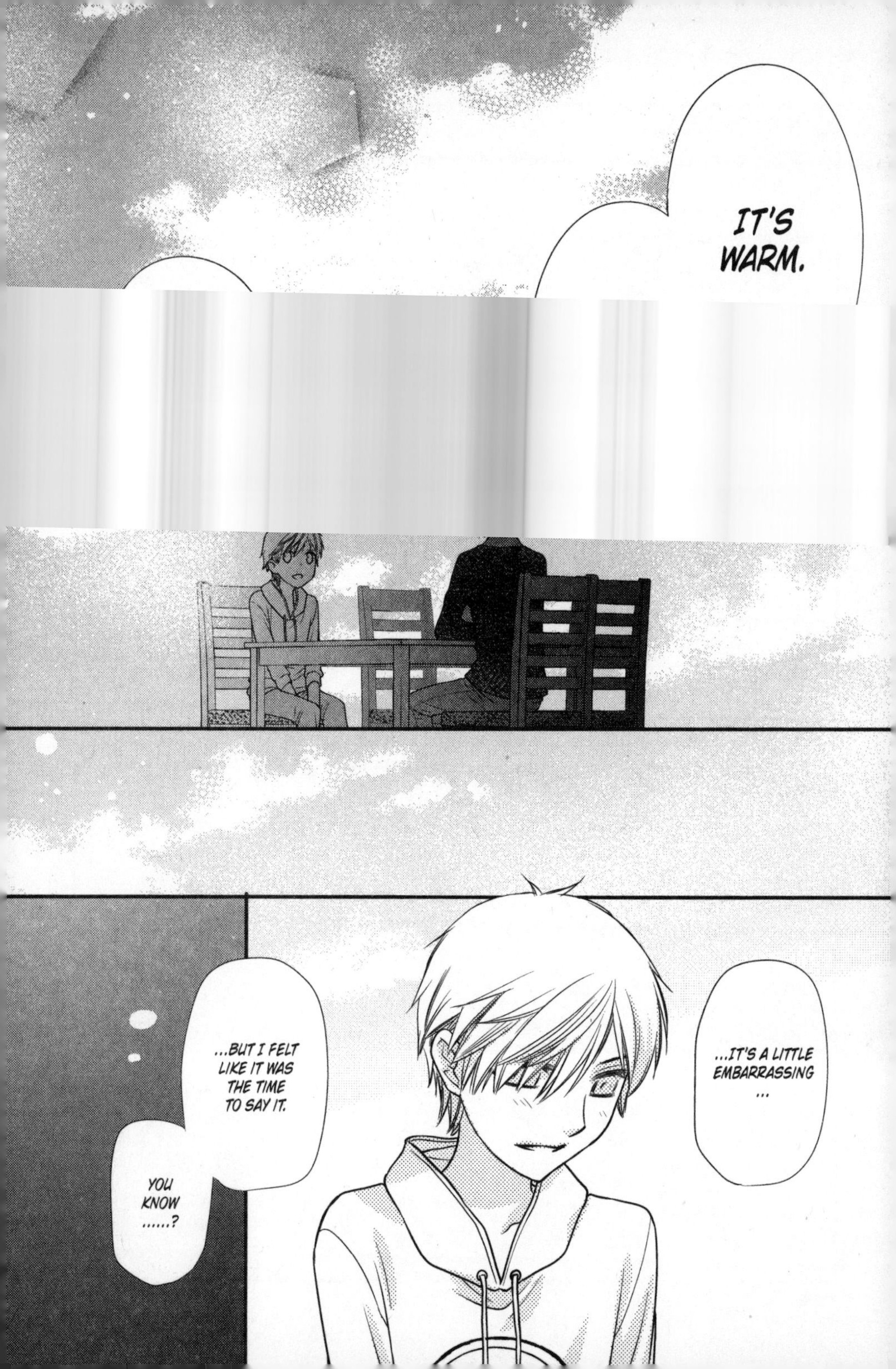
IT'S WARM.
...IT'S A LITTLE EMBARRASSING ...
...BUT I FELT LIKE IT WAS THE TIME TO SAY IT.
YOU KNOW ......?

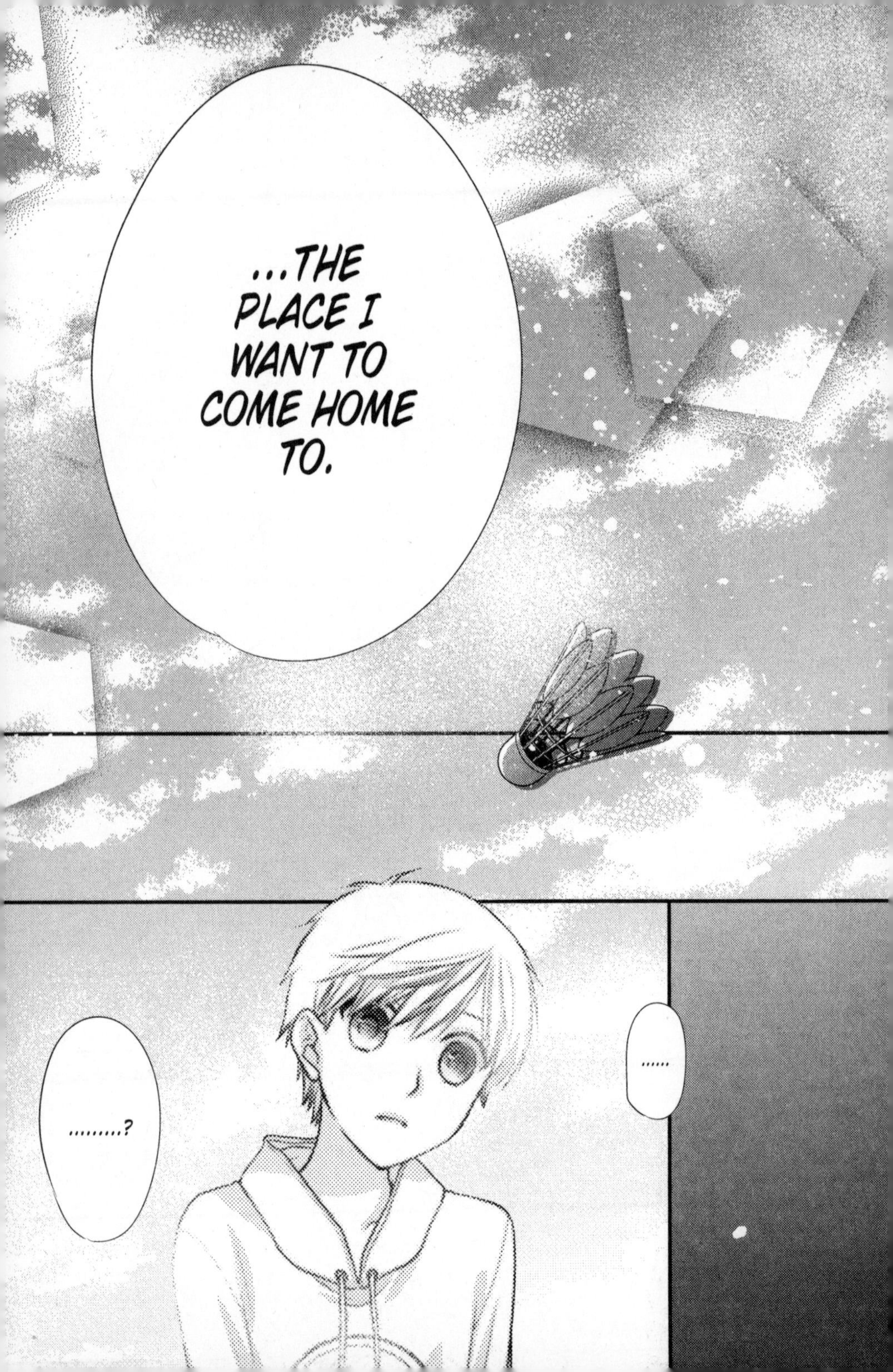
...THE PLACE I WANT TO COME HOME TO.
......
.........?

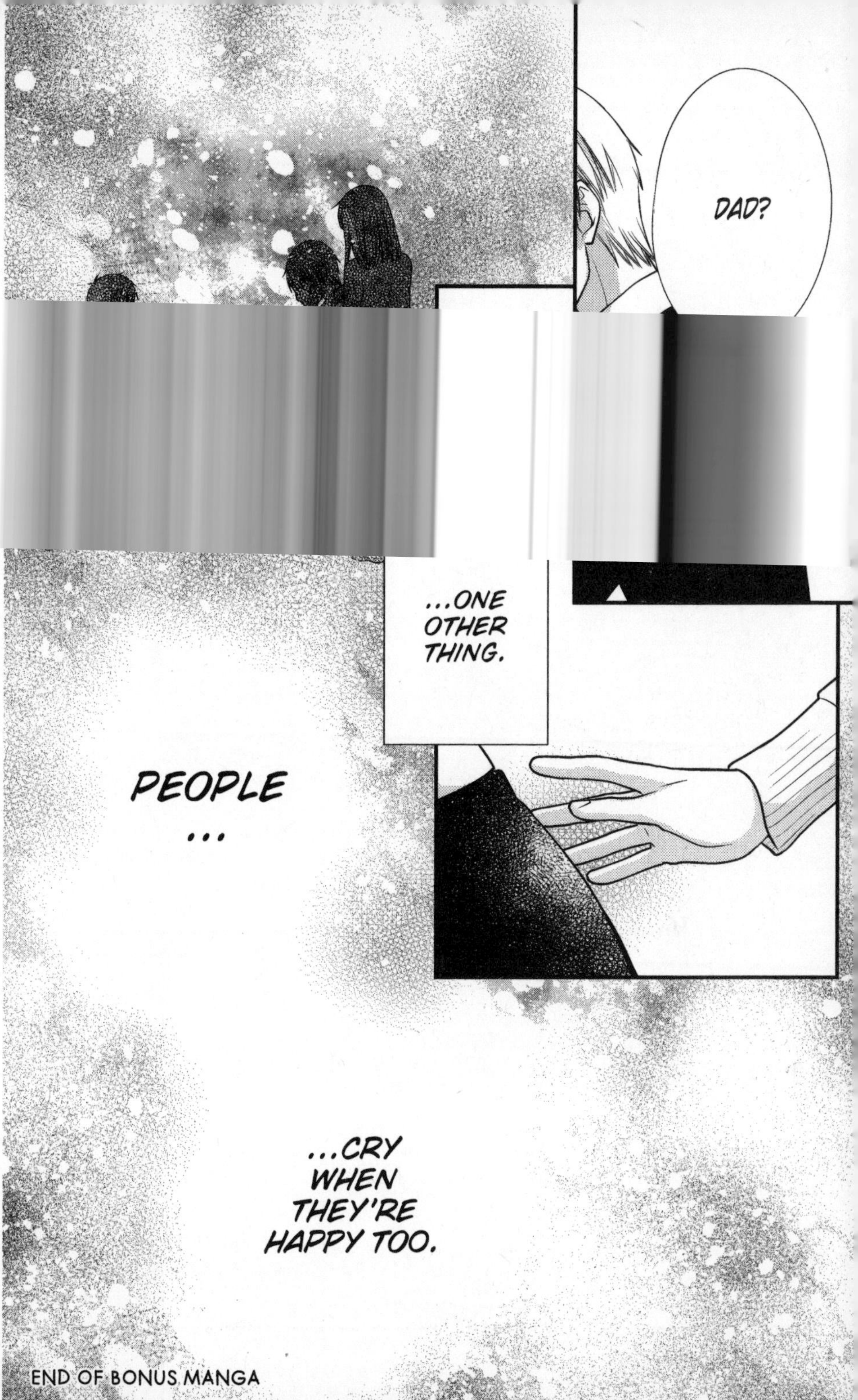
DAD?
...ONE OTHER THING.
PEOPLE ...
...CRY WHEN THEY'RE HAPPY TOO.

END OF BONUS MANGA

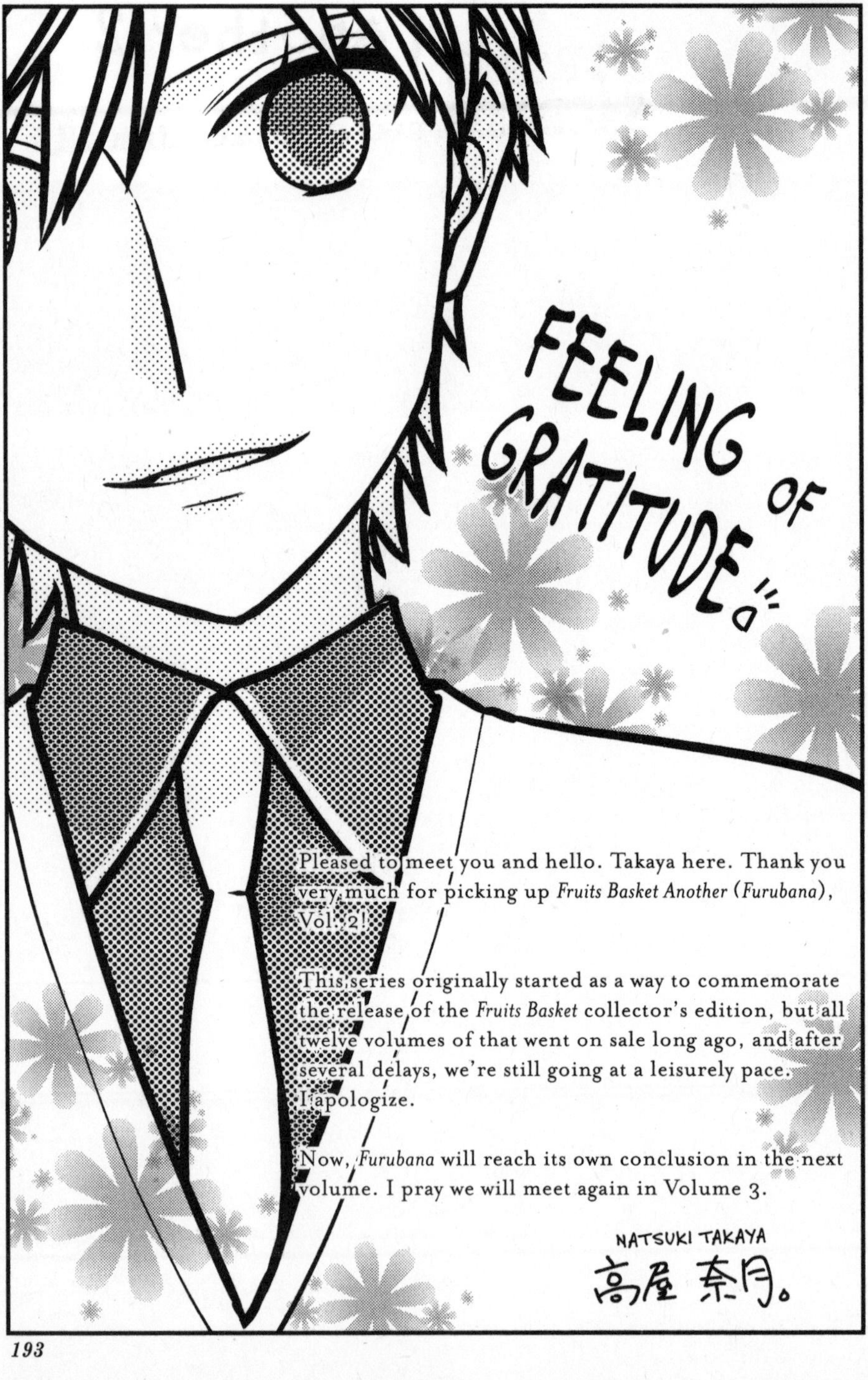
FEELING OF GRATITUDE

Pleased to meet you and hello. Takaya here. Thank you very much for picking up *Fruits Basket Another* (*Furubana*), Vol. 2!

This series originally started as a way to commemorate the release of the *Fruits Basket* collector's edition, but all twelve volumes of that went on sale long ago, and after several delays, we're still going at a leisurely pace. I apologize.

Now, *Furubana* will reach its own conclusion in the next volume. I pray we will meet again in Volume 3.

NATSUKI TAKAYA
高屋奈月。

Fruits Basket

NATSUKI TAKAYA

Translation: Alethea and Athena Nibley ✳ Lettering: Lys Blakeslee

Yen Press
1290 Avenue of the Americas
New York, NY 10104

Visit us at yenpress.com
facebook.com/yenpress
twitter.com/yenpress
yenpress.tumblr.com
instagram.com/yenpress

First Yen Press Edition: November 2018

Yen Press is an imprint of Yen Press, LLC.
The Yen Press name and logo are trademarks of Yen Press, LLC.

The publisher is not responsible for websites (or their content) that are not owned by the publisher.

Library of Congress Control Number: 2018939354

ISBNs: 978-1-9753-8224-7 (paperback)
       978-1-9753-8226-1 (ebook)

10 9 8 7 6 5 4 3 2 1

WOR

Printed in the United States of America